BTEC national

2nd Edition

Uniformed Public Services

Book 1

Debra Gray
Dave Stockbridge
John Vause

www.harcourt.co.uk

✓ Free online support
✓ Useful weblinks
✓ 24 hour online ordering

01865 888118

Heinemann is an imprint of Harcourt Education Limited, a company incorporated in England and Wales, having its registered office: Halley Court, Jordan Hill, Oxford OX2 8EJ. Registered company number: 3099304

www.harcourt.co.uk

Heinemann is the registered trademark of Harcourt Education Limited

Text, Unit 1 © Debra Gray, 2007
Text, Unit 2 © Debra Gray, Dave Stockbridge, 2007
Text, Unit 3 © Debra Gray, 2007
Text, Unit 4 © Debra Gray, 2007
Text, Unit 5 © Debra Gray, John Vause, 2007
Text, Unit 6 © Dave Stockbridge, 2007
Text, Unit 7 © Debra Gray, Boris Lockyer, 2007
Text, Unit 8 © Debra Gray, 2007
Text, Unit 12 © Debra Gray, 2007
Text, Unit 13 © John Vause, 2007

First published 2007

12 11 10 09 08 07
10 9 8 7 6 5 4 3 2 1

British Library Cataloguing in Publication Data is available from the British Library on request.

ISBN 978 0 435499 45 7

Typeset by 𝓣 Tek-Art, Croydon, Surrey
Original illustrations © Harcourt Education Limited, 2007
Illustrated by 𝓣 Tek-Art
Picture research by Sally Cole
Cover photo/illustration © Getty Images/Taxi
Printed in the UK by Scotprint Ltd

Websites
The websites used in this book were correct and up-to-date at the time of publication. It is essential for tutors to preview each website before using it in class so as to ensure that the URL is still accurate, relevant and appropriate. We suggest that tutors bookmark useful websites and consider enabling students to access them through the school/college intranet.

Crown copyright
Crown copyright material reproduced with permission of the Controller of Her Majesty's Stationery Office and the Queen's Printer for Scotland

Contents

Acknowledgements

I would like to thank the following people who have helped with the production of this book:

From Heinemann – Raegan Muskett, Pen Gresford, Faye Cheeseman and Liz Cartmell whose editing skills, patience and support have been invaluable.

From Dearne Valley College – Julie Williamson, Charlotte Baker, Paul Meares, Boris Lockyer, John Vause, Mick Blythe, Barry Pinches, Kelly Ellery, Dave Stockbridge and Nick Lawton; you make me proud to be part of the public services team at DVC.

From the Services – PC Paul Jenkinson, South Yorkshire Police; Lance Corporal Kelly Stevens, 38 Signal Regiment; Lis Martin, Skills for Justice. A really big thank you to all the services who have contributed their knowledge and skills to the development of the public service programmes at DVC over the years. Phil Campbell, Jack Mitchell, Jonty Morissey and all the other members of Justice UK for the endless quests they completed on my behalf.

The biggest thank you of all goes to my family, Ben, India and Sam, who make every day brighter.

Debra Gray

Many thanks to the two women in my life; my wife Kerry and my daughter Neve – your support and understanding has been a great motivator. I would also like to thank the public services team at DVC for sharing their expertise, knowledge and resources as without you the book wouldn't be the book it is. A final shout goes out to the Wilson, Carter and Ward clans as you help me to have a healthy work–life balance.

Dave Stockbridge

To Mick Lee of Constant Security for his help and advice.

John Vause

The authors and publisher would like to thank the following individuals and organisations for permission to reproduce photographs:

Alamy / ACE STOCK LIMITED p 328(bottom); Alamy / Andre Jenny p 212; Alamy / Ashley Cooper p 186; Alamy / Bubbles Photolibrary p 315(bottom), 316(right); Alamy / David Anthony p 325; Alamy / David Moore p 366; Alamy / Dominic Burke p 159; Alamy / Guy Harrop p 101; Alamy / Imagebroker p 103; Alamy / Image Source p 256; Alamy / Jack Carey p 319; Alamy / Janine Wiedel Photolibrary p 222, 224; Alamy / Jeff Morgan Education p 116–7, 141; Alamy / Jeff Morgan Social Issues p 89(top); Alamy / Jon Arnold p 54; Alamy / Larry Lilac p 328(top); Alamy / Martin Beddall p 144–5, 182; Alamy / Martin Mayer p 254; Alamy / Mikael Karlsson p 341; Alamy / Pablo Paul p 97; Alamy / Patrick Ward p 44; Alamy / Paul Doyle p 184-5, 226; Alamy / Paula Solloway p 190(right), 213; Alamy / Photofusion Picture Library p 168, 205, 315(top); Alamy / Si Barber p 210; Alamy / Steve Skjold p 316(left); Corbis / Alan Lewis p 10; Corbis / Andrew Parsons / epa p 89(bottom); Corbis / Ashley Cooper p 315(middle); Corbis / Corporal Adrian Harlen RLC / epa p 357; Corbis / Hulton Archive p 69; Corbis / Hulton-Deutsch Collection p 188; Corbis / Jim Craigmyle p 130; Corbis / Peter Turnley p 288; Corbis / REUTERS / Dadang Tri p 290; Corbis / REUTERS / Jerry Lampen p 301; Corbis / Reuters / Jose Manuel Ribeiro p 369; Corbis / REUTERS / Mohamad Torokman p 282; Corbis / REUTERS / POOL / Andrew Parsons p 303; Corbis / REUTERS / Richard Cohen p 295; Corbis / Russell Boyce / Reuters p 152; Corbis / Thorne Anderson p 277; Corbis / Tim Fisher, The Military Picture Library p 150; Corbis / Tim Graham Picture Library / Pool p 8; Corbis / ZEFA / Ull Weismeier p 261; Department of Transport p 109; Getty Images / AFP / Adrian Dennis p 134; Getty Images / Bruno Vincent p 346-7, 380; Getty Images

/ Chris Jackson p 2–3, 39; Getty Images / Christopher Furlong 308–9, 343; Getty Images / Francois Lo Presti p 74; Getty Images / Garry Hunter p 333; Getty Images / KARIM SAHIB p 289; Getty Images / PhotoDisc p 119, 157, 228–9, 267; Getty Images / Torsten Blackwood p 42–3, 81; Harcourt Education Ltd / Jules Selmes p 199; Harcourt Education Ltd / Tudor Photography p 190(left); Metropolitan Police Authority p 299; PA Photos p 258; PA Photos / Andy Zakeli / PA Archive p 364; PA Photos / Claire Mackintosh / Empics p 350; PA Photos / Sean Clee / PA Archive p 175; PA Photos / Sean Dempsey / PA Archive p 84–5, 113; Photofusion p 215; Photofusion / Brenda Prince p 92; Rex Features p 5; Rex Features / Alex Segre p 111; Rex Features / Alisdair Macdonald p 179; Rex Features / F. Sierakowski p 93; Rex Features / John Wright p 172; Rex Features / Philippe Hays p 90, 149; Rex Features / Sierakowski p 270–1, 305; Rex Features / Steve Maisey p 169; Rex Features / Tony Kyricaou p 91; Richard Smith p 193; Science Photo Library / David McCarthy p 238(bottom); Science Photo Library / Susumu Nichinaga p 238(top); www.eoc.org.uk / Betina Skovbro p 67;

'Consider this' icon – Corbis; 'Case study' icon – Corbis; 'Grading tips' icon – iStockPhoto.com / Nick Schlax; 'Knowledge check' icon – Photos.com; 'Remember!' icon – Richard Smith; 'Theory into practice' icon – Harcourt Education Ltd / Debbie Rowe; 'Thinking points' icon – Harcourt Education Ltd / Jules Selmes

Every effort has been made to contact copyright holders of material reproduced in this book. Any omissions will be rectified in subsequent printings if notice is given to the publishers.

Introduction

Welcome to this BTEC National Uniformed Public Services course book, specifically designed to support students on the following programmes:

- BTEC National Award in Uniformed Public Services
- BTEC National Certificate in Uniformed Public Services
- BTEC National Diploma in Uniformed Public Services.

This book includes all the core units for the BTEC National Award, Certificate and the Diploma, as well as a number of specialist units.

You will find further specialist units in Book 2. These are:

- The planning for and management of major incidents
- Responding to emergency service incidents
- Uniformed public services employment
- Understanding the criminal justice system and police powers
- Understanding behaviour in public sector employment
- Communication and technology in the uniformed public services

- Custodial care of individuals
- Understanding aspects of the legal system and law making process

The aim of this book is to provide a comprehensive source of information for your course. It follows the BTEC specification closely, so that you can easily see what you have covered and quickly find the information you need. Examples and case studies from the public services are used to bring your course to life and make it enjoyable to study. We hope you will be encouraged to find your own examples of current practice too.

You will often be asked to carry out research for activities in the text, and this will develop your research skills and enable you to find many sources of interesting information, particularly on the Internet.

In some units of the book you will find information about different jobs, roles and responsibilities across the range of uniformed public services. We hope that this information will be of practical help when making your career choices.

Unit	Unit title	Award	Certificate	Diploma
1	Government, policies and the public services	Core	Core	Core
2	Team leadership in the uniformed public services	Core	Core	Core
3	Citizenship, contemporary society and the public services	Core	Core	Core
4	Team development in public services	Specialist	Core	Core
5	Understanding discipline within the uniformed public services	Specialist	Core	Core
6	Diversity and the public services	Specialist	Specialist	Core
7	Physical preparation and fitness for the uniformed services	Specialist	Specialist	Specialist
8	International perspectives for the uniformed public services	Specialist	Specialist	Specialist
12	Crime and its effects on society	Specialist	Specialist	Specialist
13	Command and control in the uniformed public services	Specialist	Specialist	Specialist

Guide to learning and assessment features

This book has a number of features to help you relate theory to practice and reinforce your learning. It also aims to help you gather evidence for assessment. You will find the following features in each unit.

Assessment features

Grading icons

Throughout the book you will see the **P**, **M** and **D** icons. These show you where the tasks fit in with the grading criteria. If you do these tasks you will be building up your evidence to achieve your desired qualification. If you are aiming for a Merit, make sure you complete all the Pass **P** and Merit **M** tasks. If you are aiming for a Distinction, you will also need to complete all the Distinction **D** tasks. **P1** means the first of the Pass criteria listed in the specification, **M1** the first of the Merit criteria, **D1** the first of the Distinction criteria, and so on.

Preparation for assessment

Each unit concludes with a full unit assessment, which taken as a whole fulfils all the unit requirements from Pass to Distinction. Each task is matched to the relevant criteria in the specification.

Activities and assessment practice

Activities are also provided throughout each unit. These are linked to real situations and case studies and they can be used for practice before tackling the preparation for assessment. Alternatively, some can contribute to your unit assessment if you choose to do these instead of the preparation for assessment at the end of each unit.

 **Case study:** Appraisal

The use of appraisal is widespread among the public services. It is an organisational version of a personal action plan which is usually conducted by your immediate line manager. In general it follows the following structure:

Identify strengths and weaknesses
↓
Ensure that the role you fulfil makes use of your identified strengths
↓
Identify how your weaknesses could be overcome by training

Kerry is a new recruit to the fire service. In the 12 months she has served so far she doesn't feel she has made a major impact on the role and feels that other male recruits who started at the same time as her have adapted better to their role. She is concerned that her team leader thinks very little of her and this is causing Kerry to lose confidence in her abilities and make mistakes while on duty. The ongoing training and physical demands of the job are causing Kerry a great deal of distress and she believes she is falling further and further behind the other new recruits. Kerry is due to have an appraisal shortly and she wants to make the most of it to improve her performance and rebuild her confidence.

1. **How should Kerry prepare for her appraisal?**
2. **What questions should she ask during her appraisal?**
3. **What support should she ask for?**
4. **What type of feedback is she likely to encounter with regard to aspects of her job performance?**
5. **What could she do to help improve her performance after the appraisal?**

Assessment activity 2.5

1. You have been asked by your tutor to create a visual display in order to describe the different types of teams and stages of team development. **P6**

 Grading tips

P6 To achieve P6 you need to describe at least two different types of public service teams and describe clearly Tuckman's stages of team development and how they relate to public service teams.

Knowledge check

1. Explain in detail one of the main leadership styles used by the uniformed public services.
2. How does the democratic approach differ from the laissez-faire approach?
3. What are the main consequences of poor leadership?
4. What are the signs of an effective team?
5. List the main components of non-verbal communication and give three examples of effective body language.
6. Explain how you would conduct a briefing for a large team.
7. Explain how you would conduct a debriefing for a small team.
8. What are Belbin's main team roles and which one best fits you when working in a team?
9. List and describe the main qualities and skills a leader will need in the following roles:
   - prime minister
   - England cricket captain
   - chief executive of a multinational corporation.
10. Explain five different types of teams found within the uniformed public services.
11. Evaluate how effective Tuckman's theory is in explaining how a team develops.
12. List five common barriers to effective team performance and explain how they could be overcome.

It is important to evaluate as it helps the team to remember the goals initially set and determine whether they have been achieved. It also helps the team to praise each other and celebrate success, along with identifying any problems or weaknesses that could be rectified in future tasks.

Key terms

Evaluation A process used to gather information to determine whether or not the team has been successful and achievement of its aims has occurred.

Evaluating is an effective way of gathering information as a team, which can then be used to set group boundaries, devise improvement strategies and identify individual development issues. Individuals can acknowledge the benefits of team work, reflect on their own performance, plan for future development and make adjustments to how they work and interact within a future group situation.

To ensure that the team's performance is assessed you could, as the team leader, ask a series of questions which will encourage discussion, reflection and improvement.

Theory into practice

As a team leader it is important that you and the team reflect on the task. This can be done either informally or formally by asking a series of questions. You could try using some of the questions from the list below when assessing the team's performance – these questions should stimulate discussion amongst the team.

1. What were the main objectives of the task?
2. How much time did you spend on planning the task and completing it?
3. How did you go about making choices on how to complete the task?
4. What changes did you make during the planning or task stage?
5. What elements of your plan seemed to be effective or ineffective?
6. What additional support did you need and who provided it?
7. What qualities and skills did you bring to the task?
8. How did individuals contribute to the task (highlight main contributions)?
9. What do you think was your most valuable contribution to the task?
10. What have you learnt from the task and how will this help you in the uniformed services?

Figure 2.10 Ask questions that will encourage discussion, reflection and improvement

Learning features

Case studies

Interesting examples of real situations or companies are described in case studies that link theory to practice. They will show you how the topics you are studying affect real people and the services they provide.

Knowledge check

At the end of each unit is a set of quick questions to test your knowledge of the information you have been studying. Use these to check your progress, and also as a revision tool.

Theory into practice

These practical activities allow you to apply theoretical knowledge to travel and tourism tasks or research. Make sure you complete these activities as you work through each unit, to reinforce your learning.

Key terms

Issues and terms that you need to be aware of are summarised under these headings. They will help you check your knowledge as you learn, and will prove to be a useful quick-reference tool.

Consider this and Take it further

These are points for individual reflection or group discussion. They will widen your knowledge and help you reflect on issues that impact on public services. The 'Take it further' activities in particular will help you to obtain the knowledge and practice the skills required for the higher levels of achievement.

Government, policies and the public services

Introduction

This unit provides an introduction to the political structure of the UK and highlights the ways in which government policies affect the work of the uniformed public services. In order to understand this you will examine a variety of important political issues.

You will consider the different levels of government in the UK, such as central, regional and local government, and understand their impact on the work of the public services. You will find out how political representatives are elected to power and what their main roles and responsibilities are. This unit will also highlight the importance of government departments to the work of the uniformed public services and explain what their roles are in relation to a variety of services. You will also have the opportunity to identify how government policies are developed, the external factors that influence public policy and the impact that these policies can have on the work of the services.

After completing this unit you should be able to achieve the following outcomes:

- Understand the different levels of government in the UK and the democratic election process at each level
- Know the responsibilities government departments and other levels of government have for specific public services
- Know the processes involved in developing government policies and the influences that can affect government policy decisions
- Understand government policies in the UK and how they impact upon the uniformed public services.

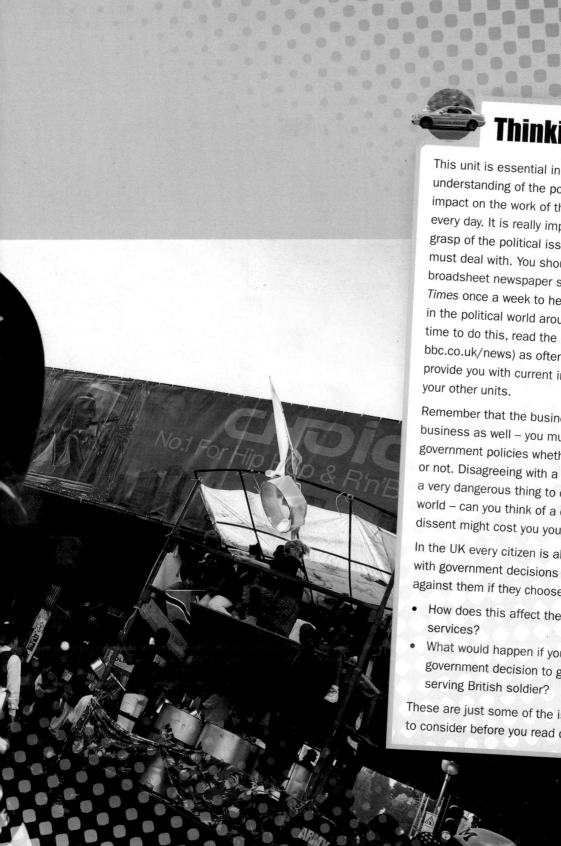

Thinking points

This unit is essential in providing you with an understanding of the policies and influences that impact on the work of the uniformed public services every day. It is really important that you have a clear grasp of the political issues that the public services must deal with. You should consider reading a broadsheet newspaper such as the *Guardian* or *Times* once a week to help you become educated in the political world around you. If you don't have time to do this, read the BBC news website (www. bbc.co.uk/news) as often as you can. It may also provide you with current information for many of your other units.

Remember that the business of government is your business as well – you must live and work under government policies whether you agree with them or not. Disagreeing with a government policy can be a very dangerous thing to do in some parts of the world – can you think of a country where political dissent might cost you your life?

In the UK every citizen is allowed to disagree with government decisions and protest peacefully against them if they choose.

- How does this affect the role of the public services?
- What would happen if you disagreed with a government decision to go to war but you were a serving British soldier?

These are just some of the issues you might want to consider before you read on.

Levels of government and their responsibilities

There are many different levels of government which exist and have a direct or indirect impact on people's lives and the work of the uniformed public services. The table below describes those levels.

This unit focuses on the UK government, so we will be focusing our attention on the following levels:

- central/national
- regional
- local.

Each level contains a variety of different organisations and branches of government which help to keep the country and the public services running smoothly and efficiently. Figure 1.1 shows the aspects of government we will examine.

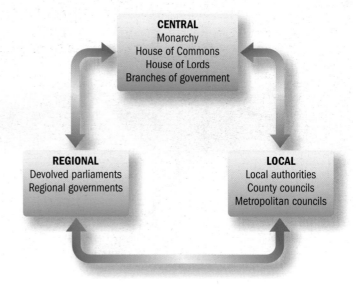

▲ Figure 1.1 All aspects of the governmental process interact and influence each other. This makes understanding and interpreting levels of government quite complex at times

Level	Description
Local	The managing of local resources to benefit local communities; usually carried out by the local council.
Regional	The management and distribution of resources over a larger geographical area. There are associated issues of independence and self-determination, for example regional assemblies or parliaments.
Multi-regional	Several different geographical regions sharing common interests or in conflict about shared resources, for example an issue which affects several local councils or counties.
Central/National	Issues which affect an entire nation such as changes in law and policy or taxation, for example new laws made in Parliament.

Table 1.1 Levels of government

Central government

Central government is the level of government that operates at a national level. It is usually located in the country's capital city and has very specific responsibilities which no other level of government has. These include, for example:

- signing treaties or agreements with other nations
- making laws
- defending the nation.

Consider this

Why are the responsibilities listed above the role of central government? What would happen if all levels of government had those powers?

▲ Question time in the House of Commons allows MPs to raise issues or seek information about the Government's plans

The central government of the UK is based in London at the Palace of Westminster. It contains the major central political institutions of the UK, the House of Commons and the House of Lords.

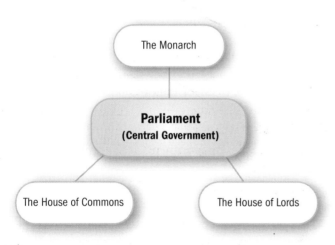

▲ Figure 1.2 These three institutions are known as Parliament

■ The House of Commons

The House of Commons (often just referred to as 'the House') consists of 646 elected members of Parliament (MPs) who represent a broad spectrum of political parties. Each MP represents a localised geographical area called a constituency. Constituencies can change boundaries to become bigger or smaller or sometimes disappear altogether. At the May 2005 general election, 13 constituency seats disappeared on the advice of the Boundary Commission for Scotland.

Consider this

All MPs must swear allegiance to the Queen. The oath reads: 'I swear by Almighty God that I will be faithful and bear true allegiance to Her Majesty Queen Elizabeth, her heirs and successors, according to law. So help me God.'

The five elected members of Sinn Féin have not sworn allegiance to the Queen so are not allowed to take their seats in Parliament or use their vote. Sinn Féin representatives are Republicans, which means they do not believe in the power of the monarchy.

- Do you think it is important that MPs swear allegiance to the Queen, or should allegiance to the public be an MP's first duty?

Election to the House of Commons

There are two ways in which you can be elected to the House of Commons:

- during a general election, representatives from all constituencies are elected simultaneously. A general election happens every five years or so

- a by-election takes place when the current representative of a constituency dies, retires or resigns and a new representative is needed for that one constituency only. A by-election can occur at any time.

A whole range of political views and interests are represented in the House of Commons. This enables the House to ensure that legislation and decisions are well debated by a variety of individuals holding different political views. The majority party is called upon to form the government and this party sits to the right of the Speaker while the opposition and smaller parties sit on the left of the Speaker. The Speaker is an MP who is elected to serve as the Chair of the House. They monitor discussions and ensure rules are followed. If a party has a majority of MPs they can pass laws almost unopposed, so the variety of parties represented does not always mean that unfair or flawed law will be stopped.

The role of the House of Commons

The House of Commons has several main roles to fulfil, as shown in Table 1.2 below.

Remember!

- The House of Commons is based in London at the Palace of Westminster.
- There are currently 646 members of parliament and nine parties represented in the House of Commons.
- All MPs must swear an oath to the Queen before taking their seat.
- The House of Commons performs a variety of functions such as making laws, scrutinising the work of government and controlling finance.

■ The House of Lords

The House of Lords dates to the fourteenth century and has a long, distinguished and, more recently, controversial history. The House of Lords can have a variable amount of members; currently there are around 730.

There are four different types of Lords:

- *Life peers*. These are Lords for their lifetime only; they cannot pass their title on to their children. These individuals are appointed by the Queen on the advice of the Prime Minister and they make up the majority of the Lords; there are currently around 600 of them.

Function	Explanation
Making laws	Nearly 50 per cent of the time of the House of Commons is spent on making new laws. These laws can have an extremely wide impact on the country and public services alike.
Controlling finance	The House of Commons controls the raising of finances through taxation and the selling of government assets. It must also give its approval to any plans the government has to spend money. The House can also check up on the spending of government departments through the Public Accounts' Committee.
Scrutiny	The House of Commons scrutinises the work of the government. The government must explain its policies to the House and be prepared to accept criticism and questioning. This ensures that all decisions have been examined by a variety of individuals before they happen.
Delegated legislation	The House does not have the time it needs to debate, discuss and pass all the laws needed by the country. The solution to this problem is the creation of delegated legislation – the House creates the parent law and then monitors how delegated legislation is implemented by local authorities and councils.
Examining European proposals	The House of Commons must examine all proposed European laws in order to assess their likely impact on the UK, its population and its public services.
Protecting the individual	Members of the House of Commons are often contacted by individuals with difficulties. In addition, large petitions are often put forward to the House on a variety of issues of importance to individuals, such as road building, reducing taxes and changes to law.

Table 1.2 The main roles of the House of Commons

- *Law Lords*. These are salaried full-time senior judges. They are also known as 'the Lords of Appeal in Ordinary'. The Queen appoints these judges on the advice of the Lord Chancellor; although the Independent Judicial Appointments Board is due to take over this role in 2007. There can be up to 12 Law Lords but this function of the House of Lords is due to end in 2008 when a separate UK Supreme Court is likely to be established.
- *Bishops and archbishops.* There are currently around 25 bishops and archbishops who represent the Church of England in the House of Lords. They pass their title on to the next most senior bishop when they retire.
- *Elected hereditary peers*. These Lords received their title through inheritance from a family member. Hereditary peers lost the right to vote on House of Lords matters in 1999, but around 90 of them currently remain.

Consider this

- Since there are representatives from the Church of England in the House of Lords, should other religions have an automatic right to be represented? Give the reasons for your answer.
- The House of Lords used to consist of hereditary life peers. In essence our upper chamber was made up of the aristocracy. This is no longer the case. What are the advantages and disadvantages of hereditary life peers?

The House of Lords is currently undergoing a series of radical reforms. These proposals are still under development, however, it is likely that all members of the Lords will be elected in the near future.

The role of the House of Lords

The House of Lords carries out a variety of roles. Some are similar to those of the House of Commons while others are quite different, as the table below shows.

Role	Description
Judicial work	The House of Lords is the most senior court of law in the UK, although this will change with the establishment of the UK Supreme Court in 2008.
Law creation	The House of Lords plays a large part in the process by which a bill is created (this is described later in the unit). The Lords spend around 60 per cent of their time on this kind of work.
Scrutiny	As with the Commons, the House of Lords scrutinise the government, using questioning and criticism as a form of control of government.
Independent expertise	The Lords conduct a variety of investigations and inquiries. They have a range of expertise which can be used on government business.

Table 1.3 The roles of the House of Lords

Remember!

- The House of Lords contains four different types of Lords – Law Lords, elected hereditary peers, bishops and life peers.
- There are currently around 730 Lords.
- The House of Lords acts as a check on the House of Commons.
- It plays a key role in the creation of law.
- It offers independent expertise to the government.

■ The monarch

The UK is a constitutional monarchy which means that the Head of State is the current reigning monarch. However, laws are generated and approved by an elected body – in the UK, the Houses of Parliament.

The current monarch is Her Majesty Queen Elizabeth II who has reigned since 1952. Her formal title in the UK is 'Elizabeth the Second, by the Grace of God of the United Kingdom of Great Britain and Northern Ireland and of Her other Realms and Territories, Queen, Head of the Commonwealth, Defender of the Faith'.

The Queen has several important formal and ceremonial governmental roles including:

- opening each new session of parliament
- dissolving parliament before a general election
- appointment of the Prime Minister
- final approval of laws via 'royal assent'
- appointment of peers
- advice and guidance to the Prime Minister.

▲ The Queen carries out various public duties in her role as monarch

Devolution and the decentralisation of power

Devolution is a process whereby power is transferred from a centralised governmental organisation to a regional organisation. Devolution consists of three elements:

- the transfer of power to another elected body which is lower down the chain of authority
- the geographical move of power from the capital to another city or town
- the transfer of roles and responsibilities of government from central to regional assemblies.

The powers of regional assemblies are defined by central government. They rarely include major financial powers or large scale law-making powers. In effect, regional assemblies are very much a junior power in the process of government.

Advantages of devolution	Disadvantages of devolution
Regional assemblies can reflect and take into account cultural and linguistic differences between the region and central government.	Establishing regional assemblies is very expensive. Why create an organisation to do what central government already does?
Regional assemblies are more in touch with the needs of their people; laws will be fairer and more readily accepted by the people.	Regional assemblies lack the decision-making experience of central government.
Reduces the burden on central government.	There may be conflict between regional and central government.
Because regional assemblies only deal with the work of the region they can focus more effectively on this than central government.	Devolution may lead to the break up of the UK.
Central government can concentrate on issues of national importance rather than being concerned about the regions.	Low voter turnout in devolution referendums indicates a lack of popular support for regional assemblies.
The combative politics seen in centralised government may be reduced in regional assemblies where parties share common goals.	

Table 1.4 The advantages and disadvantages of devolution

Key Terms

Devolution When central government decides to pass governmental powers to a lower level elected body.

Regional government When decisions about what happens in a particular region are made at a local level.

In the UK there are three main national assemblies which have devolved power. These are:

- the Scottish Parliament
- the Welsh Assembly
- the Northern Ireland Assembly.

■ The Scottish Parliament

In 1707 the Acts of Union created a new state, the Kingdom of Great Britain, by merging the Kingdom of Scotland and the Kingdom of England. The Acts also saw the merging of the Scottish and English parliaments to form a new Parliament of Great Britain, based at Westminster in London.

The Acts of Union occurred a century after Scotland and England had first shared a monarch. After Elizabeth I died in 1603 leaving no English heir, the throne of England had passed to her cousin, James VI of Scotland, who then became James I of England.

The history and clan culture of Scotland was quite different from England. The Acts of Union ensured that much of this individual character would survive, including a separate legal system, education system and Church organisation. However, the institutions of Westminster took control of Scottish political life and in essence Scotland was ruled by the UK Parliament. This state of affairs continued for almost 300 years until the Scotland Act 1998 established the Scottish Parliament.

Today, the Scottish Parliament is empowered to deal with devolved matters such as education, health, civil and criminal law, environment, housing and local government. The Scottish government is self-contained which means it can pass laws without needing authorisation from the UK Parliament. The UK Parliament has reserved powers, which means it still has jurisdiction on matters that affect the UK as a whole or have an international impact.

The Scottish Parliament is currently made up of around 130 elected members of the Scottish Parliament (MSP). As with the English Parliament, the party which has the most representatives forms the government, which is also called the Scottish Executive. The majority party selects a representative from their ranks who is appointed as First Minister by the Queen.

- Scotland became subject to the laws of Great Britain in 1707.
- The Scottish Parliament was created by the Scotland Act 1998.
- It consists of around 130 members (MSPs).
- The leader of the Scottish Parliament is called the First Minister.
- The Scottish Parliament deals with devolved matters such as housing, health and education.

Consider this

Why do you think Wales and England have had a much closer administrative and political relationship than England and Scotland?

■ The Welsh Assembly

The Act of Union between England and Wales was signed in 1536, almost 170 years before the union between Scotland and England. This means that England and Wales have traditionally been much closer in terms of culture and institutions than Scotland. The Welsh Assembly was established by the Government of Wales Act 1998 after a Welsh referendum showed public support for the idea.

The Welsh Assembly has about 60 members, 40 of whom are elected constituency members. Twenty additional members are elected on a regional basis to ensure that the overall number of seats awarded to a party in an election represents the overall number of votes received by that party.

Like the Scottish Parliament, the Welsh Assembly has considerable scope to deal with regional issues such as transport, health, education and the environment. Wales also has a First Minister who is elected by the whole executive and is usually the leader of the largest political party. One substantial difference between the Scottish Parliament and the Welsh Assembly is that Wales does not have jurisdiction over its own criminal and civil law; it is subject to English law in this area.

■ The Northern Ireland Assembly

The Northern Ireland Assembly was created by the Northern Ireland Act 1998. This Act was based on a referendum of the Belfast Agreement (more often referred to as The Good Friday Agreement). There are currently about 108 members, made up of 6 representatives from each of the 18 constituencies in Northern Ireland.

▲ The Belfast Agreement was a major political development in the Northern Ireland peace process

As with Scotland and Wales, the Northern Ireland Assembly has responsibility for education, health, agriculture, housing and so on. The Assembly is based at Stormont and there are around 10 political parties represented within it. Like the other regional assemblies it has a First Minister who is elected by all members and is usually from the dominant party. The conflict between the different parties in Northern Ireland in the past has led to an unstable assembly.

■ Regional assemblies in England

There are eight regional assemblies in England which were created by the Regional Development Agencies Act 1998; they are as follows:

- East of England Regional Assembly
- North East Assembly
- South East England Regional Assembly
- West Midlands Regional Assembly
- East Midlands Regional Assembly
- South West Regional Assembly
- North West Regional Assembly
- Yorkshire and Humber Assembly.

London has its own regional system which works differently from those listed above.

▲ Figure 1.3 Regional assemblies in England

Case study: The London region

Arrangements for regional governance in London are different to those for the other eight regional assemblies in England. London has the Greater London Authority (GLA) which is a city-wide form of government with an elected mayor and a separately elected assembly. The Mayor of London plays a key role in the development of the city's policies on a variety of issues such as transport, emergency planning and budgets for key public services such as the Metropolitan Police Authority and the London Fire and Emergency Planning Authority.

The assembly acts as a form of scrutiny on the actions of the mayor to ensure that what he or she is doing is correct and in the best interests of London. To this end the assembly must:

- approve all of the mayor's budgets

- have the opportunity to question the mayor at a monthly question time
- investigate and publish reports on issues which affect Londoners.

1   Why do you think that the London region needs a different form of regional assembly from the other eight regions?

2   Is it important to have a Mayor of London who acts a spokesperson for the capital?

3   Why would the activities of the Mayor require scrutiny?

4   Are there issues which affect Londoners which don't affect the rest of the country?

The membership of regional assemblies varies from region to region. About 70 per cent of the members are elected local authority councillors and 30 per cent are drawn from businesses, voluntary groups, religious groups and environmental organisations. Regional assemblies are funded through central government although some also receive money from local authorities.

Consider this

What are the implications of allowing devolution to continue to other regions which have distinctive culture and language such as Cornwall?

The role of regional assemblies

Regional assemblies perform four main roles:

REGIONAL PLANNING
They are responsible for developing, monitoring and reviewing regional planning and transport strategies.

REGIONAL HOUSING
They make recommendations to the government on housing priorities in their area.

ADVOCACY AND POLICY DEVELOPMENT
They provide a voice for the regions in parliament and at European level. They also promote regional partnerships.

ACCOUNTABILITY
They check and monitor the work of regional development agencies.

▲ Figure 1.4 The four core roles of the regional assemblies

Theory into practice

Regional assemblies may also fulfil a variety of other roles and responsibilities which are unique to their region. If you go to the English Regions website at ern.smartregion.org.uk you can find out more about your own regional assembly and the work that it does.

■ Local government

There are many forms of local government such as county councils, metropolitan councils, parish and district councils. Many of the roles and responsibilities they perform overlap, as shown in the table below.

Type of council	Roles and responsibilities	
County	• Education • Emergency planning • Highways and traffic • Libraries • Planning and development	• Public transport • Refuse disposal • Social Services • Trading standards
District	• Registration of births, deaths and marriages • Cemeteries and crematoria • Education • Environmental health • Planning and development	• Housing • Recreation and amenities • Refuse collection • Registration of electors • Tax and Council Tax collection
Parish	• Street lighting • Local transport and traffic services • Allotments • Cemeteries • Recreation grounds	• War memorials • Seating and shelters • Rights of way • Tourist information centres
Metropolitan	• Registration of births, deaths and marriages • Cemeteries and crematoria • Education • Emergency planning • Environmental health • Highways and traffic • Housing • Libraries • Planning and development	• Public transport • Recreation and amenities • Refuse collection • Refuse disposal • Registration of electors • Social Services • Tax and Council Tax collection • Trading standards
Unitary authorities	• Registration of births, deaths and marriages • Cemeteries and crematoria • Education • Emergency planning • Environmental health • Highways and traffic • Housing • Libraries • Planning and development	• Public transport • Recreation and amenities • Refuse collection • Refuse disposal • Registration of electors • Social Services • Tax and Council Tax collection • Trading standards

Table 1.5 Roles and responsibilities of local government

Assessment activity 1.1

An advert for a public services liaison officer at your local council grabs your attention, and it seems like your dream job. When the application form arrives it is clear that you will be required to give a 10-minute formal presentation on your understanding of the levels of government. You will need to cover the following:

- central government
- devolved parliaments
- county councils
- regional governments
- local authorities
- metropolitan councils
- other institutions in the government process such

as the House of Lords, House of Commons and the monarchy

- the main roles at government levels, such as the Prime Minister and council members.

1 Make notes to describe the different levels of government. Be sure to cover the ones listed above.

2 Create a PowerPoint or similar slide to show how they relate to each other.

3 Produce a handout which explains the responsibilities of different levels of government and local councils in the UK. **M1**

Grading tips

P1 This task asks you to outline your knowledge of the different levels of government. An outline is a brief overview or description of the information; in this case, the responsibilities of each level of government. Make sure that you cover all the levels in the list above, from elected bodies in local councils to national government. Your slide could contain a diagram

to show the relationship between the levels of government – a hierarchy chart or similar could be used.

M1 To achieve a merit you need to show that you understand the different levels by explaining in your own words how each of the responsibilities are managed.

Branches of government

The UK is a liberal democracy. This means that competition and plurality are encouraged and the interference of the state is kept to a minimum. There are three forms of power involved in the running of a liberal democracy.

1. Legislative

This is the power to make laws. In the UK the body with legislative power is Parliament. Parliament makes laws through a multi-stage process, which is outlined later in this unit. In addition to the

power to make new laws, Parliament also has the legislative power to reform old laws.

2. Executive

This is the power to suggest new laws and ensure existing laws are implemented. This power is invested in government departments and the Civil Service, who deal with the day-to-day running of the country. Laws are suggested via green papers, which open discussion about potential new laws, and white papers, which set out blueprints for potential laws.

LEGISLATIVE

JUDICIAL

EXECUTIVE

BRANCHES OF GOVERNMENT

▲ Figure 1.5 The three forms of power in the UK

3. Judicial

This is the power to interpret the laws that have been made and make unbiased judgements on whether laws have been broken. This power is given to the court system and is implemented by judges in all courts in the UK.

These three powers work together to ensure the smooth running and stability of the nation.

The main roles in government

The government in its current form could not work effectively without people who fulfil the main roles needed to ensure the country works effectively and decisions are made and implemented. The key roles you are required to examine are:

- Prime Minister
- government ministers
- MPs
- mayors
- council members.

Key Terms

Prime Minister The leader of the political party with the most seats in the House of Commons.

Minister Usually MPs appointed by the Prime Minister to take charge of a government office such as Defence, or the Home Office.

Cabinet Committee of the twenty or so most senior government ministers who meet once a week to support the Prime Minister in running the country.

■ The Prime Minister

The individual who is appointed to the office of Prime Minister (PM) is usually the leader of the political party with the highest number of representatives in the House of Commons. Currently this is Gordon Brown who is the leader of the Labour party. The role of PM is complex and difficult, involving a variety of administrative, bureaucratic and public duties such as:

- allocation of duties to ministers
- appointment and dismissal of ministers

- appointment of chairs of national industries
- the giving out of honours
- setting agendas for government business
- control of information released to the Cabinet, Parliament and the public.

As leader of the government, the Prime Minister has a large impact on the public services. This includes everything from day-to-day operations and uniforms to pay and pensions. The Prime Minister does not run the government alone, but it is his or her vision that informs government policies which affect the way that public services operate.

The power of the PM

The Prime Minister is a very powerful figure. Although power is supposed to be distributed throughout the cabinet, in effect the PM is extremely influential and dominant. The PM also plays a significant role on the European and World stage, meeting with other heads of state to discuss foreign and financial policies which can have implications far beyond UK borders.

However, it is important to note that the PM does not have an entirely free rein – as a public servant he or she is answerable to the Queen, his or her political party and the public. Furthermore, the PM should not appoint anyone he or she likes to ministerial posts but should take account of advice given by senior advisors and ensure that the individuals appointed are competent and do not create substantial political imbalance within their own party. Ministerial appointments are often given to those who have been loyal supporters of the PM or who share their political ideology.

The influence of the media

The increased concentration of the media on high profile politicians such as government ministers and the Prime Minister means that their activities are closely scrutinised and the majority of their choices are in the public domain. Thus the PM must balance personal conscience with public demands. The general public often favour or disfavour issues based on biased media information rather than a real analysis of the facts. Leaders must be aware of this and sometimes be prepared to take a political stance which is in opposition to the wishes of the public.

■ Government ministers

There are many government ministers but the 20 or so most important ministers are called 'the Cabinet'. This is the central committee of the UK government. Cabinet members are selected by the Prime Minister; the majority are elected MPs from the House of Commons who have been selected by virtue of their expertise and experience to head up particular departments, or ministries, such as the Ministry of Defence. The Cabinet also consists of a few members of the House of Lords and so it is representative of both chambers of Parliament.

Some ministers have considerable influence on the work of the public services, other ministers less so. Ministers with the greatest influence on the services are those who head up the sections of government which are directly responsible for the emergency and armed services, such as the Home Secretary and the Minister of Defence. It is the role of these ministers to lead the implementation of new policy and initiative for the services, and to monitor spending and budget allocations.

The structure of the Cabinet

The role of the Cabinet is sometimes difficult to distinguish from the role of Prime Minister. While the Cabinet is a group of individuals with equal collective responsibility for policy, the final judgment of the PM can be the decisive factor.

In addition, it has been argued that the Cabinet is informally divided into two groups. The first comprises between 6 and 10 very senior ministers who carry tremendous authority. This group would usually include ministers such as the Chancellor of the Exchequer and the Home Secretary. The second consists of 10 to 12 ministers with much less influence and authority.

The role of the Cabinet

The role of the Cabinet is:

- to make important government and policy decisions
- to review decisions which have already been made to assess their impact on policy areas
- to ensure that key social problems are reviewed, such as rising crime rates, inflation and the state of the NHS
- to help ensure that all government ministries are able to communicate freely with each other, thereby ensuring that decisions taken by one department do not have unintended consequences on another department.

Ministers must show public unity and coherence in decisions if they are to retain public confidence, and the Cabinet also helps to reinforce this.

It can be difficult for a cabinet to address social problems in depth because of the many time pressures that Cabinet ministers are under. For example, some Cabinet meetings only happen once a week for a few hours and it may be difficult to carry out an in-depth review with all Cabinet members. Some problems may be referred to a separate Cabinet committee which will feedback to the main cabinet on its findings.

There are some issues which overlap many government departments, for example terrorism. On issues such as these, ministries try to work in close coordination to ensure that the overall government response to a situation is sensible and provides a good service to citizens.

Key government positions

Key government departments include HM Treasury, Transport, Education, Health and Media.

Departments which have a large impact on the public services are:

- the Treasury – controls public spending, customs and excise
- the Home Office – responsible for police, immigration, and counter-terrorism
- the Ministry of Defence – responsible for the Armed Forces, peacekeeping
- the Ministry of Transport – responsible for HM Coastguard

- the Ministry of Health – responsible for the Ambulance Service
- the Ministry of Justice – responsible for probation, prisons and the Courts.

All government departments are headed up by a Secretary of State (senior minister) who may or may not be part of the Cabinet. The Secretary of State is supported by several junior ministers who are responsible for specific areas of the minister's responsibilities.

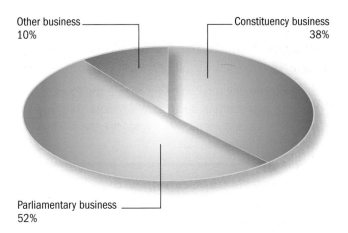

Other business 10%
Constituency business 38%
Parliamentary business 52%

▲ Figure 1.6 The duties of an MP are split between working in the constituency where he or she was elected and working in the House of Commons itself

Theory into practice

The 646 elected members of Parliament cannot run an effective government by themselves. The actual machinery of government, which sees decisions implemented, lies with the 500,000 or so civil servants who execute government decisions.

The role of the civil servant is complex and wide ranging:

1 What responsibilities do civil servants have, to allow ministers to do their jobs?

2 What would happen without the civil service?

Consider this

Who is your local MP? What role does he or she play in your local area?

■ Members of Parliament

Although the role of MP is largely decided by the individual themselves, there are several key functions which they may choose to perform. Many MPs spend a great deal of time in their constituency listening to and acting upon the concerns of their constituents. This is particularly true of MPs who do not have an official role in government.

One of the benefits of the UK's current voting system is that MPs are strongly tied to a particular geographical area and a particular local population. This means they need to make sure they address the concerns of their constituents. However, MPs are often powerless to address local concerns which constituents are likely to raise, such as rubbish collection or poor repair of council houses, since these issues are the province of local councillors.

Another of the key roles performed by MPs is that of advocate. Although they have limited power to directly address individual constituents' concerns, MPs are able to act as advocate for sectional groups. Sectional groups are groups of people with specific shared interests such as businesses, charities or pressure groups. The MP as advocate can be very useful to the sectional groups concerned, as their MP can raise their profile and influence changes in law and policy.

MPs also spend a great deal of time on public business. This includes the creation of legislation and membership of committees which evaluate potential law. These roles can have a large impact on the public services. The creation of new law can sometimes mean substantial changes to the way the public services operate and what they are allowed to do.

■ Mayors

A mayor can have a variety of roles. They are normally appointed or elected for a period of one year and their role is often largely ceremonial. The main duties of a mayor are:

- representing the council on civic and ceremonial occasions
- chairing meetings of the full council
- promoting the area and being the council's spokesperson
- teaching civic pride to young people
- supporting charities and community groups.

The impact that mayors have on public services is minimal, but they can and do have an impact on the local community by encouraging people to respect and improve their locality. This may have an indirect effect on some services by reducing crime and nuisance behaviour.

The role of the Mayor of London is different, as you will have noted from the previous detail on the London assembly and its mayor.

■ Council members

Councillors are elected by the local community to conduct the business of the council. They try to improve the quality of life in their area where they are elected by making decisions about local issues such as transport, education and public services. They are often community leaders and promote community groups and charities in their area.

They may also act as advocates by speaking on behalf of individuals or groups who are in need.

One of their most important roles is to decide on the policies which will be implemented by the council. This can have far reaching effects both on ordinary citizens and the work of the public services. For example, local councils are responsible for setting council tax for their region. Some of this tax will be used to finance services such as the police

and fire service. It is the responsibility of local councils to ensure that council tax is sufficient to meet the funding needs of public services.

Remember!

- Government is made up of many departments which have responsibilities for key policy areas. These departments are called ministries.
- Each department is headed by a Secretary of State who is supported by several junior ministers of state.
- Key departments include HM Treasury, Transport, Education, Health and Media.
- Departments which have a large impact on the public services are the Treasury, Home Office, Ministry of Defence, Ministry of Transport and Ministry of Health.
- The decisions of the Cabinet and individual ministries are performed by the Civil Service.

Democratic election processes

In order to be a democratic society the representatives who serve on our behalf in government must be elected by the people of the nation. In order to understand the election procedures of the UK it is important to examine the following factors:

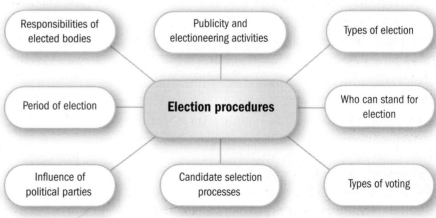

▲ Figure 1.7 Factors involved in election procedures

Types of election

There are several types of election in the UK but the most common are general elections and local elections.

- A general election is where all the seats in the House of Commons are open for re-election. The maximum term that a Parliament can sit is 5 years and 3 weeks without a general election, so this type of election tends to happen every 3½–5 years depending on when the party in power think they might have the best chance of winning. It is the Prime Minister who decides when the next election will be within the proper time period.
- Local elections follow a four-year cycle but not all councils elect at the same time.

Who can stand for election?

Who can stand for election depends on the type of election.

- For a general election where all UK constituencies are open for re-election, the candidate must be over 21 years of age and a British, Commonwealth or Republic of Ireland citizen. They must be nominated by at least 10 of the registered electors in the constituency and if they want to stand for a particular party they must receive authorisation from that party. If you don't have authorisation from a party you are classed as independent. In addition, a candidate must pay a £500 deposit when they register as a candidate; they will only get this money back if they receive over 5 per cent of the votes cast. You may not stand for election if you are a prisoner serving a sentence of over 12 months.
- For a local election the candidate must satisfy similar criteria but an individual who is a citizen of a European Union nation may also stand. A person is not eligible to stand for local election if employed by the local authority, subject to bankruptcy restrictions or previously sentenced to a prison term of three months or more.

Candidate selection procedures

If you are standing as an independent representative there are no candidate selection procedures; as long as you are eligible you may stand for office.

Existing MPs who want to stand for re-election are normally automatically approved.

The political parties often have more potential candidates than they need to fill the seats they are hoping to win. This is when some form of selection procedure becomes necessary to ensure that the best candidate, or the candidate most likely to win the seat, is selected. There are many methods of doing this. One method is that the party selects a list of centrally approved candidates from which the local branch can then choose. Candidates are decided in a rigorous way which, in many ways, mirrors the public services selection procedure. They are subject to a paper sift of their CV and application form; there may be a weekend of aptitude tests; they may also undergo a background check.

Another method involves the local branch of the party interviewing the potential candidates to find the one they want to serve their area. Sometimes a party will draw up a shortlist containing only women in order to improve the numbers of women serving in Parliament, but this can be controversial.

Consider this

What are your views on women-only shortlists?

Period of election

Periods of election in the UK can range from 1 to 5 years depending on the post the candidate is elected to. Mayors typically serve for 1 year, councillors for up to 4 years and MPs for up to 5 years before they must stand down or be re-elected.

Types of voting

Most people are familiar with the tradition of going to a polling office (usually a church, school or community centre which has changed purposes for the day). Here, voters mark a ballot slip by placing a cross next to the name of the candidate they wish to vote for. Votes are cast in a voting booth, to guarantee privacy.

As technology evolves there are more ways to cast a vote than ever before. Today, alternative voting options include postal voting and electronic voting in some cases. There is also the facility to have someone cast your vote for you; this is called voting by proxy.

The influence of political parties

Political parties have a tremendous amount of influence on the election process. Most importantly, the political party in power at the time is the one who chooses to have a general election in the first place. This means they can call a general election at any time within a five-year period that best suits them and makes it more likely that they will win. They also have a tremendous amount of funds for backing their candidates in terms of publicity and resources. This puts smaller parties and independent candidates at a distinct disadvantage.

Responsibilities of elected bodies

The responsibilities of elected bodies are described earlier in this unit (see pages 4–7).

Publicity and electioneering activities

It is important that a candidate becomes well known in the area he or she is hoping to represent. To this end candidates will often undertake a great deal of publicity work, such as leafleting houses, displaying posters and canvassing door-to-door for votes. This is obviously helped if there is money available to pay for a team of people to support the candidate – hence larger, more wealthy parties have an advantage. In addition, during a general election you will often see party political broadcasts for the main parties outlining their policies (although broadcasts may concentrate on why you shouldn't vote for the other party – this is called negative campaigning).

Remember!

Political parties have the most significant influence on the election process and candidate selection.

Assessment activity 1.2

It is election time and your college has asked you to write an article for the student magazine. The article should enable learners who do not study politics to become familiar with the electoral process. Remember to include the following information:

- who can stand for election
- how candidates are selected
- the influence of parties on elections
- period of election
- publicity activities
- voting systems
- responsibilities of elected bodies
- election day activities.

Your article should be divided into three sections:

1 Write an introduction which describes the electoral process for one level of government in the UK. **P2**

2 Write a middle section which compares the electoral processes for at least two different levels of government in the UK. **M2**

3 Write a conclusion which analyses the responsibilities and electoral processes of two different levels of government in the UK. **D1**

Grading tips

P2 You only need to describe one election process, but you must clearly state which one you have chosen, and describe it accurately and in detail from the initial application to stand, to the election and the declaration of the vote.

M2 Don't forget to compare the electoral processes. This means examining the differences and similarities between them. It is not enough to produce a list of the similarities and differences; you should discuss your comparison in detail.

D1 To achieve D1, you must analyse the responsibilities and processes of two different levels of government in the UK. To do this, you must examine the issues covered in P1, P2, M1 and M2 in detail, showing evidence of your own views.

Government departments with responsibilities for the public services

Each government department has responsibility for one or more public services. The table below highlights the main government departments and their responsibilities to the uniformed public services.

Remember!

The uniformed public services fall into several different ministries. This is one of the reasons why they are subject to different terms and conditions of employment.

Assessment activity 1.3

In a group, in pairs or on your own, find out more about the responsibilities of different government departments. You should choose at least three departments from the following:

- the Ministry of Defence
- the Home Office
- the Department of Communities and Local Government
- HM Revenue and Customs
- the Immigration and Nationality Directorate
- the Department of Health
- the Ministry of Justice.

Once you have researched your chosen departments, you should complete the following task:

1 Produce a poster describing three government departments and their responsibilities for uniformed public services. **P3**

Government department	Responsibilities for the public services
Ministry of Defence (MOD) (www.mod.uk)	Has responsibility for the British Army, the Royal Navy and the Royal Air Force. It is headed by the Secretary of State for Defence and three junior ministers: • the Minister of State for the Armed Forces • the Under Secretary of State and Minister for Defence Procurement • the Under Secretary of State for Defence and Minister for Veterans. The MOD decides on budgets, policy and procurement (the acquisition of resources) for all three armed services. It therefore has tremendous influence on the armed services, deciding everything from pay and working conditions to equipment and locations of service.
The Home Office (www.homeoffice.gov.uk)	Has primary responsibility for the majority of UK civilian public services such as the police and immigration service. It contains the Immigration and Nationality Directorate and Passport Office, and has responsibility for homeland counter-terrorism.
Department of Communities and Local Government (www.communities.gov.uk)	This is where primary responsibility for the UK's Fire and Rescue services lies. It is headed by the Secretary of State for Communities and Local Government and several junior ministers. It has responsibility for: • allocating local governments with resources to fund their fire and rescue services • developing fire and rescue national policies and priorities • local government; while non-uniformed it is nevertheless an essential public service.
Department for Health (www.doh.gov.uk)	Has overall responsibility for the National Health Service (NHS). From a uniformed public service point of view, this gives them responsibility for the Ambulance Service.
HM Revenue and Customs (www.hmrc.gov.uk)	This government department has responsibility for the collection of taxes. From a public service point of view, it has responsibility for customs and excise.
Ministry of Justice (www.justice.gov.uk)	Has responsibility for the prisons, probation service and courts. It was created in May 2007 after the Home Office was split in two.

Table 1.6 Responsibilities of government departments to the uniformed public services

Grading tip

P3 In order to achieve a pass, you need to describe at least three different government departments. For each department include basic information such as the full name of the department, the minister in charge, the public service it is responsible for and a short description of the responsibilities.

The roles of individuals and responsibilities to the uniformed public services

In addition to the responsibilities of government departments, there are many individuals who have a responsibility towards the public services. These people include:

- the Prime Minister
- the Deputy Prime Minister
- government ministers
- civil servants
- councillors
- mayors.

Here we will examine the influence on the public services of the Civil Service and the Deputy Prime Minister.

The Civil Service

The Civil Service is a vital mechanism of government. It is split into departments which are attached to particular ministries. The civil servants in these departments are directly responsible to the minister in charge of that department and work for him or her in carrying out government policy. The structure of the Civil Service is very hierarchical and many civil servants make a career from progressing through the ranks.

Civil servants perform a variety of roles such as:

- consulting with pressure groups on specific issues
- providing advice to ministers
- preparing speeches for ministers
- dealing with a minister's correspondence
- research on specific issues of ministerial importance
- helping a minister prepare for questions they may face from the media
- costing of government proposals
- technical aspects of implementing policy.

The Civil Service is a very powerful organisation; government would be unable to deliver policy initiatives without it. Civil servants are meant to be politically impartial and as a consequence they are not allowed to stand for political office. They are privy to highly sensitive information, particularly in the Home, Foreign and Defence ministries, and because of this must abide by the Official Secrets Act. This means they are forbidden from discussing their work with the general public and media, since this could cause serious embarrassment to the government and possibly compromise national security.

Consider this

The effect of the Civil Service on the public services is enormous. It is a public service in its own right and provides underpinning support for all of the ministries responsible for helping the public services to do their job. This includes:

- budgets and finance
- procurement of equipment
- pay and conditions
- the national strategy of the services
- national policy initiatives
- the implementation of new laws.

The UK has no formal office of Deputy Prime Minister and the role exists at the discretion of the current Prime Minister. The role belonged to John Prescott until June 2007. Following constitutional changes announced on 5 May 2006, the Department for Communities and Local Government replaced the Office of the Deputy Prime Minister.

The accountability of the uniformed public services

Since the uniformed public services are funded with public money and are designed to serve the needs of the public, it is important that there are checks and balances on their behaviour. Some of the public services have tremendous power over the lives of individuals so it is essential that they are seen to act in a fair and consistent manner. Equally, it is important to note that the public services cost billions of pounds of taxpayers' money each year and the taxpayer has a right to know if that money is being used effectively.

The government recognises this and has set up a variety of inspectorates and monitoring commissions which are designed to establish whether the public services offer value for money and if they are effective in the job they are supposed to do. These inspectorates may also offer the public the opportunity to make a complaint about poor or unfair treatment, which can then be investigated impartially by a complaints agency.

There are three main aspects to investigating how the public services are monitored:

- inspectorates
- local organisations
- documents of accountability.

INSPECTORATES
Defence Vetting Agency
Police Complaints Commission
Health Care Commission
HM Inspectorate of Probation
HM Inspectorate of Constabulary
HM Inspectorate of Prisons

LOCAL ORGANISATIONS
Police authorities
Health authorities
Fire and Rescue
authorities

DOCUMENTS
Annual reports
Objectives
Mission statements
Internal complaints
Management procedures

Figure 1.8 Public services are monitored through inspectorates, local organisations and documents of accountability

Inspectorates are set up by the government on a national basis to ensure the smooth running of specified public services.

■ The Defence Vetting Agency (DVA)

The DVA exists to carry out national security checks. This kind of check might be applied to:

- anyone who wishes to join the armed services
- civilians who work for the Ministry of Defence
- civilian contractors who will potentially build on MOD land or supply MOD services
- individuals in government departments.

The DVA conducts around 140,000 checks on individuals each year which makes it the largest government vetting agency.

■ Independent Police Complaints Commission (IPCC)

The IPCC was created in 2004 to replace the Police Complaints Authority, although it gains its regulatory powers from the Police Reform Act 2002. It is funded by the Home Office but remains entirely independent of it. This ensures that any decisions it makes are free of government influence.

The IPCC can investigate in several different ways. It can choose to supervise a case being investigated by a police service internally or it can independently investigate if the complaint is about a serious matter. Serious complaints might include:

- incidents involving death or injury
- police corruption
- police racism
- perverting the course of justice.

The IPCC allocates teams of investigators to certain regions so they can deal with complaints quickly and efficiently as they arise. In 2005/6 a total of 26,286 complaints were received; this represented a 15 per cent increase on the previous year. The most common causes of complaints were:

- neglect or failure in duty (22 per cent)
- incivility, impoliteness and intolerance (20 per cent)
- assault (16 per cent)
- oppressive conduct or harassment (7 per cent)
- unlawful/unnecessary arrest or detention (5 per cent)
- breach of codes of practice on detention, treatment, questioning (4 per cent).

(*Source*: Police Complaints Statistics for England and Wales 2005/6)

■ Healthcare Commission

The Healthcare Commission promotes improvements in the healthcare sector in England and Wales. They are effectively the inspectorate of healthcare services including the ambulance service. They also have a role in dealing with complaints made against the National Health Service (NHS). They inspect all NHS organisations including GP surgeries, pharmacists, hospitals, school health services, private healthcare providers and ambulance services.

■ Her Majesty's Inspectorate of Probation for England and Wales

HM Inspectorate of Probation was originally established in 1936. It receives funding from the Ministry of Justice and reports directly to the Justice Minister, although it is independent of the government. The inspectorate exists to assess the performance of the National Probation Service and Youth Offending Teams in reducing re-offending and protecting the public. It also works very closely with the Inspectorate of Prisons to assess the effectiveness of offender management.

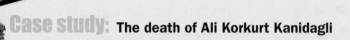

Case study: The death of Ali Korkurt Kanidagli

A complaint was made to the IPCC about the death of Mr Ali Korkurt Kanidagli in London on 12 November 2005, when he was hit by a Metropolitan Police vehicle which was responding to an emergency call. The speed at which the police vehicle was travelling and the tightness of the corner it was turning resulted in the officer losing control of the vehicle and mounting the pavement where it struck Mr Kanidagli causing fatal injuries. Another pedestrian also received injuries and the second officer in the police vehicle suffered minor injuries. The officer responsible was fined £500 and given 6 penalty points on his licence after pleading guilty to Driving Without Due Care and Attention.

1 Why is it important that the IPCC is fully independent of the police in situations such as this?

2 Do you think a complaint should have been raised against the officer – or was he simply doing his job?

3 Do you think the punishment was fair and appropriate?

■ Her Majesty's Inspectorate of Prisons for England and Wales

HMI Prisons is also funded by and reports directly to the Ministry for Justice while maintaining its independence. Although inspecting prison establishments is its main priority it also has a responsibility to inspect immigration holding centres and has been invited to inspect the military prison at Colchester.

In terms of its main responsibilities HMI Prisons must inspect every prison in England and Wales at least once every five years. However, there are a variety of different types of inspection, only some of which the prison will know about in advance. A prison cannot refuse entry to the inspectorate.

Types of prison inspection include:

- *Full inspection* – information is collected from a variety of sources including statistical data, prisoner accounts, and visitor and prison staff testimony.
- *Follow-up inspection* – if there has been a problem with an institution it might receive a follow-up evaluation to see if the situation has improved.
- *Short follow-up inspection* – brief visits to see whether small problems identified at full inspection have been corrected.

The purpose of the inspections is to ensure that the prison is fulfilling its aims. A prison should be safe for the inmates and provide an environment where they are treated with respect and dignity. The prison should provide activity and education which may lead to the rehabilitation of the offender and prepare him or her for release into the community.

Consider this

Prisons are not open to the public. If the inspectorate did not exist, nobody would know how prisoners were being treated.

■ Her Majesty's Inspectorate of Constabulary for England, Wales and Northern Ireland (HMIC)

HMIC is one of the oldest inspectorates in England. It dates back to the County and Borough Police Act of 1856. It is funded by and reports to the Home Office while maintaining its independence.

The role of HMIC is to formally inspect and assess the 43 police services in England and Wales and support the Chief Inspector of Criminal Justice in Northern Ireland. However, it also fulfils an inspection role for other bodies including:

- Central Police Training and Development Agency
- Civil Nuclear Constabulary
- British Transport Police
- Ministry of Defence Police
- Serious Organised Crime Agency.

HMIC is able to conduct several different types of inspections:

- *Thematic inspection* – a particular aspect of performance is measured across several different police constabularies, for example child protection or training of police officers.
- *Best value inspection* – focuses on whether a police authority is allocating and spending money in a manner which could be considered best value.
- *Command unit inspection* – focuses on leadership and management.
- *Baseline assessment* – monitors the improvement or deterioration in performance against a pre-established baseline.

Local organisations

■ The police authority

There are 43 police authorities in England and Wales, one for every police constabulary. They make sure that the police service in that area runs efficiently.

A police authority can vary in the number of representatives it has, but most have around 17 members who are made up of local councillors, local magistrates and lay people from the community. The police authority has a real impact on the work of the police service as it sets the strategic direction of the force and holds the Chief Constable accountable for the performance of his or her organisation. Another important function of the police authority is deciding how much council tax is needed to pay for the police service. This is crucial – without funding the police service could not operate.

Strategic Health Authorities (SHA)

There are currently 10 SHA in England and Wales, which almost matches the Regional Assembly areas discussed earlier in this unit (see pages 11–12); the only difference is the addition of a South Central region between the South West and the South East.

The SHA were created in 2006 after smaller health authorities were merged to form much larger ones. The role of the SHA includes:

- strategic oversight and leadership of the healthcare system in a particular region

- ensuring better value for money for taxpayers
- leading service improvements
- accountability to the Department of Health for providing high quality healthcare
- reducing health inequalities.

Fire and Rescue Authorities (FRA)

FRA are similar to police authorities in that they are made up of local representatives from the council. Most FRA have between 12 and 30 members depending on the size of the area they manage.

Their primary responsibility is to be accountable to the public in providing an efficient and effective fire and rescue service. The authority must ensure that the fire service has all the firefighters, equipment, premises and vehicles it needs to fulfil its duty to the public. It also has a responsibility for ensuring equality and diversity, and plays a key role in brigade recruitment and training policies.

How public services are accountable

The public services are held accountable via the documentation they produce.

Document	Explanation
Objectives	Many organisations set themselves a series of targets with the aim of reducing response times or making financial savings, for example. These targets are called objectives and increase accountability by making it easier to see if an organisation has achieved what it set out to do.
Annual report	Document produced by an organisation on either a voluntary or compulsory basis. It is made available to the community and tells interested parties how well the organisation performed in a given year. It usually details financial and performance targets and states how well an organisation has fulfilled its aims.
Mission statement	This is intended to summarise the core values of an organisation and tell people who read it why that organisation exists. The organisation should then endeavour to do what the mission statement says.
Internal complaints procedure	Procedure an organisation has for dealing with complaints that are made to it. Not all complaints will be referred to government complaints bodies as this would be too time consuming; often it is better to resolve a problem locally, where possible, to ensure speed and efficiency of response.
Management procedures	Management procedures exist to formalise how individuals should behave in a given situation and the procedures they should follow to deal with a set of events. They improve accountability by ensuring all staff know the guidelines they are expected to work within.

Table 1.7 Accountability documentation

Government policy can be generated by a number of factors, such as:

- a need identified by the public or organisations
- a reaction to an issue in the media
- a new issue such as terrorism which forces change in the way the government must run the country.

The creation of law and policy can be a complex procedure and there are many parts to it. This section aims to discuss policy-making procedure in the UK so you understand how laws and policies are generated.

Development processes

Initially policies begin life as ideas on how to change or manage a situation. These ideas can come from a variety of sources including:

- the public
- the media
- the public services
- politicians
- experts.

Meetings

If the policy is needed and the idea has merit, it becomes subject to a great deal of discussion in governmental meetings such as cabinet meetings and parliamentary committees and subcommittees. If the idea is still considered to be worthwhile after these discussions then the procedure becomes more formal – the idea is put into a green paper.

Green papers

A green paper is a document about a proposed change in the law, which is distributed to interested parties to gather their views on the change and open up a period of consultation and debate. This debate might take the form of public meetings, specialist consultation meetings or open enquiries. Sometimes the discussions around a green paper make it clear that the policy or law would not be welcome or is not needed, and the policy stops there. However, sometimes the discussions show that there is a need for the law and it moves ahead to the next stage – a white paper.

White papers

These contain a set of formal proposals on the new law or policy. White papers are the drafts of what will become known as bills in later stages of development.

Representation from outside government

Ways in which the new public policy can be influenced from outside government include:

- letters to MPs
- seeing an MP in their surgery
- taking into account the views of the opposition.

Bills

All potential statutes begin life as a bill. A bill is a proposal for a piece of legislation. There are three kinds:

- public bill
- private bill
- private members bill.

■ Public bill

A public bill is usually a proposal for a large piece of legislation which will affect the whole country. They are created by the government currently in power. They are sometimes preceded by a green paper which allows interested parties to consult and comment upon the ideas put forward. Examples of public bills are the Crime and Disorder Act 1998, Police and Criminal Evidence Act 1984 and the Theft Act 1968.

■ Private bill

A private bill is typically proposed by a local authority or large corporation and will usually affect only the people who proposed it in the first place. For instance, a private bill might deal with the compulsory purchase of land by a local authority in order to build a new motorway. An example of a private bill involving a large corporation is the Henry Johnson, Sons and Co. Limited Act 1996 which allowed the said company to transfer to France.

■ Private members' bills

A private member's bill is usually prepared by ordinary members of Parliament who have to enter a ballot in order to be guaranteed the time in Parliament that it takes to introduce a bill. This allocated time is very important – the reason private members' bills often fail is lack of time for them to be debated. Sometimes private members' bills are introduced as a way of drawing attention to a particular public concern, for instance the Wild Mammals (Hunting with Dogs) Bill drew massive public attention even though it did not succeed in becoming law in that parliamentary session. Examples of private members' bills are the Abortion Act 1967 and the Activity Centres (Young Persons Safety) Act 1995.

The legal process used to create legislation

The drafting of the statute

There are seven stages through which a bill must proceed before it can become law, as shown in Figure 1.9 on page 28.

Remember!

- Statute law is made by parliament.
- Statute is another name for law or policy.
- It is created via three kinds of bills; public, private and private members' bills.
- It is approved by a seven-stage procedure concluding with royal assent.
- The Monarch has not refused to sign a statute law since 1707.

Setting dates of implementation and issuing guidance and directives to public services

Making a new law or policy does not automatically mean that the public services will know how to implement it. It is important to have a period during which the public services can become familiar with the new law, undertake relevant training if necessary and be ready for when the bill becomes law. For this reason laws are rarely implemented immediately on being signed but instead have an implementation date. For example, the Human Rights Act 1998 didn't actually come into force until 2000. Before new laws come into force the government issues guidance and directives to the public services that are affected by the law, identifying to them what the changes are and what they will be responsible or accountable for.

Advertisements in the media to publicise the law

It is also important that the general public have the opportunity to become familiar with the new law. If the public were not informed about the law, they would fail to abide by it. Consequently the whole process of making the law would become rather pointless. A key way in which changes to the law are promoted to the public is through the use of the media.

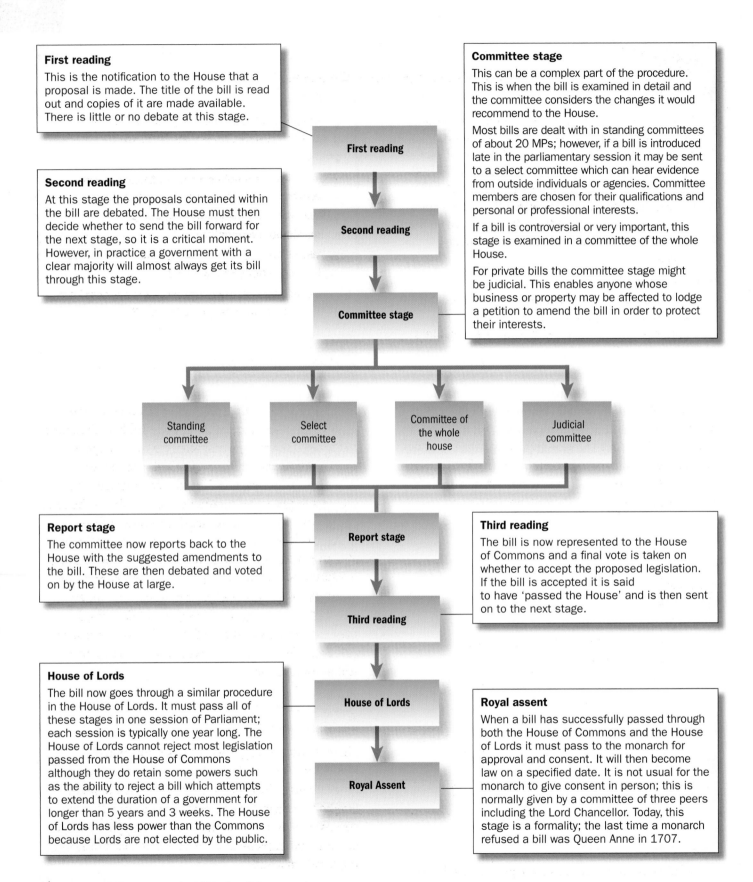

First reading

This is the notification to the House that a proposal is made. The title of the bill is read out and copies of it are made available. There is little or no debate at this stage.

Second reading

At this stage the proposals contained within the bill are debated. The House must then decide whether to send the bill forward for the next stage, so it is a critical moment. However, in practice a government with a clear majority will almost always get its bill through this stage.

Committee stage

This can be a complex part of the procedure. This is when the bill is examined in detail and the committee considers the changes it would recommend to the House.

Most bills are dealt with in standing committees of about 20 MPs; however, if a bill is introduced late in the parliamentary session it may be sent to a select committee which can hear evidence from outside individuals or agencies. Committee members are chosen for their qualifications and personal or professional interests.

If a bill is controversial or very important, this stage is examined in a committee of the whole House.

For private bills the committee stage might be judicial. This enables anyone whose business or property may be affected to lodge a petition to amend the bill in order to protect their interests.

Report stage

The committee now reports back to the House with the suggested amendments to the bill. These are then debated and voted on by the House at large.

Third reading

The bill is now represented to the House of Commons and a final vote is taken on whether to accept the proposed legislation. If the bill is accepted it is said to have 'passed the House' and is then sent on to the next stage.

House of Lords

The bill now goes through a similar procedure in the House of Lords. It must pass all of these stages in one session of Parliament; each session is typically one year long. The House of Lords cannot reject most legislation passed from the House of Commons although they do retain some powers such as the ability to reject a bill which attempts to extend the duration of a government for longer than 5 years and 3 weeks. The House of Lords has less power than the Commons because Lords are not elected by the public.

Royal assent

When a bill has successfully passed through both the House of Commons and the House of Lords it must pass to the monarch for approval and consent. It will then become law on a specified date. It is not usual for the monarch to give consent in person; this is normally given by a committee of three peers including the Lord Chancellor. Today, this stage is a formality; the last time a monarch refused a bill was Queen Anne in 1707.

First reading

Second reading

Committee stage

Standing committee | Select committee | Committee of the whole house | Judicial committee

Report stage

Third reading

House of Lords

Royal Assent

Figure 1.9 The stages of a bill before it becomes law

Case study: The use of mobile phones while driving

On 27 February 2007, new legislation came into force which increased the penalties which drivers receive if they use a hand-held mobile phone while driving. The new policy means offenders will receive a £60 fine and 3 penalty points on their driving licence. Penalties are much worse if the case goes to court and worse still if the offence was committed by a bus driver or the driver of a heavy goods vehicle.

A national multimedia campaign began on 22 January 2007 using the radio, television and Internet. The government also targeted key employers and industries with leaflets and posters.

Road safety officers and the police were heavily involved in promoting the change in law to the public.

1 Why did the media campaign begin a month earlier than the actual change in law?

2 Why did the government decide on a multimedia campaign?

3 Which form of advertising do you think would be most effective and why?

4 Do you think the government was successful in promoting the change to the law?

The case study above highlights the use of road safety officers and the police to promote a change in road safety law. Other organisations which may be involved in promoting change or implementing a new law include the Probation Service and the National Association for the Care and Resettlement of Offenders (NACRO).

Consider this

Why is it important that new laws have an implementation date rather than just being introduced immediately?

Other influences affecting government policy decisions

Demonstrations and strikes

These allow certain sections of the general public to show their displeasure at the government by publicly protesting against its decisions. Sometimes a public protest will make the government rethink its decisions, but more often the government will not change its agenda. However, strikes in particular can reveal loopholes in legislation which the government can then act to put right. An old example of this is the 1919 Police Act which made it illegal for police officers to strike. This law was introduced after a series of strikes about pay and conditions had led to social breakdown in some areas. At the time police pay and conditions were extremely poor and although the government made positive changes to these, one of the things they recognised was that in future the police must be prevented from striking – hence the new law which is still in force today.

Financial constraints

Finance affects every aspect of government and public service operations. One key consideration for government is the expense of introducing a new law weighed up against the benefits it would bring. If the government doesn't have the money to implement the law, it might implement a partial version of it or not implement it at all.

Immigration

Immigration is a necessary part of the UK's cultural life. Not only do immigrants enrich UK culture, they also carry out specialist jobs where there is a shortage of workers, for example in medicine. The policy on immigration must adapt to an increased global climate of movement. It must also take into account the people who choose to emigrate abroad and try to strike a balance between individuals coming into the UK and those leaving it.

The laws and policies on immigration in the UK are strict and are contained in the Immigration Act 1971, although there have been several updates and amendments since that time.

Terrorism

The terrorist attacks of 11 September 2001 against the USA had far reaching consequences in terms of changes to UK laws. The London bombings of 7 July 2005 also had a significant impact on policy changes.

- The Prevention of Terrorism Act 2005 supports the fact that terrorist incidents can trigger new laws which enable the public services to have more power.
- The Terrorism Act 2006 gives tremendous power to certain public services in their pursuit of terrorist suspects and terrorist intelligence.

Although it is widely recognised that there is a need to prevent terrorism, there has been a lot of debate about whether these laws give the public services too much power over the public.

Multinational corporations

Multinational corporations can be extremely big and powerful; some of them have annual profits larger than the economy of a Third World nation. Their wealth and power means they can exert influence over governments to change laws. The threat of multinational corporations pulling business out of a country and leaving thousands jobless, as well as the impact on the national economy, can be a very persuasive tool when getting a government to amend its policies.

The European Union

The EU has a big impact on UK policy making. The UK is subject to some laws and guidance which come from Brussels, and events in Brussels can trigger new laws here. For example, the Human Rights Act 1998 was originally the European Convention on Human Rights which was issued as guidance to all EU members and translated into law by the UK government. Also, the UK government was forced to change its policy about not allowing homosexuals to serve in the armed forces after several gay and lesbian armed service personnel took their case to the European Court of Human Rights and won.

The media

The media is watched, listened to and read by millions of UK citizens, so can have a significant impact on the development of new policy. If the media support and promote a new law or change in policy then it is likely to find favour among the public. An example of this was the push for Sarah's Law after the tragic murder of 8-year-old Sarah Payne in July 2000. The campaign was heavily backed by the *News of the World* and supported the principle of controlled access to information on paedophiles living in local communities; however, in spite of the campaign the government does not allow this information to be made public. An example of the media promoting a negative stance towards a change in policy can be found in its reporting of congestion charges, motorway toll charges and taxes on petrol.

Assessment activity 1.4

1 Produce a series of notes about the following steps in the process of producing a policy:

- meetings that will occur
- white and green papers
- representations from outside government
- the drafting of a statute
- the process a bill goes through to become a statute
- implementation
- accountability
- promoting the new law.

You will need to:

a) explain how government policies are developed **P4**

b) analyse this process. **M3**

2 Use your notes to help you make clear and effective contributions to a small group discussion focusing on the development process of government policies. Remember also to discuss how government policy can be influenced by factors outside the government itself. You may wish to choose from the following examples:

- demonstrations
- financial constraints
- immigration
- terrorism
- multinational corporations
- the European Union
- the media.

After your group discussion, produce notes describing, with two examples, how government policy making can be influenced by factors outside the government. **P5**

Grading tips

P4 To achieve P4, you will need to clearly explain each of the factors involved in the development of government policies. Make sure that you have a comprehensive set of notes explaining the full procedure a policy goes through before it becomes law.

M3 To achieve M3, analyse the processes by which government policies are developed. How effective are they? How fair are they? What problems might arise?

P5 You will need to make clear notes of your discussion, describing two examples of how government policy making can be influenced by factors outside government.

This part of the unit will examine how policies made by the government impact on the uniformed public services:

- Policies affecting all the services
- Policies affecting the military services
- Policies affecting the emergency services.

Policies which affect all of the public services

▲ Figure 1.10 Policies affecting all services

Human rights

The uniformed public services have a tremendous amount of power over people's lives. They can take away people's freedom, investigate their private lives,

monitor their actions and use the information they find out to prosecute. These powers must be carefully regulated to avoid abuses by the state and its public services against ordinary members of the public.

In a democracy there must always be checks and balances on power to ensure that no one agency or service has too much power and that the public are able to challenge that power. Generally speaking, the UK's public services operate with the consent and cooperation of the public – they are respected and respectful. However, even with highly trained and knowledgeable officers there can still be breaches of human rights. This is why there is the need for laws and policies such as the Human Rights Act 1998.

■ Human Rights Act 1998

This Act ensures that all UK citizens have certain rights. These include the rights to:

- life
- prohibition of torture
- prohibition of slavery and forced labour
- liberty and security
- a fair trial
- no punishment without law
- respect for private and family life
- freedom of thought, conscience and religion
- freedom of expression
- freedom of assembly and association
- marry
- prohibition of discrimination
- protection of property
- education
- free elections
- abolition of the death penalty.

If these rights are broken by the public services, then the individuals concerned have the right to take the service to court and challenge its actions.

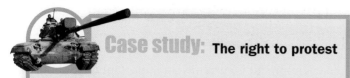

Case study: The right to protest

In March 2003, three days after the invasion of Iraq began, coaches containing 120 anti-war demonstrators travelled from London to RAF Fairford in Gloucestershire. The protesters intended to join a peaceful demonstration against the war but were detained by the police for more than 2½ hours and prevented from participating. The police argued that they were protecting the demonstrators' right to life since the American forces at the base had reserved the right to use 'deadly force' if the base was breached. The protesters argued that the detainment violated their right to freedom of speech and assembly and freedom from arbitrary detention. The House of Lords agreed with the protesters and found the police in breach of the Human Rights Act 1998.

(*Source*: Indymedia.co.uk)

1 **Do you think the police made a sound case for wanting to protect the lives of the protesters?**

2 **Why do you think the protesters felt the need to take the case to court?**

3 **What impact did this case have on the police?**

4 **In your opinion did the House of Lords make the right decision?**

Financial reductions or increases

At the heart of the work of the public services is finance. The public services could not operate if they did not have the resources to:

- pay the personnel
- buy and maintain equipment
- support a complex infrastructure which allows the services the UK needs to be delivered as and when they are needed.

The financial policies of the government therefore have a tremendous impact on the public services. It goes without saying that if the public money used to fund the services is reduced, then this will have a direct impact on the work the services can afford to do – less officers may be appointed, they may have less specialised training and equipment and be less able to respond effectively to social or military problems. If public spending is increased then the reverse will be true.

Equal opportunities

All of the public services today place great emphasis on the importance of equal opportunities. Equal opportunities legislation, such as the Equal Pay Act, the Sex Discrimination Act and the Race Relations Act, has fundamentally changed the way the services interact with their officers and the public. These changes are designed to ensure the public services reflect the communities which they serve. For example:

- Many public services are actively recruiting women and those from ethnic minority groups. This policy is designed to enrich the service and make it more representative of the general public, although there is still some way to go on this.

- Uniform requirements have changed to accommodate different religious groups. For example, female Muslim police officers may wear a dark-blue head-covering under their police hat, while male Sikh police officers may wear a dark-blue police turban with the badge of the force clearly displayed upon it.

- In the armed services, equal opportunities legislation has impacted on ration packs, with kosher and halal meals available for Jews and Muslims respectively.

Consider this

Why is it important that the public services are representative of the people that make up UK society? What benefits could this bring?

Civilianisation is a process whereby police officers (or other public service officers) are released from completing non-operational tasks which don't require their specialist expertise or training. These officers are then able to be deployed to an operational role. This makes the use of such staff more efficient since they are doing the job they were trained to do rather than routine administrative work. Routine administration or non-specialist support is then provided by civilians employed by the service. In effect, it is cheaper to employ a civilian on non-operational duties than to use a public services officer. This approach, while not always perfect, has gone some way to putting the officer back where he or she ought to be – policing the streets, or similar.

Key Terms

Civilianisation The process of freeing up public service personnel by employing civilians to do non-operational work.

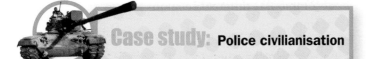

Case study: Police civilianisation

In 2005, civilians working in Scotland's eight police service areas voted for strike action. Almost 4000 staff voted for the strike after pay negotiations were unsuccessful. The civilians perform tasks such as dealing with emergency 999 calls, forensics and crime scene work. They provide an essential support network which allows frontline officers to be released for active duty.

1 **Do you think civilian public service workers ought to be banned from striking (in the same way as some public services are)?**

2 **What might be the implications of a strike like this on frontline policing?**

3 **What does this case study highlight about the disadvantages of civilianisation?**

The environment is currently an important issue about which the government must be seen to act. In line with this, the public services have become more aware of the need to recycle resources and move to manoeuvres and exercises which limit damage to the environment. In addition, some MOD land houses protected species which may not have a chance to thrive elsewhere.

Key Terms

Exercise Another name for a simulation. It provides opportunity for the public services to practise their skills and knowledge in a simulated battle situation.

Policies which affect the military services

A declaration of war will have a large and immediate impact on the military services. They will begin to be deployed almost immediately to a particular battle zone along with their resources and equipment, in order to fight for an aim or set of aims specified by the government. The armed services exist as servants of the government; they can only go into military action when ordered to do so by the government. They do not get to pick and choose where or when they serve.

The implications on the services of the decision to go to war are far reaching.

- First, there is the constant risk to the lives of serving solders in combat or in an area of global instability. In essence, military personnel may be killed or seriously injured by the enemy, by civilians who resent the military presence or by allied troops ('friendly fire').
- Families of military personnel may experience extreme stress and anxiety about the welfare of their loved ones.
- War is a tremendously expensive prospect and can quickly use up a variety of resources, including ammunition and protective equipment.

Increased use of reserve forces

Until the late 1990s, military reserve forces were rarely used on active duty. However, as the commitments of the armed services have grown over the last decade with operations in Afghanistan and Iraq, reserve forces have had to be used as an essential component of the UK fighting force. In 2006, reserve forces numbered 36,000. The largest proportion of these was the Territorial Army and regular reserves (former full-time army personnel who can be called up to serve, of which there are around 52,000). The National Audit Office report on reserve forces in 2006 notes that over 12,000 reservists have been deployed in Iraq since 2003 and they contribute approximately 12 per cent of the fighting force. Reservist medical personnel have been even more important, staffing up to 50 per cent of the field hospitals in the conflict.

Key Terms

Reserve forces Volunteer troops who may be called up in time of conflict but otherwise lead a normal civilian life.

The use of reserve forces carries advantages and disadvantages. Commanding officers have noted that reservists may be physically less fit to cope with the demands of the conflict. There have also been problems when reservists have not been trained and were deployed with a regular unit. On the plus side, reservists bring a wealth of experience from their civilian lives which can enhance the service greatly. The government is committed to maintaining reserve forces although they are considering policy changes on how they are trained and deployed to try to bring them in line with their regular counterparts.

Increased use of technology

The armed services have always been at the forefront of technological development. They have been the impetus for developing many technologies which otherwise might not have caught on. It is also true to say that war and conflict drive technological change as each side seeks advantage over the other. This has become particularly true in the war against terrorism where advanced technology and surveillance equipment has been used by both military and civilian counter-terrorist specialists to try and protect the public.

Links with international services

As a result of the coordinated policy of the North Atlantic Treaty Organisation (NATO), of which the UK is a founder member, the UK is required to maintain collective defence capabilities. This means that NATO forces must be able to integrate into operations seamlessly where possible. To this end UK troops often exercise with NATO troops from allied nations in combat simulations. This ensures they can be more combat-effective should a situation arise where they have to collaborate. The UK's three armed services also regularly train and exercise together since they are reliant on each other for a variety of roles. See *Unit 8* for further information on international perspectives and the United Nations.

Policies affecting the emergency services

Police regionalisation

Police regionalisation was a very controversial policy put forward by the Labour government. It involved the radical restructure of the police service from the current 43 forces to 24 larger ones. This plan was supposed to make the police service more efficient; however, the forces themselves were very much against the move and argued that it would harm the quality of policing they could offer to the community. The government abandoned the plans in the face of the opposition but not before the police service had spent in excess of £6.1 million preparing for the event.

The policy has also been applied to the fire service where the changes have gone ahead despite opposition from the Fire Brigades Union. This has led to the closure of local 999 fire service response teams and the teams being moved to a central location within a government region. There is also the issue of fire station closures which are examined next.

Fire station closures

There has been a recent spate of fire station closures, particularly in smaller rural areas, as an efficiency measure. This is despite concerns from local residents that if local stations are closed it could take longer for a fire crew to reach the area in times of emergency.

Case study: Fire station closures in South Yorkshire

Fire authorities have to create a three-year corporate plan which demonstrates improvement to the Services and shows that the Services are offering value for money to the taxpayer. The 2006–09 corporate plan for South Yorkshire Fire Authority included the closure of Ringinglow Fire Station, despite enormous local opposition. The area in question is rural and local people were extremely concerned that response times during an emergency would increase, potentially putting lives and property at risk. South Yorkshire Fire and Rescue Authority's rationale for closing Ringinglow was that it was a station with consistently low call-out rates and the firefighters and equipment could be better deployed elsewhere without compromising the safety of people in the area.

1   **Should public services have to produce a corporate plan like a business?**

2   **What are the potential problems with closing fire stations in rural areas?**

3   **What is the likely impact on the community of such a closure?**

4   **In your opinion were the South Yorkshire Fire and Rescue Authority correct in closing the station and redeploying the resources elsewhere?**

Target-setting standards

All of the public services have an incredible amount of targets set for them by central government. They are also made to set numerous targets for themselves on a range of things, including 999 response times, ethnic minority recruitment, female recruitment, budget expenditure,

reductions in crime or fires, patient survival rates and many more. This can lead to a tremendous amount of pressure on all levels of the public services to meet the targets or face the possible consequences.

If you examine the fire service case study above, the main reasons for deploying the crew from Ringinglow was that the brigade was not meeting 999 response times in certain other areas of South Yorkshire and so needed to move the under-utilised resources to a place where they would have a better impact on targets. Hence another aspect of the fire authority's corporate plan was to open a new Dearne Valley station which would help it meet response times in the area. In this way you can see that government and local targets have a real influence on the operation of the services.

Assessment activity 1.5

Public policy can have a direct or indirect impact on public services, affecting how they operate.

1   Produce and deliver a ten-minute PowerPoint presentation which describes and explains how two government policies have impacted on different uniformed public services.   **P6** **M4**

You can choose from the following policies:

- environmental
- civilianisation
- equal opportunities
- human rights
- financial increases or decreases.

There are also policies which directly affect the military or emergency services, which were explained earlier in the unit (see pages 34–36).

Extension activity

To achieve D2, you need to justify the introduction of two government policies in relation to their impact on the uniformed public services.   **D2**

You could do this in either of the following ways:

- add it to your presentation and deliver the information verbally
- put it on a handout for your audience to read after you have delivered the presentation.

Grading tip

P6 To achieve P6, you will need to describe two government policies and their effects on different uniformed public services.

M4 To achieve M4, you must provide an explanation of how your chosen government policies have impacted on the uniformed public services.

D2 For D2, 'justify' means to consider whether something is necessary, so you will need to tell your audience *why* the two policies you have chosen to examine are needed.

Social responses to government policies

Although many aspects of government policy are open to public consultation, many decisions are made which some of the public do not agree with. There will also be some decisions which the public feel so strongly about they are prepared to take action.

There are several responses a society or an individual can make in response to a policy, as described below.

Civil disobedience

This is the deliberate and planned breach of policy or law by an individual or group of people. It is usually done peacefully to highlight how inappropriate a law is and promote the need for a change in the law.

Civil disobedience was a common tool in the black civil rights movement in the USA in the 1960s. Black people would deliberately break the racial segregation laws to show how deeply unfair they were and how much the law needed to change. A good example of this is the case of Rosa Parks, who in December 1955 refused to give up her seat on a bus to a white man when asked to do so. She was arrested and her arrest sparked a chain of events which led to the US Supreme Court decision in 1956 that racial segregation on transportation was illegal.

Demonstrations and meetings

Meetings to discuss problems with government policy are very common. They are a way for like-minded individuals to air their concerns. Meetings can be held outside and include a march or demonstration to show the government or local authority the depth of public feeling against a decision. A good example of this would be the rallies and protests organised by the Countryside Alliance since the UK government placed a ban on foxhunting.

Terrorism

Terrorism is an extreme response to public policy. It involves an individual or group using violence or the threat of violence against civilian and military targets in order to force the government to change its policy. It is usually the last resort of a group which has already tried civil disobedience and demonstration to no effect.

Governments do not respond well to terrorism; many have a policy of not negotiating with terrorists under any circumstances. An example of this in the UK was the situation in Northern Ireland in the second half of the twentieth century. Loyalist and Republican terrorist groups were active in Northern Ireland and on the UK mainland, with great cost to civilian and military life and property, yet the UK government refused to give in to their demands. One of the worst atrocities committed was the Omagh bombing in 1998 which killed 29 people.

Picketing

Picketing is when striking workers gather together outside their place of work. This is a common way for employees to show their unhappiness with a policy decision made on national or local issues; the focus is usually pay, redundancies or working conditions. The Fire Service strikes in 2002 are one example.

Sit-ins

Sit-ins are a peaceful way of demonstrating against an issue by causing great inconvenience and delay to the people trying to implement the decision. They are a tool often used by environmental protesters who oppose the building of new roads. By building camps underground and in trees, the protestors make it difficult for work to begin safely. For example, in 1995–6, environmental protestors effectively disrupted work on the Newbury bypass. The protest included 29 camps with tree houses and a tunnel network. Although the protesters failed to stop the eventual building of the bypass at Newbury, their actions led to a change in government thinking on the building of new roads. Consequently plans for the Salisbury bypass were stopped on the basis of the environmental impact.

Knowledge check

1 What are the responsibilities of central government?

2 What is the role of an MP?

3 Who can stand for election?

4 What public services do the Home Office have responsibility for?

5 What is the role of the Prime Minister?

6 What is the general role of an inspectorate?

7 Describe what green and white papers are.

8 What is royal assent?

9 What factors can affect government policy?

10. How does civilianisation benefit the public services?

11 What impact does target setting have on the public services?

12 How can people respond to a government policy if they don't like it?

Preparation for assessment

The police service is made up of 43 forces in England and Wales. Each force may have different policies and procedures on staff training and development. It is vitally important that police officers at all levels understand the importance of the role of the government and the impacts of its policies on the service as a whole.

You are working with the police training officer who has responsibility for ensuring that all police officers in your force area understand these important issues. You have been asked to oversee the next issue of the force magazine, *Policing Today,* to ensure that everyone gets a consistent message.

Ensure the next issue of *Policing Today* contains the following information:

1 Outline the different levels of government in the UK. **P1**

2 Explain the responsibilities of different levels of government and local councils in the UK. **M1**

3 Describe the electoral process for one level of government in the UK. **P2**

4 Compare the electoral processes at different levels of government in the UK. **M2**

5 Analyse the responsibilities and electoral processes of two different levels of government in the UK. **D1**

6 Describe three government departments and their responsibility for specific uniformed public services. **P3**

7 Explain and analyse the development process of government policies. **P4 M3**

8 Describe how government policy making can be influenced by factors outside the government, giving two examples. **P5**

9 Describe and explain how two government policies have impacted upon different uniformed public services. **P6 M4**

10 Justify the introduction of two government policies in relation to their impact on the uniformed public services. **D2**

Grading criteria	Activity	Pg no.		
To achieve a pass grade the evidence must show that the learner is able to:			To achieve a merit grade the evidence must show that the learner is able to:	To achieve a distinction grade the evidence must show that the learner is able to:
P1 Outline the various levels of government and elected bodies from local councils to national government	1.1	13	**M1** Explain the responsibilities of each level of government in the UK	
P2 Describe one election process and identify which level of government it relates to	1.2	19	**M2** Compare the election process for the elected representatives at at least two levels of government in the UK	**D1** Analyse the responsibilities and electoral processes for different levels of government in the UK
P3 Identify a minimum of three government departments and explain their responsibilities for specific uniformed public services	1.3	20		
P4 Explain the development process of government policies	1.4	31	**M3** Analyse the development process of government policies	
P5 Describe how government policy making can be influenced by factors outside the government	1.4	31		
P6 Describe how two government policies have affected different uniformed public services	1.5	36	**M4** Give an explanation of government policies and their effects on the uniformed public services	**D2** Justify the introduction of two government policies and consider their effects on the uniformed public services

Team leadership in the uniformed public services

Introduction

This unit is intended to give you an insight into team leadership by looking at its key principles in a relevant and public services context. You will identify and investigate the different styles of leadership and how and when they may be used in the uniformed public services.

You will gain a clear understanding of team aims and goals and explore the benefits of working in teams as opposed to working as an individual. You will look at effective communication, both verbal and non-verbal, and understand its importance within a group setting, especially when giving instructions and feedback. Throughout the unit you will develop your interpersonal skills helping you to interact and deal effectively with team members, whether this is through giving feedback, group encouragement or individual support. You should take every opportunity to reflect on your performance and identify the skills needed to develop and become a more effective leader.

You will also identify a range of barriers to effective teamwork and look at solutions and techniques in overcoming them. Finally, you will look at using the above mentioned skills to carry out planning sessions and demonstrate your ability to conduct group and individual evaluations.

After completing this unit you should be able to achieve the following outcomes:

- Understand the styles of leadership and the role of a team leader
- Be able to communicate effectively to brief and debrief teams
- Be able to use appropriate skills and qualities to lead a team
- Understand what makes a successful team.

Thinking points

The unit is essential in developing your skills in leading a team. Leadership is a critical component when working in a uniformed public service team and different services will use different leadership styles. For example, the Armed Forces are likely to take a more autocratic approach to leading soldiers, especially in dangerous situations, while senior police officers will adopt a more democratic approach, allowing their officers to make important decisions and demonstrate their expertise.

You should be able to put the theory of the unit into practice both in and out of an educational setting. This means that you should have the opportunity to explore and reinforce the skills used in group situations.

- Think about the skills a leader needs, such as communication, how poor communication can lead to poor performance and how a failure to be assertive can lead to aggression and conflict amongst the group.

Leadership skills are essential as uniformed public services employees often work in teams that rely on each other to carry out their individual roles effectively. This is often in stressful situations, such as major incidents, when multiple services will be involved.

- Could you remain professional and motivated at all times?
- Can you continue to lead when faced with challenging and difficult situations by tackling any barriers that could be in the way?

You should also expect to be given feedback from others about your leadership skills and you will have to deal with it.

- Think about the type of feedback you are likely to receive from the team and your peers.

Leadership studies have developed rapidly over the last 100 years. They have led to a set of theories which have been used widely in many workplaces, including the public services, in order to promote efficiency, cost effectiveness and accountability. The issues raised by leadership studies are crucial for all organisations and groups to understand if they wish to achieve goals and get the best from people. They are equally significant for the uniformed public services due to the rigidity of their hierarchical structures, the necessity of obedience, the following of lawful orders and the dangerous nature of the roles they perform.

Consider this

Before you read about leadership, take the time to write your own definition of it, perhaps in pairs or small groups. Once you have created your definition, compare it to others.

Key terms

Leadership A fluid and dynamic action, which listens and responds to the needs and demands of individuals and the organisation. It allows the team in turn to meet its goals and objectives in an open and non-oppressive manner.

Leadership styles

A leadership style is the manner and approach of providing direction for a team, implementing plans and motivating people to complete a task. There are several different leadership styles, each with its own set of advantages and disadvantages. The public services are constantly changing due to changes in public expectations, the law and the current political environment and it is to be expected that the styles of leadership they use will change and evolve too.

Here we will describe some of the more commonly known and used styles.

Authoritarian leadership

Sometimes this style is also called autocratic. It is often considered a classic leadership style and is used when a leader wishes to retain as much power as possible and maintain control over the decision-making process. It involves the leader telling the employees what they must do without any form of consultation and negotiation. Employees are expected to obey orders without receiving any explanation. Appropriate conditions when you might use this leadership style include:

- when you have all the information to solve the problem

▲ **Authoritarian leadership in action**

you are working to a tight deadline

the team is well motivated.

Generally this approach is not considered to be the most appropriate way to get the best response from a team in ordinary working life, but it has distinct advantages for the public services, such as the Armed Forces. It tends to work best in situations where there is great urgency and pressure to achieve. Autocratic leaders often rely on threats or intimidation to ensure that followers conform to what the leader requires. In addition, this approach devalues employees by ignoring their expertise and input and discouraging demonstrations of initiative. Many of the public services encourage leaders to utilise this particular leadership style for very sound reasons:

It maintains order and discipline.

It allows public services to be deployed quickly and efficiently.

It allows young and inexperienced recruits to know what to do and when to do it.

It allows large scale coordination with other shifts or units.

It ensures that decisions are made by those best equipped to make them.

It enables decisions to be made very quickly.

However, although this style might be appropriate in public service life, it does not transplant easily to other environments. Some of the drawbacks of the authoritarian/autocratic approach are as follows:

Team members rely on the leader for instruction and do not develop initiative.

Team members have less responsibility for their own actions.

Team members may feel angry and resentful at being ordered to perform tasks without explanation.

It can lead to high staff turnover and absenteeism.

Staff may feel devalued and fearful of punishment.

Staff morale may decline leading to poor job performance.

Most uniformed services have moved away from this approach over the last 30 years but it is still a preferred organisational and individual leadership style in the Armed Forces, such as the Army, the Royal Navy and the Royal Air Force where high discipline and readiness to act are crucial factors in operational effectiveness.

Consider this

After examining the authoritarian style of leadership described above, consider how well you would respond to this particular style. How would you feel if you were working under it?

Figure 2.1 The advantages and disadvantages of authoritarian leadership

Bureaucratic leadership

Bureaucracy is a system of leadership in which authority is diffused among a number of departments or individuals and there is strict adherence to a set of operational rules. This is also considered to be a classic leadership style and is often used in organisations that do not encourage innovation and change, and by leaders who may be insecure and uncertain of their role. It involves following the rules of an organisation rigidly. People who favour using this style of leadership are often very familiar with the many policies, guidelines and working practices that an organisation may have.

If a particular situation arises that is not covered by known rules and guidelines then a bureaucratic leader may feel uncomfortable as they like to 'do things by the book'. They may feel out of their depth and will have little hesitation in referring difficulties to a leader higher up in the chain of command.

This approach is commonly found in many uniformed and non-uniformed public services. Often the public services are very large and bureaucratic themselves and, although it may seem unlikely, there are several situations where the bureaucratic leadership style may be useful, for example, when:

- a job is routine and doesn't change over a long period of time

- a job requires a definite set of safety rules or working guidelines.

However, if the bureaucratic style is used inappropriately it can have very negative consequences, leading to a lack of flexibility, an uninspired working environment and workers who only do what is required of them but no more.

The modern public services and the leaders within them have to deal with a constantly changing social and political environment and a rigid approach isn't always effective in view of this. However, the public services are the guardians of our safety and security and it is entirely appropriate that they should have to follow bureaucratic procedures, which ensure the safety of the public and protect against the misuse of power. A balance must be found when using this leadership style in which rules and procedures are obeyed and understood without compromising flexibility, responsiveness and creativity.

Consider this

Consider an occasion when you have been subject to a bureaucratic style of leadership. Describe the situation to a fellow learner and then discuss how it made you feel.

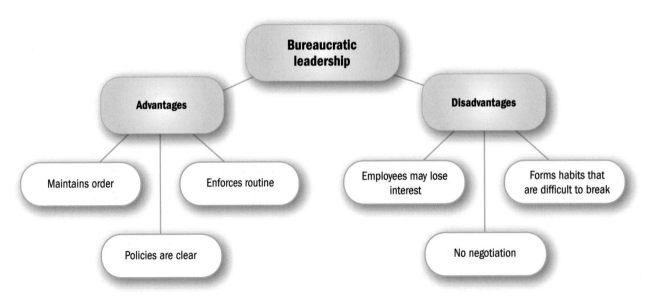

▲ Figure 2.2 The advantages and disadvantages of bureaucratic leadership

Democratic (participative) leadership

In this approach the leader encourages the followers to become a part of the decision-making process. The leader still maintains control of the group and ownership of the final decision but input from team members is encouraged and the leader informs team members about factors which may have an impact on them, the team and the project. This encourages a sense of responsibility in team members who feel that they have a vested interest in the success of the project or operation. This approach allows a leader to draw upon the expertise and experience of a team in order to achieve the best results for all and it also helps to develop people's skills. The democratic approach is viewed very positively as it gains employees' respect and it can produce high quality work over long periods of time from highly motivated teams. Employees and team members also feel in control of their own destiny, such as gaining promotion and progressing up the ladder. However, its application in the field of public service work is slightly more problematic and its drawbacks are as follows:

- Democratic discussion takes time. A public service may have to respond very quickly so gathering the views of all members may not be a viable option.

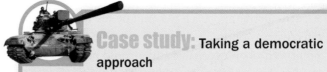

Case study: Taking a democratic approach

Simon is a senior community police officer involved in an initiative to reduce the amount of youth crime occurring in the centre of a large city. He has called a meeting to discuss what the current problems are, how effective current preventative action is and to create a plan to move forward in achieving the local authority's goals. Many organisations are involved in this initiative such as Social Services, youth action groups, the Probation Service, Victim Support and local business owners. All of them have sent senior representatives to this important meeting. After reviewing his preparation notes for the meeting, Simon decides to take a democratic approach to the meeting rather than using another style.

1. Why do you think Simon chose to employ a democratic style for the meeting?
2. What are the advantages to Simon in using this style?
3. What are the disadvantages to Simon in using this style?
4. What are the advantages to the project as a whole in using this style?

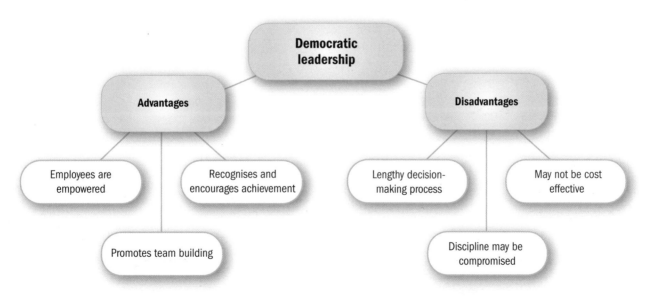

▲ Figure 2.3 The advantages and disadvantages of democratic leadership

- A participative approach may not be the most cost effective way of organising a service. The time of police officers is expensive and it could be better for public perceptions and government funding if our uniformed services are actually doing the job that they are paid to do rather than talking about *how* to do it.

- This approach is not really appropriate if the safety of team members is paramount. Safety is not open for negotiation; a public service must endeavour to protect its members from harm wherever operationally possible. Equally, when members must risk their personal safety in the defence of others, it is not open to discussion.

Although this style wouldn't necessarily be appropriate for use among the lower ranks of the public services, it certainly has application in meetings or projects involving senior officers who will expect to be consulted with and listened to.

Laissez-faire leadership

The laissez-faire approach can also be called the hands-off approach, free-reign approach or the delegative approach. This style differs from the others in that the leader exercises very little control over the group and leaves them to establish their own roles and responsibilities. Followers are given very little direction but a great deal of power and freedom. They must use this power to establish goals, make decisions and resolve difficulties should they arise. This style is difficult to master as many leaders have great difficulty delegating power and authority to others and allowing them the freedom to work free from interference. It is also a difficult approach to use on all groups of followers as some people experience great difficulty working without a leader's direction and projects or goals may fall behind schedule or be poorly organised.

In general, a laissez-faire approach is most effective when a group of followers are highly motivated, experienced and well trained. It is important that the leader can have trust in their followers to complete tasks without supervision and this is more likely to happen with a highly qualified team or individual.

It is also a good approach to use when dealing with expert staff that may know a great deal more about a subject than the leader themselves. In a public service context, a good example of this would be a murder enquiry where the supervising officer would employ a laissez-faire approach to a scene-of-crime officer or a forensic investigator. The experts know what they are there to do and can be safely left to get on with it, leaving the supervising officer free to attend to other tasks.

However, there are situations where a laissez-faire style may not be the most effective style. An example of this would be when a leader lacks the knowledge and the

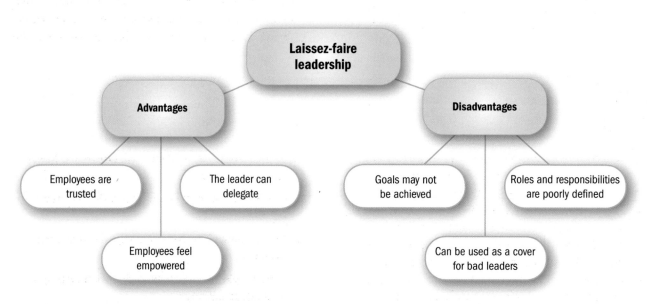

▲ Figure 2.4 The advantages and disadvantages of laissez-faire leadership

skills to do the job and employs this style so that the work of the followers or employees covers the leader's weaknesses. In addition, it would be inappropriate to use this style with new or inexperienced staff that may feel uncomfortable if the direction of a leader weren't readily available. For instance, a CO would not approach the training of new recruits with a laissez-faire manner but as an individual progresses through a rank structure they will become more skilled, experienced and trustworthy and they may encounter this style more often.

Take it further

A small infantry unit of six men is trapped behind enemy lines in desert conditions. They must maintain radio silence so that they are not detected by the enemy. They have enough water and rations for 72 hours but the journey they must make to return to safety is approximately six days long. Two of the men are experienced in desert conditions but three are relatively new recruits. The CO must lead them to safety.

1. Describe how an 'authoritarian' leader might handle this situation and assess how effective it would be.
2. Describe a 'bureaucratic' leadership response to this situation and assess how effective it would be.
3. Compare the two approaches.
4. How effective do you think a combined approach would be and which styles would you combine?

Apart from the more common leadership styles already mentioned, there are some other styles that you may not be aware of. They are explored below.

Transactional leadership

This is similar to autocratic but not as extreme, even though transactional leaders, like autocratic leaders, are direct and dominating and spend a great deal of time telling others what is expected of them. Transactional leaders are very common in businesses where people receive rewards such as bonuses, training or time off if they demonstrate good performance.

Transactional leaders use conventional rewards and punishments to gain the support of their team. They create clear structures whereby it is obvious what is required of the team and what incentives they will receive if they follow orders (salary, benefits, promotion or praise). Team members who perform adequately or accomplish goals will be rewarded in some way that benefits their own self-interest. Those who don't perform or meet the standard required will be punished by the leader through the 'management by exception principle', whereby, rather than rewarding work, they will take corrective action against those who don't work to the required standards.

Transactional leadership is more of an individual management strategy and can be used by any of the leaders within the uniformed services to one degree or another. However, it is probably best suited to the

Case study

Jack has been a leading fire fighter with Green Watch for the last two years. While attending a warehouse fire at night, his sub officer is injured and rendered unconscious leaving Jack in command of 15 other fire fighters. Green Watch is a close-knit group who work together extremely well and are experienced and competent. There is no immediate risk to the public as the warehouse is empty and the surrounding area is deserted due to the late hour. However, there is substantial threat to neighbouring property if the fire cannot be contained.

1. **Assess how effective a democratic approach would be.**
2. **Assess how effective a laissez-faire approach would be.**
3. **Which style do you think is the most appropriate for Jack to employ?**

services that have strict discipline codes such as the Armed Forces.

The transactional leader offers his or her team members 'a trade'. For example, an Army officer participating in military simulations might offer his team additional recreation time if they perform well, whilst a pay rise could be offered in exchange for additional or substantial changes in a personal role.

Good points	Bad points
• The leader actively monitors the work and each individual's performance. • People are motivated by being rewarded for exceeding expectation. • There is a clear chain of command. • Formal systems of discipline are in place. • The team is fully accountable for its actions and will be punished for failure. • It ensures that routine work is done reliably.	• Leaders tend to be action oriented and focus on short-term tasks. • Team members don't get job satisfaction because of the reward and punishment ethos. • It has serious limitations for knowledge-based or creative work but remains a common style in many organisations. • Team members do exactly what the manager tells them to do and have no authority. • The team might not have the resources or capability to carry out a task. • The style assumes that people are motivated by money and not by emotional and social factors. • The leader could manipulate others to engage in unethical or immoral practices and control others for their own personal gain. • It creates an environment of power versus perks.

Table 2.1 The good and bad points of transactional leadership

Transformational leadership

Transformational leaders aim to make us better people by encouraging our self-awareness and helping us to see the bigger picture of what we do. They want us to overcome self-interest and move towards achieving the common goals and purposes which we share with the group.

Transformational leaders are often charismatic with a clear vision. They spend a lot of time communicating and gaining the support of the team through their enthusiasm. This vision may be developed by the leader or the team, or may emerge from discussions. Leaders will want to be role models that others will follow and will look to explore the various routes to achieve their vision. They look at long-term goals rather than short-term goals. They are always visible and will be accountable for their actions rather than hiding behind their team. They act as mentors and demonstrate how the team should behave and work together through their own good practice. They listen to the team and often delegate responsibility – they trust their team enough to leave them to grow and solve the problems through their own decisions.

The fire and rescue service have adopted this approach over a traditional transactional approach. This is to meet the needs of their expanded role of ensuring overall community safety. The fire service, like all uniformed services, must annually review how their services are delivered with an emphasis on quality, innovation, efficiency and productivity.

Good points	Bad points
• People will follow transformational leaders because of their passion, energy, commitment and enthusiasm for the team and their vision. • They add value to the organisation through their visions and passion. • A person with vision and passion can achieve great things. • They care about their team and work hard to motivate them – this reduces stress levels and increases well-being. • They have belief in others and themselves. • They spend time teaching and coaching the team.	• The team may not share the same vision if they are not convinced by it. • If the team do not believe that they can succeed, then they will lack effort and ultimately give up. • There will be failures along the way and many dead ends. • Followers need to have a strong sense of purpose if they are to be motivated to act. • Leaders believe their vision is right, when sometimes it isn't. • Large amounts of relentless enthusiasm can wear out the team. • They see the big picture but not the details. • Leaders can become frustrated if transformation is not taking place.

Table 2.2 The good and bad points of transformational leadership

Consider this

What are the main differences between transactional and transformational leadership? When are the public services likely to use transactional leadership? When are the public services likely to use transformational leadership?

People-orientated leadership

The people-orientated leader is totally focused on organising, supporting and developing the team. They are competent in their role and inspire others by unlocking their potential. They allocate roles based on a person's strength and individual skills. This style of leadership is participative and encourages good teamwork, loyalty and creative collaboration and helps to avoid work-based problems such as low morale, poor communication and distrust. The style has a human element and good relationships are crucial to its success. The key to this style is people power and the organisation is successful by utilising the knowledge, skills, abilities, life experiences and talents of the individuals and groups. A people-orientated style also looks to develop a person's skills and help them acquire new ones through continuous and regular training.

Police services can be well served by this concept as modern policing provides opportunities for individuals of many different backgrounds to undertake a worthwhile career in this public service. For example, if a chief inspector wants to change an organisation from a task-orientated (see below) to a people-orientated organisation, they need to promote relationships and people need to get to know each other. This requires leaders to use communication skills to encourage effective interaction with all of the teams rather than concentrating solely on the technical and tactical performance of the officers. Policing is an incredibly complex profession and often officers, as well as managers, are expected to be masters of all trades. However, key roles can be allocated within the service to best suit individuals' strengths. For example, officers with extremely good communication skills would be best suited to policing within the community while officers who have extremely good organisation skills would be best suited to investigative work.

Task-orientated leadership

Task-orientated leaders focus mainly on getting the task done, whether it is structured or unstructured. They will define the work and the roles required, put structures in place, plan, organise and monitor with little thought for the well-being or needs of their teams. This approach can have many flaws, such as difficulties in motivating and retaining the team.

This style of leadership is the opposite of people-orientated leadership. In practice, most leaders use both task-orientated and people-orientated styles of leadership.

Figure 2.5 The people-orientated leader at work

Consider this

List possible situations when the public services will use a task-orientated approach and situations in which they would use a people-orientated approach to lead teams.

As an example, a police inspector organising crowd control at a football match may use a task-centred approach but back at the station, when dealing with junior police officers, he might employ a people-centred approach.

Remember!

Choosing the right leadership style depends very much on the situation but to help you select the most appropriate style you need to consider the following:

- The authoritarian approach tells others what to do and how to do it.
- The bureaucratic approach has clearly outlined procedures which must be followed if you are to know what to do and how to do it.
- The democratic approach discusses with others what to do and how to do it.
- The laissez-faire approach lets followers decide for themselves what to do and how to do it.
- The transformational approach encourages individuals to share the goals of the organisation and work towards its success.
- The transactional approach rewards people for good performance and punishes those who don't perform well.
- The people-orientated approach focuses on the needs, problems and skills of team members and identifies the support individuals will need.
- The task-orientated approach focuses on getting the task done and the leader considers what needs to be done to achieve this.

As you can tell, all of the theories of leadership have evidence to recommend them and all of them have difficulties which need to be overcome, if a leader using that style is to be effective. There is no such thing as a right or wrong theory and there is more than one opinion on what might work best. Employing the right approach in the right situation is crucial if a leader is to successfully achieve their aims. The costs to a public service organisation of bad leadership can

be phenomenal in terms of finance, goodwill and motivation and the benefits of effective leadership cannot be bought with any amount of money.

Leadership in the public services	
Benefits of effective leaders	**Costs of bad leaders**
• Organisations will retain good quality staff. • Staff will go that extra mile in order to do a good job. • Efficiency and cost effectiveness are achieved. • Staff feel valued. • Tasks are completed successfully. • Discipline is maintained. • Teamwork is encouraged and team members support each other. • Teams will work towards common objectives. • Teams will perform better in highly pressurised or dangerous situations.	• Staff will leave. • Staff will not be motivated to do a good job. • Resources such as time and money will be wasted. • Tasks may not be done properly or left incomplete. • Staff may disobey or be mutinous. • Social order may decline. • Lives may be lost. • Territory and valuable assets may be lost. • Equipment may be faulty or unfit for purpose. • Teams may collapse under difficult circumstances. • Staff will be more concerned with their own self-interest rather than achieving a common goal.

Table 2.3 Benefits of effective leaders and costs of bad leaders in the public services

Theory into practice

To choose the most effective approach for you, you must consider:

- the skill levels and experience of your team
- the work involved (routine or new and creative)
- the organisational structure/environment
- how much time is available to complete the task
- working relationships – are they based on respect and trust?
- who has the information and how well you know the task
- the nature of the task – is it structured, unstructured, complicated, or straightforward?

Consider this

Consider six leaders that are familiar to you. Your list might include a football manager, a teacher, a politician, a famous political leader or a public service figure.

Which of the leadership styles outlined above relates best to each leader?

Assessment activity 2.1

Imagine you have been asked to create a leaflet which will be given out to potential recruits for the various uniformed services at a number of career and recruitment events.

1. Describe the different leadership styles and relate them clearly to the necessary uniformed services. **P1**

2. Compare two of the different leadership styles highlighted previously which are used in two different public services. **M1**

3. Evaluate the effectiveness of two previously mentioned leadership styles which are used in the uniformed public services. **D1**

Grading tips

P1 To achieve a pass you need to describe and relate the following leadership styles to the particular uniformed services:

- authoritarian
- transactional
- democratic
- transformational
- bureaucratic
- people-orientated
- laissez-faire
- task-orientated.

M1 To achieve M1 you need to expand on your knowledge of leadership styles by comparing two different styles. Comparisons should

point out key similarities and differences and highlight any impacts that these styles may have on the roles they perform.

D1 To achieve D1 you need to consider whether two of the team leadership styles are effective within the public sector.

The team leader role

Who can be a team leader?

Team leaders can be appointed in many different ways, for example, they can be promoted, nominated or delegated to do the role. They might also volunteer. In theory anyone can be a team leader although some people will make better leaders than others. However, as long as someone is interested and willing, with an idea of how to communicate well, understand the needs of others, offer support and be flexible, then they have the basics to develop their leadership skills.

What are the functions of a team leader?

There are many functions of a team leader. They range from helping the team to decide how roles and responsibilities will be divided amongst its members to helping to coordinate the task and resolving interpersonal conflicts.

The team leader is the contact point for communication between the team members. He or she should:

- encourage and maintain open communication
- help the team to develop and follow team norms and roles and keep the team focused on the task
- be an active listener and show the initiative when things become flat by building up rapport to help maximise performance
- look to delegate their authority when appropriate and follow up on any points after a task has been attempted or completed
- encourage the team members to reflect on the task.

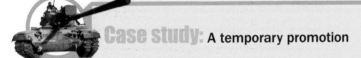

The uniformed public services have a clear rank structure to help ensure effective leadership of the organisation and the team. A full exploration of these structures can be found on pages 146–8 in *Unit 5: Understanding discipline within the uniformed public services.*

■ Commanding Officer

One example of a leadership position within a uniformed public service is that of a Commanding Officer (CO). The CO is the officer in command of a military unit, post, camp, base or station. He or she has authority over the unit and is given legal powers, within the bounds of military law, to discipline and punish certain behaviour.

A CO has a range of significant responsibilities with regard to the allocation of service personnel, finances and equipment. They are accountable to the higher ranks and have a legal duty of care to the team. COs are highly valued and progression within the service is awarded to the best officers who have worked their way up the ranks.

The CO is often assisted by an Executive Officer (XO) or Second-in-Command, who handles personnel and day-to-day matters. Larger units may also have staff officers taking up some of the responsibilities of the CO.

■ Station Commander

This person is in overall charge of running a fire station. When the other fire fighters are responding to the incident it is the job of the Station Commander to check response times and be in radio contact with the crew to give them any advice or information that they might need.

Case study: A temporary promotion

Jamila has been a police sergeant for five years working at a large city centre station. She has an excellent working relationship with the other sergeants based at the station and they work very closely together coordinating shifts of police officers to respond both to the needs of the community and the strategic direction of the constabulary. Although many of her fellow sergeants have more experience or more qualifications than her, she has been asked to 'act up' to the rank of inspector to cover for a member of staff who is on long-term sick leave.

1. **What difficulties might Jamila face from her team of sergeants if she accepts the temporary promotion?**

2. **What difficulties might Jamila face from other inspectors?**

3. **What difficulties might Jamila encounter when the inspector who is on sick leave returns and she returns to the rank of sergeant?**

4. **What strategies can Jamila employ to overcome the difficulties she might face in each situation?**

▲ Jamila has an excellent working relationship with the other sergeants at her station

Leadership qualities and skills

The qualities and skills needed by a leader will be covered later in this unit under section 3 (see pages 66–9). We need to first consider how a well-led team can benefit an organisation and the members of the team.

Benefits of teams to the uniformed public services

Working as part of a team is common in the uniformed public services and an effective team has many benefits at both an operational and an individual level. It can lead to increased efficiency, especially important when working to ever decreasing government budgets, and ultimately it maintains a high level of customer satisfaction.

The benefits to the organisation

The benefits of an effective team to the organisation include:

- The team tends to be more successful in implementing plans and strategies within a set timescale and dealing with a demanding workload.
- The team is often better at solving problems by offering solutions and is usually more productive, creative and energetic.
- The team will have open communication channels, leading to an increased knowledge and understanding of the tasks to be completed.
- The team is accountable for decisions that it participates in.
- Conflict is often avoided between team members.
- There are usually good relations with the management.
- There will be a high level of commitment and this can benefit the organisation through a lower turnover of staff and less absenteeism.
- The team will generally have little resistance to change.

All of the above ensures that the organisation has an experienced team with the necessary skills and training to deal with the demands of the job; this in turn creates a very marketable and efficient service.

The benefits to team members

A good team environment provides open and effective communication and collaboration, and a team of people who don't want to let each other down. This can create and promote a shared sense of belonging and identity and makes the workplace an enjoyable and fun environment. It helps people to feel valued and creates informal and formal support networks so that problems can be discussed openly and ever increasing stress levels can be dealt with. A good team environment also leads to errors being addressed in a constructive and professional way and better collective decisions are made because more information and expertise is shared.

Effective team	Ineffective team
• Everyone contributes. • Demonstration of good faith and good will. • Individual diversity and contributions are respected. • Competitive and assertive behaviour is encouraged. • Demonstration of open, honest, and respectful communication. • Demonstration of trustworthiness and confidentiality. • Everyone listens well – seeking first to understand rather than to be understood. • Collective decision making, with all the alternative solutions being considered. • Task-focused with a good team spirit. • Mutual support. • More likely to succeed within the time set.	• One person exercises strong leadership. • All decisions are made by one person. • Evidence of aggressive behaviour. • Some people are ignored or don't take part. • People don't take responsibility for their own behaviour or that of the team. • Constant conflict is occurring. • Failure to complete the task. • No motivation. • Working as individuals with no clear roles. • Poor time management.

Table 2.4 The common signs of effective and ineffective teams

Theory into practice

Consider a team situation you have worked in recently and use the checklist above to identify how effective the team was. If you have identified signs of ineffectiveness, state how they could be addressed in subsequent teamwork situations.

Assessment activity 2.2

All teams need a leader in order for them to function effectively and the lack of a leader can be detrimental to any organisation and its workers.

The Armed Forces have a detailed rank structure and a variety of specialist teams. The government, due to budget restraints, are looking to streamline the rank system and the variety of teams at an operational level. You are a colonel in the army, strongly opposed to any streamlining, and have been invited to attend a preliminary meeting hosted by the Ministry of Defence. To present your arguments against streamlining the Armed Forces, you need to research and prepare discussion notes based on the following question.

1. Describe the roles of a variety of team leaders found within the uniformed public services and the benefits of teams to the uniformed public services.

Grading tips

P2 To achieve P2 you need to identify the responsibilities of the various team leaders mentioned, including any relevant skills and qualities they have. You also need to state the benefits of teams to the organisation and to other team members.

Communication

It is important that a leader possesses a number of qualities and one of the most important is good communication, especially when leading and interacting with an organisation and within teams.

Effective communication is crucial for the uniformed public services, particularly as a major part of their work involves briefing and debriefing teams. Communication may take place in a variety of ways, for example, face-to-face, over the phone, emails, memos, etc.

Communication is the processing of information, usually through a system of encoding, transmitting and decoding messages. There are four basic ways of communicating:

1. speaking
2. reading
3. writing
4. listening.

We are focusing on verbal communication (which refers to what we say with words and the way we say it) and non-verbal communication (which refers to all the other ways we communicate including body language and gestures).

When we communicate, the communication is usually comprised of the words used (7 per cent), the way the words are used or stressed, for example, tone, emotions (38 per cent) and body language (55 per cent).

Verbal communication

Effective communication means that other people take you seriously and only occurs if the receiver understands the exact information or idea that the sender intended to transmit. To ensure this happens while speaking in groups, communication should be clear and concise and as simple as possible so that it is understood. Communication should be relevant to the task and clarification should be sought from the recipient, even if it is just a nod of the head. Straightforward questions should be asked to ensure the communication has been understood.

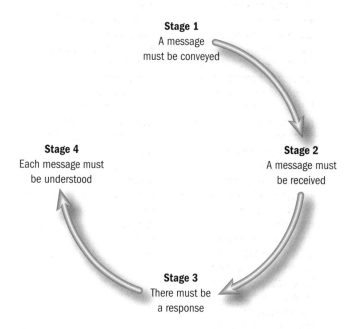

Stage 1
A message must be conveyed

Stage 2
A message must be received

Stage 3
There must be a response

Stage 4
Each message must be understood

▲ **Figure 2.6 The four elements of effective verbal communication**

The content of the message can be affected by the tone, pitch, quality and speed of your voice. You should ensure your voice complements the message that you convey to avoid misinterpretations. Use silence in between messages to help to ensure the message has reached the team. You should be enthusiastic and full of energy when you speak to the team but you should avoid shouting.

The cornerstones to effective speaking are:

- clarity
- simplicity
- preparedness
- conciseness.

To ensure that communication is active in your teams, consider the following points.

- Ensure you know the names of all members of the team as this will help the group to be responsive and supportive.
- Try to be confident in situations where you don't always feel comfortable.
- Be open and responsive to problems when they occur and be prepared to talk about them as a group.

- Respect and seek the opinions, thoughts and feelings of all members of the group or communication will break down as people feel alienated.
- Exhibit emotions such as concern, empathy, sympathy and remorse when they are needed as these put people at ease.
- Ensure that you use the right tone of voice when speaking to avoid unnecessarily upsetting or offending anyone.

Finally, always go that extra mile – be prepared and relaxed and learn from your mistakes and reflect with the group about what you've learned.

Non-verbal communication

Non-verbal communication involves all actions which accompany communication. Many of these have a recognised meaning and are used intentionally to send meaning through signs. When we communicate with others we should be aware of the gestures we make and our movement and facial expressions.

Theory into practice

How would you convey the following through body signals? Demonstrate and see if a friend can guess what they are:

- upset
- happy
- shocked
- angry
- bored.

■ Body language

This refers to the whole way in which a person's body is behaving and can tell us a great deal about someone's state of mind. For example, a nervous person is likely to fidget, pinch or tug their flesh and a defensive person is likely to cross their arms or legs and avoid eye contact. These can be valuable signs for a police officer to look out for when interviewing a person they suspect of a crime – their body language could conflict with what they are saying.

Consider this

- Imagine someone has told you a lie in the past. How would you know it was a lie? Was it because of the things they said or was it the way they acted?
- How do you let someone know that you like them, when you are too shy to speak to him or her?
- How do you know that a team leader is showing you approval and recognition for your achievement without using words?

Other examples of non-verbal communication are included in Table 2.5.

Non-verbal communication	What it might indicate
Making direct eye contact	Friendly, sincere, self-confident, assertive
Shaking head	Disagreeing, shocked, disbelieving
Smiling	Contented, understanding, encouraging, happy
Biting the lip	Nervous, fearful, anxious
Folding arms	Angry, disapproving, disagreeing, defensive, aggressive
Leaning forward	Attentive, interested
Shifting in seat	Restless, bored, nervous, apprehensive
Having erect posture	Self-confident, assertive

Table 2.5 Examples of non-verbal communication

Take it further

When briefing and debriefing a team you should consider the following non-verbal signs:

- Distance – you should not stand or sit too far away from the team. You should also lean slightly towards someone when speaking to ensure your message is clearly received.
- Orientation – you should sit within the group and ensure you can maintain clear eye contact with each member of the team.
- Posture – you should be erect and as tall as possible when interacting with the team and not slouched. You should also avoid crossed arms or legs and be relaxed, not tense.
- Physical contact – contact through shaking hands, touching or embracing demonstrates you have feelings for the team but avoid repeatedly invading their space as this can build barriers and make people feel uncomfortable.
- Expressions and gestures – you should smile and avoid expressions such as frowning or yawning if you want to ensure positive interactions with the team. Gestures should match the tone and words used – avoid aggressive gestures such as clenched fists when using your hands and steer away from constant and extreme gesturing. Using gestures and expressions helps you to deliver a message with passion and conviction.
- Environment – consider a suitable setting and arrange the objects in your environment, for example, the tables and chairs. Your surroundings should be open and comfortable so that the team can facilitate and not hinder the communication process.
- Appearance – you should be dressed appropriately for the situation and have a smart appearance.

Remember that non-verbal behaviour can be affected by cultural differences. A female Asian member of the uniformed services can legitimately refuse to shake hands with a male superior, for example.

■ Listening skills

Listening is more than just hearing. Hearing is the act of perceiving different sounds. Listening, however, is the art of consciously taking the sounds and concentrating on processing and understanding what the sounds mean.

As with any skill, listening takes practice and it will develop the more you use it. You will spend a lot of time using this skill, especially in group situations. It is worth considering that your ability and capacity to listen is four times greater than your ability to speak.

By practising your listening skills, you will also develop better communication skills. Tips for effective listening include:

- maintain eye contact as appropriate
- give your full attention
- be active and focus on the content
- avoid distractions
- use open and supportive body language
- let the speaker finish before you begin to talk
- let yourself finish listening before you begin to speak
- ask questions if you are not sure you understood what the speaker has said
- give clear feedback through signals such as nodding.

Theory into practice

Try this exercise with a friend. Start talking about any topic related to the public services for about 30 seconds. When you stop talking, ask your friend to repeat back to you the main points that you said. Then, reverse the roles and repeat the exercise. You could also increase the time or talk about a topic your friend knows little about to really test their listening skills.

Remember!

Listening is difficult – a typical speaker says about 125 words per minute and an active listener can receive 400–600 words per minute. Ensure that you listen to the full message and don't jump to a conclusion about the remainder of the message.

■ Barriers to communication

Anything that prevents understanding of the message is a barrier to communication. There are many physical and psychological barriers to communication which can mean that the sender's message does not get through to the receiver or the receiver misunderstands the sender's message.

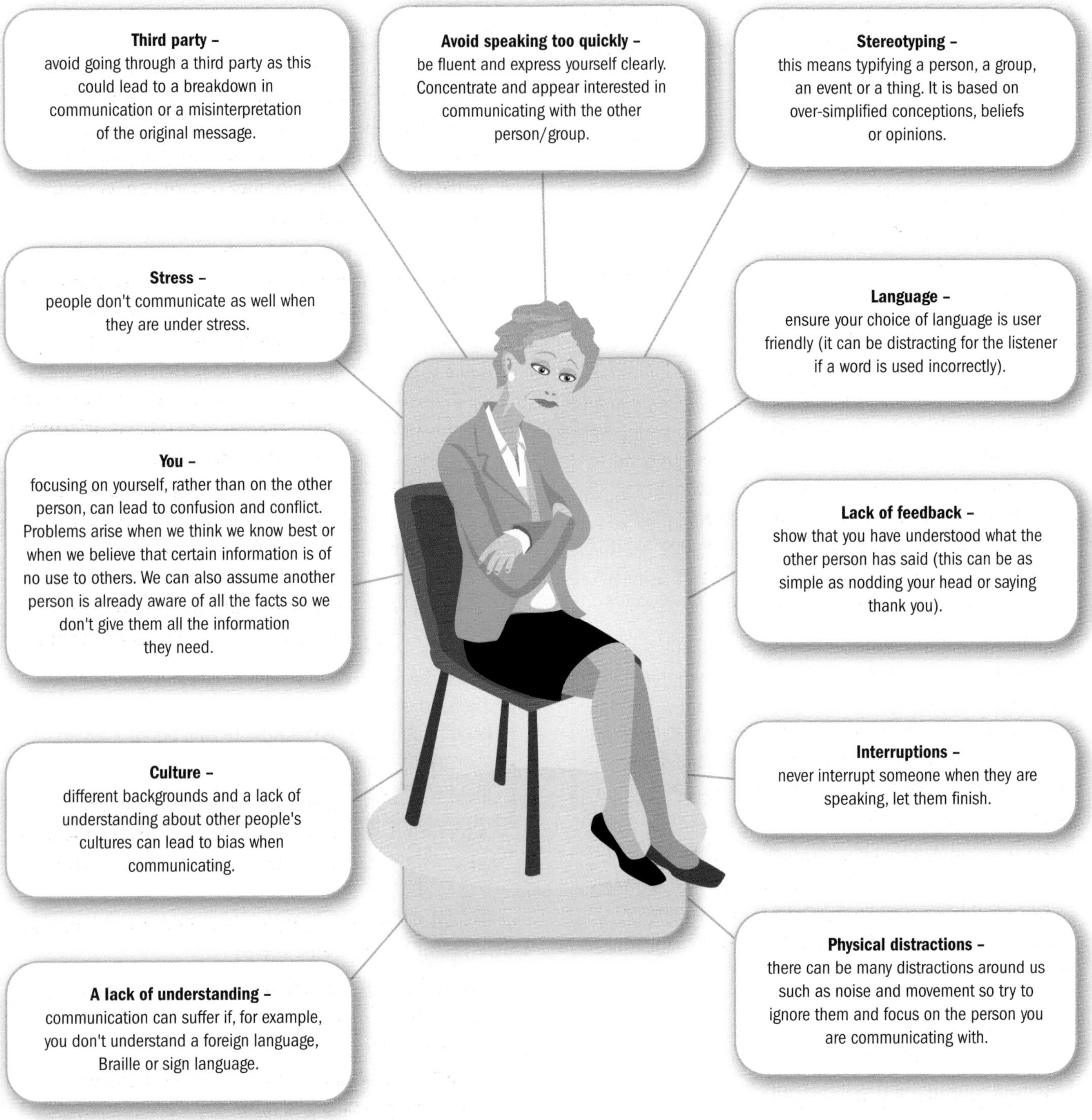

Third party –
avoid going through a third party as this could lead to a breakdown in communication or a misinterpretation of the original message.

Avoid speaking too quickly –
be fluent and express yourself clearly. Concentrate and appear interested in communicating with the other person/group.

Stereotyping –
this means typifying a person, a group, an event or a thing. It is based on over-simplified conceptions, beliefs or opinions.

Stress –
people don't communicate as well when they are under stress.

Language –
ensure your choice of language is user friendly (it can be distracting for the listener if a word is used incorrectly).

You –
focusing on yourself, rather than on the other person, can lead to confusion and conflict. Problems arise when we think we know best or when we believe that certain information is of no use to others. We can also assume another person is already aware of all the facts so we don't give them all the information they need.

Lack of feedback –
show that you have understood what the other person has said (this can be as simple as nodding your head or saying thank you).

Culture –
different backgrounds and a lack of understanding about other people's cultures can lead to bias when communicating.

Interruptions –
never interrupt someone when they are speaking, let them finish.

A lack of understanding –
communication can suffer if, for example, you don't understand a foreign language, Braille or sign language.

Physical distractions –
there can be many distractions around us such as noise and movement so try to ignore them and focus on the person you are communicating with.

▲ Figure 2.7 There are many physical and psychological barriers to communication – try to overcome them

Briefing teams

Team briefings are similar to meetings and are a verbal process of getting information to people quickly and efficiently. A briefing should be an open and two-way communication process and not just about informing the team about what they are required to do. Often there will be no written records of team briefings as they are applied to one-off situations, which are often practical in nature.

Remember that you are not addressing Parliament! This is a team you are familiar with, so the briefing should be relaxed and reasonably informal.

Tips for a successful briefing include being:

- *clear* – avoid unfamiliar technicalities and acronyms and keep communications adult to adult – never patronise or talk down
- *brief* – be precise and only repeat yourself to make sure the main points have been understood
- *in control* – be prepared and lead, keep in control by ensuring you can focus on all members of the team so that you can read their body language
- *positive* – be confident and don't appear nervous. Monitor your body language (avoid negative signs such as crossing arms or no eye contact). If things start to go wrong, or not to plan, don't panic and persevere with the task.

Successful team briefings will avoid misunderstandings and blockages. Teams who are involved in the briefing process are more likely to perform, progress and achieve the desired results as they will have clear direction and awareness of the main issues and won't need to rely on constant guidance from the team leader.

There is no single recognised model for briefing teams but a successful team briefing should follow a reasonably consistent format so that everyone knows what to expect. However, it could include the features outlined below.

Ground orientation

- Commonly used in the military.
- Involves the use of objects and models to help explain the location and surrounding area.

- Can be adapted to suit more conventional team briefings by ensuring the team is aware of the environment it is working in (including issues such as facilities and resources at their disposal).

Safety points

- A risk assessment of any location/task needs to be carried out in order to identify hazards and risks.
- Identify the precautions that should be taken to minimise the risk and decrease the likelihood of harm (for example, avoiding certain behaviours, wearing special equipment).
- Uniformed services often rely on dynamic risk assessment when working in teams. This is a process of identifying hazards and risks on a situation by situation basis and taking appropriate steps to eliminate or reduce them. This means as new risks occur, or as the circumstances change, the uniformed services will adapt the risk assessment and inform the team of any changes or requirements.
- An example of this would be fire fighters dealing with a factory fire and discovering that the factory has some highly explosive and very toxic chemicals stored in the basement. On learning this, they will adapt the risk assessment and take new measures and precautions to protect their colleagues and the public.

Summary of a situation

- When briefing a team, a clear summary of the situation should be offered – this could take the form of a brief and concise statement that presents the main points.
- It should include the things a team must and should know about the situation.
- From this, the primary aim or aims should be established (these are the most important and immediate concerns).
- An example of this is at a road traffic incident where the primary aim of the public services will be to coordinate and work together to ensure the preservation of life and safety of the people involved

or affected directly by the incident. This may mean closing the road and diverting traffic to preserve the scene for later investigation and removing the vehicles involved.

The method to achieve the aim

- Briefings should be forums for debate and this should involve the team being able to suggest possible ways of achieving the primary aims and goals.
- After all the possible solutions have been presented, discussion should take place on the pros and cons of each suggestion along with the likelihood of their success.
- It may ultimately be down to the team leader to select the method used to achieve the aim, based on the solutions offered by the group.

Designated roles

The team leader is not expected to achieve the goals and aims unaided. A team briefing will allow the team leader to delegate and designate roles based on people's strengths and abilities. One way this could be done is by using Belbin's team roles shown in Table 2.6.

For a full exploration of Belbin's roles, read pages 125–6 in *Unit 4: Team development in public services*.

Timings

It is likely that briefing will have to take place quickly and often under situations of extreme pressure and stress. (Think about how the combined uniformed services would have to respond to a terrorist attack within an urban area.) This means that resources, equipment and safety issues will need to be identified immediately and the team will need to quickly establish the situation and primary aims, along with how they will tackle the problem. In the example of a terrorist attack, the uniformed services will coordinate and designate roles based on their service's strengths. For example, the fire service will focus on search and rescue, the paramedics will deal with casualties at the scene and the police will manage the scene to bring the situation under control and ensure general safety.

Equipment

When offering solutions to problems, the team can be aided or restricted by the equipment they have available. This means that you should consider the equipment you have and ensure the team are informed of, or can see it. For example, if the team are asked to scale a ten foot wall and there is no equipment to aid them, then a solution from a team member involving the use of ropes and

Team role	Summary of role
Coordinator	Clarifies group objectives, sets the agenda, establishes priorities, selects problems, sums up and is decisive, but does not dominate discussions.
Shaper	Gives shape to the team effort, looks for patterns in discussions and practical considerations regarding the feasibility of the project. Can steamroller the team but gets results.
Plant	The source of original ideas, suggestions and proposals that are usually original and radical.
Monitor-evaluator	Contributes a measured and dispassionate analysis and, through objectivity, stops the team committing itself to a misguided task.
Implementer	Turns decisions and strategies into defined and manageable tasks, sorting out objectives and pursuing them logically.
Resource investigator	Goes outside the team to bring in ideas, information and developments – they are the team's salesperson, diplomat, liaison officer and explorer.
Team worker	Operates against division and disruption in the team, like cement, particularly in times of stress and pressure.
Finisher	Maintains a permanent sense of urgency with relentless follow-through.

Table 2.6 A summary of the team roles developed by Belbin

crates is unsuitable and can't be considered because the equipment simply isn't there.

Team motivation

A successful team is a team that is well motivated and eager to work together to implement the identified aims. There are many ways that a team can be motivated to perform.

- *Clear focus* – if the team has a clear aim and understands how to achieve that aim it is more likely to work towards its completion in a positive manner.
- *Challenge* – a team will be motivated if the task is a sufficient challenge to them but is less likely to be motivated if the task is too simple or too difficult.
- *Camaraderie* – a sense of comradeship and loyalty will help a team to work together as the members will have a genuine respect for each other and will work hard to develop and maintain this relationship.
- *Rewards* – this could be money or benefits that the team will receive upon completion of the task.
- *Responsibility and authority* – having a sense of ownership of the task and a clear role is likely to help motivate the team.
- *Growth* – if the team feels they are moving forward, learning new skills and stretching their minds then they are likely to have a high level of motivation as personal growth enhances an individual's self-esteem and self-worth.
- *Treating people fairly* – it is important that all members of the team are treated equally and are all involved in the task; this will ensure that each member is motivated and that they work as a team.

Check understanding

- During the briefing you should check understanding.
- This could be done by generally observing a person's body language and facial expressions or by asking questions for clarification.
- The team should also be encouraged to ask questions and make comments to gauge their understanding of the task.

Theory into practice

The next time you conduct a team briefing, apply the following criteria:

- assess your surroundings and consider potential risks and likelihood of harm
- summarise the task
- identify the main aim and possible ways of achieving success
- assign roles and responsibilities
- identify how long you have to complete the task and the equipment you have available
- ask questions to clarify that people understand what they are doing or are expected to do.

Debriefing teams

Debriefings were first used by the Armed Forces and involved troops giving feedback about their mission. The information generated was then assessed and the troops were instructed on what they could talk about and what information was strictly confidential. The information given was also used to assess the troop's mental condition and to determine when they could return to duty.

Debriefings with teams can be seen as reviewing what has been learnt from a task. It is a process that helps you to reflect on the completed task in order to aid personal and professional development. Successful reviewing will help you and the team to improve your interpersonal skills and work more effectively. Reviewing a task involves more than just reflecting on the task, it involves open communication between the team which leads to analysing and evaluating the task to ensure learning takes place.

Remember!

The main features of a debrief are:

- reviewing the task
- processing the task
- reflection on the task.

Reasons why you should debrief after completing a task include:

- It keeps you in touch with the team and helps maintain motivation and enthusiasm for future tasks.
- It adds value to the experience and shows that you care for and are interested in the team.
- The team benefits from discussing, reviewing and evaluating the task which will in turn increase confidence and allow the team to become more independent and more capable of self-development.
- It increases the amount of strategies and ideas that may be used in future tasks as people will be imaginative and express themselves.
- It develops your skills (such as communication, perception and observation).

- Everyone learns from the task as they will share understanding and knowledge and gain an appreciation of their own strengths and weaknesses.
- It helps to reinforce the objectives of the task and can be used to clarify and measure the amount of achievement that has taken place.
- The team is likely to work better and be successful in future tasks as they feel engaged and integrated into the process and can see the bigger picture.
- It helps people to acknowledge and enjoy success.

Feedback

One of the key aspects of any team debriefing is giving feedback. There are three common types of feedback including:

- *Negative feedback* – this should be avoided when debriefing teams as it is likely to cause conflict and a decrease in future participation by the whole group or certain members of the group.
- *Positive feedback* – this is obviously a great way of maintaining good group cohesion and output. However, it could be detrimental when there are obvious flaws in the team that go unmentioned as this could cause long-term problems.

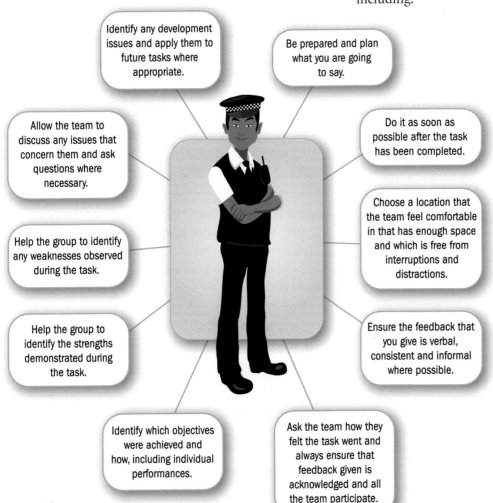

Identify any development issues and apply them to future tasks where appropriate.

Be prepared and plan what you are going to say.

Allow the team to discuss any issues that concern them and ask questions where necessary.

Do it as soon as possible after the task has been completed.

Help the group to identify any weaknesses observed during the task.

Choose a location that the team feel comfortable in that has enough space and which is free from interruptions and distractions.

Help the group to identify the strengths demonstrated during the task.

Ensure the feedback that you give is verbal, consistent and informal where possible.

Identify which objectives were achieved and how, including individual performances.

Ask the team how they felt the task went and always ensure that feedback given is acknowledged and all the team participate.

Figure 2.8 It is important to give feedback and you need to consider carefully how you do this

- *Constructive feedback* – the best approach when giving feedback is to do so in a constructive way. Reassuring the team that supportive comments will be given, even if they fail, will encourage people to take risks. Also both failure and successful experiences will be analysed so that the team can develop further and move forward.

Assessment activity 2.3

1. In a group, you have been asked by your tutor to conduct a training seminar with a variety of scenarios that describe both verbal and non-verbal communication skills and the process of a successful team briefing and debriefing. **P3**

2. You then need to conduct and demonstrate a team briefing and debriefing which incorporates effective communication skills. **M2**

Grading tips

P3 To achieve P3 you need to describe the necessary communication skills that are needed to brief and debrief a team and state why briefings and debriefings are important. You also need to outline the processes for both and why each part of the process is necessary.

M2 To achieve M2 you need to demonstrate your communication skills in briefing and debriefing a team and ensure you follow the correct procedures for both as identified in P3.

Key terms

Skill A skill is an ability that is demonstrated and used to perform a task successfully.

Quality An inherent and essential characteristic or attribute that distinguishes one person from another.

Leadership qualities

A leader will demonstrate a range of leadership qualities and, depending on the type of leader and type of organisation, there will be different qualities that a person will demonstrate.

The following leadership qualities are a selection of those that are practically important to the uniformed services because these leaders will have influence over a team and are often expected to lead in dangerous and crisis situations.

Decisiveness

A leader within the uniformed services needs to demonstrate good judgement by making effective, timely and sound decisions in response to situations that arise. Decisions need to be made quickly and include consideration of the impact and implications of their decision. Many decisions need to be made proactively before a problem arises. Even if the data is limited and they have little time to weigh up the pros and cons, the decision should always be in the interests of the organisation, even if there are unpleasant consequences for the team. All decisions should be made in a calm and professional manner and never half-heartedly or subjected to change.

Adaptability

A leader within the uniformed services needs to be able to adjust any long-term plans when new information is available and constantly apply critical thinking to address any new demands and prioritise and reprioritise tasks in a changing environment to fit any new circumstances. This is particularly important in public services where the political climate or operational conditions can change with very little or no warning.

Courage

A leader within the uniformed services needs courage to accomplish tasks, especially when he or she is faced with tough decisions and has to take action in difficult circumstances. Leaders need to use courage to manage dangerous situations whilst appearing calm to the rest of the team at all times, even when under stress.

Integrity

A leader within the uniformed services needs integrity as they need the trust and admiration of the team. They must demonstrate the organisational values of the service within their work ethic in the hope of being a role model for others.

Accountability

A leader within the uniformed services should be accountable for their actions and give individuals credit where it is due and accept personal responsibility for failures. They need to make all members of the team feel equally valuable to avoid low self-esteem or making certain team members feel inferior.

Consistency

A good leader is consistent in their approach to tasks and their manner with staff. Leaders should not display favouritism or show dislike openly and avoid swings of mood, which can leave staff feeling uncertain or wary. A good leader is a solid and stable rock which staff can revolve around and refer to while working towards goals. This does not preclude them from being innovative or dynamic but it does mean they should remain level headed and professional at all times.

Trust

Before anyone will fully open up they need to trust and have faith in you and feel that you trust them. This can be done in a number of ways, for example, showing a person respect. This is achieved by valuing everybody's opinion within the group and being open and honest with your ideas, concerns and values. It is also done by supporting each other – team work can be stressful and different team members will want help at different stages of a task and on different types of task. Support is an important element because it means that any problems are dealt with sensitively and not aggressively – supporting each other generally leads to behaviour which is consistent and acceptable by all. Showing loyalty and depending on people's individual strengths can also lead to trust – displaying loyalty to a member of your team, or the whole team, shows that you value them and lets people get on with the task by ensuring they perform to their strengths with little or no interference. This is important as it will eliminate potential conflict and prevent frustration.

Commitment

A leader within the uniformed services needs commitment. This is demonstrated by the time and

▲ **A lead fire fighter needs to display many leadership qualities**

energy they put into the job and leading from the front. They put effort into the task until a level of success has been achieved.

Take it further

When leading a team-building exercise within your college, you will demonstrate a range of leadership qualities. Why are the qualities listed below important when working in such a situation?

- openness
- creativity
- honesty
- inspiration
- fairness
- broadmindedness
- knowledge
- imagination
- forward-thinking
- self-confidence
- assertiveness
- ability to listen
- empathy
- persuasion
- foresight
- altruism
- charisma
- compassion
- enthusiasm
- dedication
- competency
- a sense of humour.

Consider this

Looking at the leadership qualities above, identify in order of importance the qualities needed by a lead fire fighter.

Think about another position within an alternative uniformed service and repeat the exercise.

Compare your two lists and discuss any similarities and differences with a fellow learner.

Leadership skills

There are many skills associated with leadership and the skills demonstrated will vary from situation to situation. For example, the skills needed by a commanding officer in a conflict situation may vary from the skills needed by a station officer in charge of the day-to-day running of a fire station. But no matter what the different skills needed are, these skills will serve them well in their daily lives and careers.

Here are some common skills often demonstrated by leaders which help them to instruct their team and achieve their goals.

Motivation

To create a motivated team you need ground rules. However, these should not be too complex or rigid in order to avoid confusion. Any dysfunctional behaviour should be stamped out and communication should be clear and consistent. Also team members should be given team roles that suit their personalities and complement their strengths.

Morale has a profound effect on a team. When it is high, a team will be enthusiastic about its work and function better by being more productive as its members will be committed and confident of success. Good morale makes communication easier, clearer and more energetic. When a team is happy, all the members will feel a sense of pride in being a member of that team. Good morale gives your team a good mindset and good team spirit. This often means team members become friends. Morale can be observed directly through people's behaviour and the productivity of the group.

If team morale is low, or needs building, you can try to do this by offering treats or incentives to complete

Remember!

It only takes one member of the team to drop their morale for it to affect the rest of the team.

tasks. If multiple tasks are being done throughout a day, morale can be maintained by celebrating when a task is completed or an objective is met.

Cooperation

To create team cooperation you need a good leader in order to avoid confusion and to create a positive environment. Team cooperation will develop when the group identity has emerged. A cooperative team is one that is involved in active decision making with well-disciplined listening and thought-provoking questions. Commitment is very important as team members need to feel that they belong to a team rather than just being individuals within a team. Finally, effective teamwork can only be achieved when individuals work together for the success of the group rather than for the success of the individual.

Time management

The 80:20 Rule (or Pareto's Principle) states that typically 80 per cent of unfocused effort generates only 20 per cent of results. The remaining 80 per cent of results are achieved with only 20 per cent of the effort.

This means that a successful team is one that manages its time, as time is the most valuable (and undervalued) resource you have. It can be managed effectively by determining which task or element of a task is most important. This will help you use your time in the most effective way you can. A well-managed team will also look to control the distractions that waste time and break the flow.

By putting these points into action you will reduce stress and be more in control of what you do. You will be more productive and hopefully you will find working in a team more enjoyable.

Delegation

Delegation is not about the leader handing over authority. It's about delegating to the team clear roles and responsibilities and leaving it to the team to manage and control their task.

To allow delegation to take place the team leader needs to establish:

- the task
- the schedule and time frame to complete the task
- people's strengths and weaknesses
- people's prior experience and expertise
- how the successful completion of the task will be assessed and monitored.

The key to delegation is to delegate as much as possible so that team members feel empowered and to delegate equally amongst the team so that everyone has a role or responsibility. Apart from giving a person responsibility for the completion of the task, you should also give them ownership.

For example, you may say something like: 'Tom, I want you to tie all the rope ends to form the sides of the rope bridge and, once that has been done, make sure that it is safe and secure. If you're not sure about anything, give me a shout or call Tim over as he is good at this kind of thing.'

Conflict resolution

Leaders must be skilled in the art of resolving conflict between all levels within an organisation and also between the organisation and customers and external contacts. Leadership is often about balancing the needs of one group against the needs of another and keeping both groups happy – not an easy task!

▲ Great leaders must have a number of important qualities

'It was the nation that had the lion's heart. I had the luck to be called upon to give the roar.'

Winston Churchill (1954)

Winston Churchill was born into a well-recognised military and political family on 30 November 1874. After serving as a military officer in three campaigns and also as a war correspondent he developed skills which set him on the road to greatness. Many of the qualities which would help him save Britain from Nazi invasion 40 years later were already emerging. These qualities included intense patriotism, an unshakeable belief in the greatness of Britain and its empire, inexhaustible energy, a strong physical constitution, a willingness to speak out on issues despite the fact that to do so would prove unpopular, meticulous organisational skills and an indomitable spirit which inspired and motivated others.

When World War I broke out in 1914, Churchill was Lord of the Admiralty and had a crucial role to play in the events of 1914–18. His experiences during World War I had educated him about political office and large-scale battle tactics and helped him come to terms with his leadership failings.

Not all of Churchill's military campaigns in World War I were successful. In 1915 he was instrumental in sending a naval and army force to Gallipoli in the Mediterranean. Gallipoli was a disaster and cost thousands of allied soldiers and sailors their lives. Admitting responsibility, Churchill resigned from both political and military office; he would not regain his pre-war political status for over 25 years. Followers who make mistakes are often forgiven but for leaders the situation is much more serious. Failures by leaders last much longer in the minds of the public than successes.

It seemed that his troubled political years helped to develop his leadership skills and mental faculties to such an extent that in the hour of Britain's crisis at the beginning of World War II, his skills and abilities matched the requirements of the situation better than those of his political contemporaries. During the 1930s Churchill spoke out vigorously on the rise of totalitarian regimes such as the Nazi party. This ensured that when confrontation between Britain

and Germany inevitably arose, Churchill stood out as a statesman who had fought against the threat of Nazism for many years while other politicians had tried to appease Adolf Hitler.

The nation felt it had found a politician who understood the situation and whom it could trust. Churchill was reappointed to head the admiralty office on the day that war broke out: 3 September 1939.

Norway fell to the Germans in April 1940 and this was quickly followed by the fall of Belgium and the Netherlands in May. Neville Chamberlain, the Prime Minister of the time, lost the confidence of Parliament and resigned. It was clear at that point that Churchill had the skills and spirit to unite and lead the nation. He was installed as Prime Minister to a coalition government headed by a war cabinet. After the fall of France, Britain stood without substantial allies and faced most of 1940 under German air bombardment and the constant threat of Nazi invasion. Churchill used his personal skills and patriotism to motivate and inspire the British public to endure the hardships they faced with fortitude and resourcefulness. Churchill also used extensive diplomacy and communication to forge alliances between nations with differing political and social philosophies. Churchill was instrumental in holding together the communist Soviet Union and capitalist US in a firm and dynamic alliance, which eventually prevailed over the axis powers.

Churchill's leadership qualities were present from the early days of his military and political career but it is fair to say that some of the decisions he made in his early career did not enhance his status as a leader. He only achieved real greatness under a particular set of circumstances. Despite his many and varied leadership skills it is unlikely that he would have risen to greatness without World War II. It was the circumstances that Churchill found himself in that allowed his best abilities to dominate in a way they might not otherwise have done.

1. **Think of a leader you have admired in your own life. List the qualities that they brought to their role and describe how those qualities made that person a better leader.**

When considering leadership skills and abilities it is important to remember that, even if an individual has a range of the skills and abilities mentioned in this section, they are not necessarily a great leader. You also need other characteristics such as personality and a good persona and the ability to act clearly in times of personal, professional or national crises.

Implementing a plan

Planning is the process by which you and the team will determine the most effective way to attempt and complete a task and the time you spend planning will often make the difference between success and failure.

You can't always plan for every eventuality as there may be unexpected difficulties but planning helps a group to achieve when others around are failing. Think about the group exercises you have done. Did you discuss the possible solutions to the problem and what you needed to do? (You might have tried **brainstorming**.) If so, you have shown some planning.

By planning effectively you can:

- **avoid wasting effort** – it is far too easy to spend large amounts of time trying to complete a task with ideas and methods that are completely irrelevant to completing the task
- **take into account and consider all possible solutions** – this ensures that you are aware of all the methods available to complete the task and that you are prepared for a variety of different eventualities. This will help your team work effectively with minimum effort
- **be aware of all possible changes and alternative solutions** – if you have a number of possible solutions to the task, then you can assess in advance the likelihood of being able to change the way you tackle the problem throughout the duration of the task
- **identify the resources needed** – by planning the task you will be able to evaluate the worth of the resources you have available and how they are to be used to complete the task and, in some cases, be able to work out if additional resources are needed.

In summary, the planning process helps you to:

- use the information available to define the task and make a workable plan
- identify precisely what the aim is and why and how it might be achieved
- encourage and discipline individuals by creating a team spirit, relieving any tension and reconciling disagreements
- identify what resources are available and needed
- detail precisely who will do what, when, and where it will be done
- select the best course of action in completing the task
- control and influence the tempo by ensuring all actions move towards the aim by keeping discussions relevant and guiding the team to a decision
- discuss the pros and cons of a proposed solution and identify whether it is likely to succeed
- evaluate the team's performance on completion and ensure that the team members evaluate their own performance along with what could have been done differently.

The reasons why teams don't plan include:

- laziness – the team is not bothered about spending time on creating a plan as they want to do the task as quickly as possible
- fear of failure – the team doesn't believe it will be able to complete the task and therefore doesn't feel it is worth planning
- inexperience – the team doesn't understand how to plan or the importance of planning
- dominance – the team is controlled by the team leader and believes that he or she knows best
- eagerness – the team is in a rush to attempt the task and starts the task with little or no planning.

Leading the team

In order to lead the team you need to:

- brief the team
- check the team has an understanding of the overall aim
- give individuals their own roles
- execute the plan
- ensure there is ongoing quality control (for example, of safety, performance etc.)
- achieve the aim
- debrief the team
- review and evaluate.

Assessment activity 2.4

You have been asked by your tutor to:

1. Organise a college event with other learners which allows you to demonstrate appropriate and effective leadership skills and qualities. **P4 M3**

2. Evaluate your own performance in a one-to-one interview with your tutor after completing the event. In this interview you will be required to: offer a summary of what the team has achieved; assess how the team performed; assess your own performance, including areas for further development and recommendation on how you might do things differently. **P5 M3 D2**

Grading tips

P4 **P5** To achieve P4 you need to demonstrate and use appropriate leadership skills and qualities with a team of people through the implementation and evidence of a specific plan, which has evidence of a specific aim. This should also include evidence of being able to correctly brief and debrief the team. To achieve P5 you also need to offer straightforward assessment of your performance and the team by answering the question set within part 2 of Assessment activity 2.4.

M3 To achieve M3 you need to demonstrate leadership of others through effective command and control techniques, which show implementation and evidence of critical and creative thinking. This should also include evidence of correct briefing and debriefing procedures as identified in P4 which motivate the team to perform.

D2 To achieve D2 you need to provide a detailed reflection and evaluation of your effectiveness as a team leader and offer realistic and achievable recommendations for your future development as a team leader.

Developing the team

In this unit so far we have focused on team leaders and the qualities and skills needed to implement a plan and brief and debrief teams.

Today we find all kinds of teams in society and they generally fall into one of two groups: permanent teams and temporary teams. We are now going to look at some of the different types of teams that can be formed within the public services.

Types of teams

■ Interdependent teams

These are permanent teams that need the help of all the team to be able to accomplish the task, and in which the success of every individual is inextricably bound to the success of the whole team. The members of an interdependent team benefit from getting to know each other, developing trust in one another, and from overcoming challenges. An example of this within the public services would be a number of fire engines and their crews dealing with a large warehouse fire, which involves rescuing employees and dealing with chemical hazards.

■ Independent teams

Independent teams are also permanent teams. However, they are the opposite of interdependent teams and involve each team member performing their own role

within a task. They are likely to help each other by offering advice or support but ultimately each person's success is primarily due to their own efforts. An example of this within the public services would be a paramedic dealing with an elderly person who has fallen at home; they will need information from the casualty, any witnesses and the command room to establish the nature of the injuries but ultimately it is down to them to deal with and manage the situation.

■ Project teams

These are temporary teams used for a defined period of time and which then disband. They are often separate from the main team and have a clear purpose and common function. Members of these teams might belong to a variety of different teams who have come together to provide various different skills and perspectives, and for the defined period of time they are assigned to the same project and become one team. Some of the members might not be full-time to the

The members of this fire crew ▶ will have developed trust in each other

project, or the project itself may not be full-time, but when the team comes together the aims of the project are their primary concern. An example of this within the public services would be the police service and other agencies coming together to form a task force to deal with a murder enquiry and working together until the murder is either solved or the operation is scaled down due to re-allocation of resources.

■ Cross-functional teams

Cross-functional teams are similar to project teams. However, they are often more permanent and work on long-term projects such as Crime and Disorder Reduction Partnerships, which are a combination of police, local authorities and other relevant agencies who work together to implement strategies for tackling crime at a local level.

■ Advisory teams

These are temporary teams who are responsible for providing support or guidance on a task. They often have part-time team members and only become involved when needed by other teams as they possess certain specialist knowledge. An example of this within the public services would be a forensic officer or a fire investigator who is brought into the team to help collect evidence and establish the facts of the case.

■ Inter-service teams

These are temporary teams that are independent of each other but rely heavily on others in working towards the same aim. They do this by supporting each other by using their teams' specialist skills and resources. An example of this within the public services would be when the Army, Navy and RAF come together to aid each other in a conflict situation as they will have their own missions and objectives but share the same primary aim.

■ Work teams

These are permanent teams who share a common mission and collectively manage their own affairs within predetermined boundaries that are in line with the team norms. Most of the time the team members will manage and direct themselves independently by performing their work on their own and managing their own time. The team leader's role is to pull the group together and brief and direct the team to ensure they are up-to-date with the main aims. An example of this within the public services would be police constables on a shift who respond and react to calls from the community by prioritising their workload accordingly.

Stages in team development

No matter what the situation is or what type of team is created, an individual needs to understand the advantages that are offered by teamwork and what kind of role within the team is likely to be appropriate for them. One of the keys to an effective team is to understand what strengths, skills and motivations each individual brings to the team; the issue of group diversity will help to make a team strong and flexible.

The cohesiveness of groups has a major impact on their functioning and generally groups go through five stages. Bruce Tuckman published his 'Forming, storming, norming, performing' model in 1965 and in 1975 he added a fifth stage, adjourning/transforming. Tuckman's theory still remains a good explanation of team development and behaviour today. The theory on team development predicts that teams must go through the whole sequence to be successful.

▲ Figure 2.9 The model of team development developed by Bruce Tuckman

Everyone who works in a team needs to know what the various growth stages of a developing team are and they should know how best to move the team through these stages. Knowing that it is normal for a team to go through a roller coaster ride to achieve their goal will help you understand and anticipate the team-building process, and take action to be more productive when working in groups in the future. Some teams will go through the first four recognised stages fairly rapidly and move from forming through to performing in a short space of time. It all depends on the composition of the team, the capabilities of the individuals, the tasks at hand and the leadership style.

Teams that go through these stages successfully should become effective teams and display:

- clear objectives and agreed goals
- openness
- support and trust towards each other
- cooperation
- good decision-making skills
- appropriate leadership
- ability to review team performance
- sound inter-group relationships
- individual development
- understanding of how to deal with confrontation and conflict.

■ Stage 1: Forming (the orientation stage)

The forming stage is the first stage of team development and happens when a newly formed team comes together with individuals who may not know each other. This means that people may feel anxious and uncomfortable. This stage is a difficult time when team members will explore the boundaries of acceptable behaviour and determine their individual role within the team. They will discuss the task and decide how it will be accomplished, and they will identify the resources or skills needed and begin to communicate openly about individual likes and dislikes and strengths and weaknesses.

A key tip for anybody taking a group through this stage is to ensure that open discussion takes place at the start of the task. This ensures that people get the chance to air their views, concerns and queries, and if it is not done at this stage then it could result in failure later.

The following points highlight what you can do as a team to ensure this stage goes well:

- Outline the task the team has to complete.
- Identify each person's role in the task by identifying people's strengths and weaknesses.
- Encourage each team member to perform.
- Ensure that the team forms a set of rules and guidelines.
- Decide on how decisions will be made.
- Decide how the team is going to give feedback on each other's performance.

■ Stage 2: Storming (the conflict stage)

This is when team members start to 'jockey' for position and when control struggles take place. The storming stage is critical as this is where things may start to go wrong. If team members have not become acquainted then they may still feel uncomfortable with their roles. For example, some team members may think the task is too hard and others may distance themselves from the group because they feel excluded. Communication may be poor as the team is not listening to each other. Conflicts may begin as simple disagreements, which then lead to more fundamental differences of opinion, meaning that the group becomes divided. Although conflict may damage or destroy a team, conflict is a natural consequence of team membership and it may, in fact, strengthen the team as the members learn to accept and constructively resolve their differences.

Storming is a challenging phase and this is where leadership qualities are tested as the storming usually arises as a result of goals, roles and rules becoming confused and unclear. This can lead to conflicts with the potential of creating factions within the team and decreased productivity. To deal with this problem you must go over the agreements made by the team during the forming stage and ensure that the understanding is uniform across the team. The earlier in the storming stage this is revisited, the more likely you are to achieve a successful outcome.

Remember!

If things are going wrong then you should go back to the forming stage and re-establish or modify your ground rules (norms) and if necessary clarify or re-negotiate roles and responsibilities.

If the disagreements and concerns continue, get the team together and openly thrash out what the concerns and disagreements are. Remember it is never a bad idea to let the team 'bleed' a little and then begin the healing process by facilitating their coming together.

■ Stage 3: Norming (the cohesion stage)

This stage is when rules are finalised and accepted and when team rules start being adhered to. The norming stage is where team members accept the team and its ground rules, along with their individual role within the team. The team works cooperatively with a willingness to confront issues and solve problems and constructive criticism replaces conflict. There is a sense of team spirit and identity which ensures everyone is working together. Members are highly involved and member satisfaction is at its highest. Not only are members pleased with the team, but they themselves may experience higher self-esteem and lower anxiety as a result of their participation in the team. At this stage the group will look at more detailed planning for completing the task.

The norming is the calm after the storm. The team is calm and focused on the goal, roles and rules are clarified and understood by all and relationships become stronger as people are more aware of each other's strengths and weaknesses.

■ Stage 4: Performing (the task-performance stage)

This stage is when the team starts to show productivity through effective and efficient working practices. This occurs late in the developmental life of the team as team members at this stage have a clear understanding of each other's strengths and weaknesses and are able to avoid conflict as they are aware of how to resolve differences by utilising each person's individual talents and opinions.

It is at the performing stage where team members really concentrate on the team goals. This is a period of potential personal growth among team members as there is a good deal of sharing of experiences, feelings and ideas.

Not every team makes it to the performing stage. Many get stuck at the norming stage because there is often a lack of momentum and motivation towards achieving goals.

■ Stage 5: Adjourning and transforming (the dissolution stage)

This stage is when team dissolution occurs. It can happen for a number of reasons; for example, when the team has either completed its task, exhausted its resources/ideas, members are unable to resolve conflicts, members have grown dissatisfied and depart or when repeated failure makes the team unable to continue.

As teams perform it is almost inevitable that fatigue, tension and conflict will develop. Fatigue will set in if the task is physically demanding or boredom will develop if it is too easy. Tension and conflict will develop when alternative approaches need to be considered and applied because the first approach was unsuccessful.

Finally the team will enter a transforming stage. This is where the successful achievement of the task takes place and is acknowledged. The team celebrates and reflects on their achievement before dispersing and using the experience in future tasks with different teams.

Barriers to effective performance

There are many possible barriers to a team's successful performance of a given task. Some of these problems are relatively easy to rectify while some can cause long-term resistance and continual poor performance.

Common barriers include:

- Team members simply don't understand their role or all have similar roles which leads to disorganisation, conflict and a disjointed team structure.

- Teams can also be affected by being unclear about the exact aims of the task or by a lack of support from the team leader. This could lead to the team lacking focus and wasting valuable time.

- If the team or individual members don't have the appropriate skills or abilities to complete the task, they may refuse to cooperate with the rest of the team. This lack of skills or abilities could be simply down to the fact that they lack prior knowledge or are poorly prepared.

- Poor relationships between certain team members or with the team leader can create barriers to performance and lead to a breakdown in communication along with a non-conducive working environment, especially if the team leader tries to control the group through a dictatorship style approach.

- Little or no recognition can make a team member lose enthusiasm and commitment for future tasks as they may not feel valued. This can lower their self-esteem, especially if others do receive recognition or reward for their participation.

- Barriers can also be created when the team question the credibility of the team leader as this will lead to them having little confidence in the team leader and competition may arise for the team's leadership.

- Further barriers can also be created if certain team members have hidden agendas or individual interests that go against the group ethos.

- Teams that have low standards and little expectation of success, along with no accountability for the team's performance, will create a blame culture. This can lead to conflict or ultimately the group will completely break down.

- Teams that receive and give little or no encouragement to their members, especially when things are tough, can lead to a drop in motivation. Team members will become fragmented and discouraged from performing the task.

- Inconsistent teams can also be problematic as in one task they will work well together and in the next task they will not perform. This could be due to the nature of the task – the team may perform well in a task that involves a mental challenge but, due to a lack of overall fitness, they may perform poorly or choose not to take part in a physical challenge.

Finally there are some factors that can affect the team's performance that are purely out of their control. These include:

- A lack of adequate resources to complete the task (which may be down to financial constraints) leading to having no resources at all, poorly qualified staff or substandard equipment.

- The environment and facilities can also affect team performance, especially when attempting outdoor tasks, as bad weather or poor conditions can make the task more challenging and test the group's resolve.

Consider this

In a small group, identify and list the main barriers to effective team performance and create a PowerPoint presentation for your class group which gives clear strategies on how the barriers could be challenged.

Evaluation methods

Reviewing your team's performance is an important part of team development and is particularly valuable if you are going to work again as a team.

Often when a task is being attempted, everyone will make observations about what is going well and how things could be better, but most of the time they will not reflect and discuss these issues together as a team.

It is important to evaluate as it helps the team to remember the goals initially set and determine whether they have been achieved. It also helps the team to praise each other and celebrate success, along with identifying any problems or weaknesses that could be rectified in future tasks.

Key terms

Evaluation A process used to gather information to determine whether or not the team has been successful and achievement of its aims has occurred.

Evaluating is an effective way of gathering information as a team, which can then be used to set group boundaries, devise improvement strategies and identify individual development issues. Individuals can acknowledge the benefits of team work, reflect on their own performance, plan for future development and make adjustments to how they work and interact within a future group situation.

To ensure that the team's performance is assessed you could, as the team leader, ask a series of questions which will encourage discussion, reflection and improvement.

Theory into practice

As a team leader it is important that you and the team reflect on the task. This can be done either informally or formally by asking a series of questions. You could try using some of the questions from the list below when assessing the team's performance – these questions should stimulate discussion amongst the team.

1. What were the main objectives of the task?
2. How much time did you spend on planning the task and completing it?
3. How did you go about making choices on how to complete the task?
4. What changes did you make during the planning or task stage?
5. What elements of your plan seemed to be effective or ineffective?
6. What additional support did you need and who provided it?
7. What qualities and skills did you bring to the task?
8. How did individuals contribute to the task (highlight main contributions)?
9. What do you think was your most valuable contribution to the task?
10. What have you learnt from the task and how will this help you in the uniformed services?

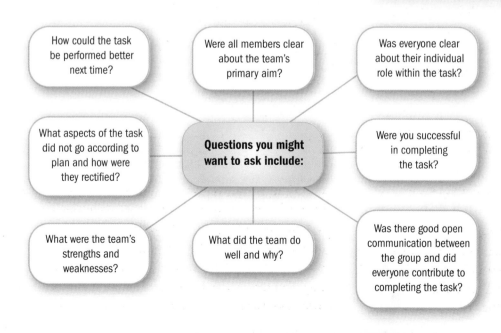

Figure 2.10 Ask questions that will encourage discussion, reflection and improvement

Case study: Appraisal

The use of appraisal is widespread among the public services. It is an organisational version of a personal action plan which is usually conducted by your immediate line manager. In general it follows the following structure:

Identify strengths and weaknesses
↓
Ensure that the role you fulfil makes use of your identified strengths
↓
Identify how your weaknesses could be overcome by training

Kerry is a new recruit to the fire service. In the 12 months she has served so far she doesn't feel she has made a major impact on the role and feels that other male recruits who started at the same time as her have adapted better to their role. She is concerned that her team leader thinks very little of her and this is causing Kerry to lose confidence in her abilities and make mistakes while on duty. The ongoing training and physical demands of the job are causing Kerry a great deal of distress and she believes she is falling further and further behind the other new recruits. Kerry is due to have an appraisal shortly and she wants to make the most of it to improve her performance and rebuild her confidence.

1. **How should Kerry prepare for her appraisal?**

2. **What questions should she ask during her appraisal?**

3. **What support should she ask for?**

4. **What type of feedback is she likely to encounter with regard to aspects of her job performance?**

5. **What could she do to help improve her performance after the appraisal?**

Assessment activity 2.5

1. You have been asked by your tutor to create a visual display in order to describe the different types of teams, stages of team development and barriers to effective performance. **P6**

Grading tips

P6 To achieve P6 you need to describe at least two different types of public service teams and describe clearly Tuckman's stages of team development and how they relate to public service teams. You should also include descriptions of possible barriers to a team's successful performance of a given task.

Knowledge check

1. Explain in detail one of the main leadership styles used by the uniformed public services.

2. How does the democratic approach differ from the laissez-faire approach?

3. What are the main consequences of poor leadership?

4. What are the signs of an effective team?

5. List the main components of non-verbal communication and give three examples of effective body language.

6. Explain how you would conduct a briefing for a large team.

7. Explain how you would conduct a debriefing for a small team.

8. What are Belbin's main team roles and which one best fits you when working in a team?

9. List and describe the main qualities and skills a leader will need in the following roles:

   - prime minister
   - England cricket captain
   - chief executive of a multinational corporation.

10. Explain five different types of teams found within the uniformed public services.

11. Evaluate how effective Tuckman's theory is in explaining how a team develops.

12. List five common barriers to effective team performance and explain how they could be overcome.

Preparation for assessment

At the end of the unit you will be attending a two day, one night team-building residential at a location away from your college.

You will be put into teams of eight and you will all have the chance to lead the team for part of the residential. To be able to do this successfully you have been asked to create a portfolio which will be completed during the unit (although some sections will be completed after the residential is over).

Your portfolio needs to address the following questions and be divided into the following sections.

Section one

1. Describe leadership styles and their use in the uniformed public services. **P1**

2. Compare two different leadership styles used in the uniformed public services. **M1**

3. Evaluate the effectiveness of two different leadership styles in the uniformed public services. **D1**

Section two

4. Describe the role of the team leader and the benefits of teams to the uniformed services. **P2**

5. Describe different types of teams and the stages of team development, including barriers to effective performance. **P6**

Section three

6. Describe the required communication skills and the process used to brief and debrief a team. **P3**

7. Demonstrate effective communication skills and the correct process when briefing and debriefing a team. (*To be conducted and assessed during the residential.*) **M2**

Section four

8. Use appropriate skills to lead a team in the practical implementation of a plan. (*To be conducted and assessed during the residential.*) **P4**

9. Demonstrate effective leadership skills when leading a team in the practical implementation of a plan to achieve a given task. (*To be conducted and assessed during the residential.*) **M3**

10. Describe evaluation methods used to assess effective team leadership. **P5**

11. Evaluate your own ability to provide effective team leadership, making recommendations for your development and improvement. (*To be conducted and assessed during the residential.*) **D2**

Grading criteria	Activity	Pg no.		
To achieve a pass grade the evidence must show that the learner is able to:			To achieve a merit grade the evidence must show that the learner is able to:	To achieve a distinction grade the evidence must show that the learner is able to:
P1 Describe leadership styles and their use in the uniformed public services	2.1	53	**M1** Compare two different leadership styles used in the uniformed public services	**D1** Evaluate the effectiveness of two different leadership styles in the uniformed public services
P2 Describe the role of the team leader and the benefits of teams to the uniformed public services	2.2	56		
P3 Describe the required communication skills and the process used to brief and debrief teams	2.3	65	**M2** Demonstrate effective communication skills and the correct process when briefing and debriefing a team	
P4 Use appropriate skills to lead a team in the practical implementation of a plan	2.4	72	**M3** Demonstrate effective leadership skills when leading a team in the practical implementation of a plan to achieve a given task	**D2** Evaluate own ability to provide effective team leadership, making recommendations for own development and improvement
P5 Describe evaluation methods used to assess effective team leadership	2.4	72		
P6 Describe different types of teams and stages of team development	2.5	80		

Citizenship, contemporary society and the public services

Introduction

Citizenship has become an important political concept over the last 20 years. This unit aims to help you understand the strong focus on it by discussing specific definitions of citizenship and relating them to the public services. You will also examine the UK's position on legal, humanitarian and political views of citizenship.

It is important that you are fully aware of the rights that citizenship gives to an individual and the impact that these rights might have on the public services. The public services are called upon to protect these rights but there is also the potential that they might breach them in the course of their duties. You will also explore what a 'good' citizen is, the personal qualities they might have and the activities they might undertake. You will look at the benefits of good citizenship to the public services and to society as a whole.

Finally, one of the most important aims of this unit is to assess how the media and current affairs can affect the work of the public services. This includes how the media portray the services and the impact of national and international events such as terrorism and natural disasters.

After completing this unit you should be able to achieve the following outcomes:

Thinking points

The modern public services are dynamic and changing organisations. New government initiatives, national and international issues and pressure groups can all affect the way they are allowed to operate.

When you attend a public services interview they will expect you to be aware of the current issues that are important, not only to them, but to society as a whole. It is important to keep up-to-date with national and international current affairs if you are to be successful in an interview. One of the best ways of doing this is to read a broadsheet newspaper such as the *Guardian*, *Independent* or *Times* at least once a week and more often if you can. Try and make a point of doing this throughout your study of this unit – you will be surprised how many other subjects you are studying will also benefit from your reading.

Understanding the issues and problems that the modern public services face will help you to start your career.

- Understand how different views of citizenship have developed in contemporary society
- Know the legal and humanitarian rights that 'citizenship' provides for an individual in the UK and its impact upon the public services
- Understand how the qualities of a 'good citizen' may be demonstrated in contemporary society and the benefits of these qualities to society and the uniformed public services
- Understand how national and international current affairs are highlighted by the media and influence the public services.

Different views of citizenship

Citizenship is concerned with many issues that are important to the public services today. It involves questioning rather than accepting your role in society and trying to understand complex topics such as:

- your role as a citizen
- your influence on society and how much power you have to change things
- what is going on in society and how it will affect you personally and in your professional life
- what makes a good citizen and how citizenship can benefit society.

Citizenship is concerned with debates, discussions and evaluation of evidence. It will make you more socially and politically aware, a vital quality in any potential public service recruit and one you should be actively seeking to develop.

The concept of citizenship is difficult to define. Legal citizenship lays down requirements that enable you to claim nationality and citizenship in a particular nation. The moral and political view of citizenship centres on how a person should operate within society. There cannot be a great deal of debate about legal requirements in this context because they are created by parliament and are relatively fixed and static, but the moral and political definitions of citizenship are constantly changing and developing.

Legal view

The government department responsible for nationality issues is the Immigration and Nationality Directorate. There are several pieces of legislation which create the legal basis for citizenship. These are acts of law including:

- The British Nationality Act 1981
- The British Overseas Territories Act 2002
- Nationality, Immigration and Asylum Acts 2002, 2006.

The British Nationality Act 1981 came into force on 1 January 1983. It replaced 'Citizenship of the United Kingdom and Colonies' with three separate types of citizenship which are outlined below:

- British citizenship, for people closely connected with the UK, the Channel Islands and the Isle of Man
- British Dependent Territories citizenship, for people connected with the British overseas territories
- British Overseas citizenship, for those citizens of colonies without connections with either the UK or the British overseas territories.

In 2002, the British Overseas Territories Act changed the name of British Dependent Territories citizenship to British Overseas Territories citizenship. It automatically gave full citizenship and 'the right of abode' to all citizens living in our overseas territories. (Overseas territories include places such as the Falkland Islands and Gibraltar.) British citizens are the only group of people who have the right to live in Britain permanently (this is called the 'right of abode'). They are free to leave and re-enter the UK as many times as they choose to.

The chart in Figure 3.1 from the UK Border and Immigration Agency shows how individuals who were born in the UK can achieve British citizenship.

If you do not fall into one of the categories above (for example, you may have settled here because of work or as an asylum seeker) you may wish to apply for British nationality. There are two main ways to do this:

- *Registration*. This is a way of becoming a British citizen if you already have some connection with the UK, such as being a British overseas citizen or a British protected person. You can also register if you have previously given up British citizenship and want to have it back.

What will be the **citizenship** of people who are born in the United Kingdom?

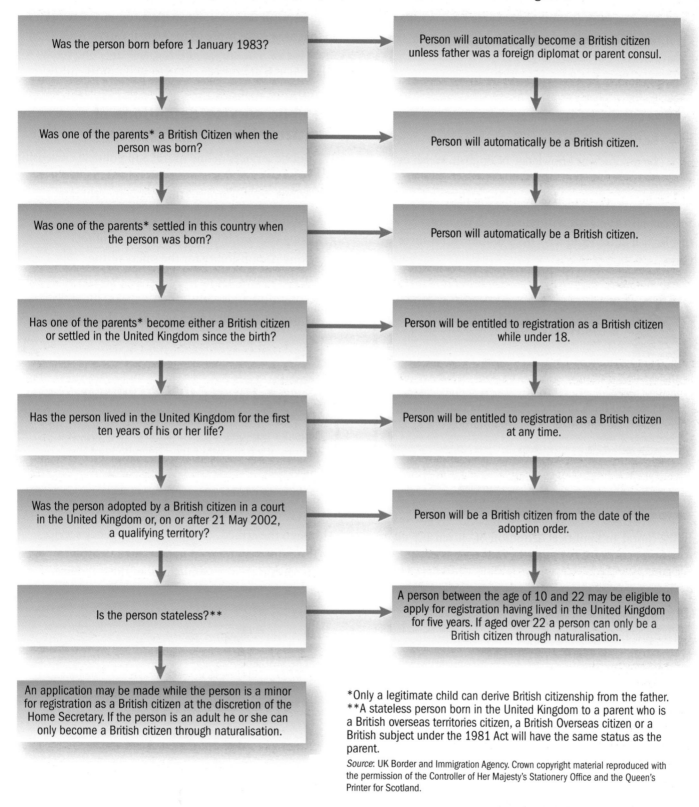

Figure 3.1 How individuals born in the UK can become British citizens

- *Naturalisation.* Individuals who have no connection with the UK, including people from Eire and the Commonwealth nations, must apply for a certificate of naturalisation. In order to qualify for a certificate you must:
  - have lived legally in the UK for five years
  - be 18 or over
  - be of sound mind
  - be of good character
  - have sufficient knowledge of English, Welsh or Scottish Gaelic
  - stay closely connected with the UK.

You can also apply for naturalisation if you are married to a British citizen and have lived in the UK for three years.

Consider this

Why do you think there is a three year wait for naturalisation if you are married to a British citizen? What do you think might happen if you automatically became a British citizen when you married one?

How organisations view citizenship

In the moral and political definition of citizenship all of us are citizens, even if we are not old enough to vote. We all have a variety of roles that make us citizens, as Figure 3.2 below shows.

All of these roles help to support the nation and ensure that we are economically stable and socially aware. Without them, society as we know it could not function – taxes need to be paid in order to fund public services, students need to learn in order to take on specialised roles such

as becoming a doctor or a barrister, families need to raise the next generation in order to ensure the continuation of society. All these roles provide a support network so that as we give more to the state it can provide more for us. The citizen and the state are completely interdependent, one cannot exist without the other.

■ Public service definitions of citizenship

The public services define moral and political citizenship in much the same way as everyone else. Usually these definitions revolve around the following criteria:
- community involvement
- taking responsibility for the safety of others
- taking responsibility for the safety of the environment
- a commitment to continually develop life skills
- a positive attitude which welcomes challenges.

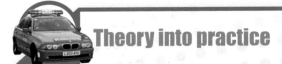

Theory into practice

Consider approaching your local armed services careers office to gather their definitions of citizenship.

Although the armed services and emergency services perform different tasks in society, their definitions of citizenship are very similar. All of them require

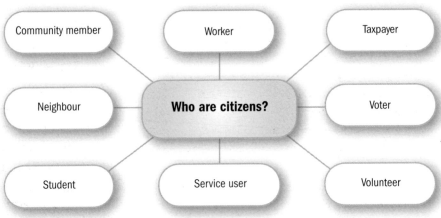

Figure 3.2 The many roles of a citizen ▶

Community member · Worker · Taxpayer · Neighbour · **Who are citizens?** · Voter · Student · Service user · Volunteer

The Neighbourhood Watch Scheme is a good example of people getting involved with their community and their local police service

active citizens to fulfil the criteria listed on page 88. It is important that the services set a good example of citizenship to civilians, not least because of the power and influence they have. Many young people aspire to join a uniformed service, so you must remember that you will have a much better chance of being recruited if you are an active citizen. Members of the public services often have to deal with situations which are challenging, dangerous and emotionally draining. Although they receive training to help them deal with difficult situations, they must be able to demonstrate many key citizen qualities in order to be considered suitable for entry in the first place. These key qualities underpin the training they receive making it more effective. So what citizenship qualities do the public services look for? Have a look at the case studies below.

Case study: The British Transport Police (BTP)

The British Transport Police in action

The BTP has responsibility for policing Britain's railway infrastructure. They deal with well over 100,000 offences each year including all major crimes such as murder and rape, and minor crimes such as graffiti and theft. The BTP also deals with specific railway issues including trains being obstructed, the transport of sports fans and issues of safety being compromised on tracks and at stations. The force has over 2000 officers in eight operational areas. The key citizenship qualities they look for in potential recruits are:

- diplomacy
- management skills
- decisiveness
- flexibility
- versatility
- determination
- personal responsibility and discretion
- good communication skills
- excellent interpersonal skills
- teamwork
- the use of initiative
- good sense and balanced judgement
- personal responsibility.

Only about 5 per cent of potential recruits actually become BTP officers which demonstrates the rigorous nature of the recruitment process and highlights the importance of possessing good citizenship qualities before you apply.

1. **How do you think the BTP would describe citizenship based on the information given above?**
2. **How could you improve your citizenship skills if you wanted a career in the BTP?**
3. **How would the skills listed above make you an asset to your community and to the service?**
4. **Are good citizenship skills the same as having good interpersonal and leadership skills? Explain your answer.**

▲ The fire service in action

The fire service has a varied role including emergency response to fires, responding to other emergency situations which threaten life or property, inspection/safety matters and fire prevention education. Because of the varied and demanding role of a fire fighter, good citizenship skills are naturally very important. They look for qualities in potential recruits such as:

- teamwork
- community involvement
- reliability
- flexibility
- understanding
- the ability to act quickly.

Fire fighters go to work every day with the knowledge that they may be required to compromise their own safety to ensure that of others. The mark of a good/active citizen is that they are prepared to compromise their own needs for the greater good of the society or community they live in.

1. **Why are good citizenship qualities important to the role of a fire fighter?**

2. **How do you think the fire service would describe citizenship based on the roles they fulfil?**

3. **Do you think you have the necessary citizenship skills to become a fire fighter? Justify your answer.**

■ Religious groups

It can be difficult to comment on how individual religious groups view the concept of citizenship since they are very diverse and often have different perspectives on a whole range of issues, not just citizenship. On a general level, religious or 'faith-based citizenship' does not differ a great deal from the types of concepts we have already discussed. It revolves around concepts such as volunteering, speaking up on behalf of others, voting and participating in the activities of wider society with the goal of making society a better place in which to live. From a religious perspective, the basis for being a good citizen is one of strong moral and ethical beliefs. Ideally these beliefs should respect the rights of others to hold opposing or different points of view.

There are many people in public and political life who hold strong religious views. In a secular society such as the UK, these views do not form part of their role as a public servant. Religious citizenship, like conventional citizenship, should promote respect, acceptance of diversity and compromise in achieving a just and fair society that benefits *all* its members, not just a particular social or religious group. In a democracy, personal religious beliefs, no matter how strongly felt, cannot influence policy and law: only a mandate from the public can do that. This can lead to problems for religious citizens who find themselves involved in carrying out policy that they may morally and ethically disagree with; for example a doctor whose religious beliefs are anti-abortion, or a soldier whose faith prevents them from serving in a particular conflict.

■ Pressure groups

A pressure group is an organisation or collection of individuals who seek to influence or change government

▲ **Amnesty International protested against the Guantanamo Bay prison camp in January 2007, in London**

policy on a particular cause or interest. Pressure groups can be:

- very large international organisations such as Greenpeace, Friends of the Earth and Amnesty International
- smaller national organisations such as the Confederation of British Industry (CBI) which represents around 150,000 businesses
- very small local organisations which only have a dozen or so members and campaign on local issues such as pollution or traffic management.

Pressure groups do not aim to achieve political office themselves: they merely seek to influence those who have the power to make decisions. Figure 3.3 highlights the kind of roles pressures groups undertake.

Pressure groups are effectively groups of concerned citizens who are prepared to stand together in order to change an issue or an aspect of society.

Take it further

Is there a particular 'citizenship' issue that you are interested in – perhaps connected to the environment, poverty or human rights? Research a pressure group of your choice to find out more about how they help your cause. You could use the websites of organisations such as Greenpeace, Friends of the Earth or Amnesty International or ask your college to organise a visit from a member.

Consider this

Can you think of a change to the law which was brought about by a pressure group?

Roles of pressure groups

- Act as a source of specialist information
- Influence and shape policy
- Promote discussion and debate
- Represent minority groups
- Educate about specific issues
- Create public support for issues

▲ **Figure 3.3 The roles of pressure groups**

Government initiatives to identify citizenship

Government initiatives to identify citizenship have focused around the three main elements which are discussed below.

▲ Carrying out your civic duty could involve checking on the welfare of an elderly neighbour

■ Social and moral responsibility

This is the development of behaviour that is respectful towards others, including peers and those in authority. It also includes the understanding of the concept of civic duty – this is the responsibility you have for helping the people in your community and the responsibility they have to help you. This ensures that all community members can live safe and productive lives, helping and supporting each other. It could include acts such as checking on the welfare of elderly neighbours, or reporting a crime that you witnessed against a community member's property. It is about treating others as you would wish to be treated by them.

■ Community involvement

This is about taking an active interest in your community by becoming involved with the life and concerns of your neighbourhood through giving service to it. This could mean things like volunteering in your area, taking part in community initiatives such as Neighbourhood Watch or becoming involved in environmental issues that may have an impact on your community.

■ Political literacy

This is about understanding the political life of society locally, regionally and nationally. It involves understanding the way local and national governments work and being clear about the role you can play in democracy in terms of participation in political issues and encouraging social change that might benefit your community. This may involve speaking to your local MP or councillors about a variety of issues, or it may involve you becoming politically active yourself. At the very least it involves understanding how your vote in an election works and why it is important to use it.

These three overarching principles have created numerous schemes and initiatives that the government has used to promote the concept of citizenship, two of which are highlighted in Table 3.1.

Initiative	Description
National Curriculum	All secondary schools in England were given notice in 1999 that Citizenship was to become a compulsory part of the national curriculum from September 2002. The government chose three strands of citizenship education on which schools should concentrate: • community involvement • political literacy • social/moral responsibility. There were increasing concerns about the levels of participation in local and national elections and the alienation of youth culture. This led to a call for values to be placed centre stage in the education of young people. Citizenship education works by creating links between the pupils' learning in class with wider social and political events, both nationally and internationally.
Citizenship training/ adult classes	Individuals who wish to become British citizens are required to undertake citizenship training to equip them for a life in modern Britain. This includes studying such topics as: • how to manage in everyday Britain including the NHS, schools and how people get help or support • employment in Britain, including citizens' rights and the minimum wage • the basics of the English or Scottish legal system and the 'rights and duties of a citizen' • the basic history of UK institutions such as the role of the monarch, Parliament and government • the face of Britain, particularly its modern history as a multicultural society and its principles of equality, fairness and justice. Once a potential new citizen has attended citizenship classes they are invited to attend a ceremony where they are formally awarded their British citizenship. The first ceremony in the UK took place in 2004 and it is seen by the government as a way of reinforcing the bond between the individual and their new country.

Table 3.1 Government initiatives that promote the concept of citizenship

Current concepts of citizenship

Although citizenship in a strictly legal sense applies only to the UK it should be apparent that social and moral citizenship is not bound by geographical borders. Increasingly sophisticated communications technology such as the media, the Internet, chat rooms and online gaming mean that it is possible to be a citizen of a much broader social world than ever before. More and more we are seeing the development of concepts such as global or environmental citizenship – these place a duty on the individual to behave in a way that benefits others across the globe. This could include recycling, reducing energy usage or campaigning against human rights violations in other parts of the world.

Increasingly sophisticated communications technology mean ▶ that it is possible to be a citizen of a much broader social world than ever before

Assessment activity 3.1

For this assessment activity you are required to produce a written report which discusses different views of citizenship in contemporary society. You must ensure you include the following content:

- Different views of citizenship – legal views, views of different organisations, government initiatives to identify citizenship, concepts of global and national citizenship.

You should use this content to answer the following question in your report:

1. Describe different views of citizenship in contemporary society. **P1 M1 D1**

Grading tips

P1 For this criteria you need to make sure you have explored a variety of views about citizenship. You should aim to explore a minimum of three different views such as those of the public services, religious groups and pressure groups.

M1 M1 is a straightforward extension of P1 except that you have to analyse rather than describe. This means providing more in-depth and detailed work which shows evidence of you making interpretive comments and conclusions.

D1 D1 is an extension of M1 but it requires you to evaluate the different views of citizenship in contemporary society and identify how they affect the public services. This means weighing up the positives and negatives about the issues and their effect on the services. Ensure you draw your own conclusions.

Human rights

It is important in any examination of citizenship to consider the issue of human rights. One of the most fundamental human rights documents was developed by the United Nations. It is called the Universal Declaration of Human Rights (UNDHR) and, although it was created at the end of the Second World War, it remains the universal standard of acceptable conduct across the globe. The UNDHR and the United Nations are covered in detail in *Unit 8: International perspectives* on pages 272–4 and 300–02.

Consider this

Are breaches of human rights linked to the social structure? Are most breaches of human rights committed against those at the bottom of the social structure?

You will see from the discussion of human rights in *Unit 8* that people's rights can be compromised for a variety of reasons ranging from their ethnic origin to their beliefs and values (including their religion and sexuality). It is important to remember that human rights abuses are often committed against those with the least amount of power in society, either because they are a minority ethnic group or because their beliefs and values marginalise them from the government and the wider community.

Legal rights

There are several pieces of legislation which influence the legal rights of citizens, such as the immigration Acts covered earlier in this unit and the Human Rights Act 1998 covered in *Unit 8*. Another key piece of legislation you are required to examine is the Police and Criminal Evidence Act 1984.

The Police and Criminal Evidence Act 1984 (PACE)

PACE is a key piece of legislation which both provides the police with powers, and creates safeguards against the misuse of these powers.

PACE provides guidance on several key areas of policing practice which are important to the rights of citizens. PACE is interesting in the sense that, as well as providing powers for the police on a whole range of policing issues, it also provides safeguards against the misuse of those powers. This means that the public are protected against over zealous police officers who may decide to stop and search on the basis of ethnic group or age, rather than genuine suspicion of wrongdoing.

Remember!

- The public services are like ordinary citizens in that they are accountable for their actions.
- There are a variety of laws which give the public services their powers and a variety of laws which regulate their powers.
- One of the most important pieces of law which provides the police with powers is PACE 1984. PACE also protects the public by safeguarding human rights.
- PACE governs areas such as stop and search, arrest, seizure and detention.

Police and Criminal Evidence Act 1984	
Area of law	**Details of the powers and safeguards it conveys**
Stop and search	PACE introduced a general power of stop and search for persons or vehicles, on the basis of reasonable suspicion of finding stolen or prohibited articles. The suspect has to be informed of the reasons for the search and accurate written records must be kept.
Entry, search and seizure	Premises may be searched for evidence or in order to make an arrest. Reasons must be provided for the searches and full and accurate written records of the conduct of the search and any seized property must be kept.
Arrest	PACE rationalised arrest powers. The basis for arrest is reasonable grounds for suspicion or where a summons is impractical. A summons is a formal call to appear in court.
Detention	This is only permissible where it is necessary to secure or preserve evidence. It usually involves more serious crimes or a crime where there may be a threat to the victim or witnesses. For most offences only 24 hours without charge is allowed. The custody officer who ensures the detainee's welfare must be independent of the investigation.
Questioning and treatment of suspects	Detainees have a right to legal advice and to have someone informed of their detention. They should not be interviewed before they have received legal advice if they have requested it. Accurate records must be kept. In addition, juveniles or individuals with a mental disorder must be interviewed in the presence of an appropriate adult.
Accountability and supervision	PACE stresses the need for accountability and supervision of the police. Full custody records must be kept for each detainee and the Act created the Police Complaints Authority (PCA) which supervises investigations into allegations of police misconduct.

Table 3.2 Key aspects of the Police and Criminal Evidence Act 1984

Documentary records

All citizens are required to have a set of documents which provide evidence of their citizenship. Citizens do not have to have all of the documents but they are part of everyday life and they can be requested by a variety of official government agencies and private businesses such as the police, schools and employers.

Document	Description
Passport	In the UK a passport is an official government document which is issued to a citizen and allows them to travel outside of the UK and return when they see fit. It confirms the identity of the holder and acts as proof of their nationality. It also reassures other governments that the person who holds the passport is a UK citizen and is unlikely to become permanently resident in their country as an illegal immigrant.
Birth certificate	In the UK, a birth certificate is an official copy of the information registered when a person is born, including who their parents are and the date and place of birth. It is a legal requirement in the UK to register a new birth within 42 days. If the parents are married then either parent can register; if the parents are unmarried then the mother must register the birth. Birth certificates are commonly used as a way of proving an individual's identity and age.
National Insurance number	National Insurance is a system in the UK which allows you to pay money out of your wages in order to be entitled to certain benefits at a later date, such as the state pension or unemployment benefit. In order for your contributions to be identified and not given to someone else, each person who is resident in the UK should have a unique national insurance number. This is usually issued to individuals just before their 16th birthday and it makes sure that all the money you give to the government is properly recorded on your account. It acts as a reference number for the whole social security system and it is also a way of identifying you to employers and the government.
Visa/work permit	A work permit is fairly self-explanatory: it provides someone who is not a UK citizen with the right to work in the UK for a specified amount of time. Most EU citizens can work in the UK without one, so it mainly applies to individuals from outside the EU who might choose to work in the UK for a period of time. A visa is a document which individuals from some countries need in order to enter the UK. The visa contains a variety of information such as why you are coming to the UK and how long you intend to stay. Individuals who are not part of the EU and don't have a UK passport might be refused entry if they don't have a UK visa.

Table 3.3 Citizenship documentary records

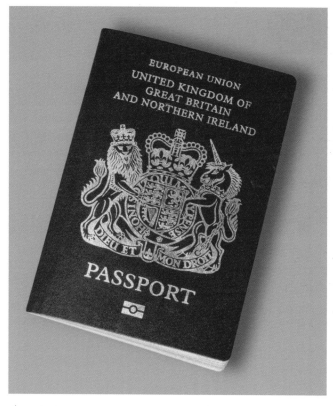

▲ A UK passport

Theory into practice

All of the documents in Table 3.3 contain important and confidential information about us which could lead to identity theft if they were to fall into the wrong hands. Investigate how the Data Protection Act 1998 helps protect our personal information.

of the uniformed public services. It is the role of the services to protect the freedoms that the public are entitled to (such as freedom of speech) while ensuring that these freedoms are not used to harm the wider community. It can be a difficult balancing act to ensure that one person's freedom of speech does not cause a riot which would harm the freedoms of many other individuals.

The public services have several roles in upholding our civil rights. These roles include:

- implementing the laws which provide individuals with their rights
- ensuring that these rights are protected by enforcing the law when needed
- providing an ongoing system of monitoring to ensure that all citizens receive the rights they are entitled to by law.

Impact on public services

Human rights legislation and laws which provide citizens with freedoms have a direct effect on the work

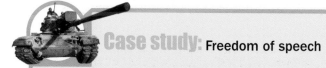

Case study: Freedom of speech

In February 2006, protests took place in London about a series of cartoons that were published in a Danish magazine which satirised the Islamic Prophet Mohammed. Around 300 Muslim protesters gathered to condemn the cartoons as Islamophobic and offensive. However, some individuals in the crowd began chanting slogans such as 'Bomb the USA, Bomb Denmark' – several held placards with similar slogans on. The police intervened and several protesters were arrested and charged with inciting racial hatred. The Crown Prosecution Service (CPS) who prosecuted the cases were quoted as saying that they are always mindful of free speech in such circumstances, but that free speech 'should not be misused to insult, abuse or threaten people in such a way that it will stir up racial hatred'.

1. **Why is the right to protest important?**
2. **Were the police correct in arresting some of the demonstrators?**
3. **Explain the difficulties faced by the CPS when deciding to deal with offences by protestors.**
4. **Explain how the police balance the rights of the protestors with the rights of the wider community.**

Assessment activity 3.2

Imagine you are to take part in a local radio programme to highlight the role that public services play in human rights in the UK. In small groups, divide up the roles of programme presenter (interviewer) and representatives of human rights organisations.

You should include the following content as part of your discussion:

- human rights – United Nations and the UNDHR, beliefs and values, social structure
- legal rights – immigration Acts, the Human Rights Act 1998, PACE 1984, documents, data protection.

You should use this information to structure your discussion to answer the question below.

1. Describe two legal and two humanitarian rights of citizens in the UK identifying how they affect the public services. **P2 M2**

Grading tips

P2 Remember that in a small group discussion you should ensure each member has an opportunity to participate. For P2 you are required to describe: this means that you should provide a brief description of the rights citizens have, and make reference to conflicts between individual's rights and the needs of society.

M2 M2 is simply an extension of P2. M2 requires you to 'explain' the rights, so your discussion should be in greater detail and you should consider producing a set of discussion notes as part of your evidence.

3.3 How the qualities of a 'good citizen' may be demonstrated in contemporary society and the benefits of these qualities to society and the uniformed public services

We hear lots in the media and in education about good citizenship and the positive impact it can have on communities and on society as a whole. But what is good citizenship and what kind of activities do good citizens take part in?

Recognised qualities

There are many well-recognised qualities of a good citizen.

Quality	Explanation
Responsibility	A good citizen takes personal responsibility to improve the community in which they live. They don't complain about litter and how poor their local council might be in dealing with it – they move the litter themselves or organise a group of people to work with them to achieve the task. Good citizens see themselves as responsible for changing things for the better – they do not wait for someone else to do it for them.
Dedication	Good citizens don't give up on tasks – they persevere until change is achieved. They are dedicated to the task at hand and set themselves on a course of action that they are prepared to see through.
Attitudes to other people	Good citizens have a positive attitude to others in their community. They are helpful, respectful, considerate and non-judgemental. They are not racist or homophobic, they welcome diversity as enriching a society and don't judge people by their colour, age or religion.
Participation in community activities	A good citizen participates fully in community activities such as Neighbourhood Watch programmes, community fundraising and environmental campaigns.
Awareness of the needs of others	Good citizens are aware that we are not all the same and that some people need more support than others in contributing to a community because of issues such as poverty, language or disability needs. They are aware of and sensitive to these issues and help to provide a supportive inclusive community which values all its members such as minority ethnic groups, children, teenagers and the elderly.

Table 3.4 The qualities of a good citizen

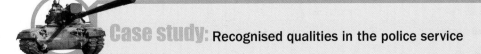

Case study: Recognised qualities in the police service

The police have a complex and challenging role. Figure 3.4 shows some of their main responsibilities.

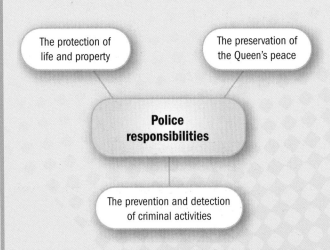

▲ **Figure 3.4 The police have a complex and challenging role**

There are many laws which grant the police extraordinary powers which set them apart from the rest of the general public, including PACE 1984. As a result, the government and the public have the right to expect them to uphold the highest standards of behaviour. This means that the police must follow internal regulations regarding their behaviour, such as the Police (Conduct) Regulations 1999 which set out the citizenship qualities that a good police officer needs to display at all times. These qualities include:

- *Honesty and integrity*. Officers should be open and truthful in their dealings because it is vital that the public can have faith and trust in them.
- *Fairness and impartiality*. Police officers must treat everyone with fairness and impartiality. This includes dealings with the public and with their own colleagues.
- *Politeness and tolerance*. The police must treat the public with courtesy and respect and must not demonstrate abusive or deriding attitudes. They must avoid favouritism and all forms of harassment (this not only applies to their treatment

of the general public but also that of lower ranked officers).

- *Confidentiality*. The police are privy to extraordinary amounts of confidential data about members of the general public and the public need to be certain this information is held in confidence. Police officers must not use private information for personal gain. In addition, they should not divulge confidential policy or operational information about the police force unless authorised to do so.
- *Following lawful orders*. The police service can only operate effectively when it is a disciplined body. This means that unless there is good and sufficient cause they must obey all lawful orders given to them. They must support their colleagues in the execution of lawful order and oppose improper behaviour, reporting it where appropriate.
- *Sobriety*. While on duty officers must be sober and must not consume alcohol unless it becomes necessary for the proper discharge of their duties; for example, if a police officer working undercover needed to drink in order to appear convincing.
- *Smart and professional appearance*. Officers should always be well turned out and clean and tidy unless they are fulfilling duties which dictate otherwise.
- *Reasonable use of force*. Officers should never knowingly use more force than is deemed reasonable, nor should they abuse their authority.
- *Conscientious performance of duties*. Officers should attend work promptly when they are on duty and carry out their designated duties with diligence. In addition, whether on or off duty, a police officer should not behave in a way which is likely to bring discredit to the police service.

1. **Do you think this list is a sensible guide to the behaviour of a police officer?**

2. **Can you think of anything else you might want to include which would help a police officer to interact better with the public?**

3. **Do you think you uphold these standards of behaviour?**

4. **What could you do better in your own life to meet these challenging requirements?**

Figure 3.5 The many roles of a ▶
'good citizen'

Activities of a good citizen
- Community work
- Youth work
- Advocacy
- Environmental issues
- Volunteer work
- Working with the services
- Charity work
- Informing others

Consider this

Look at the diagram above which describes some of the roles good citizens may fulfil. Explain how each of the roles could contribute to the well-being of your local community. In addition, consider how many of these roles you personally fulfil in your everyday life.

Volunteers in the public services

There are many opportunities to volunteer in the public services in a variety of roles such as:

- Special Police Constable
- Retained fire fighter
- Territorial Army
- St John's Ambulance
- Lifeboat volunteers
- Mountain/cave rescue.

Activities of a 'good citizen'

Good or active citizens often fulfil a variety of roles, such as those set out in Figure 3.5. An active citizen may take part in some or all of the following activities:

- education
- campaigning
- donating and raising money
- protesting
- lobbying government
- publicising issues
- volunteering.

One of the most important of these to the public services is the role of the volunteers. There are two main types of volunteer in the public services context: volunteers in the services themselves and community volunteers.

▲ Unpaid volunteers provide extremely valuable support to the public services

Although some of these involve paid work (such as the Territorial Army) most are unpaid and are carried out entirely in the spare time of the volunteer or when they are called upon to attend an emergency incident. Volunteers provide essential support to the regular services and often serve alongside them doing exactly the same role. It can be very difficult for ordinary members of the community to volunteer as they may already be juggling a family and a full-time job. These people deserve our respect – they volunteer to make society a better place and they don't do it for the money.

■ The Territorial Army volunteer

'I left school at 16 and went straight into working in a factory. I didn't really have any idea what I wanted to do so I suppose I followed the crowd and did what my friends did. After working for a few years I found myself in a real rut – I was unfit, unhealthy and going nowhere. I knew I needed a change but I had no idea what to do about it. I saw one of the TA adverts on the telly and it just caught my eye. I liked the idea of being part of a team and learning new skills and challenging myself in a totally different environment. It took a lot of courage to go to the TA centre and get myself signed up and I was really worried about the fitness but it was the best thing I ever did. That was four years ago and since then I have travelled all over Europe taking part in Army competitions and overseas training exercises. My fitness is now excellent and I have a lot more confidence and self assurance than I did before. The best thing about the TA is the people. You work together as a team and because we are all volunteers and are there because we want to be, not because we have to be, it makes for a good working environment. We have the opportunity to serve on tours of duty alongside the regulars and many TA volunteers have served in Iraq and other conflicts. The TA have a vital role in supporting the regular services and I'm proud to be part of that.'

Source: Lance Corporal Kelly Stevens, 38 Signal Regiment

Volunteers in the community

There are thousands of people who give up their time to volunteer in their local communities on a range of issues including youth work, environmental activities and charity work. There are also organisations which promote voluntary work in the community such as the Duke of Edinburgh Award Scheme and Millennium Volunteers. Volunteering is a very worthwhile way to contribute to society and to help you achieve valuable skills which you may also be able to transfer into your paid employment.

Key terms

Millennium Volunteers These are young people aged between 16–25 who give up their time to volunteer in their local communities for a variety of activities such as working with the elderly, protecting the environment or coaching a sports team. The idea is that by volunteering in the community the person can gain skills and abilities which will help them in the workplace.

Duke of Edinburgh Award Scheme This is a programme for people aged between 14–25 who want to develop their confidence and knowledge in a variety of areas such as:

- service (volunteering to help people in the community)
- skills (a hobby or personal interest)
- physical recreation (sport and fitness)
- expeditions.

The scheme fits in extremely well with the Nationals in Public Services and it is worth exploring whether you can combine the two.

Consider this

Do you do any volunteer work? How could volunteering help your chances of getting into the service of your choice? Research the Millennium Volunteers or the Duke of Edinburgh Award Scheme on the Internet and see what they might have to offer you.

▲ Taking part in the Duke of Edinburgh Award Scheme can be fun and challenging

Benefits of a good citizen to society

There are many benefits that a good citizen brings to society:

BENEFITS OF GOOD CITIZENSHIP

MAKE A POSITIVE DIFFERENCE

RAISED SELF ESTEEM

CHALLENGE INJUSTICE

PROMOTE FAIRNESS

IMPROVE SOCIETY

PROTECT ENVIRONMENT

INCREASED KNOWLEDGE

HELPING OTHERS

HELPING YOURSELF

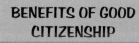 Figure 3.6 Good citizens help to build a better society

Benefit	Explanation
Adds value to improve society and makes a positive difference	Good citizens make our society a better place by improving the social environment we live in. They provide a sense of community to an area and a sense of pride in the surroundings. They may do this by very simple things such as ensuring their property is well maintained and presentable or they may act as role models for younger people.
Protects the environment	Good citizens are conscious of the importance of the environment on several levels. At a local level they may clean up litter and ensure their dogs don't foul the pavement, making the area cleaner and safer. They may engage in local projects such as recycling initiatives or cleaning up wasteland and encourage their friends and neighbours to do the same. On a larger scale they may support renewable energy initiatives or support environmental charities and pressure groups such as Greenpeace or Friends of the Earth.
Challenges injustice and brings about fairness	Good citizens should aim to challenge injustice and the origins of injustice. This might mean challenging people who use racist or homophobic language. It might mean acting as an advocate for someone who may have difficulty speaking for themselves, such as an elderly neighbour. A good citizen supports the principle of fairness and equality and encourages others to do the same. In the long-term, this makes for a fairer more inclusive society.

Table 3.5 The benefits that a good citizen brings to society

Assessment activity 3.3

Imagine that you are a Millennium Volunteer and that you have been asked to help with recruitment in your school or college. You know that volunteering is an enriching experience that has a positive impact on the community. Create a leaflet that helps to promote the benefits of volunteering to other students. (If you volunteer for a particular organisation already, you could write about that instead.)

You should include the following content:

- recognised qualities – responsibility, dedication, attitude to other people, participates in community activities, awareness of others' needs
- activities – volunteers in the public services, volunteers in the community
- the benefits of a good citizen
- relevance to the services – the concept of the importance of volunteers, support to services, reduction of crime, fires and injury.

Use this content to produce your leaflet which answers the following question.

1. Describe how different activities will demonstrate good citizenship and benefit uniformed public services and society. **P3**

Grading tips

P3 This is a straightforward pass criteria which doesn't link to any merits or distinctions. Ensure you cover the content and offer a clear description of how different activities benefit both the services and the community.

Media representations of the uniformed public services

The public services are portrayed in a variety of ways by the media depending on the situation they find themselves in and the type of media which is reporting. There are many types of media including:

- newspapers
- magazines
- television
- radio
- Internet
- books
- journal articles
- service magazines.

The coverage can be both 'real' (in that it highlights actual members of the public services performing the actual job that they are employed to do) or it can be a fictional portrayal which may not be based on the real experience of many public service officers. All the public services are portrayed by the media but the police and the portrayal of crime dominate real and fictional representations. A study by Ericson *et al* (1987) in Canada found around 45 per cent of stories in the written media were crime or deviance related. In the UK, Williams and Dickinson (1993) found that tabloids portray more crime than broadsheets. The *Sun* had 30.4 per cent of crime news, compared to 5.1 per cent in the *Guardian*. What this highlights is that a substantial proportion of media time and energy is spent on the portrayal of public services and, in particular, the police role in solving crime.

Portrayals of the public services take up a great deal of air-time, but how are the services themselves actually shown? A US-based National Television Violence study found that, over a four year period, every reality-based police show contained acts of visual violence. This included shoot-outs, dangerous car chases and assaults. It also included portrayals of murder, sexual assault and robbery at a much higher rate than that which actually occurs in real life. The study also found that police shows depicted 33 per cent of police officers using or threatening physical aggression compared with only 10 per cent of criminals. This clearly highlights the media portrayal of police officers as aggressive or brutal at times.

Consider this

Are police officers as brutal as they are portrayed in fictional police shows? Explain your answer.

However, the findings of the US National Television Violence study also found that the media portrayal of the police was positive in some regards. For example, it found that on the reality-based police shows around 60 per cent of the crimes were solved. In reality the number of crimes solved by the police is generally a great deal lower. Police work is also portrayed as a job which involves continual excitement – TV audiences often see dramatic snapshots of the police capturing a suspect, executing a warrant or receiving calls on the radio to mobilise. This gives a false impression of real police work which is generally routine and increasingly involves a great deal of paperwork.

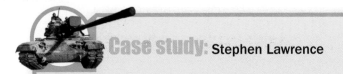

Stephen Lawrence was an 18-year-old A-level student who was attacked and killed by a gang of white youths in April 1993. The investigation which followed led to one of the most tense situations between the police and urban ethnic communities since the early 1980s. It also led to the most damning report on the activities of the metropolitan police ever published. As the case progressed it became clear that the media saw the Lawrence murder as a potentially explosive situation which could rock British race relations. The murder of Stephen and the ensuing investigations and reports, including the Macpherson Report which claimed the Metropolitan Police were institutionally racist, continually made newspaper headlines throughout the mid to late 1990s. The media made great use of the Macpherson Report and highlighted the failings of the Metropolitan Police in the Lawrence case, as well as many other racist allegations made against the police. The results of the media examination into this case have been largely positive, even though it was a negative portrayal of the police themselves. This is because it has encouraged and fostered change within the service and put the issue of police racism firmly in the public domain. However, it did have a direct effect on police morale – although individual officers were named in the Macpherson Report, the force as a whole came under heavy political and media criticism. This affected many officers who had worked hard to build up community and ethnic relations and who felt as though the time and effort they had put in had been dismissed. Equally, the accusation of racism left police officers uncertain of how to approach minority ethnic individuals who they suspected might have committed a crime – the media attention on the issue at the time meant any genuine error might be reported in the press as a racist incident.

1. **Why was the investigation of the murder of Stephen Lawrence flawed?**

2. **Why did the media cover this story in detail?**

3. **Do you think the media has helped improve the situation for reporting racist incidents to the police?**

4. **What were the negative impacts of the media coverage of this case?**

5. **What were the positive impacts of media coverage of this case?**

Media representation of compensation

The issue of compensation for police officers who are injured in the line of duty is one that the media feels very strongly about. This is especially so after officers who attended the Hillsborough football stadium disaster were able to claim hundreds of thousands of pounds after they developed post traumatic stress disorder (PTSD) in response to the events they witnessed. The media had a great deal to say about this and were scathing at times in their coverage, noting that the families of the victims received one hundred times less than one of the officers who claimed PTSD. The media in this instance opened the debate on whether or not public service workers should be entitled to any compensation at all since the activities which are likely to cause PTSD are an integral part of the job that they sign on to do. However, the issue of PTSD is not the only police compensation issue to appear in the papers. There have also been headlines surrounding pension fraud and malingering in order to claim sick pay. In January 1999, *Police Review* had the following to say about compensation in the media: ' *... according to our friends in the media, bobbies no longer look for criminals, but cracks in the pavement to fall over or polished station floors to slip on'.*

The media have often portrayed the issue of public service compensation negatively. However, officers, like other employees, are entitled to compensation for workplace injuries. It could be argued that, due to the hazardous nature of public service work, it is even more important that they are able to claim compensation.

Positive images of the public services

The public often only hear about the negative aspects of the public services. The outstanding contribution that the vast majority of the public services make to social order, stability and personal safety on a day-to-day basis is not something you often read about or see on the news. The public services operate 24 hours a day, 7 days a week, 365 days a year, performing acts of tremendous courage, bravery and self-sacrifice.
For example:

- the death of fire fighter Rob Miller from Leicester Fire and Rescue service who died in 2002 while searching a burning factory to see if anyone was trapped
- Fleur Lombard, a fire fighter in Avon, who died in a supermarket blaze in 1998
- PC Andrew Jones of South Wales police who was fatally injured by a car while chasing a burglar in 2003
- the six Royal Military Police officers who were killed in 2003 in Majar al-Kabir in Iraq.

The list of public service officers who have given their lives for the protection and safety of others is long and distinguished. While the press don't often comment on the excellent day-to-day performance of the public services, they do pay respect to remarkable acts of bravery such as those described above. This helps to create admiration and respect among the public for the services.

Consider this

Do you think that the media treat the public services fairly? Explain your answer.

Assessment activity 3.4

To achieve this assessment task, research, prepare and present a 10-minute PowerPoint presentation (with supporting notes) on how the media reports on events and how the reporting can influence the services. Ensure you include the following content:

- media representation of the uniformed public services by different types of media.

Make sure you answer the following question:

1. Compare reports from three different sources of news about a current national or international situation to show how media reporting can vary and how it influences the public services. **P4 M3**

Grading tips

P4 You should select three news reports and show how they vary in their tone and content about the same issue. You don't have to choose just written sources – video or audio reports are also acceptable and could be included as part of a visual presentation which shows the audience the comparisons you are making. The key thing is to remember to compare – you could do this in a table to make it easier.

M3 M3 is an extension of P4 – it requires you to analyse the news reports. This means you will have to go into more detail and give your own opinion on the value of the reports, the bias contained in them and the overall quality of the reporting.

How the public services use the media

In addition to being portrayed in the media, the public services are also increasingly using the media to help them do their job. This is important to mention in any discussion about the relationship between the public services and the media as it should be recognised that it is not one way. The public services make use of the media in the same way that the media use the public services – to achieve the goals of the organisation. These might range from selling more papers or reducing crime. Some of the ways in which the public services use the media are described in Table 3.6 below.

As you can see, the services use the media extensively. In effect, they have a mutually advantageous relationship: the media relies on the services for inspiration for drama, entertainment, comedy and news while the public services use the media as a vehicle to connect with the public.

Use of media	Description
Public safety campaigns	• The public services support government public safety campaigns. Good examples of this include the drink driving, road safety for children and crime prevention campaigns. These take the form of billboards, posters, newspaper advertisements and TV and radio commercials. • Government figures highlight that in 2005 there were 560 drink driving fatalities – a large scale publicity campaign can help the public be aware of the issues surrounding drink driving and the consequences of it. • These campaigns extend to children as well. Traffic is one of the largest killers of children under the age of 14 and government safety campaigns can help make children more aware of the dangers they face when they encounter traffic. These campaigns are supported by police officers who go into schools to promote the messages behind them. • It is not just the police who advise on and support public safety campaigns: the fire service are heavily involved in promoting the government's fire safety campaigns on issues such as smoke alarms, kitchen fires, careless smoking, fire evacuation plans and hoax callers.
To improve public relations	All of the public services rely on civilian support to help them do their jobs whether this takes the form of dialling 999, pulling over to let an emergency vehicle pass or working in a paid or voluntary capacity for them. Services that come into contact with the public on a frequent basis need to be particularly aware of their public image. A negative image of a service can harm recruitment and retention of officers – it can also cause tremendous resentment among the public with the possibility of civil disorder or attacks on officers. Public relations can be harmed by many things, such as service corruption, incompetence and poor treatment of members of the public. The services use the media for damage limitation in circumstances like this and to promote the positive aspects of their work.
Appeals for information	The services, particularly the police, may call upon the media to help solve a crime by publicising it to the general public and appealing for information on it. This may take the form of a press conference, a news story or a programme such as 'Crimewatch', which exists purely to help the police connect with the public on a large scale. There are many instances where the police need to inform the public to be vigilant, perhaps in the case of a sighting of a dangerous criminal or the abduction of a child. Equally, many crimes have witnesses who don't even know that they are witnesses until an appeal for information goes out.
To inform the public	The public services use the media to inform the public on a whole range of issues from crime prevention to dealing with emergencies to traffic congestion.
Disaster management	The public services use the media extensively in a disaster management situation for any or all of the following reasons: • to inform the public to stay indoors in the event of a chemical or biological contamination • to make a call for off-duty medical professionals to report to their hospitals • to provide information on casualties and fatalities • to warn the public to stay away from a disaster site • to publicise helpline numbers for concerned individuals • to reassure the public that a disaster is being dealt with quickly and efficiently • to coordinate evacuation plans • to call for specialised assistance such as counsellors or utility workers.

Table 3.6 The ways in which the public services use the media to achieve their own goals

"You're not driving anymore..."

Enjoy the football.
But if you're drinking, take a taxi home.

THINK!
Don't Drink and Drive

Source: The Department of Transport

National and international issues affecting public services

There are many national and international issues which affect the UK public services as shown in Figure 3.7.

The BTEC National in public services is a wide ranging qualification and you will find that many of these issues are covered in depth in other units of this book and *Book 2*, such as:

- *Unit 1* Government policies such as civilianisation, reduction in regiments, financial and budget decisions
- *Unit 8* Terrorism; rapid reaction groups; activities of international organisations such as NATO and the UN; the role of the services in supporting the international organisations with activities such as initial response and training overseas police officers or military officers
- *Unit 12* Increases in crime
- *Unit 14* Major disasters at home and abroad such as hurricanes, earthquakes and tsunami
- *Unit 21* Prison overcrowding.

When you are discussing current affairs it is important that you use examples which are as up-to-date as possible. Use the topics listed in the above units as a guide only, and make sure you keep up with the news as

▲ Figure 3.7 National and international issues which affect the UK

much as you can by reading a broadsheet newspaper or a reputable news website such as the BBC. You should also remember that many issues cannot be divided neatly into national or international issues – they are both.

Asylum seekers and illegal immigrants

The issue of immigration is a local, regional, national and international subject, which is often misunderstood by both the general public and the public services alike.

Asylum seekers are individuals and families who have to flee from their homes in the face of persecution, war, religious intolerance, racial hatred or any number of other factors which may harm them or their children. Being an asylum seeker means that your life may be under threat in your home country – it is not about individuals who want to gain entry into more economically affluent nations. While there is nothing wrong with being an economic migrant (after all most of us will move around the UK to get a better job or a better standard of living) they should not be confused with genuine asylum seekers whose situations are much more complex and desperate. Illegal immigrants are sometimes termed **economic migrants** as they want to go to another nation to have a better standard of living but they do not go through the legal channels in terms of applying for a visa. This is because the majority of illegal immigrants would not qualify for a visa so the only way they can stay in the country is to do so illegally.

Some people believe that the UK is being swamped by people claiming asylum, a belief that is often supported by both politicians and the media. The media portrays a situation in which asylum seekers are pouring into our small country and using up resources such as jobs, education and medical services, leaving our own citizens without the vital public services they need.

However, the UK takes far less asylum seekers than many other nations. Oxfam (2002) details the fact that Pakistan takes in ten times as many refugees as we do and of 13 European nations whose asylum figures were analysed by Oxfam, we came eighth on the list. So most European nations accept many more refugees than the UK. It is ironic but true that it is often the poorest nations which take the most asylum seekers. For instance, individuals fleeing persecution in Iraq will often head to neighbouring Iran. In Africa alone there are an estimated 8,000,000 refugees from war, conflict and famine, all taken in by neighbouring nations who may themselves be extremely poor.

It is also important to understand that most asylum seekers are kept in detention centres, which operate along the lines of prisons, and those that are not kept in such centres have a very restricted standard of living. There are arguments about whether this breaches their fundamental right to freedom. The basic allowances for asylum seekers are as follows:

Person aged 18–24	£31.15 per week
Person aged 25+	£39.34 per week
Couple	£61.71 per week

Only £10 a week of this money is available as cash, the rest is provided in voucher form. In addition, asylum seekers are not allowed to seek employment for 6 months and when they are able to, most asylum seekers will struggle to get a job due to language, transport and literacy difficulties. Therefore the notion that asylum seekers have more than British citizens or are taking British jobs is not supported by the evidence. You should also remember that illegal immigrants do not receive any benefits at all, if they tried to register for them they would be arrested and possibly deported back to their home nation.

Key terms

Asylum seeker Individuals who have fled their home nations due to conditions such as war, persecution, famine or drought to name just a few. Their home nation is not a safe place for them to be. When they arrive in the UK they may be given asylum by the UK government if it agrees their home nation is too dangerous for them to return to. Asylum is not a permanent situation; if the home nation becomes stable and safe the asylum seekers are repatriated back to their original home.

Economic migrant Individuals who move to another nation to earn money and provide a better standard of living for themselves and their families. Many economic migrants are in the UK with permission to work from the government. However, some immigrants are in the country illegally and do not have permission from the government to live or work here.

Demographic changes

Rather than asylum seekers being unwelcome and unwanted there are those in society who argue that if our society is to survive we should be taking in more asylum seekers not less. The UK's population is getting older and the birth rate is getting lower, meaning that at some point there may not be enough young people working to support the public services which take care of those who do not work, such as the very young and the very old. A study by the University of Swansea has suggested that we need to increase immigration by a fifth if we are to prevent population decline and avert an economic crisis.

Remember!

Many social and contemporary issues are interlinked. Immigration and asylum have an impact on demographic changes to society, such as housing, policing strategies, possible increases in social unrest and crime and terrorism to name a few. Don't look at each issue in isolation, try and see the links it has to other issues and the possible impact it might have on the public services.

What is the impact on the public services?

Issues such as immigration, illegal immigration, asylum and refugees have a substantial impact on some services and minimal impact on others. In general, social contemporary issues such as these tend to affect the police service, social services and local authorities more than other services; and they tend to affect urban and city-based services more than rural ones.

Consider this

Can you think why social contemporary issues tend to have an impact on the city-based police services more than other uniformed services?

▲ The police attend large public events like the Notting Hill Carnival in London

Service	Impact
Police	Policing is a very challenging job. It becomes even more challenging when you may be required to police a geographical area which could contain over 100 spoken languages, 40 different nationalities and a variety of different cultural attitudes and understandings. The police service must offer the most effective service it can to the immigrant and refugee population, especially as these groups may have faced significant persecution from the public services in their home state and may be afraid of the police. This could include strategies such as: <ul><li>the use of interpreters</li><li>producing publicity materials in a variety of languages</li><li>a high visibility team who work with the community to solve their problems and address their concerns</li><li>building effective relationships based on mutual trust and understanding.</li></ul>
Social Services	Social Services have a large part to play in organising and delivering social support including advice on benefits and entitlements and integration into existing communities.
Local Authority	The local authority is responsible for housing and education: these will be key issues for any new immigrant or refugee to the UK. Some refugees are unaccompanied children who have no primary carer so the local authority must ensure that they are taken care of.

Table 3.7 The impact of immigration on some UK services

Assessment activity 3.5

In order to achieve this assessment criteria you should produce a large poster which examines the effects of national and international issues on the services. You should include the following content:

- national issues such as illegal immigration, gun crime, housing, demographic changes, government actions

- international issues such as terrorism, major disasters and international organisations.

Use this information to produce a poster which answers the question below.

1. Identify three examples of contemporary issues and explain their likely effects on specified public services. **P5** **M4** **D2**

Grading tips

P5 You need to choose three issues which are relevant to the services, such as those outlined throughout this book and *Book 2,* and explain each one clearly on your poster ensuring you provide an explanation of the effect it may have on the public services.

M4 To achieve M4 you need to analyse the effect of contemporary issues on the public services, so more detail is required and you should be looking for relationships and links in your answer. You may want to provide additional notes to accompany your poster.

D2 To achieve D2 you need to compare and contrast the news reports – this means examine the similarities and differences between them. You could do this as a table and hand it in with your poster and notes.

Knowledge check

1. What is legal citizenship?
2. What does PACE stand for?
3. List three things the government has done to promote citizenship.
4. What is a visa?
5. What qualities does a good citizen have?
6. List the types of volunteer work you can carry out in the public services.
7. How can the services use the media?
8. How does the media portray the services?
9. List some contemporary issues which might affect the services.
10. List the ways in which you can volunteer in the community.

Preparation for assessment

Produce a citizenship magazine designed to be read by new public service recruits which answers the questions below.

1. Describe and analyse different views of citizenship in contemporary society. **P1 M1**

2. Evaluate different views of citizenship in contemporary society identifying how they affect the uniformed public services. **D1**

3. Describe and explain two legal and two humanitarian rights of citizens in the UK identifying how they affect the uniformed public services. **P2 M2**

4. Describe how different activities will demonstrate good citizenship and benefit the uniformed public services and society. **P3**

5. Compare reports from three different news sources about a current national or international situation to show how media reporting can vary and how it influences the uniformed public services. **P4**

6. Analyse three news reports about a current national or international situation to show how media reporting can vary and how it influences the uniformed public services. **M3**

7. Identify three examples of contemporary issues and explain and analyse their likely effects on specified uniformed public services. **P5 M4**

8. Compare and contrast different news reports about three contemporary issues including the effects that they might have on specified uniformed public services. **D2**

Grading criteria	Activity	Pg no.		
To achieve a pass grade the evidence must show that the learner is able to:			To achieve a merit grade the evidence must show that the learner is able to:	To achieve a distinction grade the evidence must show that the learner is able to:
P1 Describe different views of citizenship in contemporary society	3.1	94	**M1** Analyse different views of citizenship in contemporary society	**D1** Evaluate different views of citizenship in contemporary society identifying how they affect the public services.
P2 Describe two legal and two humanitarian rights of citizens in the UK identifying how they affect the public services	3.2	98	**M2** Explain the legal and humanitarian rights of citizens in the UK identifying how they affect the public services	
P3 Describe how different activities will demonstrate good citizenship and benefit the uniformed public services and society	3.3	104		
P4 Compare reports from three different sources of news about a current national or international situation to show how media reporting can vary and how it influences the public services.	3.4	107	**M3** Analyse three news reports about a current national or international situation to show how media reporting can vary and how it influences the public services.	**D2** Compare and contrast different news reports about three contemporary issues including the effects that they might have on specified public services.
P5 Identify three examples of contemporary issues and explain their likely effects on specified public services.	3.5	112	**M4** Identify three examples of contemporary issues and analyse their likely effects on specified public services.	

Team development in public services

Introduction

Teamwork is a key component of the uniformed public services. Each service you examine on your course will revolve around a team of individuals who come together to achieve a goal or an objective. This might be securing a border against terrorism, policing a football match or responding to a disaster scenario but, whichever objective a public service has to achieve, one thing remains constant throughout – the goal is not achievable by one person alone.

Where goals are not achievable by an individual, a team of people ranging from just one other person to hundreds or thousands must be deployed to achieve it. Therefore, ensuring that teams work together effectively is a crucial element in any public service career.

This unit helps you to understand what teams are, how they can work together effectively and the benefits they bring to a uniformed public service. A key part of this unit is about you personally taking part in at least five teamwork activities to demonstrate your own strengths and areas for development in a teamwork situation.

After completing this unit you should be able to achieve the following outcomes:

- Understand the use of teams and teamwork activities within the uniformed public services
- Understand team development
- Know how teamwork supports performance
- Be able to work as a team member.

Thinking points

Consider the public service you want to join – how does it use teamwork? Are your current teamwork skills and abilities up to the job?

What could you do to get a realistic view of how you behave in a team environment? Consider asking people with whom you have worked in teams for an honest assessment of your teamwork skills – you might be surprised at what you find out.

What have your experiences been of working in a team so far? What have been the positives and negatives of a team environment from your point of view?

This section aims to explore how teams and teamwork activities are used in the uniformed public services to achieve goals and objectives.

Types of team

Teams can occur in a wide variety of settings and for very different purposes. There are many definitions of what a team is. For example:

- a group of people who have complementary skills and who are committed to a common purpose
- a group of individuals who are brought together to achieve a task or goal
- a group of individuals who have a common goal and feel mutually accountable for achieving it.

Type of team	Description and example
Formal	• Formal teams have a clear membership and a defined structure. They have clear goals and objectives and there are monitoring systems in place to ensure that goals are reached in a timely fashion. • Formal teams have the backing of senior management and may have been created by management to solve a particular problem. • An example of this would be a multi-agency safer-city partnership team who work together across a variety of organisations to combat antisocial behaviour on behalf of the Government.
Informal	• An informal team may have more elastic membership allowing individuals to move in and out of the team with some flexibility as their particular skills are needed. • The goals and structure may be less well-defined but the informal nature of the team allows for innovative and new ideas to be considered. • An example of this could be a best-practice working group.
Size	• The size of teams can vary greatly from two individuals working on a task to thousands working towards achieving the same goal. Increased human resources doesn't mean the job will get done any quicker or better – two people working on a small task may work much more efficiently than two thousand people on a large task. • The size of the task largely dictates the size of the team. For example, securing a border against terrorism would need a great many uniformed public service officers while responding to a non-emergency call would take only one or two.
Temporary	• Temporary teams come together for a short space of time to solve a particular problem and then disband once the objective has been achieved. • It can be difficult for temporary teams to work well as they do not know each other's strengths and weaknesses in the same way as permanent teams do. However, they can be efficient at troubleshooting as they sometimes see things differently from established teams. • An example of a temporary team in the public services might be operational, tactical and strategic command teams at the site of a major incident. These groups come together for the duration of the incident only and then disband once the situation is resolved.
Project	• Project teams are very like temporary teams – they come together to achieve a specific task-based project and they may disband as soon as the project is finished or they may then move on to another task. • Project teams are usually made up of specialists and a project manager who runs the schedule and ensures objectives are met. • A project in the fire service might be to ensure all primary schools in a region have a visit from a fire-safety team to warn about the dangers of fires and hoax calls.
Permanent	• Permanent teams are very common in the public services; many shifts, watches and regiments can have predominantly the same members for years at a time. • They are considered strong teams who know each other's strengths and weaknesses and who can use that knowledge to its best effect in achieving aims and goals. On the downside they can become set in their ways and it can be difficult to change how a permanent team works.

Table 4.1 Types of team

What all these definitions have in common is that the team is committed and accountable for its performance and agrees on what the final goal is. Unfortunately, teams are rarely as clear-cut as this: some members of the team may not agree on the goals, some may not feel accountable for achieving them and some may not want to be part of the team at all.

The definitions above show that teams naturally evolve but the majority of teams in the public services and elsewhere are made up of people who have been placed there by line managers and given goals to achieve by the same managers. This means the team may not have much control over what they actually do. However, this does not mean that the team cannot be successful.

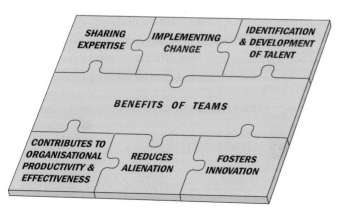

Consider this

Are you a member of any of these kinds of team in college or in part-time work? How does that team work? What are its strengths and weaknesses?

Benefits of teams

If teams were not beneficial to organisations then they would not be used.

SHARING EXPERTISE • IMPLEMENTING CHANGE • IDENTIFICATION & DEVELOPMENT OF TALENT

BENEFITS OF TEAMS

CONTRIBUTES TO ORGANISATIONAL PRODUCTIVITY & EFFECTIVENESS • REDUCES ALIENATION • FOSTERS INNOVATION

▲ **Figure 4.1 There are many benefits to effective team working**

Contribution to organisational productivity and effectiveness

Teams are a vital part of making an organisation flexible and responsive to new challenges and customer needs and the public services have plenty of customers –around 60 million in the UK alone. Every man, woman and child is a consumer of our public services and their services must be ready to respond to their needs. Teams can be a key element of identifying and implementing new ways to serve the public and take advantage of the skills and expertise the organisation already has to promote new ways of working. Being part of a good team can lead to an individual being more positive and accountable for their role and therefore more effective as a team member. It is also important to note that some organisational objectives simply cannot be met by an individual alone – a team is required to achieve them.

Reduction of alienation

Psychologists would argue that humans are social animals by nature – we like to be part of a social group, to belong to a team. This includes all manner of things

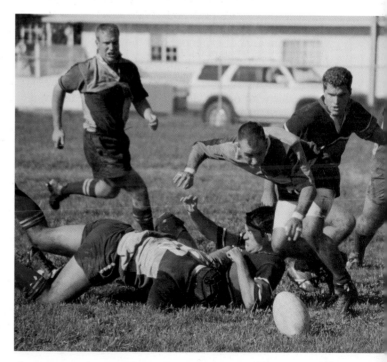

▲ **Teams allow individuals to feel that they belong**

such as sports clubs, churches, pressure groups and hobby groups. Effective teams can allow individuals to express their ideas, educate themselves about the organisation they work in and become part of it on a wider scale by having a say in policy-making procedures. Teams foster strong commitment to a goal and to team mates because their success is your success and their failure is your failure; it is hard to feel isolated in circumstances such as this.

Fostering innovation

Innovation is about new ideas and new approaches to both old and new problems. Teams can be very good places to foster innovation as they allow for brainstorming activities between several individuals in a critical yet supportive environment. All team members get to throw ideas into the pot and have them examined and evaluated by others to see if they would work in practice. This can lead to brand new approaches to issues which have traditionally been hard to solve.

Sharing expertise

Being able to share expertise is one of the greatest benefits of being part of a team. All team members, whether young or old, experienced or inexperienced, will have an area of expertise that they know more about than others in the team. In an effective team situation each person gets to share their expertise and specialist knowledge with others. This has two benefits: firstly, it educates other team members whose knowledge might not be as up-to-date and, secondly, it allows experts to have their say on how certain goals and objectives can be achieved.

A good team leader will value these contributions rather than feel threatened by them. It can be difficult for team members to share their knowledge if they come from a strictly hierarchical organisation like the uniformed public services where the discipline and structure may lead to the belief that the individual with the highest rank knows best – this is not always the case. A good team leader will understand that sharing power to gather information and ideas is not the same as surrendering their authority.

Implementing change

The role of the uniformed public services, and indeed any large customer-focused organisation, is dynamic and ever-changing. The services are subject to the changes made by successive governments, funding plans, target-setting, social changes and global needs. They do not stay the same and nor does the role they fulfil.

This means that a fundamental role of teams is to bring about change. Organisational change does not happen by itself – it must be driven by people with the vision and knowledge to understand why the changes must take place and with the communication and interpersonal skills to help others understand why the change needs to take place. Change can be perceived very negatively by some people in organisations (especially if they have a 'if it's not broken don't fix it' attitude). However, in the competitive target-driven society we live in, an 'acceptable' level of service has ceased to be acceptable; now all organisations must strive to meet challenging targets and prove they are worth the amount of public money that is spent on them each year. Teams are the key focus for change – only they can make effective and binding change happen.

Identification and development of talent

Teams are only as good as the individuals who make them up. It is therefore very important to identify team members who have talent in a particular area and ensure that they attend the right training events to develop it. For example, a manager might spot that a new police recruit manages difficult situations very well and may ensure he or she receives training and opportunities in their career which help to develop those skills still further. This is not so very different from talent-spotting in the sports world where talented young players are

Remember!

Talent is not just about intelligence; some people can be very clever but have no idea of how to get a job done. Consider the following case study.

observed by sports clubs and are trained by them if they are deemed to be good enough. Organisations can even get software which helps them to spot individuals who perform well at certain online tasks to make the job of talent identification easier.

Case study: The Apollo Syndrome

A researcher called Meredith Belbin noticed an occurrence in teams which was subsequently termed the Apollo Syndrome. The Apollo Syndrome is a trend whereby teams of extremely talented and clever individuals under-perform against teams of 'ordinary' individuals. When this phenomenon was looked at in more detail, it was discovered that Apollo team members often undermined each other's strategies while trying to achieve their own solutions to a group problem. They were essentially working as individuals in competition rather than as a united team pulling together. Experiments such as this made it clear that the intelligence, talent and understanding of the team were not the only factors in its success.

1. **Why do you think that groups of talented individuals perform less well against those who are less talented?**

2. **Why did individual Apollo team members believe their own goal was the right one to pursue?**

3. **Why did Apollo team members undermine each other?**

4. **What would you do to improve teamwork if you were in charge of an Apollo type team?**

The work of Meredith Belbin will be looked at in more detail later in this unit on pages 125–6.

Consider this

Are you a member of a team in college or at work? What are the personal benefits you reap as a result of being part of a team? Do you think there might be disadvantages to teams? What might they be?

Assessment activity 4.1

In this activity you are to choose the uniformed public service that you wish to join and research the following:

- types of team
- benefits of teams.

Once you have researched this content you should use it to produce a PowerPoint presentation which answers the following question:

1. Describe the types of teams that operate within a named uniformed public service and their associated benefits. **P1**

Grading tip

P1 How you approach this task will depend on the service you choose to examine. Each service has different kinds of team. Describe several types of team and then describe in your own words the benefits they bring to the organisation.

Remember!

- Teams are used to achieve goals that individuals could not achieve alone.
- They add to the efficiency and productivity of an organisation.
- Teams need training, support and clear goals if they are to work well together.
- Teams vary by size, duration and style of operation.
- Teams can be places of conflict as well as cooperation.

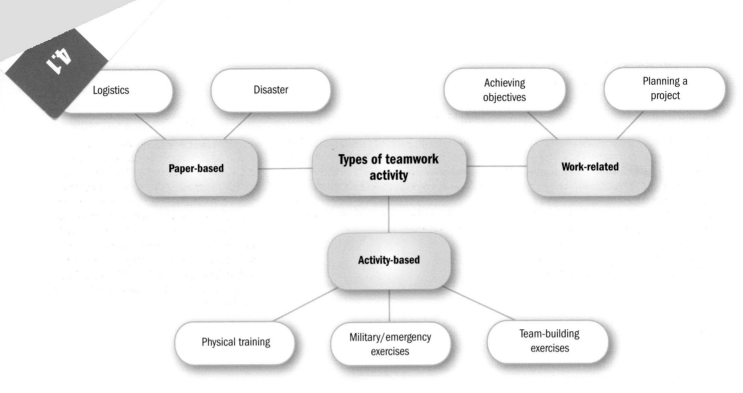

▲ Figure 4.2 Types of teamwork activity

Types of teamwork activities

There are many types of teamwork activity that can be undertaken. These include the following:

Paper-based exercises

- **Logistics:** this is the process of managing and tracking the raw materials and components needed for a project. For the Armed Forces this might be the movement of troops and equipment to a battle zone along with all the support services such as medical, housing, catering and chaplaincy support. This can involve the movement of thousands of troops and millions of pounds' worth of equipment in a situation where time is critical and in which mistakes may compromise the safety and security of service personnel. The best way to ensure the move goes as planned is to have a team of logistics experts plan it out prior to the actual move. Although it is called a paper-based activity it is much more likely to be done using computer software these days.

- **Disaster:** there are two main kinds of paper-based disaster teamwork scenario.

  1) **Seminar:** this is a discussion-based exercise that is designed to outline to all the agencies involved exactly what their roles and responsibilities are and what the procedures would be in dealing with a particular major incident. This can be done as part of a large team or services attending can break down into smaller groups to discuss one particular aspect of the emergency response or focus on the responsibilities of one particular service.

  2) **Tabletop:** this is similar in nature to a seminar exercise but it generally involves smaller teams. The public services and any other agencies talk through their responses to a specified major incident in the order in which they would occur if the incident were real. They generally conduct these exercises around a conference table, hence the name of the exercise. Tabletop exercises are effective for testing major incident plans as they highlight any weaknesses in a safe environment where lives are not at risk.

Activity-based exercises

Physical training	Team-building exercises	Military/emergency exercises
Physical training is an excellent way of promoting effective teamwork. Competitive sports such as football, basketball and rugby encourage team members to work together to achieve the goal of winning a match. Team sports can also foster a sense of camaraderie and encourage less physically able members of the team to strive to improve and encourage more physically able members of the team to assist them.	Team-building exercises can be any activity which is used to bring a team together and make it work more efficiently. This could include activities such as outward bound training courses or bringing in consultants who will help the team find better ways of working together.	Live exercises can test a small part of a major incident or military response plan (such as an evacuation) or they can test a full-scale response. The exercise is carried out as realistically as possible including fake casualties and a simulated media response. This provides all the service teams involved with an opportunity to get to grips with the problems arising from a major disaster or military incident and attempt to solve them in real time, just as they would need to do in a real incident.

Table 4.2 Activity-based exercises

Work-related team activities

Achieving work objectives	Planning and achieving a project
A major goal of teams in the workplace is to achieve the objectives set by the organisation. These objectives could range from reducing patient waiting times, to reducing the instances of self-harm in prison, to securing a building against terrorist activity.	Projects and initiatives that require planning and implementation are common in the workplace. Teams are largely responsible for developing a strategy to achieve a project and for monitoring its success. They are also accountable if the project is unsuccessful.

Table 4.3 Work-related team activities

Consider this

What kinds of team-building activities have you taken part in? How did they make the team bond? Would you recommend the activity to others?

Assessment activity 4.2

To complete this assessment activity you must research the following content:

- paper-based exercises
- activity-based exercises
- work-related team activities.

Use this research to help you work in small groups to prepare and deliver a 20-minute discussion which answers the following question:

1. Describe the different types of teamwork activities.

Grading tip

P2 This is a very straightforward grade to achieve. Ensure you record your discussion or produce discussion notes as supporting evidence for your tutor to assess.

Types of teams in the public services

Each public service has its own way of structuring and deploying teams in order to help it achieve the organisational objectives set for it by the Government. The types of teams in the service you wish to join will be very different from the types of teams in another service. Some of the most common names for teams are as follows:

- divisional
- departmental
- sectional
- geographical
- multi-disciplinary
- regiment
- brigade
- force

- multi-agency
- specialist (for example, search and rescue).

It can be very difficult to work out what these names mean and which service they relate to. Some of these types of team relate to all the services and some relate to just one. In addition, some of these terms can mean different things to different services which can also make things difficult.

Theory into practice

Using a search engine such as Google, gather web-based definitions of each of these types of team and use the results to draw up a table which explains each term and describes which service you would be most likely to find it in.

This outcome concentrates on understanding how teams develop, the roles individuals can play in teams and how teams perform.

Roles in teams

Different kinds of teams require different kinds of members. For example, a committee might need a chairperson, a football team might need a captain and a government needs a prime minister or president. Each person in a team usually has a specific role to play: that role might be the leader, the expert or the researcher and each role is equally important. There are several researchers who have examined team roles in detail; in this unit we will look at the research of Dr Meredith Belbin.

Belbin's team roles

'What is needed is not well-balanced individuals but individuals who balance well with each other.'
(Dr Meredith Belbin)

Belbin's book *Management Teams*, written in 1981, was the result of a long study into the ways in which team members interacted during team games at a management college. Belbin concluded that, in order for a team to be successful, nine key roles must be fulfilled. These nine roles are as follows:

- **Plant** – a person who generates ideas. They are often free-thinking individuals who may come up with new and innovative solutions to problems. The drawback of plants is that they may struggle to communicate these new ideas clearly enough for the rest of the team to understand.
- **Resource investigator** – an enthusiastic person who is able to network and make contacts very easily. They have a very outward focus and will look to other organisations for a solution rather than create one of their own. Resource investigators can lose enthusiasm towards the end of the project.
- **Coordinator** – a mature and confident individual who often falls into the role of managing a team. They are able to delegate to the right people by recognising each person's abilities and they are able to clarify decisions and enable other team members to focus on the tasks in hand. They could be viewed as being manipulative at times and may delegate too much work to others.
- **Shaper** – a great motivator of others. They have the interpersonal skills to move a project forward and overcome obstacles. Unfortunately they may be less sensitive to the needs of other team members.
- **Monitor evaluator** – an individual with the skill of being able to detach him or herself from being biased and who can see and evaluate a variety of options without reference to personal opinion. However, they can be difficult to motivate and they don't always have the skill of being able to motivate others.
- **Teamworker** – essential to a good team. They help resolve conflict and are diplomatic and concerned about others. They may lack decision-making ability at times.
- **Implementer** – the team member who makes things happen. They take the ideas of the others and make them a reality. They can be very self-disciplined and will always deliver work to deadlines. Some people might consider them to be inflexible as they can be unwilling to change or modify their plans.
- **Completer/finisher** – the perfectionist of the team. They want to make sure everything is just right. They can often be considered picky by their team mates and may not delegate work because they don't trust anyone to do it as well as they could.
- **Specialist** – the individual with expert and in-depth knowledge on a subject which they are happy to share with the team. They are likely to lose interest in anything which is not part of their specialist subject.

Consider this

Do you recognise yourself in any of Belbin's team roles? Remember that you might find yourself fulfilling more than one role in a team. In fact, in smaller teams, individuals may fulfil several of these roles at once.

Most organisations today, whether public services or not, are run on the basis of decisions made by management teams. This collaboration of individuals with very different backgrounds, cultures, languages and approaches can be difficult to manage. However, it is essential that the team who makes the decisions and who has the responsibility for implementing them is able to work together coherently.

One of the important things to note about Belbin's work is that he acknowledged that any strength exhibited by team members usually had a counterbalancing weakness. He also noted that some combinations of roles worked well together and some worked less well (see the Apollo Syndrome case study on page 121). It therefore follows that organisations which place a priority on recruitment, induction, training and development of teams will have far more success in achieving their objectives than organisations which have teams simply to fulfil a functional or business need.

Team building

As we have just seen, organisations which make staff development and team building a priority tend to be more successful than those which do not.

1. Recruitment

Recruitment of the right individuals is a key aspect of building and maintaining a successful team. The right person is not always the best qualified or the most confident – it is the person who has the right mix of abilities and social skills to be able to improve an existing team. Recruiting a new team member can be fraught with difficulties. There are usually two options available: firstly, you can appoint a brand new member of staff from outside the organisation or, secondly, you can search within an organisation to find an existing member of staff with the right skills and qualities. Unless you are in a position to try these new members out on a trial basis, there can often be no way of knowing if they will be the right choice until after they are given the post. This means your recruitment process must be rigorous. The public services have a very long and involved recruitment process which can take many months and this is because the consequences of appointing the wrong person to the post could be disastrous.

2. Induction

Induction is the process by which new employees become familiar with their new workplace. Some employers don't place a great deal of emphasis on induction but it is a vital part of ensuring a new employee knows what they are supposed to do and how they are supposed to do it. It ranges from simple things such as canteen arrangements, to learning about company policy and procedures, to where to go for help if you are struggling with your job role. Induction is important in the public services and they often have lengthy probationary periods or terms of basic training for new staff to learn how things are done.

3. Training/coaching

Training and coaching are key aspects of any job role in the public services. Many of the tasks employees are expected to do are highly specialised and require extensive training and knowledge in order to do them properly. This might involve the use of complex technical equipment, legal knowledge or tactical knowledge. In the public services, training is an aspect of the job that never stops – an employee is never fully

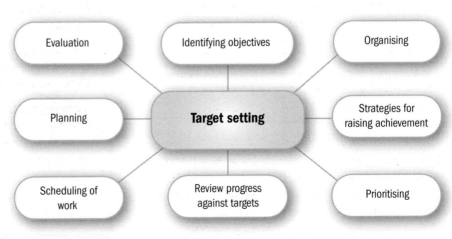

Figure 4.3 There are several key elements to building an effective team ▶

trained. New laws, new equipment and new theatres of battle all mean than training and coaching will be ongoing for an entire public service career.

4. Mentoring

Mentoring means having a more experienced colleague to whom an employee can turn for advice. A good mentor will never be a person's line manager as there may be a conflict of interests. The mentor offers advice on how to deal with difficult work-based inter-personal situations or how to achieve an objective to best effect. Some organisations do not have mentors at all.

5. Motivation

Once a team member is recruited, inducted, trained and has a mentor if required, it is crucial that they are motivated to keep performing their role well. There are two kinds of motivation: intrinsic and extrinsic. Intrinsic motivation is the desire to do a job well and job satisfaction is the reward. Extrinsic motivation is influenced by factors outside the individual's control such as financial reward and promotion. A motivated team will work more efficiently than a demotivated team. Intrinsic motivation is a key aspect of any public services work – the hours can be long and the tasks are thankless at times so it is important that an employee is able to keep themselves motivated.

Consider this

How well do you motivate yourself? Are you a person who is intrinsically or extrinsically motivated?

Team knowledge and team building

Team knowledge is about understanding the strengths and weaknesses of your team and using this knowledge to get the best performance out of them. Only by knowing what members of your team do well can you allocate tasks and responsibilities efficiently. The team-development process is an interesting one – teams do not develop overnight. Simply assembling a group of individuals and assigning them to a task will not make them an effective team; they must go through a team-development process which establishes relationships and provides them with the team knowledge they need to work effectively. One of the better known models of team development is the model developed by Bruce Tuckman.

Case study: Team building

You are a lance corporal at the local Territorial Army base. Recently, a new recruit has joined and is experiencing difficulty fitting in with the established team. After speaking to members of the team it is clear they do not like the new recruit. Although she is competent in her role she comes across as arrogant and rude which is leading to her being alienated and ridiculed by the rest of the team. After speaking to the recruit directly you form the impression that she is young, insecure and overcompensating by trying to be better than everyone else. This situation cannot be allowed to continue as the young recruit risks being bullied and the team is becoming increasingly offended by her behaviour.

1. **What could you do to help the new recruit fit in?**

2. **Do you think a mentor would help in this situation? Explain why.**

3. **How could you encourage the team to be more accepting of the new recruit while she is learning to improve her teamwork skills?**

4. **Considering the recruitment, induction, training and mentoring process, where do you think the process has failed the new recruit and the team and why?**

Tuckman's teamwork model is described in detail in *Unit 2: Team leadership*. However, a summary is included below.

■ Tuckman – the forming, storming, norming, performing model

Dr Bruce Tuckman first published this model of team development in 1965. It is effectively a theory of how teams develop from the very start of a project to the end. It describes four main stages, although he added a fifth stage (adjourning) later in his career. The stages are described below:

- **Stage 1 – forming**

  In this stage the team may be meeting for the first time. They will have a high level of dependency on the leader and roles and responsibilities will not be particularly clear. The processes that the team should follow will not be known and the majority of information and guidance comes from the leader as they explain why the team exists and what it is intended to do.

- **Stage 2 – storming**

  As the name suggests this can be a very turbulent stage in a team's development. During this stage, individuals might be struggling for position and power with other team members and there may be some challenges to the authority of the leader. Personal relationships are starting to form, both good and bad, and the team needs to be very goal-focused otherwise it may become distracted by these internal difficulties.

- **Stage 3 – norming**

  This is a much calmer stage. There is usually clear consensus and agreement and the leader is not challenged so much. Aims and objectives are clear and team roles and responsibilities are established. Commitment to the team is strong and there is a sense of bonding and unity between team members.

- **Stage 4 – performing**

  This is a crucial stage of team development as it is where the team really begins to work like a well-oiled machine. The team is able to work positively towards its goals and resolve conflict in a positive and constructive way. Team members support each other and look for new and innovative ways to develop.

The fifth stage that Tuckman added is often not seen as part of the main theory but organisational change happens quickly in the public services and teams can be broken up routinely once they have achieved their objectives. Hence, it is important to examine it:

- **Stage 5 – adjourning**

  This is the stage when the team breaks up to move on to new projects (group turnover). The original team goal has hopefully been achieved and the team is no longer needed. This can cause tremendous insecurity in team members, particularly if they like the team they work in and have formed strong bonds with their colleagues. It is a stage which needs to be dealt with sensitively to ensure that all team members can move on to pastures new with no ill feelings.

Team building in the public services is just like team building in any other sector. There are many tools that can be used to enhance team cohesion such as:

- away days
- residential experiences
- meetings
- social events
- group training.

The best technique is to bring the team together as often as possible so that team bonding on a social level can happen alongside team building on a professional level.

Team performance

There are many ways of measuring the performance of teams (for example, self-evaluation, appraisal and ongoing managerial monitoring) but the most common method of measuring team performance is against **performance indicators** and target setting.

Key terms

Performance indicators A set of figures designed to measure the extent to which performance objectives and agreed targets are being met on an ongoing basis.

Performance indicators in the public services can be things such as:

- customer satisfaction ratings
- emergency response times
- crime statistics
- measurement against the performance of other similar services.

Performance indicators for teams are usually set around a specific theme. For example, for a police team it might be the reduction of incidents of antisocial behaviour by 10 per cent in a six-month period or for a healthcare team it might be to reduce incidences of MRSA in patients by 35 per cent in a three-month period. Although the performance indicators will vary from service to service, what they have in common is that the indicators will follow a SMART target-setting process. SMART targets are:

- **S**pecific – clear and direct, they say exactly what a team is going to achieve
- **M**easurable – so that the team knows when they have been achieved
- **A**chievable – they can be reached in a realistic timescale
- **R**ealistic – they are genuinely in the team's control and they can actually take action on them
- **T**ime-related – there are clear deadlines for completion.

Consider this

Do you use SMART targets yourself? Do you think they might help you plan your college work and time?

Once performance indicators have been decided and clear targets have been set, the next step is to ensure that progress towards the targets is monitored on an ongoing basis, both by the team itself and by management. This ensures that the team is on track to meet the targets set and allows it to adjust the pace of work or develop new ideas to combat problems if it is unlikely to hit the targets. This ongoing review process at a strategic point in the project lifecycle means that there are no nasty surprises at the end of the project – all team members are aware of how well the team is doing based on comparing its current performance to the targets it has been set. If team performance is dipping and targets might not be met, it is an ideal opportunity for the team leader to consider new strategies to support and develop team members who may be struggling to meet the targets either individually or collectively. This could be additional training or coaching or the allocation of a mentor to help with any inter-personal work difficulties.

Team performance in the public services is monitored in exactly the same way as described above with the use of performance indicators and target setting. Services will also use benchmarks which are national performance indicators that inform the public and other services how well a similar service is performing. For example, there are 43 police constabularies in England and Wales, each of which will be able to compare itself against the performance of the other 42 to indicate how well or poorly it is performing compared to the national average. The school league tables use a similar system where all schools are ranked in terms of 5 GCSE A–C passes. In reality, these statistics do not take into account the particular circumstances of a constabulary or school. For example, the Metropolitan Police Service may deal with far more violent crime than a predominantly rural police service such as Devon and Cornwall. This doesn't mean that the rural police service is better because they have less crime, it just means that they are policing in very different circumstances. Similarly with schools, a school which has an 89 per cent pass rate at GCSE is not necessarily better than one with a 45 per cent pass rate once you factor in the location and socio-economic background of the school and its pupils.

Team cohesion

Team cohesion is the process of team bonding. It is what makes a team stick together and achieve goals even when everyone is tired, under pressure or experiencing difficulties and challenges. There are many aspects to promoting a strong team bond and some of these are outlined in Table 4.4.

Feature	Description
Clear vision and team understanding	The team needs a clear idea of why it exists, what it is there for and how it is intended to work together. Without this knowledge the team is aimless and will find it harder to bond.
Clear goals	The team must have SMART targets which it can strive to achieve in unity but each team member should have individual targets too. This ensures all team members pull their weight and contribute equally to team performance.
Role satisfaction	In order to promote team cohesion, team members must have satisfaction in their role and feel valued and needed within the team. Roles should be clear or this can harm team bonding.
Positive work environment	The work environment should be positive and happy. Working in teams can require a keen sense of humour and there should be opportunities for socialising and laughter. Some teams also respond well to having a unique identity within a larger organisation. Again this can help the team to bond.
Positive and cooperative relationships.	Team members need to trust and rely on each other. Personal respect and trust can promote team cohesion more than anything else. If the members of a team genuinely like each other, they will perform better as there is likely to be less conflict.

Table 4.4 Ways to promote a strong team bond

Group conflict

Conflict is unavoidable in any team. This might be conflict about choosing goals, achieving goals or other work-related issues. Some conflicts are inter-personal and are based on a clash of personalities. The important thing to remember is that conflict is not necessarily a bad thing. Conflict can be a tremendous help to a group as it can challenge old ideas and bring forward new and innovative ones.

▲ Remember that conflict is not always a bad thing if it is productively managed

Conflict is not necessarily a challenge to a leader's authority or group cohesion – resolving conflict well can often lead to a stronger more unified team. And it is always better to resolve conflict where you can rather than leaving it to simmer under the surface and harm team and individual performance. Resolving conflict positively can have several benefits for teams including:

- **An increased understanding of other team members** – resolving the conflict through constructive discussion can help to improve an individual's awareness of the points of view and needs of other team members. It can help an individual to know how to achieve their own goal without undermining the goals of others or harming overall team performance.
- **Improved team cohesion** – if conflict is resolved constructively and successfully it can strengthen the team. Individuals can develop more respect for other team members and have more faith in the team's ability to work together as a whole.

- **Increased self-awareness** – conflict can be very challenging and, at times, upsetting. However, it can also make people explore their own motivation and help them to understand why they behave in certain ways which might create a poor impression.

How teams are led is a significant factor in their performance. You can find out much more about this in *Unit 2: Team leadership*.

Assessment activity 4.3

In order to achieve P3, M1 and D1 you should research the following topics:

- roles in teams
- team building
- team performance
- team cohesion.

You should use this information to produce a written report which answers the following questions:

1. Describe ways of developing cohesive teams in the uniformed public services with reference to relevant theorists. **P3**
2. Analyse the importance of team cohesion in effective team performance, with examples from two named public services, with reference to relevant theorists. **M1**
3. Evaluate how team performance is monitored and team cohesion is encouraged within a named uniformed public service, with reference to relevant theorists. **D1**

Grading tips

P3 This is a straightforward task. You have to describe in your own words how cohesive teams are developed and ensure you mention theorists such as Belbin and Tuckman.

M1 This part of the question asks you to *analyse*, which means look at the topic in greater detail. You also have to choose examples from two different services of why team cohesion is important. You also need to make reference to theorists such as Belbin and Tuckman.

D1 In order to gain a distinction you have to evaluate how team performance is monitored. This means looking at the advantages and disadvantages of types of monitoring and review. You also have to discuss how team cohesion is encouraged and mention theorists such as Belbin and Tuckman.

This section is intended to show you how effective teamwork makes strong performance more likely. Much of the content of this section has already been covered in section 2 and will not be repeated here.

Target setting

As you have already learnt, the process of target setting is very important if teams are going to achieve their goals. If you don't know what a target is, how can you plan your time and resources to make sure you achieve it?

▲ Figure 4.4 There are many aspects to target setting

In addition to the information provided in section 2, Table 4.5 provides some additional detail on these factors:

Aspect of target setting	Description
Identifying the objectives	In order for a team to be successful they must know what their objective is and ensure SMART targets are put into place to clarify what needs to be achieved. All members of the team must be very clear on their ultimate individual and group aims for the project to be a success.
Organising	It goes without saying that any team undertaking requires organisation. This includes human and practical resource allocation, office space, meeting times, planning and scheduling. Many projects have a project manager who takes on the bulk of this stressful role, enabling the technical specialists to do their job without worrying about administrative issues.
Raising achievement	In some cases the team may already be meeting its targets but, in today's dynamic economic and social climate, targets can frequently be changed, requiring public service teams to produce better results without any additional money or staffing. The key is to consider where improvements can be made which don't require additional resources and to target those areas for improvement. Alternatively, the senior officer or project manager might have to try and secure additional resources to make the improvements possible.
Prioritising	In any teamwork situation where goals have to be achieved, there will usually be an order in which it is most sensible to achieve them. For example, if an education team needs to raise retention, achievement and success in their students, it makes sense to target retention first because, if the students leave, they can't achieve anyway. Another example would be the implementation of a new law which the police service must enforce: the key priority here would be training for officers on how to implement the law. Without that as a priority, the officers wouldn't have the knowledge to enforce the new legislation. Prioritising can be very difficult, especially if competing goals seem to demand the same level of priority. The senior officer or team leader will usually be the one who makes a judgement call on this, based on discussions with the team and other stakeholders.
Review progress and evaluation	Any team objective must be subject to an ongoing cycle of review and evaluation to ensure that it is on track to achieve its objectives. It makes sense to check throughout a project that it is on track and to make adjustments as necessary rather than get to the end and fail to meet the objectives. Evaluation also includes looking at what the team can learn from the process in order to perform better next time. In the public services there are often specific methods of evaluation which we will examine in more detail a little later.
Scheduling of work and planning	All teamwork, whether it is routine everyday activities or a specialised project, needs to be planned and scheduled in advance. Without a clear schedule of targets and achievements it would be very easy for teams to lose sight of their aims and find it difficult to achieve them. Scheduling should be clear and tight and show each member of the team what they are supposed to have done and by when.

Table 4.5 Factors that are important in target setting

Individual evaluation in the public services

For individuals, most services have a professional review or appraisal system in place. Appraisals can range from very informal chats with a manager to a formal and nerve-racking interview with your line manager. It is an opportunity for both parties to assess the professional progress of an employee and to set goals against which future performance can be measured. In effect, it is an evaluation of your workplace performance. Generally speaking, an appraisal serves four primary functions:

- It is a source of information on which to base decisions about where a person will work most effectively and whether they should be promoted.
- It is a basis on which to allocate rewards.
- It enables selection methods and training programmes to be evaluated.
- It enables managers to tell staff how well they are performing and offer opportunities to improve.

Some staff find appraisals help them to clarify their aims and set out on the next year's projects with a sharp focus. For others, appraisals are something to be feared and are viewed as an opportunity for line managers to criticise them and withhold rewards. Some staff simply do not think appraisals are worth the time but do them because they have to. As a potential manager in the public services, you will have to evaluate the performance of all three types of people.

Group evaluation in the public services

Group evaluations can be more complex as they involve several individuals and sometimes different teams from different agencies. They usually try to evaluate a project or an incident to see what can be learnt for next time from the experience the team has just had. For example, in the aftermath of a major incident, many questions are likely to be asked about what the causes were and how such events could be avoided in the future.

The public services go through a similar procedure, questioning and evaluating their own performance and the effectiveness of their major incident plan. This procedure is called a debrief and it provides all of the organisations and agencies involved with an opportunity to discuss and comment on various aspects of the combined response and the overall operation. Debriefings do not just happen as a result of major incidents – the services use them routinely to evaluate group performance at any level.

Debriefings perform several useful evaluation functions:

Function	Detail
Collect evidence for an enquiry	Major incidents or other significant issues are often caused by criminal or neglectful actions. Evidence must be gathered that establishes the causes of the incident and where responsibility for the incident lies. Debriefings can highlight some of these issues.
Improved response	Debriefings allow the services to review their response to an incident and evaluate their individual and collective performance in order to improve their response for the next time. This is a very important aspect of debriefings.
Identify staff development needs	A debriefing identifies areas for development of staff skills. It may be that some staff need equipment training, while others require increased competence in public relations or have other needs. The debrief highlights these needs and then the agencies concerned can address them.
Improve future training and development	The debriefing of a team will allow future training and development to be improved on the basis of accurate experience in the field. Senior officers will know which aspects of an issue were at fault and can identify areas in which efficiency could be improved.

Table 4.6 Debriefings as an evaluation tool

An effective debrief is concerned with learning lessons which can then be used to improve the response to the next project or set of objectives. Debriefings come in many forms and may occur at all levels within an organisation or agency.

On 17 October 2000, a GNER train travelling from London to Leeds was derailed 1 mile outside Hatfield train station in Hertfordshire. The incident killed four people and injured many others.

All of the subsequent debriefings conducted by the services were synthesised and pulled together by Hertfordshire Emergency Services Major Incidents Committee (HESMIC) into one debriefing report. This could then be widely circulated and have its recommendations acted upon. Some of the issues and concerns raised in the debrief are described below:

- There was confusion in communication between the emergency services and Railtrack over the safety of power lines which was not resolved for over an hour into the incident.
- There were many people milling around in the inner and outer cordons who had no role to perform and who were not challenged on their legitimacy to be present.
- A helicopter was used but the noise of its rotors meant that safety instructions could not be easily heard by emergency services on the ground.
- The identification of silver/tactical commanders was difficult as many individuals were wearing similar high-visibility tabards.
- Some survivors of the derailment had to complete their onward journey by train.
- Although the clergy were put on standby to help survivors in the reception centres, they were not deployed.
- The Queen Elizabeth II Hospital was put on standby but it was never given the signal to activate its major incident response. The hospital made the decision to activate the plan itself when the casualties began to arrive.

These are just some of the issues raised by the Hatfield debrief. It is clear that there is no such thing as a perfect incident response – there are always lessons to be learnt in an ongoing cycle of development.

1. Why was it inappropriate for a major incident survivor to continue their onward journey on the same form of transport that was involved in the incident?

2. How has this evaluation debrief helped improve a response for next time?

3. What is the benefit of detailed debriefs for all the uniformed public services?

4. What might be the consequences if the uniformed services did not monitor and evaluate their performance in relation to significant incidents?

Take it further

Research the Armed Forces for an evaluation or debrief of an incident such as the Deepcut situation. Do the Armed Forces use debriefs in the same way or are there differences?

Monitoring

Monitoring has been covered in detail in this section and in sections 1 and 2.

Assessment activity 4.4

In order to achieve P5 and M2 you should research the following topics:

- target setting
- monitoring.

You should use this information to take part in a small group discussion which addresses the following questions:

1. Describe how targets are set and how team performance is monitored. **P5**

2. Assess the value of different methods of monitoring the performance of a team. **M2**

Grading tips

P5 In your own words, describe how a team might set a target and how they might monitor their progress towards it.

M2 This question asks you to evaluate the different methods teams and individuals have of monitoring themselves such as appraisals and measuring performance against targets.

This section examines your own abilities to communicate and interact as part of a team.

Communication

Another aspect of teamwork which is particularly relevant for individuals wishing to have a career in the uniformed public services is the field of **communication**. Communication is an integral part of all of our lives and is a critical factor in most areas of employment. This is particularly so when the job involves substantial contact with the public and teamwork situations with colleagues, both of which occur almost all the time in public service work. Communication is a very complicated process although most people don't give a thought to the complexities involved in it simply because they communicate all the time and don't notice it. Communication is not just about being understood, it is a mechanism to both give and receive messages and articulate ideas, which we need in order to interpret the situation and environment around us and act accordingly.

When we communicate with others we do not simply speak to them. In fact, studies suggest that the actual literal content of our communication is far less important than how we speak, the tone of our voice, our facial expression and body language. Our senses are involved in giving and receiving communication all the time, although we may often not be directly conscious of it. This is a major part of how we present ourselves to others – the manner in which we communicate can mark us out as worthy of respect or it can make people dislike us. These impressions can be hard to change once they have been made by our team members so it is important to take care in how we present ourselves to others. (More information on communication is given in *Unit 2: Team leadership*.)

Key terms

Communication This is about making yourself understood to others via verbal and non-verbal skills.

Consider this

How well do you think you communicate? What impression might you give to others by how you speak to them?

Effective listening

Studies have found that listening accounts for between 42–53 per cent of the time that an average individual spends communicating. This indicates that the auditory sense has tremendous importance in the reception of messages. When you hear communication you are not simply hearing and understanding the spoken word – you are listening to the tone of the communication and the sentiment behind it. Understanding the tone of communication is crucial in most societies but especially so in the UK where sarcasm and irony are natural forms of humour.

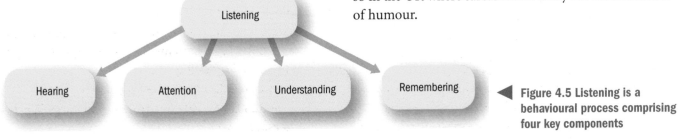

Figure 4.5 Listening is a behavioural process comprising four key components

You must hear what is being said, pay attention to the speaker, understand the content of the message and be able to remember it. This process is very important on several levels. Firstly, if you don't listen, you are placing yourself at risk and increasing your vulnerability – if you are told not to touch a piece of electrical equipment which carries live electricity, and you do not listen, the consequences could be fatal. Secondly, in a public service situation it is of vital importance that you listen to the commands of your senior officers. If you do not, you may compromise the safety of yourself, your colleagues and the general public. Thirdly, listening and paying attention are also crucial factors in the success of teams.

Listening can be divided into two main categories:

- active
- passive.

Active listening

This can be summarised as listening with a purpose. It involves paying attention to what is being said and questioning the speaker to ensure real understanding has been achieved. **Active listening** requires as much energy as speaking and it is a skill that requires practice and development if it is to be perfected.

Key terms

Active listening Listening with a purpose – active listening is a crucial skill in teamwork.

Consider this

You are a public service employee and a complaint has been made against you by a member of the public. You are anxious to defend yourself and go to see your line manager at the earliest opportunity. Your line manager hears what you say but her eyes continually wander and she stifles a couple of yawns. Explain how this makes you feel and why it is important that she actively listens.

Active listeners generally possess the following skills:

- They do not finish other people's sentences.
- They do not daydream or 'wander' while others speak.
- They do not talk more than they listen.
- They may make notes to help them remain focused.
- They ask questions for clarification.

Passive listening

This type of listening simply involves hearing what has been said – the listener is not motivated to respond or check understanding. This type of listening occurs when you are watching TV or listening to music – or possibly when you are in class!

Consider this

Are you generally an active or passive listener? How might being an active listener help you develop your team of staff? How could being a passive listener detract from the potential your team has to succeed?

The list below describes other ways to improve your speaking and listening skills:

- Be sure you know what you want to say before you say it.
- Speak clearly so that you can be heard and understood.
- Get into the habit of having general conversations with your family and friends.
- Learning when to say nothing is as important as speaking when it is appropriate to do so.
- Be sure what you say is what you mean.
- Be conscious of the fact that people interpret words differently and use techniques such as questioning to ensure understanding.
- Try to be polite and respectful in verbal communication – if you are others are more likely to respond to you.

- Do not drone on excessively, you will bore people.
- In a work situation, consider using a written back-up such as a memo or email to reiterate and clarify the verbal message.

Building confidence and morale

Communication in teams is very important in building confidence and morale; positive feedback given at the right moment can lift a team's performance. Equally, negative feedback can demoralise a team and harm their performance. Even if you need to be firm with a team about their behaviour or performance, it is still possible to do this with tact, sincerity and with concern for the feelings of the team members. Effective communication is also essential in resolving conflict (as discussed earlier in this unit).

Theory into practice

Ask three people you trust to give you an honest opinion of how well you communicate. Take on board their comments and make an action plan of how you could improve your communication skills.

Personal organisation

Personal organisation is very important to teamwork in the uniformed public services. Teamwork relies on each individual member being ready and prepared to pull their weight. If you are not personally prepared to do your part, you are letting the team down and harming the overall team performance. Working in a public services team might mean that you are working alone for periods of time such as being on the beat, maintaining equipment or speaking to the public. You might not always have others to rely on so it is doubly important that you are personally organised.

The following questionnaire should give you an indication of how personally prepared you are in terms of teamwork. The highest score is 80 and the lowest score is 16 – the higher your score, the more personally prepared you are to be part of a team.

Grade your answer 1–5 with 1 being a skill you are not good at and 5 being a skill you are very good at.

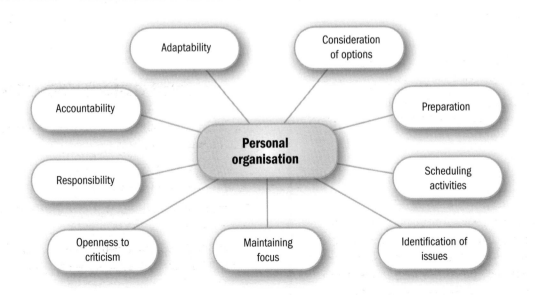

Figure 4.6 Personal organisation can help to make you a better team member

Personal organisation questionnaire					
STATEMENT	**ANSWER**				
1. I always bring the right equipment with me to college or work.	1	2	3	4	5
2. I am always punctual and reliable at college or work.	1	2	3	4	5
3. I keep an assignment diary so I know what work is due in and when.	1	2	3	4	5
4. I always attend events I have agreed to go to because I put them on my calendar.	1	2	3	4	5
5. I always take notes in class or during work training.	1	2	3	4	5
6. I can summarise information easily.	1	2	3	4	5
7. I can pick out the key point of what someone else is saying.	1	2	3	4	5
8. I am able to organise others when I work in a team.	1	2	3	4	5
9. I am accountable and can accept responsibility for my own actions.	1	2	3	4	5
10. I do not blame others for teamwork problems.	1	2	3	4	5
11. I feel accountable for how well my team performs.	1	2	3	4	5
12. I can adapt quickly to changes that need to be made.	1	2	3	4	5
13. I always consider my options before I act.	1	2	3	4	5
14. I can concentrate for long periods of time without getting distracted.	1	2	3	4	5
15. I can accept criticism.	1	2	3	4	5
16. I can give constructive criticism to others.	1	2	3	4	5

If you have scored less than 50 points on this self-assessment, you could consider drawing up an action plan which will help you to improve your personal organisation. This in turn will make you a more effective team member.

Take it further

Give a copy of the self-assessment to one of your friends, your tutor and someone you have worked with in a team and ask them to complete it on your behalf. Sometimes we don't see ourselves the way others see us – how does their assessment of you differ from your own?

Assessment activity 4.5

Research the following topics and use them to prepare a fact sheet on communication:

- communication
- personal organisation.

Use these topics to produce a fact sheet which answers the question below.

1. Identify the communication skills and personal organisation required when working in a team.

Grading tip

P4 This is a very straightforward question. Be sure to identify all the different communication skills you will need such as active listening, tact, sincerity etc. and discuss personal organisation skills such as preparation, planning and adaptability.

Assessment activity 4.6

1. In order to achieve this grade you must take part in five team activities, with support. **P6**

2. In order to achieve M3 you must take part in the team building activities confidently. (That is the only difference between P6 and M3.) **M3**

3. To achieve D1 you must evaluate your own performance in team activities, recommending personal development for future teamwork activities. **D1**

Knowledge check

1. What is a team?
2. List five benefits of teams.
3. What types of team activity are there?
4. What types of teams exist in the public services?
5. Summarise Belbin's team roles.
6. Explain the importance of team building activities.
7. How can you measure team performance?
8. How can you build team cohesion?
9. Why is communication important in the uniformed public services?
10. What factors can improve your own personal organisation?

Preparation for assessment

You have been invited for a formal public services interview. The interview panel has asked you to deliver a formal presentation on aspects of developing teams which you must deliver on the day. Your presentation must cover the following:

1. Describe the types of team that operate within a named uniformed public service organisation and their associated benefits. **P1**

2. Describe the different types of teamwork activities. **P2**

3. Describe ways of developing cohesive teams in the uniformed public services with reference to relevant theorists. **P3**

4. Analyse the importance of team cohesion in effective team performance, with examples from two named uniformed public services, with reference to relevant theorists. **M1**

5. Evaluate how team performance is monitored and team cohesion is encouraged within a named uniformed public service, with reference to relevant theories. **D1**

6. Identify the communication skills and personal organisation required when working in a team. **P4**

7. Describe how targets are set and team performance monitored. **P5**

8. Assess the value of different methods of monitoring the performance of a team. **M2**

9. Take part in five team activities, with support. **P6**

10. Take part in five team building activities confidently. **M3**

11. Evaluate your own performance in team activities, recommending personal development for future teamwork activities. **D2**

Grading criteria	Activity	Pg no.		
To achieve a pass grade the evidence must show that the learner is able to:			To achieve a merit grade the evidence must show that the learner is able to:	To achieve a distinction grade the evidence must show that the learner is able to:
P1 Describe the types of team that operate within a named uniformed public service organisation and their associated benefits	4.1	121		
P2 Describe the different types of teamwork activities	4.2	123		
P3 Describe ways of developing cohesive teams in the uniformed public services with reference to relevant theorists	4.3	131	**M1** Analyse the importance of team cohesion in effective team performance, with examples from two named uniformed public services, with reference to relevant theorists	**D1** Evaluate how team performance is monitored and team cohesion is encouraged within a named uniformed public service, with reference to relevant theorists
P4 Identify the communication skills and personal organisation required when working in a team	4.5	139		
P5 Describe how targets are set and team performance monitored	4.4	135	**M2** Assess the value of different methods of monitoring the performance of a team	
P6 Take part in five team activities with support	4.6	140	**M3** Take part in five team building activities confidently	**D2** Evaluate your own performance in team activities, recommending personal development for future teamwork activities

Understanding discipline within the uniformed public services

Introduction

Discipline is vital to the effectiveness of the uniformed public services. This unit explores the need for discipline, its role within the uniformed public services and the nature and influences of conformity and obedience. It looks at what constitutes personal self-discipline, the nature of authority and the role that legislation plays.

After completing this unit you should be able to achieve the following outcomes:

- Understand the need for discipline in the uniformed public services
- Know what conformity and obedience mean, highlighting their place in the uniformed public services
- Understand the importance of self-discipline in the uniformed public services
- Know the complex nature of authority in the uniformed public services.

Thinking points

Whether you choose a career in public services or not, exploring the subject of discipline will help you to understand how people respond to different situations.

Before you read on, answer the following questions – you could work individually or in small groups.

- What is discipline? Can you think of the different forms that discipline takes? Why is discipline needed?

- What does it mean when someone conforms? What is the difference between conformity and obedience?

Discipline is needed in the uniformed public services to ensure that each service is run efficiently – the hierarchical structure relies on it. Each service has a rank structure, with clearly defined roles and responsibilities. These are outlined below.

Table 5.1 shows the hierarchical rank structure of the emergency services, namely, the police, fire and ambulance with the most senior ranks at the top. The rank structure for the police service applies to territorial or county services. The higher ranks for the Metropolitan Police Service are structured slightly differently where the ranks from chief superintendent are: commander, deputy assistant commander, assistant commissioner, deputy commissioner and commissioner.

Police	Fire	Ambulance
Chief Constable		
Deputy Chief Constable		
Assistant Chief Constable	Brigade Manager	Duty Station Officer
Chief Superintendent	Area Manager	Team Leader
Superintendent	Group Manager	Emergency Care Practitioner
Chief Inspector	Station Manager	Paramedic
Inspector	Watch Manager	Emergency Medical Technician
Sergeant	Crew Manager	Emergency Medical Dispatcher
Police Constable	Fire Fighter	Ambulance Person

Table 5.1 The hierarchical rank structure of the emergency services

The police

All police officers, regardless of rank, are constables and they all have the same purpose and responsibility: the protection of life and property, the maintenance of the Queen's peace, the prevention and detection of crime and the prosecution of offenders against the peace.

A police constable has many duties to perform and these include: routine patrol, attending road traffic accidents, taking witness statements, investigating crime and dealing with sudden deaths.

A police sergeant's role is a supervisory one, often supervising a small team of constables, and although a sergeant is senior in rank in the hierarchical structure, they both have the same powers in executing their duty to the public.

Inspectors and chief inspectors are classed as middle managers and they are responsible for managing sergeants and constables in performing their duties. While most of their time is likely to be spent in a police station, where they organise and plan the work of their colleagues, they often go out on patrol in the company of sergeants and constables.

Police officers above the rank of chief inspector are regarded as senior management, with overall responsibility for policing a division (or district), or with responsibility for a certain area. For example, CID or Road Traffic will be commanded by a chief superintendent who, in turn, would be accountable to an assistant chief constable.

The fire service

It is the duty of all fire service personnel, regardless of rank, to protect life and property from fire or other hazards by carrying out rescues and preventing the escalation of hazards. They are also responsible for conducting risk assessments and advising on matters relating to public safety, as well as enforcing safety legislation.

A fire fighter works as part of a crew consisting of five or six fire fighters. Their duties include attending emergencies and dealing with fires, flooding, terrorist incidents, road and rail crashes, bomb alerts, dangerous spillages, as well as testing hydrants and checking emergency water supplies.

A crew manager is still a fire fighter but has the extra responsibility for supervising or managing the crew.

A watch manager is responsible for a 'watch', which is a number of crews that work on the same shift.

A station manager is in charge of all the watches (there could be four or five) that operate from a fire station. The station manager could be the fire officer in charge of an incident, unless it is a very large or serious incident where the fire officer in charge could be the brigade manager. The fire officer in charge of an incident is responsible for assessing the situation and deciding upon the best plan of action, directing the crews as necessary and completing a report of the incident.

The ambulance service

The ambulance service is accountable to the NHS and it is responsible for providing accident and emergency cover by responding to emergency 999 calls and major incidents. The ambulance service is also responsible for transporting non-emergency patients to and from their hospital appointments.

The armed forces

The British Army, Royal Navy (including the Royal Marines) and Royal Air Force are known collectively as the British Armed Forces and they are responsible for protecting the UK and its overseas territories by land, sea and air. They are also responsible for promoting the UK's security interests, as well as supporting international peacekeeping. Table 5.2 shows their hierarchical rank structures.

Army	Royal Navy	Royal Marines	Royal Air Force
Field Marshall			Marshall of the RAF
General	Admiral of the Fleet	General	Air Chief Marshall
Lieutenant General	Admiral	Lieutenant General	Air Marshall
Major General	Vice Admiral	Major General	Air Vice-Marshall
Brigadier	Rear Admiral	Brigadier	Air Commodore
Colonel	Commodore	Colonel	Group Captain
Lieutenant Colonel	Captain	Lieutenant Colonel	Wing Commander
Major	Commander	Major	Squadron Leader
Captain	Lieutenant Commander	Captain	Flight Lieutenant
Lieutenant	Lieutenant	Lieutenant	Flying Officer
2nd Lieutenant	Sub-Lieutenant	2nd Lieutenant	Warrant Officer
Warrant Officer Class 1	Warrant Officer Class 1	Warrant Officer Class 1	Flight Sergeant
Warrant Officer Class 2	Warrant Officer Class 2	Warrant Officer Class 2	Sergeant
Colour Sergeant	Chief Petty Officer	Colour Sergeant	Corporal
Sergeant	Petty Officer	Sergeant	Senior Technician
Corporal	Leading Rate	Corporal	Junior Technician
Lance Corporal	–	–	Senior Aircraftman/woman
Private	Able Rate	Marine	Leading Aircraftman/woman

Table 5.2 The rank structure of the Armed Forces

HM Prison Service

The role and responsibility of HM Prison Service is explicit in their mission statement:

> 'Her Majesty's Prison Service serves the public by keeping in custody those committed by the courts. Our duty is to look after them with humanity and help them lead law-abiding and useful lives in custody and after release.'

Source: www.hmprisonservice.gov.uk

HM Coastguard

HM Coastguard is an emergency organisation that is always on call and is responsible for performing search and rescue missions at sea, as well as assisting people in risk of injury or death on cliffs or the shoreline of the UK. HM Coastguard is responsible for coordinating and organising the necessary resources for dealing with emergency situations within the waters or shores of the UK.

Table 5.3 shows the rank structures of HM Prison Service and HM Coastguard.

HM Prison Service	HM Coastguard (full-time)
Chief Officer Grade 1	Regional operational Manager
Chief Officer Grade 2	Area Operations Manager
Assistant Chief Officer	District Operations Manager
Principal Prison Officer	Watch Manager/Sector Manager
Senior Prison Officer	Watch Officer
Prison Officer	Watch Assistant
	HM Coastguard (volunteers)
	Station Officer
	Deputy Station Officer
	Team Leader
	Auxiliary Coastguard

Table 5.3 The rank structures of HM Prison Service and HM Coastguard

HM Revenue and Customs

HM Revenue and Customs is responsible for the administration and collection of all taxes and duties in the UK including: income tax, National Insurance, VAT and excise duties (for example, tax on alcohol and tobacco). The organisation is also responsible for maintaining the security of the UK's frontiers in terms of preventing smuggling, as well as import and export prohibitions.

HM Revenue and Customs have the following ranks which are equivalent to the police ranks shown in Table 5.4.

Police rank	HM Revenue and Customs title
Sergeant	Anti-Smuggling Officer Cargo Team Member Drug Dog Unit Team Leader Excise Fraud Investigation Team Member Excise Verification Officer Local Value Added Tax Office Investigation Team Officer Passenger Services Division Team Member Road Fuel Testing Officer Specialist Investigator
Inspector/ Chief Inspector	Anti-Smuggling Team Leader Cargo Team Leader Excise Fraud Investigation Team Leader Excise Verification Unit Team Leader Passenger Services Division Team Manager Road Fuel Control Officer
Superintendent	Anti-Smuggling Manager Cargo Operational Manager Investigation Team Leader Passenger Services Division Operations Manager

Table 5.4 The ranks of HM Revenue and Customs

Private security services may have ranks, depending on the size of the firm and the nature of the security work.

Figure 5.1 A typical rank structure in a security firm

The need for discipline

'Obedience to authority' is one definition of discipline. However, discipline can be used in many different contexts. For example, it may be used as an order, a deterrent, a threat, or to control or train, and it may or may not have the authority of a written law to reinforce it.

Rules and regulations

For any organisation to operate efficiently there must be a system of **rules** and **regulations**, which are strictly followed, particularly if an organisation serves the public.

Key terms

Rule A principle to which an action should conform. Rules may be written laws or they could be customs or codes of conduct that have been adopted by a particular society or culture.

Regulation A direction given by someone in authority. For example, there are many regulations that govern the conduct of serving police officers. Disciplinary action may be taken against someone who infringes the regulations.

To ensure that rules are followed correctly, organisations impose a penalty on those who break them. This could take several forms including verbal reprimand, loss of privileges, suspension or dismissal. Penalties are usually fixed and written into the rules that govern conduct, in the same way that penalties are fixed by law for certain crimes.

In this sense, discipline is a way of making people conform to rules and regulations. It is important to note that discipline does not mean the same as punishment; discipline is a way of producing efficiency, uniformity and order and is applicable to all personnel in the uniformed services, irrespective of rank.

Why orders need to be followed

During the course of normal duty for any of the public services, decisions have to be made about many complex and potentially dangerous situations. Delegation of tasks, clear instructions and the ability to follow orders are all key to ensuring that unnecessary risks are avoided and that efficiency and public confidence are maintained.

Failure or refusal to carry out a lawful order not only undermines that authority but it also means the service is less efficient, resulting in disorganisation and confusion. To avoid this happening, the uniformed public services have codes of discipline to ensure that lawful orders are obeyed.

In the event of a house fire, where fire fighters concentrate on extinguishing the fire and rescuing anyone trapped inside, the watch manager considers the broader picture and assesses the risk of the fire spreading to adjacent premises. If he or she decides the risk is high,

▲ Discipline ensures that colleagues and the public are not put at unnecessary risk

Transporting troops, supplies and equipment requires meticulous planning and the maintenance of order

then they could give an order to the lower ranks for the evacuation of neighbouring premises.

Discipline in this context, then, is needed to bind personnel to the authority of lawful orders and to ensure that colleagues are supported in the lawful execution of their duty.

Maintenance of order

We have already seen how discipline may be used to ensure that rules and regulations are followed, as well as orders. Where order is required, that is, when something needs to be done in a systematic or orderly fashion, discipline can be used to achieve it. There may be written rules and regulations that govern orderly conduct (for example, there may be certain rules regarding making a noise after a certain time in barracks).

In the public services, it is not unusual for large numbers of personnel to be transported to a particular area – an area that is foreign to the personnel and even to those in charge of them.

Consider this

When you have taken part in a fire drill, either at school, college or work, you will have been told not to run or panic. If you did run or panic, which rule would you be breaking? Would it be a written rule or would you be going against good advice?

Consider this

In 2003, the UK government sent 45,000 Armed Forces personnel to fight in the Gulf War. Considering the large number of personnel and the huge amount of supplies required, what would be the logistical challenges of transporting them safely? How would discipline ensure these challenges were overcome effectively?

Rewards

A reward is generally regarded as some kind of positive reinforcement for performing a good deed; it is a token of appreciation of someone's efforts. In the Armed Forces, for example, personnel may be granted extended leave after a tour of duty abroad. This is a way of saying thank you for the personal sacrifices they have made by being away from their friends and families for long periods. Where a member of the uniformed public services performs a task of a heroic nature, something that is beyond the call of duty, then their reward could be in the form of a celebrated medal.

However, it is not only those individuals who have performed especially good deeds who can expect to be rewarded. By merely performing their duty according to their contract and behaving appropriately, members of the uniformed public services can expect recognition. This could be in the form of good conduct medals and long-service medals, as well as medals to reflect their contribution at a particular conflict, for instance in Afghanistan.

In this context, discipline can be seen as a positive reinforcer; a way of training members of the uniformed public services to behave correctly by rewarding their good behaviour.

Punishment

If a reward is the positive reinforcement for good deeds and proper behaviour, then punishment is the negative reinforcement for wrongful acts, such as neglect of duty or inappropriate behaviour. In each service, a system of rules and regulations ensures that *all* members behave correctly and professionally. Failure to comply with these rules and regulations could result in punishment.

Discipline through punishment can take several forms, some of which may include confinement to quarters, cancellation of leave, reduction in pay, reduction in rank, reprimand or dishonourable discharge. The purpose of punishment is to show the person who has committed a wrongful act, through negative reinforcement, the error of their ways

Consider this

As a new recruit in the Army, you are undergoing your initial training. You are looking forward to your first weekend leave and spending some time with your friends and family. However, on three occasions you have failed to observe the lights-out rule and as a punishment your Commanding Officer has cancelled your weekend leave. All your friends are going home because they have conformed to the rules and regulations.

How would this make you feel? Would it make you obey rules in future?

Consequences of a lack of discipline in the public services

Part of the effectiveness of the uniformed public services is that all members comply with rules and regulations. Without discipline, there would be no means of bringing to account those members of the services who did not abide by them. The same could be said of those who do not follow orders – it would be impossible to impose punishment. The rank structure would be pointless and promotion to the higher ranks would be worthless because the higher ranks would have no authority over the lower ranks to ensure that they complied with the rules of the organisation.

Take it further

In 2004, during the conflict with Iraq, several US soldiers humiliated some Iraqi prisoners by abusing them and publishing photographs. Look for information about this event on the internet (a sample website appears below). Think about what these actions did for the reputation of the US forces.

http://en.wikipedia.org/wiki/Abu_Ghraib_prisoner_abuse

Our uniformed public services are part of the public sector and are therefore ultimately responsible to the public. Discipline, hierarchy and structure, rules and regulations all play their part in maintaining accountability and public trust.

Effect on social order and anarchy

Social order is maintained in the UK because of the efficiency and dedication of our uniformed public services in enforcing the laws of the land. Social disorder can easily lead to **anarchy**.

Key terms

Anarchy This literally means 'without rule' and it is used to describe a state of political or social disorder.

■ In summary

Discipline may be used to:

- ensure rules and regulations are followed
- ensure orders are followed
- maintain a hierarchy of authority
- maintain social order
- ensure loyalty and a sense of duty.

▲ Lack of discipline in the uniformed public services could lead to civil disturbance or anarchy

Consider this

Think about the following questions then discuss them with your group.

- How is social order maintained in an orderly society?
- Why could lack of discipline in the uniformed public services lead to social disorder and anarchy?
- What would society with no social order be like?
- If we lived in a society without rules, then how would we protect our families, our home and our property?
- If anarchy prevailed, how could we bring wrongdoers to account?

The role of discipline

Team spirit

Many young people aspire to join the uniformed public services because of what the services have to offer in terms of security, promotion prospects, adventure, job satisfaction and a sense of belonging. However, the demanding nature of the work means that gaining entry and acceptance is not easy. It requires certain attributes such as courage, physical fitness, reliability, determination, integrity and confidence. Once you have been accepted and earned your uniform, you will have a sense of pride knowing that not everyone is fortunate enough to be accepted and you will have a feeling of camaraderie with other colleagues which is built on mutual trust, respect, loyalty, pride and the interests of the service into which you have been selected. This is known as *esprit de corps* or team spirit – and should be preserved by introducing rules and regulations. For example, the Police Discipline Regulations ensure that officers have a duty to act in a manner that will not bring the reputation of the police service into disrepute. They must not discredit the police service, or any of its members, whether on or off duty.

Sense of duty and honour

If you choose to join the public services, you do so because a particular service appeals to you. For example, you might like the prospect of a career that is challenging and varied, with good promotion prospects and security. Whatever your reasons, you must not lose sight of the fact that there is a job to do. You must acknowledge that there is a sense of duty and that life within the public services is not one big adventure with no mundane tasks involved.

As a uniformed public service employee, the manner in which you carry out your duties can affect many people, sometimes with serious consequences. Whatever your role within a uniformed public service, you have a duty to your colleagues, the service and the public. While life in the uniformed public services may appear to be glamorous and adventurous most of the time, there are other times when it may seem tedious and unrewarding but you must still perform your duty to the best of your ability.

Serving the public

Each of the uniformed public services has evolved to serve the public. You have only to look at the mission statements of the services to see that the public is the focus of the services' aims and objectives. For example, part of the police and fire services' roles include protecting life and property, while the Armed Forces are there to defend the UK, its overseas territories, its people and interests.

By committing yourself to work within a service you undertake to serve the public by protecting them and looking after their interests in a courteous manner, without prejudice or reward. This is to say that you are expected to treat everyone as equal, regardless of race, colour or creed, and without seeking financial or personal gain. For example, you would not expect a fire fighter to give preference to someone trapped in a burning building because they had promised some kind of reward. In this context, discipline has the role of ensuring that the public is served in a fair and courteous manner.

Rules/procedures/policies/legislation

We have already seen that without rules, regulations and legislation there can be no enforcement of social order. Similarly, if rules and regulations do not govern the conduct of members of the uniformed public services, then discipline cannot be encouraged or enforced.

The rules of conduct for the Armed Forces and the police service make it clear that, amongst other things, members are encouraged to remain professional, loyal to each other, their service and the public and not to bring their service into disrepute.

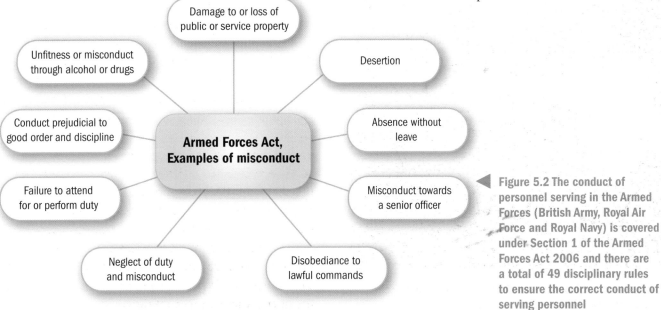

Figure 5.2 The conduct of personnel serving in the Armed Forces (British Army, Royal Air Force and Royal Navy) is covered under Section 1 of the Armed Forces Act 2006 and there are a total of 49 disciplinary rules to ensure the correct conduct of serving personnel

The police service has a Code of Professional Standards for police officers, drawn up in 2006 by a working party of the Police Advisory Board. The new code sets out ten principles that govern the conduct of serving police officers. These are listed below.

1. Police officers are personally responsible and accountable for their actions or omissions.
2. Police officers are honest, act with integrity and do not compromise or abuse their position.
3. Police officers obey lawful orders and refrain from carrying out any orders that they know, or ought to know, are unlawful.
4. When police officers use force it is only to the extent that is necessary and reasonable to obtain a legitimate objective.
5. Police officers do not abuse their powers or authority and respect the rights of all individuals. Police officers act with self-control and tolerance, treating members of the public and colleagues with respect and courtesy.
6. Police officers act with fairness and impartiality. They do not discriminate unlawfully on the grounds of sex, race, colour, language, religion or belief, political or other opinion, national or social origin, association with a national minority, disability, age, sexual orientation, property, birth or other status.
7. Police officers treat information with respect and access or disclose it only for a legitimate police purpose.
8. Police officers when on duty or presenting themselves for duty are fit to carry out their responsibilities.
9. Police officers on duty act in a professional way. Police officers do not behave in a manner which brings, or is likely to bring, discredit on the police service or that undermines or is likely to undermine public confidence in the police, whether on or off duty.
10. Police officers challenge and, when appropriate, take action or report breaches of this code and the improper conduct of colleagues.

Now answer the following questions:

1. **A police officer is struggling to arrest a man who has just assaulted a shopkeeper. You see the police officer kneeling on the detainee's back in order to place the handcuffs on him. The man is shouting and complaining that the officer is hurting him but the officer continues to kneel on his back while wrestling to overcome him. Has the officer contravened the fourth principle? If not, why not?**

2. **You are having a drink in a café when you overhear two off-duty police officers talking about a woman they have just arrested for shoplifting. You happen to know the woman they are talking about. Which principle will the officers have breached?**

3. **Give three examples of when a police officer would be in breach of principle 8 with a relevant explanation for each.**

Assessment activity 5.1

Design a leaflet in which you describe the different applications of discipline within the uniformed public services. You should ensure that you cover the following three sections:

1. *Uniformed services*
   The hierarchical command and rank structure of each service including: police, fire, ambulance, Army, Royal Navy, Royal Marines, Royal Air Force, HM Prison Service, HM Revenue and Customs, HM Coast Guard and private security services.

2. *The need for discipline*
   Definitions of discipline, the necessity for rules and regulations, why orders need to be followed, the maintenance of order, rewards, punishment, the consequences of a lack of discipline in the public services and the effects on social order, and anarchy.

3. *The role of discipline*
   Team spirit, sense of duty and honour (to your service, to your colleagues and to the public), serving the public, rules/procedures/policies/legislation in the uniformed public services to encourage discipline.

P1 **M1**

Grading tips

P1 To achieve this grade you need to show the rank structure of the uniformed public services listed in section 1, as well as using the content in sections 2 and 3 to describe the need for and role of discipline. Your leaflet should describe the need for and role of discipline in the uniformed public services.

M1 M1 is an extension of P1. As well as describing, you have to analyse, which means you have to go into greater depth and explain the sections in detail, reasoning and giving conclusions.

D1 D1 is a continuation of M1 but you need to weigh up the positive and negative aspects of discipline and say what impact this might have in the uniformed public services. However, you cannot achieve the full D1 until you have included self-discipline, which is dealt with at the end of section 3 on pages 168–70.

Conformity

What exactly do we mean when we say that someone is conforming? Since the 1930s, psychologists have been interested in the nature of conformity and obedience and one psychologist, Crutchfield (1955), attempted to formulate a definition of conformity as: 'yielding to group pressure'(i.e. giving in to the demands of a group). Much later, Zimbardo and Leippe (1991) proposed a definition as:

> 'A change in belief or behaviour in response to real or imagined group pressure when there is no direct request to comply with the group nor any reason to justify the behaviour change.'

> *Source:* Cited in Gross, R., McIlveen, R. (1988)
> *Psychology A New Introduction:* Hodder & Stoughton: Oxford

A summary of the key concepts of conformity would be:

- There is no clear or direct requirement to act in a certain way.
- It is normally peers or equals who influence us.
- The emphasis is on acceptance.
- Conformity regulates the behaviour among those of equal status.
- The behaviour adopted is similar to that of peers.

Studies have shown that conformity is influenced when a person:

- has low self-esteem
- is worried about social relationships
- has a strong need for social approval
- is attracted towards other group members
- is afraid of ridicule.

Consider this

In terms of the points just mentioned, when have you conformed and why?

Compliance

When we comply with something we act in accordance with a request or command to perform a task; such a request or command could be spoken or unspoken. When you have completed the task requested or ordered, you have performed an act of compliance. Members of the uniformed public services comply with common practices every day, possibly without even realising it. For example, lower ranks salute their officers as a mark of respect and the officers return the salute – it is a common practice. Another common practice in the uniformed public services is for males to have short hair and females, if they have long hair, to have it tied back. However, when you comply with certain practices (which could be practices that you are bound to follow by law or simply practices that have evolved through tradition) you may be said to be conforming, simply because some of the key elements that apply to conformity also apply to compliance.

The key thing to remember is that with conformity there is no explicit request.

Theory into practice

Look at the following examples and decide which of them refers to conformity or compliance (or both).

1. Jamie was smoking a cigarette at the bus stop but his friends started coughing and grimacing with disgust so he put it out.
2. Sally was new to the area and wanted to make friends. She noticed that many of the girls in the neighbourhood had had their tongues pierced and she believed that by having her tongue pierced she would be accepted as a friend.
3. Scott was a new recruit in the Royal Marines and although his hair was short he noticed his friends had had their heads shaved. The next day he went to the barbers and had his head shaved.

▲ Social integration allows us to develop our interactive skills, to communicate, to evaluate and to compromise

Social norms

It is a well-known fact that humans are social creatures, who like to share beliefs and attitudes and live in societies. When we are integrated into society we feel that we belong – we have a sense of purpose – and this gives us a sense of being in control of our lives, which makes us happy and confident.

However, for those who are unable to socially integrate, feelings such as loneliness, failure, vulnerability and deficiency may result, or it might simply be the case that a person is not comfortable with a particular culture and so chooses another one. Some psychologists believe that:

'Every culture contains a set of ideas and beliefs about the nature of human beings, what motivates them to act, the way they perceive the world, how their minds work, and the emotions that are natural to them.'

Source: Hewitt, J.P. (1998) *The Myth of Self-Esteem: Finding Happiness and Solving Problems in America*: St Martin's Press: New York

What is it that influences us into adopting social norms?

According to psychologists Deutsch and Gerard (1955) there are two main types of social influence that affect conformity, namely, Informational Social Influence (ISI) and Normative Social Influence (NSI).

ISI is the theory that we have a basic need to weigh up information and opinions but when we are in a strange environment we are susceptible because we don't have the information that makes us feel comfortable and in control. Instead, we have to pick up on the thoughts and behaviour of others as a measure of the behaviour that is expected of us. In other words, we turn to others for direction and tend to behave according to the majority. For example, suppose you were waiting to cross the road with a crowd of people at a pedestrian crossing and you couldn't see the lights because someone was obstructing your view. When the crowd begins to cross the road, you join them without even checking to see if the lights are in your favour. You look to others for guidance of how to behave and you tend to conform to the behaviour of others. If you are familiar with an environment, then you are less likely to rely on the behaviour of the majority, and, hence, you are less likely to conform.

The NSI theory claims that we conform because we have a fundamental need to be accepted by others and we may only be accepted by making a good impression and, usually, this will be by saying what the majority want to hear or behaving in a manner that meets their approval. It's difficult to imagine succeeding in a job interview by saying 'no' and frowning, when you ought to be saying 'yes' and smiling.

Closely related to ISI and NSI is the theory of internalisation – when a private belief or opinion is consistent with public belief and opinion. However, in Asch-type experiments (see page 162), the naïve participants faced conflicts and complied publicly with the stooges but what they said publicly was not necessarily what they believed privately.

Abrams and others (1990) argue for a social influence known as Referential Social Influence. Social influence occurs when we see ourselves as belonging to a group that possesses the same beliefs and characteristics and uncertainty arises when we find ourselves in disagreement with group members. In other words, it is more likely that we will take notice of and be influenced by a group with which we have an affinity than one with which we don't. When we categorise ourselves in groups in this way, we are concerned, above anything else, with upholding the norms of the group.

The role of self-esteem

Do you have a good opinion of yourself? Are you confident? If you can answer 'yes' to both of these questions, then, according to the dictionary definition, you have high self-esteem, that is, you consider yourself to have self-respect and a sense of worth.

Self-esteem comes from the way we are seen to conform to, or comply with, norms. Our behaviour is guided by comments such as, 'Well done, that was a really good effort' or 'Perhaps it would be better if you did it this way'. By receiving positive feedback, our self-esteem rises and we gain confidence in our own ability.

If you lack self-confidence or self-respect, you may be tempted to act out of character in order to gain the respect of others. For example, impressionable teenagers might decide to take up smoking or drinking alcohol because that is what the members of their group do. While this will harm them physically, it will show the group that they are conforming, which may persuade the group to accept them as a member.

However, this is not to say that all people who conform are suffering from low self-esteem or some kind of anxiety. On the contrary, it is believed by many psychologists that conformity to socially accepted demands is perfectly normal and is one of the main ways in which we develop our character and recognise our role in society.

Low self-esteem has been described as an illness in which people have negative perceptions of themselves and are more likely to feel frustrated and out of control in their lives. This may result in people losing confidence or having a reduced self-awareness.

The purpose of uniforms

It is generally considered that uniforms are a symbol of unity, pride and authority, especially those worn by public service employees. They are instantly recognisable and members of the public can relate to the personnel who wear them. But some uniforms can convey power (for example, the Army helmet) while other uniforms are used to identify professional authority, such as a doctor's white coat. Powerful institutions such as the Ministry of Defence and the police invest officers with authority and this is symbolised in their uniform to

Consider this

Think of four types of uniform, outside of the public services, that may be worn by members of a profession or voluntary organisation.
- What do those uniforms symbolise?
- How do you think members of the public would view those who wear uniform?
- Does wearing a uniform mean conformity?

▲ Uniforms are worn with pride and honour

indicate the hierarchy of authority to the members of that institution.

Uniforms also offer protection and security to the officers who wear them. For example, fire fighters require special protective equipment as part of their uniform because of the nature of their work, as do the police when dealing with riots and the Armed Forces when serving on active duty.

The relevance of conformity in the public services

We have seen that conformity, from a psychological perspective, means to be accepted. In a general sense, it also means to comply with or be in accordance with something. In the uniformed public services, both senses of conformity are relevant.

Every member of the uniformed public services wants to feel accepted and that they belong to a team of professionals, otherwise they would not have wanted to join that particular service. Teamwork is an essential quality in any of the services and is vital in achieving effective outcomes. We have already mentioned team spirit, together with the need for discipline to ensure that it continues. If one member of the team does not conform to the norms of the team, it is likely to disrupt the dynamics of the team, making it inefficient or perhaps bringing the team, or even the service, into disrepute. It is in the best interests of the other members, therefore, to deal with the member who is not conforming and remind them that if they wish to continue to be accepted then they must conform to the ethos of the team.

Obedience

In the uniformed public services you are expected to obey orders and commands from those in authority.

In some respects, obedience is similar to conformity in that it is a form of compliance. Unlike conformity, obedience means that you must comply with orders and commands; you have no choice. If you do not obey a command from a higher authority, then you are likely to face disciplinary procedures for disobedience, otherwise known as insubordination.

Remember!

- With conformity there is no requirement to behave in a specific way.
- With obedience you are ordered to do something by someone in higher authority, whereas with conformity, the influence comes from your peers or equals.
- Obedience involves social power and status, whereas conformity is generally seen as a psychological need to be accepted by others.

Obedience as an act

Obedience is the act of obeying orders given by someone in authority and if you are obedient then you are carrying out, or willing to carry out, those orders. For example, if a private in the Army stood to attention on parade, on the orders of the sergeant, then the private would be said to be performing an act of obedience.

Obedience as a practice or quality

Obedience in the uniformed public services is an essential practice as it makes the service efficient and disciplined and able to respond quickly to any situation. It develops mutual trust and respect because all those involved in the organisation know that they can depend on each other to achieve their objectives effectively by playing their part. Without the practice of obedience the uniformed public services would be in chaos and the hierarchical structure within the service would have no authority.

If you are thinking of joining one of the services, you should ask yourself if you possess the quality of obedience because without it you would find a career in the services very difficult. You may have to work at this quality, especially if you are the type of person who has personality clashes or you dislike being told what to do. Obedience does not mean you are weak willed or cannot make decisions for yourself. It means that you know where you fit into the service and that you trust those in authority, who have the experience to make the correct decisions for you to carry out for the good of the service. After all, it is the rank of the person in authority that you must respect, not necessarily the person who holds the rank.

Following orders

Orders are commands given by someone in authority. Following orders is an essential part of the uniformed public services. You should remember that orders are given by those in authority with the intention of reaching an objective efficiently and effectively. The objective may be simple and uncomplicated, for instance, the refuelling of a fire engine at the end of a watch to make sure it is ready for the next watch. On the other hand, the objective could be something as complex as, say, responding to an incident like the London bombings. Each order is given for a reason and no matter how simple or how complex an order is it must be followed to prevent serious consequences to your colleagues, the service and members of the public.

Verbal commands are not the only type of orders. In the uniformed public services, the written rules and regulations concerning the conduct of personnel and the manner in which procedures are carried out are called 'standing orders.' All uniformed public service personnel should be aware of and follow standing orders. Failure to do so would be a disciplinary offence.

Conscious and unconscious obedience

When you are awake and aware of what you are doing you are said to be conscious; you are consciously aware of your actions. If you were to try and remember your actions a short time later, then you would probably remember what you did very clearly. However, if you were to perform a task so often that it became routine – a habit – then you might not remember so clearly. For example, if you had to pack eggs into boxes for eight hours a day, you would probably not recollect packing, say, the eighty-third box because the task had become so mundane that you were performing the task out of habit. Therefore, instead of you being conscious of packing the eggs into boxes, you were unconscious of doing so.

Obedience in the uniformed public services can be conscious or unconscious, depending on whether the obedience is routine or not. For example, if you were in the Royal Marines and you had followed orders to search a series of caves in Afghanistan, then that would be conscious obedience because you wouldn't normally search caves as part of your job. But when you were at the training camp doing your initial training you would have reacted to so many orders that they just became routine and you would have followed them unconsciously.

Compliance

Compliance has already been explored on page 156. As a member of the services you have to act – or comply – in accordance with orders from a higher authority. By demonstrating compliance you are showing that you are obedient and following orders as instructed.

Status as a factor in obedience

Within the uniformed public services, obedience status depends on your rank within the hierarchy of authority.

You have to obey those of senior rank, while those of a lower rank have to obey you. The higher the rank, the more responsibility you have for making decisions and ensuring your orders are carried out.

Status in the uniformed public services is a factor in ensuring obedience because if you have ambition and want promotion, you have to show that you can obey orders, just as all those of the higher ranks have done. You cannot reach a position of authority and expect the lower ranks to obey your commands if you cannot demonstrate obedience.

It is not only the lower ranks of the public services which have a role of obedience to play within the hierarchy of authority – society also gives its members a certain status. For example, as children we are taught to respect our elders and obey authority. The same is true of parents where the father might be regarded as the head of the family and brothers and sisters are ranked according to age. We are also conditioned, from an early age, to be obedient and comply with requests from those we perceive to be in authority. For example, children will wait at the side of the road until the school crossing patrol warden waves them across.

Consider this

Think of six occasions where you have obeyed the instruction or request of someone you have perceived to be in authority.

1. Age and sex groupings (infant, old, male, female)

5. Status groupings (manager, team leader)

2. Family groupings (father, sister)

4. Common interest groupings (sports clubs, patrons of public houses)

3. Occupational groupings (teacher, lawyer)

With Linton's groupings (see Figure 5.3), unlike the public services, there is no law that binds a member of the group to an act of obedience. Rather, the obedience status has been derived from tradition or culture.

◄ Figure 5.3 Linton (1945) identifies five different social groupings which all have different status and expectations

Fear

Fear is a strong influence in ensuring obedience within the uniformed public services, both physically and psychologically. Disobedience could lead to a reduction in rank or pay, loss of privileges, dishonourable discharge, suspension from duty or even imprisonment.

Apart from the fear of punishment, there is the fear that failing to obey orders could stand in the way of your career development. Furthermore, you may fear that you will be letting down your team by failing to obey orders, thus weakening the strength of the team and bringing about a feeling that you are no longer part of it.

Reward

Unlike the private sector, the uniformed public services do not receive financial rewards for performing their duty. For example, you would not expect a fire fighter to receive a bonus for the amount of fires they have fought in a week; they do their job regardless. However, as mentioned earlier, members are positively reinforced with medals for good or heroic conduct, or extended leave after a tour of duty abroad. Members don't join the services to be rewarded for doing their job; they are rewarded by the personal satisfaction they receive from doing their job well.

Love

While many people are obedient as a mark of love for the people they are obeying, this is not usually the case in the uniformed public services. A different kind of love influences obedience in the services – it is a love for their service and the camaraderie within it that influences obedience. This affection for the team and the service has developed as a result of obedience to duty.

Respect

If you respect someone you value them or admire them for what they have achieved. In the uniformed public services promotion is gained through merit, that is, loyalty to the service, hard work, experience and displaying the kinds of qualities needed for leadership. As a member of the uniformed public services you must respect the rank of seniority and what it stands for, even though you might not personally know the officer carrying the higher rank. Some people say that 'you can't respect someone until they've earned it' but in the uniformed public services respect goes with the rank because it has certainly been earned. Respect in the uniformed public services is therefore an influence on obedience.

The relevance of obedience in the uniformed public services

Just as conformity is relevant in its own way to the uniformed public services, so is obedience. When you obey an order you may be doing something that can affect a large number of people in a positive or negative way, depending on the order. For example, you may be ordered to destroy enemy buildings, which would have a negative effect on the enemy but a positive effect on your colleagues and your service. You must always remember that when obeying orders you are doing so for the good of yourself, your colleagues, the service and the public. By disobeying orders you are not only being selfish and risking disciplinary proceedings, you are letting your colleagues, service and public down. Nor should you forget that you joined a uniformed public service for the good of the service and the public, not just because it offered you a promising career.

Without obedience in the uniformed public services there would be no teamwork, team spirit, trust, respect or authority; all the things that make the uniformed public services what they are.

Research studies

Psychologists have conducted many conformity and obedience experiments, the results of which are quite remarkable. Four well-known studies are presented below.

1 The Asch Paradigm

Asch (1951) wanted to show that people's behaviour was a response to group pressure, either real or imagined. The test was a line judgement task, which involved participants being presented with two cards: one card

Milgram was astonished by the result of his experiments: every teacher administered at least 300 volts and 65 per cent administered 450 volts (a possibly lethal amount). He concluded:

> '[T]he most fundamental lesson of our study is that ordinary people, simply doing their jobs, and without any particular hostility on their part, can become agents in a terrible destructive process.'

Source: Cited in Gross, R. (1988)
Psychology A New Introduction: Hodder & Stoughton: Oxford

3 Zimbardo: the prison simulation experiment

In 1971, the psychologist Philip Zimbardo investigated human response to captivity. He advertised for student volunteers to take part in a simulated prison experiment. After being judged to be emotionally stable and physically fit, 25 male volunteers were told that they would be randomly selected to be either a prisoner or a guard, though all of them had stated a preference to be a prisoner.

One Sunday morning, the 'prisoners' were unexpectedly arrested and handcuffed by the local police and taken to a police station where they were searched, fingerprinted, charged, and taken to prison blindfolded.

The basement of Stanford University had been adapted to resemble a prison. Upon arrival, the detainees were stripped, skin-searched, issued with bedding, uniform and an identification number. They were chained and wore nylon stockings to simulate shaven heads. They were referred to only by their identification numbers and were kept in a cell shared by two others, only to be allowed out for meals, exercise, toilet and work.

The guards wore khaki uniforms and silver reflector sunglasses to prevent eye contact. They carried clubs, whistles, handcuffs and keys to the main gate, and had complete control over the prisoners. The prisoners assumed a passive nature as the guards became aggressive towards them, with roll calls in the middle of the night, for instance, to disrupt the prisoners' sleep.

As the prisoners seemed to lose control of their lives, the guards appeared to enjoy their role. One guard was quoted as saying, 'Power can be a great pleasure'. However, because of severe depression, fits of rage and uncontrollable crying, one prisoner was released after just 36 hours, with three others leaving shortly after with the same symptoms.

Although the experiment had been scheduled for two weeks it was terminated after only six days because of the emotional deterioration of the prisoners, who had initially been selected because of their emotional stability.

Source: Cited in Gross, R. (1988)
Psychology A New Introduction: Hodder & Stoughton: Oxford

4 Hofling's nurses

In 1966, Hofling *et al* conducted an experiment to see if nurses would deliberately cause harm to a patient if ordered to do so by a doctor. Hofling spoke to 22 nurses and told them about reports of a new drug, Astroten, which indicated that it was very toxic. In fact, the drug Astroten was made up by the research team; it didn't really exist. After speaking to the nurses, Hofling asked for a doctor who was familiar to the nurses to telephone each of them in turn while they were working on the wards. The doctor was told to instruct the nurses to administer 20mg of Astroten to a patient on the ward. 21 out of the 22 nurses did administer the drug (which was nothing more than a glucose substitute) in spite of the following factors:

- the nurses had been told that the maximum dose of the drug was 10mg
- hospital policy stated that drugs shouldn't be prescribed over the phone
- the drug was not on the ward stock list.

How do these studies apply to the uniformed public services? With reference to the studies of Asch, Milgram and Hofling we could conclude that most people will obey, without question, those who appear to be in authority. It seems to be the case that people have been conditioned to obey authority. Certainly, nurses (as in Hofling's study) would find nothing odd in carrying out the orders of a doctor, when that is what they are accustomed to. Personnel in other uniformed public services are also used to obeying authority without question and perhaps they feel secure in the knowledge that, if anything were to go wrong, they can say that they were only following orders.

Two of the studies tended to show obedience – the subjects were specifically asked to perform a task, which they did, and this is applicable to all the uniformed public services.

The other two tasks tended to highlight conformity – the subjects acted of their own volition, as opposed to being asked to perform a specific act of obedience. While Asch's experiment showed that individuals did not want to feel left out of the group, Zimbardo's showed a certain bonding of like-minded individuals who tended to abuse their power by bullying those in their charge. It is worth remembering that while there was no evidence to suggest it, some of the guards might have joined in the bullying because of fear of ridicule from the group. In other words, it is possible that they were conforming to the behaviour of others.

You should remember that the experiments were precisely that, experiments; it could be argued that the subjects were not behaving as they might under normal circumstances because they knew they were taking part in an experiment.

Theory into practice

In order to see if any or all of these studies apply to the uniformed public services, you will need to show that similar traits are demonstrated by personnel in the services.

If you look at the following websites you will find some strikingly similar traits of members of the uniformed public services that suggest the studies do, indeed, apply:

http://news.bbc.co.uk/1/hi/england/west_yorkshire/3565031.stm

http://news.bbc.co.uk/1/hi/uk/257693.stm

http://news.bbc.co.uk/1/hi/uk/2372983.stm

Take it further

- What was each experiment designed to prove?
- What were the similarities of the experiments?
- Which experiment did you find convincing and why?
- What are your conclusions from the experiments?
- How do they apply to the uniformed public services today?

Assessment activity 5.2

Prepare a presentation to explain conformity and obedience and how they are expressed in the uniformed public services, together with the things that influence them. You should also describe three research studies which investigate conformity and obedience.

Make sure that your presentation covers the following three sections:

1. *Conformity*
   Compliance with common practices; social norms; the role of self-esteem; the purpose of uniforms; the relevance of conformity in the uniformed public services.

2. *Obedience*
   As an act, practice or quality; following orders; conscious and unconscious obedience; compliance; status as a factor in obedience; influences, for example, fear, reward, love, respect; the relevance of obedience in the uniformed public services.

3. *Research studies*
   For example, Asch, Milgram, Hofling and Zimbardo.

P3 P4 M3 D2

Grading tips

P3 **P4** You must make clear what is meant by conformity and obedience and how they are used in the uniformed public services, together with the factors that influence them. For the research studies, you could describe three of the four case studies highlighted in this outcome.

M3 If you analyse the three studies on conformity and obedience and apply them to the uniformed public services you should achieve this grade. You could do this by explaining them in more detail and looking for similarities within the uniformed public services. For example, you might think that Hofling's nurses and Milgram's electric shock experiment showed blind obedience, so that is one aspect you could explore. Zimbardo's and Asch's experiments tended to show conformity within a group, so think of the connections with the uniformed public services.

D2 If you critically evaluate the positive and negative effects of blind obedience to authority you could be on your way to achieving this grade. You need to go into detail and criticise the positive and negative effects as much as you can. However, you cannot fully achieve this until you have included the various types and natures of authority, which is covered at the end of section 4 on pages 177–8.

Self-discipline

Self-discipline is another form of discipline and an essential quality for a member of any service. Self-discipline can be defined as the ability to apply yourself in the correct manner, including controlling yourself and your feelings. To appreciate the qualities needed for self-discipline fully, you need to understand the following areas.

Personal grooming and presentation

If you can't be bothered to take a pride in your own appearance, what message does that convey to others?

Would you like to eat in a restaurant if the waitress had dirty fingernails? In the uniformed public services, where members of the public may be looking to you for help or guidance, it is particularly important that you are of smart appearance. People form impressions and opinions about us from the way we appear to them, so if you want to create the right impression it is important that you are correctly presented.

Punctuality

In order to run efficiently and effectively, organisations have to keep to tight schedules and this means being governed by time. In the public services punctuality is

▲ When you wear the uniform of a public service you are representing your organisation and people will judge the organisation by your appearance

vital so that, at any time, someone can say where, when and how many people are on duty. At the beginning of a shift, public service personnel are briefed about any major issues that may have arisen, for example, police officers would be kept updated about a missing child. If you are late for a shift and miss the briefing, then you are preventing that organisation from operating at its full efficiency. What would happen if everyone was late for their shift?

Time management

In the uniformed public services you have to manage your time by prioritising your workload and ensuring that important reports and documents are produced on time, even if this means rearranging your work schedule or social time. For example, the emergency services are often involved in dealing with serious accidents or major incidents, which are very time consuming. Certain reports have to be completed, statements must be taken and enquiries followed up. If there are fatalities, then HM Coroner needs to be informed, as well as relatives and friends. The complex demands of such incidents mean that any other plans you might have must take second place because the matter that you are dealing with has taken priority.

Reliability

An organisation is only as reliable as its members. Uniformed public service employees must be reliable, so that an employee can be depended upon. Forgetfulness or dishonesty can bring disrepute to the entire service, thus destroying public trust and confidence.

Attendance

There may be times when we have to do something we are not looking forward to – perhaps a presentation in front of class or an important examination. It would be easy to make excuses and convince ourselves that we are not well enough to perform the task in hand and just not bother to turn up.

In the public services you are part of a team and non-attendance, without good reason, lets yourself and the team down. Previous hard work – for example, painstaking enquiries and observations – may be in vain if you don't attend on the day an arrest is to be made. Plans cannot be made for a whole team when one member has a poor record of attendance.

Composure

Can you keep your head in a crisis? As a member of the public services, you will be the person to whom people turn for help, information and attention. You can only give help and bring about order by remaining calm and thinking clearly.

◀ Composure is one of several essential qualities of self-discipline

Attitude

Can you show sympathy and understanding, even when you feel frustrated and annoyed? Police officers have to be fair, unbiased and courteous and must not allow their personal problems to interfere with their professional responsibilities. People in distress often turn to the police because they see them as figureheads – someone they believe they can trust to advise and help sort out their problems.

What would happen if people were reluctant to seek help and advice from the police because they were made to feel that they were being a burden or a nuisance? They might seek help elsewhere if they felt that going through the normal channels was of no use.

If you are sulky or offhand with your colleagues, then this could affect morale, which could have an effect on the efficiency with which you execute your duties.

This is not to say that you should always try to be happy and enthusiastic to the extent that you are overpowering. You should be able to alter your attitude to suit the mood of the moment.

Performance

You might be happy with just doing enough but members of the public or your colleagues might not be. In the public services, you not only have yourself to think about; you have a duty to perform to the best of your ability at all times. If your performance is perceived as relaxed or carefree in the wrong situation, this may affect the morale of your colleagues. Remember, you have a duty to show team spirit – you should be proud and have a high regard for your chosen service.

The performance of public service employees is always monitored in some form by members of the public. Performance instils confidence in the public, knowing that if they needed the public services, they could be relied upon to perform to the best of their ability.

Personality

When we talk about 'personality' in the uniformed public services, we mean the distinctive, attractive qualities that make us stand out from others. Just because everyone wears a uniform and has a service number, it doesn't mean that public service employees don't have personality.

You might think that we can't alter our personalities but this isn't necessarily so. As with many other qualities, we have to work at improving things by practising and then reflecting on what we did right or wrong. Your personality can make a huge difference to your role within the public services: it can make you a popular colleague to work with and it can ease relations with the public both at home and abroad.

The effects of self-discipline and the consequences on the individual and organisation of a lack or total absence of self-discipline

If you lack any of the qualities that make up self-discipline, then you cannot meet the expectations of your job. For example, poor attendance could mean that you are not fully informed of important issues at briefings, which will mean that your team cannot rely on you to respond correctly to situations. This could make you feel as though you are not accepted by the group. What would this do for team morale?

Teams in the uniformed public services are only effective if the public have confidence in them. It only takes one member to lack self-discipline and the entire team, or possibly the entire organisation, could suffer. Disciplinary action could be taken to punish an individual for breaking rules and regulations but it cannot replace the public's trust in that organisation. Trust and good reputation is built up over years of hard work and devotion to duty, yet one selfish act can ruin all that effort.

Assessment activity 5.3

For this assessment activity you are required to discuss the importance of self-discipline within the uniformed public services. Make sure you cover the following content:

- Personal grooming and presentation; punctuality; time management; reliability; attendance; composure; attitude; performance; personality; the effects of self-discipline and the consequences on the individual and organisation of a lack or total absence of self-discipline

Grading tips

P2 You should study the qualities for self-discipline so that you are familiar with them and so that you can give examples of them in your discussion. Make some notes to help you but you should not read from them in the discussion.

M2 M2 is an extension of P2 but you will need to provide further evidence as the discussion alone will not allow you to achieve this grade. In addition to describing the importance of self-discipline (as you have in the discussion) you should analyse why it is necessary for the effective operation of at least one uniformed public service. You could do this by looking at the examples in this unit, as well as thinking of some of your own. Explain in detail why it is necessary in a written piece of work.

D1 You may have already achieved part of this grade at the end of section 1 (see page 155) but to achieve the complete grade you now need to evaluate the impact of the lack of self-discipline, just as you evaluated the impact of discipline in the uniformed public services. This should be included in your written piece of work.

Authority

We have already mentioned rules, regulations and obedience to authority. Now we will consider what authority is, the nature and types of authority and various legislation that gives authority its force.

Authority, as with discipline, can have different meanings and the meaning of 'authority' is dependent upon the context in which it is used. For example:

- the power or right to enforce obedience
- delegated power
- a person whose opinion is accepted because of expertise.

Consider this

Consider the following statements and try to decide on the meaning of 'authority':

1. When Private Johnson told his friend Private Williams to get a haircut, he ignored him because he had no authority. However, he didn't ignore the sergeant, who quoted the Act and section.
2. Blue watch responded to the authority of Crew Manager Bryant because they knew the station manager was in a meeting.
3. The jury didn't believe Mrs Chambers' evidence that the deceased died of poisoning but they listened to the authority of the pathologist.

The Independent Police Complaints Commission (IPCC)

The IPCC was formed in 2004 as a result of the Police Reform Act 2002. It replaced the Police Complaints Authority as the independent body to oversee complaints against the police in the 43 police services in England and Wales. It currently comprises 15 commissioners, who are appointed by the Home Secretary for a period of five years and a team of independent investigators.

Each team of investigators is headed by a regional director in each of its four regions, covering England and Wales. The IPCC carries out investigations into serious allegations of misconduct by serving police personnel. These include allegations:

- of serious or organised corruption
- against senior officers
- involving racism
- of perverting the course of justice.

You can find out more about the IPCC by visiting their website www.ipcc.gov.uk.

HM Chief Inspector of Prisons

Her Majesty's Chief Inspector of Prisons is another independent body which reports to the Secretary of State for the Ministry of Justice on the condition

▲ HM Chief Inspector of Prisons reports on the conditions of prisons

and treatment of prisoners in England and Wales. Its authority is given under section 5A of the Prison Act 1952 and by section 57 of the Criminal Justice Act 1982.

The inspectorate is appointed by the Home Secretary for a period of five years and its authority extends to Northern Ireland, the Channel Islands, Isle of Man and some Commonwealth-dependent territories. It reports to the Home Secretary on whether the objectives for prisons are being achieved in terms of accommodation, treatment of prisoners, conditions in prisons, and the progress made by prisons in reducing re-offending through effective programmes and preparing offenders for release.

HM Chief Inspector of Fire and Rescue

The Government is currently reviewing the role of HM Chief Inspector of Fire and Rescue and it is anticipated that from the summer of 2007 the Inspectorate will be replaced by a Chief Fire and Rescue Advisory Unit.

While the former Inspectorate was responsible for inspecting fire and rescue services and reporting to the Government, the new unit will be responsible for providing Government ministers and officials with independent professional advice on matters concerning the structure, organisation, performance and future development of fire and rescue services. Furthermore, the new unit, led by a chief fire adviser, will advise ministers and Government departments during a major emergency, providing recommendations to local authorities and other interested parties.

Extent of authority

The extent of authority relates to the limit of control held by an individual or organisation. The limit of control is governed by the job description of the role, as well as the jurisdiction, with authority coming either from statute or company policy. For example, Her Majesty's Chief Inspector of Prisons has the authority under the Ministry of Justice to inspect and report to the Government on the treatment and conditions for all prisoners in England and Wales. The Inspectorate also has a statutory responsibility to inspect all holding facilities on behalf of the Immigration and Nationality

Directorate, as well as the Military Corrective Training Centre in Colchester. The authority of the Inspectorate extends to Northern Ireland, the Channel Islands, Isle of Man and some dependent territories of Commonwealth countries.

Power or right to enforce obedience

The power or right to enforce obedience means the authority of an individual or organisation to enforce obedience. It is similar to the extent of authority in that the right is granted by statute or policy and the person or organisation enforcing obedience does so within an accepted legal framework. For example, a senior police officer has the right to ensure that colleagues remain honest because such a principle is included in the Police Code of Conduct. Similarly, any officer in the uniformed public services has the power or right to enforce obedience from any officer of a lower rank provided that such an act of obedience does not contravene rules and regulations of that particular uniformed public service. Any request to perform an illegal act is not a lawful order and the person making the request has no power or right to enforce it.

Nature of authority

Power

Power, like discipline, has several applications and, again, like discipline, it depends upon the context in which it is used. It can refer to the strength or might of something or someone (for example, military strength) or it can mean the ability to persuade someone to act in accordance with a demand because the person doing the persuading has some sort of power.

Power is used as a tool of persuasion where there is a conflict of interests or an unwillingness to respond to a request. If there was no unwillingness to respond, there would be no need for power to be used as a tool of persuasion. The power may come from a lawful or unlawful source. For example, a person may be reluctant to hand over their wallet to a stranger but might do so if the stranger produces a gun to reinforce the demand.

However, power, in the context of authority, means the right to ensure an individual or organisation complies with reasonable and lawful requests, even though there may be unwillingness on the part of the individual or organisation. For example, a serving soldier may be ordered to perform a fatigue (a non-military, mundane task), such as sweeping the barrack room floor and he or she may be unwilling to do this. The soldier would not have performed this act were it not for the power of the senior officer. Hence, for power to be exerted there must be a conflict of interests before the task is completed. Without a conflict of interests there would be no need for power in order to make a person carry out a task.

The difference between the two examples above is that the power of the senior officer came from a legitimate authority, whereas the power of the gunman came from an unlawful source.

Raven (1965), (cited in Gross, R., McIlveen, R. (1988) *Psychology A New Introduction*) identified six bases of power:

- *Reward power* – we do what we are asked because we desire rewards or benefits, such as praise, a wage increase or promotion.

- *Coercive power* – we do what we are asked because we fear sanctions, such as being made to perform mundane tasks, lack of privileges or even fear of dismissal.

- *Informational power* – we do what we are asked because we are persuaded by the content of a communication (verbal or written) and *not* by any influencing figure.

- *Expert power* – we do what we are asked because we believe that the power figure has generally greater expertise and knowledge than us.

- *Legitimate power* – we do what we are asked because we believe that the power figure is authorised by a recognised power structure to command and make decisions.

- *Referent power* – we do what we are asked because we can identify with the source of influence; we may be attracted to them or respect them.

Position

When we talk about someone being in a position of authority we usually mean that they hold a certain rank or status within society or within an organisation such as the public services.

There are several ways in which a person could find himself or herself in a position of authority. For example, a priest has the authority of the church while a mother or father has parental authority over children. In the uniformed public services, positions of authority come with promotion. An officer may be promoted because of certain achievements and special attributes, such as experience in the service, good character, knowledge of the job, dedication, self-discipline and the respect of one's colleagues.

If you join the uniformed public services and are placed in a position of authority, you may lawfully command team members, who recognise your authority and their duty to obey those legitimate commands.

When authority is legitimate, there is no need to influence or use power. Indeed, if a senior officer were unable to gain the respect of a team member by command alone, then there would be no recognisable authority.

Status

Status relating to authority is closely akin to obedience status, which we have already mentioned. Many of the reasons why people obey can be applied to why we accept authority. For example, we respect the authority of those we perceive as:

- experts who are supposed to know more – those who may have answers we want or need
- people with higher status
- people with titles
- people who wear uniforms or who are of smart appearance
- people with power
- people whom we believe can punish us.

In the uniformed public services, each officer knows his or her status and the status of their colleagues and where they fit into the hierarchy of authority.

Influence

Influence is different from power because power is often used to apply pressure where there is a conflict of interests, whereas influence can make a person carry out a task or alter their ways simply by reason or evaluation. The status of a person can have an influence on someone who aspires to be like that person. On the other hand, a person can be influenced by someone without any particular status, but who holds their respect and trust.

Corruption

Corruption is where a person lacks moral fibre and may be willing to undertake acts of dishonesty. Examples could be altering documents or evidence, taking bribes and theft. Dishonesty in any of the uniformed public services is seen as an abuse of authority. Members of some of the uniformed public services have the authority to seize property, for example, the proceeds of crime, and they are entrusted to follow correct procedures to ensure the property is returned to the rightful owner. Furthermore, they have access to confidential information, which should not be used for personal gain.

Disobedience

Disobedience within the uniformed public services can be an extremely serious charge, depending on the degree. Serious cases of disobedience in the uniformed public services can lead to dishonourable discharge.

Blind obedience

Blind obedience means to follow orders unquestioningly – to carry out whatever is asked without question or thinking of the consequences. Early in their training, members of the uniformed public services are encouraged to obey orders immediately. This is so they become accustomed to obeying orders when they are in, for example, a conflict situation. If you thought about all the different consequences before carrying out orders, the result might not be what was intended by those giving the orders.

There are many occasions where lives have been saved and dangerous situations defused because members of the uniformed public services have obeyed orders immediately.

However, the problem with obedience is knowing when to speak out. At which point do you stop obeying and ask yourself if you are doing the right thing by carrying out an order? The question may be answered by balancing the consequences of disobedience with the consequences brought about by ignoring an order.

◀ Sometimes it is essential to carry out orders without thinking

There are other occasions where blind obedience does not leave us with happy memories and feelings of gratitude. We know that during World War II, Nazis behaved atrociously but when questioned they insisted that they were merely following orders.

Consider this

Can you think of other examples of appalling consequences resulting from blind obedience? You might wish to consider the psychological effects of carrying out an order that you disagree with, yet you feel duty-bound to comply with. Can you think of some examples where this might be the case? You might also think about the consequences of a service in which everyone questioned orders. What would that mean for the concept of discipline within that service?

Moral dilemmas and responsibility for decisions taken

A moral dilemma is a problem to which there is no obvious 'right' solution. For example, suppose you were walking alongside a fast flowing river and you saw two young boys apparently drowning. They were both shouting to you to save them and you could see they needed rescuing immediately. With no support and no time to make a call for assistance you wade into the river but you only have time to save one of the boys. Assuming the boys are the same age and neither of them can swim, how do you decide which one to save? This is a moral dilemma.

Sometimes you can work out the answer to a problem by weighing up the consequences. That is to say, you can try to decide if one action would bring about greater happiness to a greater number than another course of action would. So if course of action A brought about greater happiness than course of action B, then course of action A would be the morally right thing to do.

The responsibility for making decisions rests with the senior officer in charge and a good leader would accept responsibility for their decisions and stand by them.

Consider this

- What are the positive effects of blind obedience?
- What are the negative effects of blind obedience?

Questioning of orders

The public services and Armed Forces are dependent upon orders being followed for their efficiency. For example, in a conflict situation, there could be serious consequences if orders were not followed immediately and without question. If orders are questioned then the authority of those giving them is undermined and the hierarchy of authority loses its effectiveness. Similarly, in a major incident situation, the success of the response and recovery stages by the emergency services is reliant upon teams of personnel following the orders of the coordinating officer without question.

As we have seen in the hierarchy of authority, certain ranks have a right to command lower ranks and those lower ranks have a duty to carry out those orders. We should expect orders that come from a legitimate source to be carried out without question as they are issued by officers who have the experience to know what is required to bring about successful conclusions. But do the lower ranks have a right to question those orders?

While it might not be acceptable, in most cases, to question authority, you have to take into account that while those giving the orders may have people's or even the nation's best interests at heart, they are still human and prone to error, especially in times of extreme stress or extraordinary situations, where their otherwise accurate powers of judgement might be temporarily impaired.

Types of Authority

Authoritarian (autocratic)

This is a type of authority whereby a leader tells their team members what task to perform and how to perform it without consultation or advice from other parties. Used appropriately, an authoritarian style of leadership can be effective in bringing about the desired result, especially where time is limited. However, there are many occasions where this type of leadership would not motivate or command respect from those who are carrying out the task. This is because autocratic leadership does not encourage teamwork or initiative since the leader knows the answers and does not need to consult anyone to achieve the desired result.

Dictatorial

Dictatorial authority is authority that is carried out without the consent of the people whom it affects. 'Dictatorial' is sometimes used to refer to someone who is domineering and arrogant in the manner in which they give orders. To remain in power, dictatorial regimes rule by intimidation and fear.

A dictator is a ruler with unrestricted authority over the state, as well as individuals, and who has complete power to render current laws invalid and create new laws without the prior consent of the very citizens who will be affected by them. Unlike democratically elected leaders, dictators can behave in any manner they see

Authoritarian

Dictatorial

Consultative

Participative

 Figure 5.6 The four different types of leader

fit without fear of being defeated in elections as the electorate are usually helpless in preventing a dictator from remaining in power.

Consultative

Consultative authority, also known as collective authority, is where a leader might share a problem with several members of a team, either individually or in a group with a view to hearing ideas and suggestions. This form of authority is also used where a change in procedures or policy is being considered and members' views are sought on the changes. The leader will then make a decision but not necessarily one that is influenced by suggestions and ideas from the group.

Participative (democratic)

With this type of authority, the leader allows one or more employees to be included in the decision-making

Consider this

Which type of authority do you think would be applicable to the uniformed public services in the following examples? Explain why.

1. A squad of new recruits in the Army are about to undergo their first session of drill. They only have three months before their passing out parade.
2. Consider the huge exercise involved in the recovery operation following the London bombings in July 2005. The Commissioner of the Metropolitan Police Service, Sir Ian Blair, was in charge of coordinating the operation, but which form of authority would he have used?
3. The station manager has attended a multi-vehicle accident where people are trapped inside vehicles. There is a strong risk that leaking fuel could ignite but there is an equal risk that people will die if they are left trapped in their vehicles without medical care.
4. Can you think of a situation where dictatorial authority is used in the uniformed public services? If not, explain why not.

process (determining what to do and how to do it). However, the leader maintains the final decision-making authority. Using this style is not a sign of weakness, it is a sign of strength that employees will respect.

Legislation

Members of the uniformed public services are not only subject to the laws of the land, they also have to abide by codes of conduct and disciplinary rules and regulations relating to their particular service. These rules and regulations are written into Acts of Parliament.

The rules and regulations are not solely for enforcing discipline. They also exist to protect the rights of serving officers who may have broken a rule and to make sure procedures for dealing with disciplinary hearings are standardised. Furthermore, they exist to protect members of the public from such things as harassment and victimisation by clearly stating police powers of arrest and search.

Armed Forces Discipline Act 2000

This Act provides the statutory framework for discipline procedures for our three Armed Forces. The basis for this statutory framework stems from the Army Act 1955, the Air Force Act 1955 and the Naval Discipline Act 1957, which are renewed by parliament every five years and are known collectively as the Service Discipline Acts (SDAs). Essentially, the Armed Forces have their own legal system and it applies to personnel wherever they are based in the world, whether in peacetime or conflict. However, the Act does not apply only to service personnel: it may apply to civil servants and their dependants, as well as the civilian dependants of service personnel.

The Act deals with the processing and punishment of personnel who have been charged, or are likely to be charged, under disciplinary regulations. This legislation makes provision for:

- the right for the accused to apply for bail pending trial
- the trial judge to direct the accused's commanding officer to give orders for the accused's arrest

- the right to appeal against the summary award of the commanding officer
- appeals against a conviction by way of a fresh hearing
- appeals against sentence by way of a fresh hearing but only the evidence relevant to sentencing will be reheard
- the punishment from a summary appeal court cannot be any more severe than that which was initially awarded by a commanding officer
- appeals must be brought within 14 days beginning with the date on which the punishment was awarded or within such longer period as the court may allow
- the accused's right to elect trial by court martial
- where the accused elects trial, the court cannot award any punishment which could not have been awarded by the commanding officer or appropriate superior authority had the election for trial not been made.

Police Act 1997 section 50

All police services within the UK are subject to a code of conduct as set out by the Police (Disciplinary) Regulations. Below are three examples of that code:

1. Honesty and integrity – officers should not be inappropriately indebted to any person or institution and should be reliable in the discharge of their duties.
2. Fairness and impartiality – police officers have a particular responsibility to act with fairness and impartiality in all their dealings with the public and their colleagues.

3. Politeness and tolerance – officers should treat members of the public and colleagues with courtesy and respect, avoiding abusive or deriding attitudes or behaviour.

However, the National Crime Squad (NCS) is an organisation involved in tackling serious crime nationally, and does not, therefore, come under the jurisdiction of a single police service, though it does have its headquarters in London. The NCS consists of members who are seconded from different police areas and it is regulated by its own authority, the power of which is given to it by section 50 of the Police Act 1997. The Act also makes provision for the secretary of state to issue and revise a code of conduct for the NCS, as well as setting targets and objectives.

Police and Criminal Evidence Act 1984 part IX

The purpose of this Act was to standardise the rules that all police officers must follow in relation to persons whom they are searching, arresting or detaining. Part IX was introduced in 1985 to clarify the position regarding police complaints and disciplinary procedures.

It is important for the police to show honesty, fairness and politeness when doing their duty ▶

The Act sets out all the measures for investigating complaints against the police, including senior officers, from the initial stage until completion, as well as giving information on the manner of the investigation. It states when matters should be referred to the Independent Police Complaints Commission and also to the Director of Public Prosecutions.

Fire and Rescue Services Act 2004

This Act, which applies in England and Wales, replaces the Fire Services Act of 1947. It sets out a variety of duties and powers of fire and rescue authorities to promote fire safety and respond to fires, road traffic accidents and emergencies, such as natural disasters and terrorist attacks.

The legislation empowers fire and rescue authorities to respond to the needs of the community and carry out risk assessments in preparation for emergencies. To meet the demands of our modern age, authorities have the right to combine with other authorities in order to promote fire safety and to deal with emergencies where one authority does not have adequate resources.

Assessment activity 5.4

Write a report describing different types of authority and explaining the nature of authority in relation to the uniformed public services. You should ensure that you include the content in the following four sections:

1. *Authority*
   Within a range of different public services, for example, Independent Police Complaints Commission, HM Chief Inspector of Prisons; extent of authority; power or right to enforce obedience.

2. *Nature of Authority*
   Power; position; status; influence; corruption; disobedience; blind obedience, including both positive and negative aspects; moral dilemma and responsibility for decisions taken.

3. *Types of authority*
   Authoritarian; dictatorial; consultative; participative; how these forms of authority are applied to the uniformed public services.

4. *Legislation*
   For example, Armed Forces Discipline Act 2000; Police and Criminal Evidence Act 1984 (section IX); Police Act 1997 (section 50), including any subsequent amendments.

Grading tips

P5 In your report you should explain what is meant by authority, giving examples of where some of it comes from, as shown in section 1. Then you need to describe the four types of authority that appear in section 3.

P6 For P6 you need to explain the nature of authority, which appears in section 2, and then outline the legislation that appears in section 4.

M4 For M4 you must explain why it is important to recognise authority and what could happen when there is no authority within the uniformed public services. You could do this by thinking of examples to highlight the reasons for and against.

D2 You may have already attempted D2 at the end of section 2 (see page 166) but to fully achieve it you now have to critically evaluate the positive and negative effects of blind obedience on different types and natures of authority. You need to go into detail and criticise the positive and negative effects as much as you can, then give a balanced conclusion.

Knowledge check

1. How does the rank structure of the Metropolitan Police Service differ from county or territorial police services?

2. What is the difference between a rule and a regulation?

3. What is meant by anarchy?

4. What is the role of discipline in the uniformed public services?

5. How does conformity differ from obedience?

6. What did Asch's experiment try to show?

7. What did Hofling's experiment try to show?

8. What did the studies of Zimbardo and Milgram have in common?

9. Give four reasons why self-discipline is needed in the uniformed public services.

10. What is the role of the IPCC?

11. What is meant by blind obedience?

12. What is a moral dilemma?

13. What legislation regulates the National Crime Squad?

Preparation for assessment

Design and produce a leaflet, to be distributed to public service students, which will provide answers to the following:

1. Describe and analyse the need for and the role of discipline in the uniformed public services. **P1 M1**

2. Explain what is meant by conformity and obedience and how they are represented in the uniformed public services, including the factors that influence them. **P3**

3. Describe three research studies which explore conformity and obedience. **P4**

4. Analyse how three research studies on conformity and obedience apply to the uniformed public services. **M3**

5. Describe the importance of self-discipline in the uniformed public services. **P2**

6. Analyse why the qualities of self-discipline are necessary for the effective operation of a given uniformed public service. **M2**

7. Evaluate the impact of discipline in the uniformed public services. **D1**

8. Describe four types of authority. **P5**

9. Explain the nature of authority in relation to the uniformed public services. **P6**

10. Explain the importance of recognising authority and the consequences of a lack of authority within the uniformed public services. **M4**

11. Critically evaluate the positive and negative effects of blind obedience to authority. **D2**

Grading criteria	Activity	Pg no.		
To achieve a pass grade the evidence must show that the learner is able to:			To achieve a merit grade the evidence must show that the learner is able to:	To achieve a distinction grade the evidence must show that the learner is able to:
P1 Describe the need for and role of discipline in the uniformed public services	5.1	155	**M1** Analyse the need for and role of discipline in the uniformed public services	**D1** Evaluate the impact of discipline in the uniformed public services
P2 Describe the importance of self-discipline in the uniformed public services	5.3	171	**M2** Analyse why the qualities of self-discipline are necessary for the effective operation of a given uniformed public service	
P3 Explain what is meant by conformity and obedience, and how they are represented in the uniformed public services, including the factors that influence them	5.2	166	**M3** Analyse how three research studies on conformity and obedience apply to the uniformed public services	**D2** Critically evaluate the positive and negative effects of blind obedience to authority
P4 Describe three research studies which explore conformity and obedience	5.2	166		
P5 Describe four types of authority	5.4	180	**M4** Explain the importance of recognising authority and the consequences of a lack of authority within the uniformed public services	
P6 Explain the nature of authority in relation to the uniformed public services	5.4	180		

Diversity and the public services

Introduction

This unit investigates the continuing development of our society. Recent political and economic changes have affected the various uniformed public services in their working policies, procedures and practices. This includes the service provisions needed to meet these changes to support our ever-changing society by addressing the common inequalities in society.

This unit explores the historical development of the UK, including legislation concerned with discrimination and equality, along with values, myths and stereotypes. You will look at the needs of communities and individuals at both local and national levels in a diverse society. You will also explore how the public services can support the community and address equal opportunities. Particular focus is placed on discrimination in the areas of race, gender and disability and how individual rights and responsibilities are upheld and protected.

After completing this unit you should be able to achieve the following outcomes:

- Understand the term 'diversity' within a historical context
- Understand relevant legislation that protects the human rights of individuals
- Understand the role of the public services and their duty to provide equality of service to all members of the community
- Know how national and local policies, strategies and procedures address diversity issues within a chosen public service.

Thinking points

If you want a career in one of the public services, you'll need to understand the issues surrounding diversity and equality. These issues are at the forefront of the public services' recruitment processes, as there is no room in any service for people who show discriminatory behaviour. You'll need to be aware of the composition of current UK society at both local and national levels and be able to deal with all members of the community openly and fairly. You should also understand the relevant legislation and follow new government initiatives and media coverage. It is important to understand why we have developed a diverse society and to challenge any myths, stereotypes or prejudices.

- Think about times when you have witnessed stereotyping, prejudice and even discrimination.
- Are you aware of how people are protected from discrimination and negative behaviour?
- Are you aware of the roles and responsibilities of the uniformed public services in promoting and providing equality of service to all?

Diversity is about appreciating and valuing the fact that communities are made up of a range of people with different **cultures** and backgrounds. These differences can involve **race**, **nationality** and **religion** as well as **ethnicity**, age and gender. Living in a diverse society means incorporating those differences into the way we structure our lives and services. Issues of diversity are important to everyone in society and the public services need to be aware of how to interact and deal with the various groups in a fair and equal way.

Key terms

Diversity This opens people to new experiences and new ways of looking at things. Being open to other cultures enriches everyone and means that our lives are more interesting, even at such basic levels as the food we eat.

Culture The values, beliefs, customs and behaviours that distinguish a group of people.

Race People who share a common origin or heritage.

Nationality This means belonging to a particular nation.

Religion A system of faith and worship around a personal god or gods.

Ethnicity Certain characteristics that distinguish an ethnic group from the surrounding community, in particular a long-shared history and a cultural tradition of its own.

Historical developments and social attitudes

In this unit you will learn about some of the history behind Britain's diverse society and aspects of diversity including:

- immigration

- race
- religion
- nationality.

How Britain became a diverse society – a historical perspective since 1800

Britain has always been a racially and culturally mixed society. It is a nation populated by people from different countries who immigrated as long ago as the Bronze Age (5000 years ago). This early immigration was followed by invasions and occupation by Romans, Celts, Saxons, Vikings and Normans who all settled in Britain to live. Immigration still continues in Britain today with refugees from Eastern Europe and Africa arriving steadily.

▲ British society is made up of a range of different cultures

■ Timeline of immigration since 1800

1833 Parliament passes the Slavery Abolition Act, giving all slaves in the British Empire their freedom.

1850s Irish immigrants escaping the potato famine make up 3% of the British population.

1892 Britain's first non-white MP, Indian Dadabhai Naoroji, is elected to the House of Commons.

1933–9 Nearly four million European Jews settle in the UK along with 80,000 refugees from central Europe due to the rise of Adolf Hitler and the development of the Nazi state in Germany.

1939 World War II. Soldiers and workers from all over the Empire are stationed in Britain, including US troops and 100,000 Poles fighting under British command.

1943 There are 114,000 war refugees in Britain.

1945 Post-war labour shortages in Britain. The government begins looking for immigrants.

1948 SS Empire Windrush docks at Tilbury in London, delivering hundreds of men from the West Indies after the British Government gives citizenship to people from ex-colonies. This indicates the start of mass immigration to the UK and the arrival of different cultures.

mid 50s–early 60s The immigration of non-white people from the Commonwealth, in particular the Caribbean, India and Pakistan due to the labour shortages in the UK in the post-war period.

1959 First Notting Hill Carnival. Today more than one million people celebrate the three day festival.

1962 Commonwealth Immigrants Act reduces the migrants from the Commonwealth by only allowing in people who have skills that are in short supply.

1970 The non-white population of Britain is 1.4 million (approximately 2.5% of the whole population).

1972 New legislation means that a British passport holder born overseas can only settle in Britain if they have a work permit and can prove that a parent or grandparent had been born in the UK.

1972 Ugandan dictator General Idi Amin expels 80,000 African Asians from the country – 28,000 settle in the UK.

1976 Race Relations Act passed and the Commission for Racial Equality is established.

1981 The Immigration Act 1981 tightens up immigration conditions, limiting the rights of families and partners to automatically enter the UK.

1981 Race riots in Brixton. Youths riot amid resentment that the police are targeting young black men in the belief that it will stop street crime. This leads to the creation of the Police and Criminal Evidence Act 1984.

1989 British Government grants citizenship to 225,000 people from Hong Kong, mostly Chinese.

1990s Wars and persecution see new groups of immigrants fleeing from countries such as Afghanistan and Croatia. They come to seek political asylum in the UK.

1991 The beginning of stringent checks on people claiming refugee status.

1993 Murder of black teenager Stephen Lawrence leads directly to new anti-discrimination legislation.

1998 The Human Rights Act is passed.

2000 125,000 asylum seekers settle in the UK, mainly from Eastern Europe/Balkans.

2002 The minority ethnic population of London is 29%.

2006 The Commission for Equality and Human Rights is created, replacing the Commission for Racial Equality (CRE), Disability Rights Commission (DRC) and Equal Opportunities Commission (EOC).

2007 Bulgaria and Romania join the EU, allowing citizens from these countries free movement within the UK.

Millions of immigrants from Germany and Central Europe settled in the UK in the 1930s

Case study: Why minority ethnic immigrants came to Britain

After World War II, there was a general feeling of goodwill between Britain and the Commonwealth countries due to the war effort made by citizens of the Commonwealth. This was further reflected in the 1948 British Nationality Act which stated that all Commonwealth citizens were free to enter Britain, to find work and settle with their families. This meant that by the late 1950s, hundreds of thousands of people from black Commonwealth countries had settled in Britain to try and gain a better standard of living. They filled mainly low-paid jobs such as cleaning, catering and transport which were seen as undesirable to many existing white citizens.

The arrival of large numbers of people who were physically and culturally different led to fear among the white population and race riots broke out in Notting Hill in London in 1958. This led to a series of immigration Acts designed to strictly control the number of immigrants who are racially and culturally different from the white majority (see the timeline on page 187). These Acts reflect the problems our society has had in accommodating people from different cultures.

In the 1960s, Enoch Powell, a conservative MP, made his famous 'rivers of blood' speech which he believed summed up the concerns of the people at that time. He called for the repatriation (return to the country of birth, citizenship or origin) of all black immigrants who had settled in Britain.

1. **What was the main reason why immigration from black Commonwealth countries increased after World War II?**

2. **What happened during the 1960s, 1970s and 1980s with regard to immigration from black Commonwealth countries? The timeline on page 187 will help you to answer this question.**

In 2005, an estimated 565,000 migrants arrived to live in the UK for at least one year. In the same period, 380,000 people emigrated from the UK for a year or more; over half of these were British citizens. Australia was the most popular destination for British emigrants, followed by Spain and France. The difference between immigration and emigration was 185,000. This was equivalent to adding over 500 people a day to the UK population.

with the exception of 1976, there have been more births than deaths in the UK and the population has subsequently grown due to this natural change. However, since the 1990s migration into the UK from abroad has been an increasingly important factor in population change – more so than increased birth rates – and the ethnic makeup of the country has changed as a result.

Consider this

There are many factors that influence people to migrate from one country to another. Can you list some of these factors?

Many people have emigrated from the UK. Which countries have many people gone to? What are their reasons for leaving the UK?

White	92.1%	54,153,898
Mixed	1.2%	677,117
Asian or Asian British		
Indian	1.8%	1,053,411
Pakistani	1.3%	747,285
Bangladeshi	0.5%	283,063
Other Asian	0.4%	247,664
Black or Black British		
Black Caribbean	1.0%	565,876
Black African	0.8%	485,277
Black other	0.2%	97,585
Chinese	0.4%	247,403
Other groups	0.5%	230,615

Table 6.1 UK population in the 2001 Census

Source: www.statistics.gov.uk. Crown copyright material is produced with the permission of the Controller of HMSO and Queen's Printer for Scotland.

Society's attitude to diversity

■ Ethnicity

The total population of the UK rose by 17 per cent from 50.2 million in 1951 to 58.8 million in 2001. The growth has been faster in more recent years. Between mid-1991 and mid-2003 the population grew by an annual rate of 0.3 per cent. In every year since 1901,

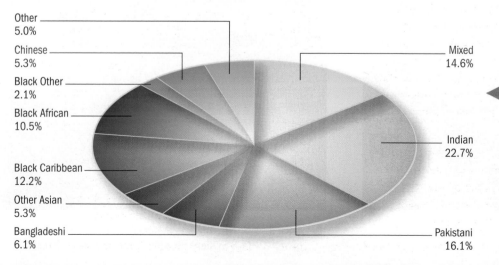

Other 5.0%
Chinese 5.3%
Black Other 2.1%
Black African 10.5%
Black Caribbean 12.2%
Other Asian 5.3%
Bangladeshi 6.1%
Mixed 14.6%
Indian 22.7%
Pakistani 16.1%

Figure 6.1 Almost 8% of the population may be categorised as coming from a minority ethnic group. The pie chart shows how that 8% is made up. The majority of these groups are people who have been born in the UK and have made a substantial contribution to the life of Britain and have enriched areas such as industry and commerce, sport and music

■ Religion

The UK supports freedom of worship with many religions crossing ethnic and cultural barriers. An understanding of religion in all its forms will help the public services address cultural issues which may cause conflict and misunderstanding in society and damage the relationship between the services and the public. It is particularly important to understand the norms and beliefs of different religions when entering places of worship or people's homes.

The main faiths in Britain today are:

- Christianity
- Hinduism
- Islam
- Sikhism
- Judaism
- Buddhism.

Just over three-quarters of the UK population report having a religion.

After Christianity and Islam, the next largest religious groups are Hindus (559,000), followed by Sikhs (336,000), Jews (267,000), Buddhists (152,000), and people from other religions (179,000). Overall, 15 per cent of the English and Welsh population reported having no religion and 8 per cent declined to answer the question.

Christianity

Christianity developed in the Middle East about 2000 years ago in the land now known as Israel. It is based on the life and teachings of Jesus who Christians believe to be Christ, the son of God. The central belief of Christianity is that Jesus was crucified as part of God's plan for saving all humans from their sins, and that he rose from the dead. There are different groups or denominations within Christianity. The Christian calendar affects daily life in the UK as Christian festivals are reflected in the timing of school holidays, for example.

▲ In England and Wales, 36 million people (nearly 7 out of 10) describe their religion as Christian

▲ After Christianity, Islam is the most common faith with nearly 3% (1.6 million) describing themselves as Muslim

Hinduism

Hinduism is one of the world's oldest religions with 750 million followers around the world. It is the main religion in India and Nepal. It began over 5000 years ago and has no single founder. It has a number of sacred writings of which the Bhagavad Gita is probably the most popular. Hindus believe in one supreme God called Brahman whose many aspects and qualities are represented by a range of gods and goddesses. Hindus believe in reincarnation and that behaviour in one life determines status in the next.

Islam

Followers of Islam are called Muslims. Muslims who adhere to the Islamic faith believe that Allah is the unique and only God and that the prophet Muhammad was Allah's final messenger on Earth. The Qur'an and Sunnah together provide an authoritative source for Muslim law. Muslims' faith also demands that they bear witness to their faith, pray five times daily, fast in the holy month of Ramadan, pay alms to the poor annually and take a pilgrimage to Mecca (the Hajj) once in their lifetime.

Sikhism

Sikhism is around 500 years old. It emerged as a result of the teachings of Guru Nanak in India. Guru Nanak's aim was to encourage all people to faithfully worship one god with the idea of individuals helping humanity. The fundamentals of the religion were then further developed by a continuous line of nine gurus who succeeded him. The last guru declared that, after him, there would be no other gurus as the Sikh holy book would be viewed as the eternal guru. The ultimate aim of a practising Sikh is to build a close and loving relationship with God.

Religion	Membership	Deity	Holy text	Main holidays	Diet	Dress	Place of worship
Christianity	2 billion	God (monotheistic)	• Bible • New Testament	• Easter • Christmas	• No specific restrictions	• No specific restrictions	Church
Islam	1 billion +	Allah (monotheistic)	• Qur'an	• Eid-Ul-Fitr • Eid-Ul-Adha	• Halal food • No pork • No alcohol	• Modest dress • Women must cover hair with headscarf	Mosque
Hinduism	750 million	Brahman (polytheistic)	• Holy scriptures • Mahabarata • Vedas • Upanishads	• Deepawali (diwali)	• Beef forbidden • Many Hindus are vegetarian	• No specific restrictions	No specific place – worship is a private matter but there are Hindu temples
Sikhism	22.5 million	God (9 gurus)	• Granth Sahib	• Diwali • Vaisakhi Birth of: • Guru Nanak • Guru Gobind Singh	• Tobacco and alcohol are forbidden • Pork banned	• Men must wear turban • 5 Ks	Gurdwara
Judaism	18 million	God (monotheistic)	• Old Testament • Talmud	• Yom Kippur • Passover • Rosh Hashana	• Kosher food • Pork forbidden	• Modest dress • Skull cap for men	Synagogue
Buddhism	665 million	No deity Worship of Buddha – the Enlightened One	• Buddha's teachings	• Wiesak • Dharma Day • Sangha Day • Parinirvana Day	• No specific rules	• No specific rules	Temple

Table 6.2 A summary of the main faiths and their cultures

Judaism

Judaism is the oldest monotheistic religion (belief in one God). According to the Torah, the central scripture for Jews, God is holy and unmitigated. The rules and traditions an observant Jew follows are known as the Halakha (the Path), which come from the first five books in the Bible (the Pentateuch or Torah). They include the Ten Commandments and a further 603 dealing with the rules for living and sharing society with others.

Buddhism

Buddhism is more than 2,500 years old and has more than 2000 sects. There are around 655 million practising Buddhists worldwide. It developed in North India around the sixth century BCE when Siddattha Gotama attained 'enlightenment' – the ultimate state called 'Nirvana' which frees people from the cycle of re-birth. He became Buddha – 'the enlightened one'. Buddhism is a major cultural influence in China and about 75% of Japanese people are Buddhists.

Take it further

Choose a religion that has been mentioned in this unit and create a fact sheet that highlights how the religious and cultural beliefs and norms may differ from your own. Consider the following areas of research: dietary requirements, hygiene, prayer, dress/jewellery, names, festivals, religious signs and symbols, origins and beliefs.

■ Sexual orientation

Society's attitudes towards gay, lesbian and bisexual people have improved but **discrimination** still exists. The Employment Equality (Sexual Orientation) Regulations 2003 and the Equality Act 2006 created laws to protect these groups from discrimination in areas such as employment, training, harassment and services.

Key terms

Discrimination The act of distinguishing one from another on irrelevant or unfair grounds such as sex

or race. Discrimination is the result of a **prejudice** combined with a power. This makes the discriminated person feel at an unfair disadvantage to another.

Equality The quality of being the same in value or status where people feel essentially equal or equivalent to others.

Ethnocentricity The assumption that an individual's viewpoint from their own cultural perspective is normal or superior, without considering that there could be other points of view.

Prejudice An attitude based on incorrect information, usually in the form of a biased attitude towards a stereotype. Often a prejudice will lead to some form of discrimination.

Heterosexism A belief that male-female sexuality is the only natural or moral mode of sexual behaviour.

Homophobia The irrational fear of homosexuals (people thought to be lesbian, gay or bisexual) or any behaviour, belief or attitude which doesn't conform to the traditional sex-role stereotypes.

■ Disability

The definition of disability is very broad and has three distinct elements. It must:

- be substantial
- be long-term (lasting more than 12 months)
- affect a person on a daily basis in areas such as mobility, manual dexterity, speech, hearing, seeing and memory.

It also covers conditions such as dyslexia, HIV and cancer, meaning that around 8.5 million people in the UK could be classed as disabled (one in seven). Disabled people may need additional support in areas such as education, health, housing, transport and finances.

Key terms

Disability Anyone with a physical or mental impairment which has a substantial and long-term adverse effect upon their ability to carry out normal day-to-day activities.

▲ The rising proportion of the elderly will have significant implications on the public services in the future especially in the areas of welfare, health and social support

■ Age

The UK has an ageing population – the result of declining birth and death rates. Medical advances tackle once fatal diseases and people now have fewer children and healthier lifestyles, all of which means that people now live longer than they did 100 years ago.

Group	Population
Under 16	11.9 million
Men 16–64, Women 16–59	36.1 million
Men 65+, Women 60+	10.8 million
All ages	58.8 million

Table 6.3 Population numbers in 2007

The average age rose from 34.1 years in 1971 to 38.6 in 2004 and is projected to rise to 42.9 in 2031. The proportion of people aged over 65 is projected to increase from 16 per cent in 2004 to 23 per cent by 2031. This is in particular because of the large numbers of people born after World War II and during the 1960s baby boom.

■ Gender

The UK population consists of 28.6 million males and 30.2 million females. This is a male to female ratio of 0.95. Before the 1981 census the ratio of men to women showed men outnumbering women at ages up to the late 40s. However, by 2001 there were fewer men than women at all ages over 21 and women are now in the majority in the UK.

■ Media representation

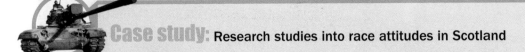

A research study at the University of Glasgow looked at how native Scots felt about other ethnic groups in the Scottish population. They gathered data to determine how much prejudice Scots displayed against minority groups such as Muslims and English immigrants who were living in Scotland. Approximately 1 per cent of the Scottish population are Muslim and 8 per cent are English.

Participants in the study were asked whether they thought a 'true Scot' had to have been born in Scotland and whether they had to be white. More than half the participants felt that being born in Scotland was a requirement, but a much lower proportion felt that a 'true Scot' had to be white.

More participants in the study displayed negative views of Muslims than they did of English immigrants. Nearly a quarter of the participants said they wouldn't be happy if a relative entered into a relationship with a Muslim, compared to only 3 per cent of Scots who would be unhappy about a relative's relationship with an English immigrant. More participants felt that Muslim immigration would threaten Scotland's national identity than felt there was a threat posed by English immigrants.

Despite these rather gloomy findings, the study included other, rather contradictory, results. Only a small number of participants felt that Muslims or English immigrants were taking jobs from Scots. Approximately half the participants felt that Muslims contributed valuable skills to Scotland with slightly more participants stating that they felt the same about the English immigrants.

The findings of the study were published by the Scottish Centre for Social Research. They did show that there was more prejudice against Muslims than against English immigrants but they also showed that a large number of Scots are not threatened by either Muslims or English immigrants. More than 60 per cent of Scots felt that discrimination against both Muslims and English immigrants should be outlawed.

1. **Does this study suggest that the concept of multiculturalism, integration and tolerance to other groups is easily accepted?**

2. **What are the key arguments against the above concepts?**

3. **What could be done to help create a more multicultural society?**

4. **What could the media do to help promote a multicultural society?**

■ Language, art and literature

The development of a more diverse society has led to an increase in the different languages spoken in Britain and it is common that people from ethnic minority groups can speak more than one language fluently. In certain areas, languages such as Punjabi are available as a subject of study within schools for all students.

The diversity found within society has greatly affected British culture, for example, in the foods we eat; think about the food you have had over the last week and consider the country of origin for the food and consider how much originates from the UK. Also think about the last book you read, the last film you watched or even the last art exhibition you attended. Consider what the influences and origins of the book, film or art were and how these are integrated into British culture.

Concepts

Integration

Integration can be defined as a process or outcome which is measured against specific factors such as economics, society or politics. In terms of population it can be measured by factors and variables which have helped or hindered the incorporation of **minority ethnic** groups into mainstream society. Successful integration is where different groups are brought together and can have their own identity within that society and are not simply forced into sharing the majority population's customs and traditions.

Key terms

Minority ethnic A group within a larger society or cultural order that is distinguished by its national, religious, linguistic, cultural and sometimes racial background. This includes all minority groups found in a particular community if their numbers are very small in comparison to the majority group.

Tolerance and multiculturalism

Tolerance involves an interest in, and concern for, the ideas and attitudes of those whose opinions, practices, race, religion, nationality, etc. differ from our own.

Multiculturalism is the practice of acknowledging and respecting the various cultures, religions, ethnicities, attitudes and opinions within a society.

Multiculturalism could be seen almost as a policy aimed at promoting the interaction and social inclusion of people from various cultures in Britain to increase mutual respect for one another as well as providing equal rights and opportunities.

This is ultimately done by reducing inequalities between the least advantaged groups and communities and the rest of society by closing the opportunity gap and ensuring that support reaches those who need it most.

Consider this

How could the public services improve their interaction with and inclusion of minority groups within a given community?

Rights and responsibilities of individuals in society

Everyone should be recognised as being a citizen from birth. This involves enjoying rights and exercising responsibilities both legally, politically and socially and being able to make informed choices and decisions, and taking action as an individual or a group.

The rights and responsibilities of individuals go hand in hand. We all have a right to be treated with respect, just as we have a clear obligation to treat others with respect. If we all have a right to voice our opinions on matters that affect our lives, then we have a responsibility to consider the views of others on matters that affect them. However, perceptions of rights and responsibilities by individuals may differ in different social groups and cause conflict. Challenging this conflict helps to better integrate society and create a real sense of citizenship and multiculturalism.

Equal opportunities

Everyone who has a legal status within the UK should have **equality of opportunity** regardless of their race, nationality, religion, gender, sexuality, disability, age or marital status. The legal route of enforcing their rights to equal treatment is covered later in the unit on pages 201–6. Many employers and service providers, including the uniformed services, will look to uphold equality by providing services and opportunities open to all, showing value to all members of society, consulting and informing the community on any relevant changes, encouraging and promoting diversity and treating people as individuals with consideration and respect for their needs.

Key terms

Equal opportunity The right to equivalent opportunities and access regardless of an individual's characteristics in areas such as employment and education and services such as healthcare.

Theory into practice

How could you, as a uniformed public service worker, challenge any negative behaviour that you witness? What strategies could you put in place to ensure you treat all sections of the community equally?

Positive action to find solutions for greater social inclusion and representation

Positive action can be used to prevent or compensate for disadvantages linked to a person's status. Positive action may vary from community to community as they may have their own strategies for social inclusion but it could include challenging segregation through the creation of mixed race schools, regenerating run-down areas, creating community projects that allow different groups to integrate and work together and encouraging groups to mix through a diverse renting and letting policy.

Corporate social responsibility

The public services have a corporate responsibility to create working practices that engage and include the local community and which recognise individual qualities, respecting age, gender, ethnicity or religion. Public service interaction within the community should involve positive action such as challenging negative behaviour and treating all sections of the community with equal respect. This is ultimately done by reducing inequalities between the least advantaged groups and communities and the rest of society by closing the opportunity gap and ensuring that support reaches those who need it most.

Diversity

Diversity is the status of being different. It is used to describe the relative uniqueness of each individual or group within a given society. Diversity encompasses such factors as age, gender, race, ethnicity, ability and religion, as well as education, professional background and marital and parental status. In conclusion, diversity refers to all the characteristics that make individuals and groups different from each other.

Diversity – as defined by the public services

All the uniformed services will have policies to ensure that diversity is maintained and encouraged within that service. The Army's equality and diversity policy is included as an example of how it might read.

'*We aim to treat everyone fairly and will not tolerate unlawful discrimination, including harassment and bullying. We recognise that everyone is unique and will respect their differences. We will give them the opportunity to develop their abilities fully, while emphasising their responsibility to the Army. We expect all our soldiers and officers to operate as members of a close-knit community, where trust, cohesion and teamwork are decisive factors in our success on operations. We rely upon leadership at all levels, and the effective contribution of every individual to achieve this.*'

Source: Equality and Diversity Directive for the Army, www.armyjobs.mod.uk

Local and national composition

It is important that the uniformed public services understand both the diversity of the local community that they serve and the composition of the country as this will help shape the way they interact with and support the community, as well as the strategies that are in place to help them conduct their job professionally and fairly.

A good way of finding out about the composition of your local area is by looking at the National Census. This is carried out every ten years and the last one was completed in April 2001. The National Census is the only survey that provides a detailed picture of the entire population and covers the following areas: population, health, housing, employment, transport and ethnic groups. The following example shows you the type of information gathered.

■ Composition of Rotherham, South Yorkshire

- The population of Rotherham has decreased by 2.2% over the last ten years while the UK population has risen by 2.4%.
- The average age of the population of Rotherham is 38.6 years.
- There are 248,179 people living in the Rotherham borough: 120,694 are male and 127,482 are female.
- 36.78% of the population of Rotherham do not have any formal qualifications while the national average is 29.1%.
- The unemployment rate for Rotherham is 3.9% while the national average is 3.4%. When broken down further the unemployment rate for men is 5.2% and the unemployment rate for women is 2.8%.
- The percentage of people in Rotherham born within the UK is 97.4% and the size of Rotherham's minority ethnic communities is 3.1% (7,712 people) while the national average is 8.7%.
- The largest minority ethnic group within Rotherham is Pakistani at 1.9% (4,704 people) and the next largest is Indian at 0.2% (497 people).
- 79.4% of the population are Christian, while 10.22% stated that they were not religious and the next largest group was Muslim with 2.18%.
- 19,306 people in Rotherham are registered as disabled with 14, 359 stating it to be a physical disability.

Source: National Census 2001. Crown copyright material is reproduced with the permission of the Controller of HMSO and the Queen's Printer for Scotland.

Take it further

Using your research skills, compare Rotherham with your local area. How does the composition of your area differ from Rotherham with regard to ethnicity, religion, gender and age?

Support groups

Many national and voluntary agencies exist to offer various types of additional support, beyond that offered by the public services.

Statutory agencies

Statutory agencies are created by Acts of Parliament and their functions are set down in law. These include local authorities that are democratically elected and answerable to the voters and central government. Their primary role is for the social well-being, economic development and health of the people they serve. Some statutory agencies include the NHS, police and fire and rescue service (not directly elected but answerable to the government).

Voluntary organisations

These are formally structured, independent, not-for-profit organisations managed by voluntary committees or boards of trustees which often have paid employees and/or volunteers. They are often registered charities and/or charitable companies. They undertake activities, provide services, offer support and/or campaign for change within the local community, depending on their nature.

■ How do statutory and voluntary agencies differ?

Statutory agencies (public) take many forms such as a branch of a central government department (Department of Health, NHS or the Inland Revenue) or a school working under a local education authority. Statutory agencies have legally binding responsibilities and are publicly accountable. Voluntary agencies (private) are often non-bureaucratic and work more closely with particular members of the local community and can often be unique to a particular area. Examples of voluntary agencies include Rape Crisis and Childline which are independent from the government. Most of the helpers are unpaid volunteers but there may be paid personnel to run the agency on a daily basis and to manage financial aspects such as fundraising and donations. These agencies may have a relatively short life as funding may only be allocated for a certain period.

Other areas of support may also come through a person's religion. Support can be offered on a variety of issues by a local church, mosque or synagogue. Local community centres may also provide facilities and clubs for developing the recreational, educational, cultural and personal welfare of community members.

The list below is not a full list – there are many other support groups. Your area may have unique services that exist to meet the needs of a certain group of people or to tackle a problematic issue in your local community.

■ Citizens Advice Bureau

The Citizens Advice Bureau (CAB) service helps people to resolve problems by providing free information and advice. The service has over 3000 centres nationwide which are run by more than 20,000 volunteers. They deal with about 5.5 million enquiries every year. Their website also receives over 400,000 visits a month. This busy support group commonly deals with employment issues, housing problems, immigration laws, consumer debt and matrimonial disputes.

■ Victim Support

Victim Support is the national charity for people affected by crime. It is a completely independent organisation, offering a free and confidential service to over 1.5 million victims a year, along with 250,000 witnesses. Staff are trained to provide emotional support, information and practical help to people who have suffered the effects of crime ranging from burglary to the murder of a relative.

Staff are also trained to provide support and information about the court process to witnesses, victims and their families, before, during and after the trial. The charity also runs a witness service in every criminal court in England and Wales.

Victim Support has two primary objectives: to provide support and assistance to individual victims, witnesses, their families and friends; and to raise public awareness and recognition of the effects of crime and promote victims' rights.

■ Sure Start

Sure Start aims to improve the health and well-being of families and children before and from birth by setting up local Sure Start programmes to improve services for families with children.

▲ Sure Start offers services including outreach and home visiting, support for good quality play, learning and childcare experiences for children, primary and community health care and support for children and parents with special needs

Sure Start is a government-funded scheme which aims to increase the availability of childcare, improve the health and development of children and help parents find employment. This is achieved by offering financial help and services for parents to meet the above aims and ensure children are not living in poverty.

Local initiatives include better access to family support, advice on nurturing, health services and early learning.

■ Samaritans

The Samaritans is a registered charity which is made up mainly of volunteers – each centre costs over £100 per day to open and maintain. The Samaritans offer support in any way they can. There are 202 branches across the country for people to come in and talk face-to-face with trained volunteers about their problems. Samaritans also offer 24-hour support via a helpline and listen to people explore their feelings in confidence without prejudice.

Terminology

The specifications list of a number of words which you must be able to define. Each of these words is explained and defined in context at appropriate points throughout this unit.

Assessment activity 6.2

Create a 5-minute presentation that explains how one voluntary agency and one statutory agency support members of the community. **P3**

Grading tips

P3 To achieve P3 you must outline how one voluntary agency and one statutory agency support members of the community.

Theory into practice

Visit your nearest town/city centre and list ten agencies that offer support to the local community. Why do you think such agencies are based in your area and who do they support?

6.2 Legislation that protects the human rights of individuals

In the UK, all individuals should have the same legal rights and obligations. However, inequalities still tend to cluster around certain groups, for example: women, minority ethnic groups, lesbians and gay men, the disabled and the elderly. A range of legislation exists in the UK to promote equality of opportunity for these groups and to combat discrimination against anyone who may be subject to it to ensure that everyone is treated equally by the law. This legislation will be covered in detail below.

The uniformed public services, like any organisation, must follow and apply the law in ensuring that all members of the community receive equality within the services they provide. They must also be able to justify why certain groups can't do certain jobs within the uniformed services. For example, the Army has to justify why only 70 per cent of its jobs are open to women and the fire service must explain why having a certain disability will exclude you from being a firefighter.

Consider this

What 'at risk' groups exist within society? Why do they need laws to protect them? Has the law done enough to protect these groups? Give examples and use media sources to argue your case.

The following Acts of Parliament promote equality of opportunity or protect the rights of particular groups of people.

The Equal Pay Act 1970

The Equal Pay Act (amended in 2003) was created to reduce the pay gap between men and women which stood at 37 per cent at the time. The Act states that men and women should be entitled to equal pay if the work is 'like work' (the same or broadly similar); if the work demands the equivalent skills, effort and decision making; and if the job is of equal value to the employer. Men and women should also receive equal terms and conditions such as bonus payments, holidays and sick leave. The Act does not give anyone the right to claim equal pay with a person of the same sex. It has had limited success – 30 years on the pay gap remains at somewhere between 15 and 20 per cent.

The Equal Pay Act 1970 (Amendment) Regulations 2003

This Act introduced two amendments to the Equal Pay Act. It allowed the six-month time limit for bringing equal pay claims to be extended in cases of concealment or disability. For example, concealment may happen when the employer lies about the fact that two people are paid unequally due to their gender when asked by an employee. It also allowed for the two-year limit on back pay to be extended to up to six years in cases of concealment and disability.

Sex Discrimination Act 1975

The Sex Discrimination Act 1975 (amended by the Sex Discrimination Act 1986) makes it illegal for employers to discriminate on the grounds of sex and marital status. It implements the principle of equal treatment for men and women in accessing employment, training, promotion, social benefits and working conditions. It is unlawful to treat a person less favourably because of their sex – this is known as **direct discrimination**. It is also unlawful to apply an unjustified condition, meaning that only a small per cent of one sex could comply with it – this is known as **indirect discrimination**.

Unlike the Race Relations Act 1976, the Sex Discrimination Act contains no express provisions in relation to harassment. However, sexual harassment is a form of direct discrimination and is dealt with in this way. A person who claims that they have been discriminated against has the right to take their case to a tribunal and claim damages. The Sex Discrimination Act applies to both men and women.

Key terms

Direct and indirect discrimination Direct discrimination is discrimination that is obvious and open whilst indirect discrimination is less obvious and could be a condition or restriction which affects a certain group more than other groups.

Sexism This is prejudicial or discriminative behaviour based on gender. This could be personal such as telling a joke or making a derogatory remark that demeans a person, or institutional such as when women are paid less than men for doing the same job.

Sex Discrimination 1975 (Amendment) Regulations 2003

Under this regulation, police officers are treated as being in the employment of the chief officer, who is therefore liable for the actions of officers (such as comments of a sexual nature) if he or she cannot prove that they took reasonable and practical steps to prevent the police officer from committing the unlawful act. These regulations also make it unlawful to discriminate against someone after the formal employment relationship has ended if the discrimination arises out of, and is closely connected to, that relationship.

Sex Discrimination (Gender Reassignment) Regulations 1999

Gender reassignment is the medical process of reassigning a person's sex by changing physiological and sexual characteristics. This legislation extends the Sex Discrimination Act 1975 to cover discrimination on the basis of gender reassignment in recruitment, employment and vocational training on the grounds that the person intends to undergo gender reassignment, is undergoing gender reassignment, or has at some time in the past undergone gender reassignment. This legislation covers only direct discrimination.

Race Relations Act 1976

The Race Relations Act 1965 made it unlawful to discriminate on the grounds of colour, race, ethnic or natural origins. It also became unlawful to incite racial hatred. The Race Relations Act 1976 went further and discrimination was also applied to jobs, training, housing, education and the provision of goods, facilities and services. It also became an offence to discriminate on the grounds of race, or to instruct, incite or induce someone else to do so. The Act also created the Commission for Racial Equality which helps people to bring legal action against alleged racial discrimination.

Race Relations (Amendment) Act 2000

This was created in response to the Stephen Lawrence inquiry report in December 1999. It extended the 1976 Act to cover the activities of the police and other public bodies. The Lawrence Inquiry first put forward the definition of **institutionalised racism** to describe the police service actions in the Stephen Lawrence murder inquiry.

It is important to realise that the above Acts deal with racial discrimination, not prejudice. They are concerned with people's actions and the effects of their actions, rather than their intentions and opinions.

Key terms

Institutionalised racism This is concerned with racism that takes place in an institution and is incorporated into its structures, policies and procedures either because of prejudicial behaviour or because of a failure and ignorance to take into account the needs of minority ethnic groups.

Racism The belief that some races are superior to others, based on the false idea that different physical characteristics such as colour or ethnic origin make some people better than others.

Racist A person who believes that there is an inherent difference between the various human races and who shows hatred or intolerance towards another race or other races due to this belief.

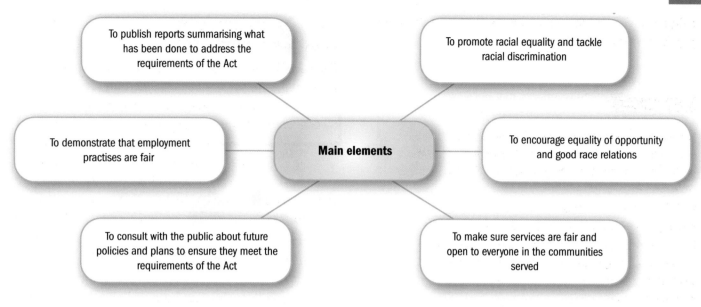

To publish reports summarising what has been done to address the requirements of the Act

To promote racial equality and tackle racial discrimination

To demonstrate that employment practises are fair

Main elements

To encourage equality of opportunity and good race relations

To consult with the public about future policies and plans to ensure they meet the requirements of the Act

To make sure services are fair and open to everyone in the communities served

Figure 6.2 The main elements of the Race Relations (Amendment) Act 2000

Consider this

What effects have the following laws had on the public services:

- Equal Pay Act 1970
- Sex Discrimination Act 1975
- Race Relations Act 1976
- Race Relations (Amendment) Act 2000?

The Public Order Act 1986

This Act created a number of offences to help the police deal with public disorder and violence such as:

- riots: where 12 or more people are threatening unlawful violence which would cause a reasonable person to fear for their safety
- violent disorder: where three or more people are doing the above
- affray: where at least one person is doing the above.

The Public Order Act 1986 also covered activities such as using threatening, abusive or insulting words or behaviour and display, publication or distribution of written materials, plays or broadcasts where stirring up of racial hatred is intended. (Racial hatred means hatred against a group of persons in the UK with reference to colour, race, nationality and ethnic or natural origins.)

Public Order (Amendment) Act 1996

This amended and limited the power of arrest of section 5 of the earlier Act.

Protection from Harassment 1997

Harassment is defined as causing alarm or distress. The legislation covers a wide range of behaviour such as racially or religiously-motivated harassment and can be used to prosecute people for certain types of antisocial behaviour where these amount to harassment, such as playing loud music, stalking and keeping noisy pets.

It also introduces several new criminal offences including harassment and putting a person in fear of violence. To be guilty of harassment, it must take place during a course of conduct (on at least two occasions), which amounts to harassment of another, which the defendant either knows, or ought to know. The same applies to being found guilty of putting a person in fear of violence.

Human Rights Act 1998

This ensures that the rights and responsibilities of citizens are clearly recognised and properly protected. The Human Rights Act contains a series of principles rather than a list of do's and don'ts. It is important that public service workers understand what our rights and responsibilities are. For more information on this important Act, see *Unit 1: Government, policies and the public services*.

Freedom of Information Act 2000

This Act creates a right of access to information from Government departments and public authorities such as the police to make recorded information held available to the public and to release this information upon request. All public authorities are obliged to ensure that information is readily available to members of the public and to inform the public of the extent of the information they have. Where information is exempt from disclosure, the public authorities must disclose it if the public interest in the disclosure outweighs the need for maintaining the exemption.

Disability Discrimination Act 2005

The Disability Discrimination Act (DDA) was originally introduced in 1995 and made it unlawful for a disabled person to be treated less favourably in employment, access to goods, facilities and services, and the buying or renting of land or property.

The law was expanded further in October 1999 to ensure that reasonable adjustments for disabled people are made, for example, by providing extra help or making changes to the way services are provided. In 2004 reasonable adjustments had to be made to the physical features of premises that offered barriers to access such as replacing steps with ramps and improving washing facilities to include disabled toilets.

In April 2005 the law was extended further to include:

- making it unlawful for operators of transport vehicles to discriminate against disabled people
- making it easier for disabled people to rent property and for tenants to make disability-related adaptations
- making sure that private clubs with 25 or more members cannot keep disabled people out, just because they have a disability
- extending protection to cover people who have HIV, cancer and multiple sclerosis from the moment they are diagnosed
- ensuring that discrimination law covers all the activities of the public sector
- requiring public bodies to promote equality of opportunity for disabled people.

The 2005 Act also introduced the Disability Rights Commission (December 2006), established to help secure civil rights and produce guidance for disabled people.

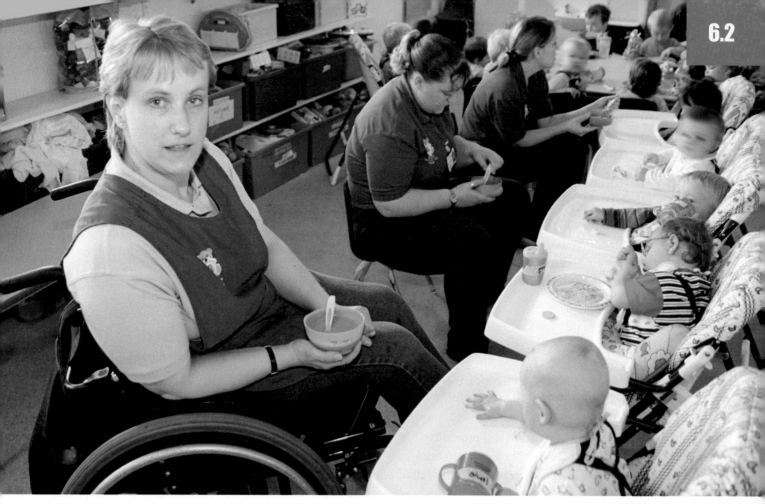

▲ **It is unlawful to discriminate against a person because of a disability**

Take it further

List ten reasonable changes that the various uniformed public services could do to ensure they don't discriminate against disabled people.

Equality Act 2006

The main element of this Act is the creation of the Commission for Equality and Human Rights (CEHR). This has replaced the Equal Opportunities Commission and the Disability Rights Commission and will replace the Commission for Racial Equality in April 2009. The CEHR will also promote other areas of discrimination such as sexual orientation, religion, belief and age by promoting human rights and equality in society (see below).

The Equality Act also makes discrimination unlawful on the grounds of religion or beliefs in the provision of goods, facilities, services, premises, education and the exercise of public functions. It has the following effects on the public services:

- It creates a duty on public services to promote equality of opportunity between men and women, and to prohibit sex discrimination in the exercise of their duties.

- This means all public services will have a general duty in the exercise of their public functions to pay due regard to eliminating unlawful discrimination, and promoting equality between men and women. This will affect activities such as employment practices and processes, recruitment policies, access to promotion and training.

- Public services will therefore need to ensure they take active steps to eliminate sources of discrimination in their own employment practices, for example, by ensuring the proportion of women they employ at a senior level is appropriate and that they pay their workforce equally.

- Public services will also have specific duties such as identifying gender equality goals and showing the action they will take to implement them. These will be published, monitored and reviewed every three years.

■ The Commission for Equality and Human Rights (CEHR)

This is a non-departmental public body covering England, Scotland and Wales. This means it assists ministers in the making or application of its equal opportunity legislation but ultimately remains independent of Parliament.

Its main purpose is to reduce inequality, eliminate discrimination, create good relations between the different groups of people and protect human rights. To do this the new focus is on educating workplaces and communities to apply fairness to all and not enforcing fairness through the courts.

It has the power to enforce legislation and promote equality for all. It will enforce equality legislation on issues such as age, disability, gender, race, religion, sexual orientation and encourage compliance with the Human Rights Act 1998. It will also campaign for social change and justice in any other areas where people face inequality.

EEC Directive on Equal Treatment, 76/205/EEC, 76/207/EEC

This European Directive established the principle of equal treatment for men and women across the European Union in accessing employment, training, promotion and working conditions. It requires all member states to ensure that men and women receive equal treatment and the Equal Pay Directive (75/117/EEC) ensures that member states offer equal pay for the same work or for work to which equal value is attributed.

The European Directive 2002/73 introduces substantial and procedural amendments to the Equal Treatment Directive 76/207 by providing clarification and definitions of key concepts such as direct and indirect discrimination and (sexual) harassment. These are very much in line with the previously mentioned UK legislation and because the UK is a member of the European Union they are also bound by European laws.

The Employment Equality (Age) Regulations 2006

The Employment Equality (Age) Regulations became effective from 1 October 2006 making it unlawful to discriminate against workers, employees, job seekers and trainees because of their age.

The Regulations cover recruitment, terms and conditions, promotions, transfers, dismissals and training but don't go as far as covering the provision of goods and services.

Under the Regulations it is unlawful to:

- discriminate directly against anyone by treating them less favourably because of their age
- discriminate indirectly against anyone by applying a provision or practice which disadvantages people of a particular age
- discriminate against someone after the working relationship has ended.

The Regulations also cover harassment or **victimisation** based on a person's age.

Key terms

Victimisation An act or exploit that occurs to make an individual feel unfairly treated.

Assessment activity 6.3

Preparing for a job in any of today's public services requires a candidate to have a comprehensive understanding and awareness of equality issues and people's rights. To help educate learners who wish to join the public services, create a leaflet which addresses the questions below.

1. Describe the main legislation that protects human rights in the UK. **P4**

2. Explain two pieces of legislation in detail and state how they impact on the various public services. **M1**

Grading tips

P4 To achieve P4 your leaflet must cover the following pieces of legislation: Sex Discrimination Act 1975 and Amendment 2003, Equal Pay Act 1970, Human Rights Act 1998, Race Relation Act 1976 and Amendment 2000, Public Order Amendment Act 1996, Disability Discrimination Act 2005, Freedom of Information Act 2000, The Employment Equality (Age) Regulations

2006, Protection from Harassment Act 1997, EU legislation – EEC directive on Equal Treatment, 76/205/EEC, 76/207/EEC.

M1 To fulfil the M1 criteria, you must explain the relevant sections of two of the following areas of legislation (sex, race or disability) and state how they have an impact on the public services.

In this section you will learn about the role that the various uniformed public services have in ensuring **equality of service** to all sectors of the community. This section covers the services offered to individuals such as aims and objectives; the concepts of fairness, **social justice**, law and morality; together with issues of personal management, discipline and accessibility.

Key terms

Equality of service/treatment Treating people with an equal level of respect (not necessarily treating people the same). This means that people should have equal access to services such as education and training, employment, housing and protection from crime.

Social justice This is an ideal of society and is based on the idea that society treats individuals and groups fairly and everyone gets a fair share of the benefits of society.

Role of the public services

As the public services provide essential support to the communities they serve, it is essential that all the services provide equality of service to the diverse groups within their communities.

Aims and objectives

The public services will have many aims and objectives set, either internally or externally, and a number of these will be particularly focused at offering a fair and equal service. Some examples of the aims and objectives that the uniformed services might have are shown below.

- **Police service**
  The police service might be asked to reduce the proportion of stop and searches of ethnic minority groups if the statistics were very disproportionate to that of the local population.

- **Fire service**
  The fire service might be asked to improve its station facilities to better cater for female fire fighters.

- **The Armed Forces**
  The Armed Forces may need to change some of their uniforms and dress codes to suit certain religious requirements.

- **Ambulance service**
  A paramedic may need to consider an individual's beliefs and culture and gain their consent before conducting certain medical procedures, for example, those which involve undressing a person or when giving them blood.

Apart from their own service aims and objectives, all services must follow Government objectives. The most influential departments are the Home Office, the Ministry of Justice and the Ministry of Defence.

The Home Office has responsibility for the police and areas such as terrorism, national security and immigration.

The Ministry of Justice, which is part of the Department for Constitutional Affairs, has responsibility for the agencies dealing with offenders such as the courts, prisons and probation service and responsibility for criminal law and sentencing policies.

The Ministry of Defence has responsibility for the Armed Forces, which comprises over 200,000 personnel. Its primary role is to defend the realm by ensuring the security and defence of the United Kingdom and its overseas territories.

These departments must work towards the following key objectives:

- protecting the UK from terrorist attack
- cutting crime, especially violent and drug-related crime
- ensuring people feel safer in their homes and daily lives, particularly through more visible, responsive and accountable local policing
- safeguard people's identity and the privileges of citizenship

- work with other government departments to create an efficient, effective and proportionate criminal justice system
- securing our borders, preventing abuse of immigration laws and managing migration to benefit the UK.

How the public services and statutory and non-statutory services are linked

Statutory services are required by law to provide a service. Non-statutory services are usually charitable agencies which offer specialist support such as advice and guidance on a variety of issues. They can become involved with people in the community through referrals from the various uniformed services such as victims of crime or terrorism.

Sometimes the uniformed public services rely on the help of statutory and non-statutory services.

Statutory Services (defined by legal statute)	Non-statutory services (add value to a statutory provision)
• Social Services • National Health Service • Police • Probation services • Criminal Justice System • Trading Standards	• Voluntary sector – charities • RNIB • Barnardos • Sure Start • Citizens Advice Bureau

Table 6.4 Statutory and non-statutory organisations

Social Services is a statutory agency responsible for helping children in need and their families, for protecting children and for looking after children who need to live apart from their parents. It is governed and funded by the Government through public money. It is supported by a number of non-statutory agencies which are not governed directly by the Government including:

- *Barnardos* – this non-statutory service supports children, families and the community through services such as family centres and playgroups, along with counselling and training services, and advice on fostering, adoption and disability
- *Sure Start* – a non-statutory service that offers universal, free, early education and childcare to families with children aged between 0–14 and who are from poor and disadvantaged backgrounds.

■ Police and Criminal Evidence Act 1984 (PACE)

This Act sets out to strike a balance between the powers of the police and the rights and freedoms of the public. It is the main framework for the powers of police officers in England and Wales, as well as providing codes of practice for the exercise of those powers. It deals with such matters as powers to stop and search, arrest, detain and interview. It was passed as a result of the recommendations of the Phillips Commission on Criminal Justice. The Act brought about the following changes:

- the requirement that the police keep records of stop and search incidents
- each police station should have a custody officer to record all that happens while a suspect is detained
- imposing strict time limits on detention by police of suspects
- interviews at the station must be tape-recorded.

This Act was significantly modified by the Serious Organised Crime and Police Act 2005, replacing all existing powers of arrest, including the category of arrestable offences, with a new general power of arrest for all offences.

■ Fire and Rescue Service Act 2004

A key feature of this Act was the new duty on all fire and rescue authorities to promote fire safety in their area by providing flexibility for fire and rescue authorities to work with others in the community. This meant that fire and rescue authorities were required to strike a balance between prevention and intervention.

The new duty means that all fire and rescue authorities must make fire prevention a mainstream activity by drawing up Integrated Risk Management Plans (IRMPs) to identify particular at-risk groups within their areas, and target resources accordingly (Home Risk Assessments).

The Act puts in place wider duties for the service that cover other forms of emergencies such as: chemical, biological, radiological and nuclear attack (CBRN);

serious flooding; incidents requiring major search and rescue; and major non-road traffic incidents.

■ Armed Forces Act 2006

This Act replaced the three separate systems of service law (Royal Navy, Army and Royal Air Force) with a single harmonised and streamlined system to govern all members of the Armed Forces. The basic elements of the discipline systems remain, meaning commanding officers deal with less serious offences, and more serious offences are tried by court martial. The main changes to the **disciplinary** system are:

- granting commanding officers in the three services identical powers to deal with matters summarily
- creating a single independent service prosecuting authority
- replacing district and general court martial with a standing court martial
- a faster, more efficient redress procedure with an independent member to sit on the services complaints panel to deal with certain cases such as bullying and harassment
- a complaints commissioner, to hear complaints and allegations from service personnel and third parties
- replacing the various boards of inquiry with one single form of statutory service inquiry.

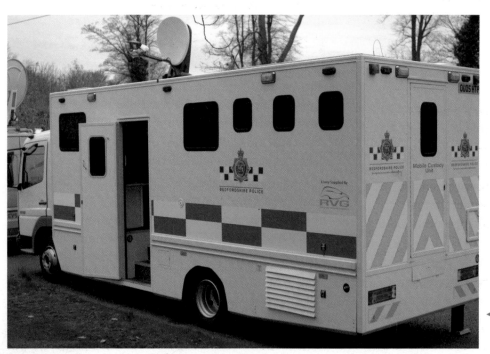

Key terms

Disciplinary A procedure in place to correct or punish breaches of discipline.

Public service responsibilities

So far we have identified that the public services need to treat all members of the community equally, meaning that certain groups shouldn't be prioritised over others. To ensure this, public service workers need to show good self-discipline, positive behaviour and professionalism at all times.

Offering a fair and equal service

The main public service that has faced scrutiny with regard to offering an equal and fair service is the police service. Below are some of the common aims and objectives that the various police constabularies will uphold in their policing plans to ensure a quality service.

- *Mobile police stations* – these are highly visible 24-hour incident rooms at major investigations. They are used at football and other leisure events and can be placed in crime problem areas to ensure easy access for all sections of the community. They provide full facilities, such as computers and telephones.
  - *Crime prevention schemes* – this includes help in setting up Neighbourhood Watch

◀ Mobile police stations are used as 24-hour incident rooms at major investigations

schemes. Information on crime prevention may be given to victims of crime to prevent repeat offences. This ultimately helps to reduce the worry about crime and increase a feeling of safety.

- *Police Community Support Officers* – PCSOs are often seen as frontline officers – 'the bobbies on the beat' – providing a visible presence on the streets and interaction with the public. They tackle antisocial behaviour, deal with misdemeanours and provide crime-prevention information.

Consider this

What are the advantages and disadvantages of having police officers on foot patrols in high-crime areas?

Self-discipline

Self-discipline is important to the public services as the action they take often challenges their emotions or opposes their fundamental moral values. A self-disciplined person is often very motivated and this can help them deal with various problems or difficulties they may face.

Personal management

Personal management has many aspects and covers the qualities and skills an individual needs to organise themselves and to conduct themselves appropriately, often by scheduling, delegating and being adaptable. Public service workers need to demonstrate professionalism, perhaps by time-keeping, or by wearing a uniform correctly so that they look approachable and smart when in the community.

■ Accountability and Public Service Agreements

The Government is accountable to the public for its actions, by way of elections to office. Public services are accountable to both the public and the Government. One of the most common ways of ensuring accountability in the public services is through Public Service Agreements (PSAs).

The objectives of PSAs are to establish a clear set of standards in order to drive up the performance of every public service and to reduce significantly the performance gap between the best and the worst performing services. PSAs are usually set within a one-year time frame.

Examples of PSAs include:

Fire service

1. To reduce accidental fires in peoples' homes by x* per cent.
2. To reduce the number of accidental fire-related deaths in the home by x* per cent.
3. To reduce deliberate fires by x* per cent.
4. To reduce hoax calls by x* per cent.

Police service

1. To reduce crime by x* per cent.
2. To reassure the public by reducing the fear of crime and antisocial behaviour.
3. To reduce the harm caused by illegal drugs including substantially increasing the number of drug-misusing offenders entering treatment.

*x can vary from service to service

Law versus morality

Apart from a legal obligation to ensure equality of service, public service workers often have to deal with moral obligations.

The word 'morality' comes from the Latin word '*mos, more*' meaning 'customs and habits'. It is defined as that which concerns the distinction between right and wrong in relation to actions, conditions and character. Morality refers to the concept of human ethics, which is the assumption of what is right and wrong and involves an individual's conscience in making sound judgments. This is sometimes referred to as moral values. One person's moral values may be similar to those of another, especially if they have shared cultural or religious beliefs. Their moral values may be very different if they are from different social groups. Morals can affect a person's behaviour, motivations and actions in a given situation, and can develop during a person's lifetime. Many things that are not against the law may go against our moral values, such as the right to have an abortion.

As society has developed, so has the law. Early (unwritten) laws were often based on people's views on right and wrong, sometimes called 'natural law'. Modern written laws still very much seek to enforce justice and support morality. Obedience from the majority of the community is achieved as people share the belief that laws need to be maintained to help society. However, modern laws are more focused on preventing harm (public morality) than on individual views (private morality).

Legal consequences

See pages 218–9 in section 6.4 for a discussion of legal consequences.

Accessibility

The public services must not discriminate against existing and potential service users on the basis of disability. Reasonable adjustments should be made to the workplace and facilities provided by the various services. Table 6.5 provides some examples.

▲ It is important to make reasonable adjustments to the workplace and facilities provided by the various services

Individual and group requirements

To ensure equality of service to all members of the public, the public services need to consider both individual and group needs. Treating people differently is often an effective way of offering equality, for example, removing your footwear if you enter a mosque (something you wouldn't do if you entered a Catholic church).

Meeting the needs of the community involves listening to them and interacting positively with the various groups in an appropriate way. The way you speak to the community would differ depending on the group involved, for example, not using common slang or complex terms when speaking to someone who doesn't speak English as their first language.

■ Community forums

These are public meetings arranged by the public services, in particular the police, and involve members of the public. They are chaired by members of the public services and normally meet several times a year. The forums could focus on a particular group such as ethnic minorities, young people or women to gauge their opinions. The forums are likely to: promote and encourage good relationships between the public and the public services; enable a better understanding of the use of available resources; discuss the public services' plans and aims; provide an opportunity for people to talk to the public services about their concerns and make suggestions. In essence, the forums provide an opportunity for discussion between the community and public services, promoting good relationships and better understanding.

General	Ethnic minorities	Disability (sensory and physical)
• Clear signposting • Open-planned • Automatic doors/double doors • Lifts • Baby-changing facilities/play area • Handrails • Wide aisles/corridors	• Use of plain English and picture symbols • Translator/multilingual staff • Multilingual leaflets/signs • Special dietary foods • Prayer room	• Wheelchair access • Disabled toilets • Dropped and raised kerbs • Hearing loops/audio speakers • Flashing doorbells/alarms • Disabled parking • Ramps • Disabled toilets

Table 6.5 Improving accessibility for all

Take it further

A recent community forum was attended by representatives from some of the main agencies that run key services, including the local council and the police and fire service. The following issues were raised by various sections of the community:

- the increase in gangs of youths hanging around at the local bus station
- the lack of facilities in the local park
- the amount of violence and noise from a local pub
- strong criticism at the proposal to merge the two nearby fire stations into one
- the lack of police patrols in the area, especially at night
- accusations that the fire service only recruits males as there are currently no female fire fighters.

For each concern, suggest action points for the police, fire service or local council to feed back to the next meeting.

▲ Work on community projects is an important part of the public services' role

■ Community projects

Another way the public services can provide equality of service is by taking part in community projects which help to enrich the lives of those who find it difficult to help themselves. Four common groups in society that benefit from such projects are young people, the elderly, disabled people and families.

Table 6.6 shows examples of projects that take place up and down the country and that involve these groups and the various public services.

Group	Examples of activities	Public service involved (police, prison, fire, Armed Forces)
Young people	<ul><li>Day trips – theme parks/outward bounds</li><li>Youth clubs</li><li>Skate parks – improving local facilities</li><li>Internet café – youth forums</li><li>Radio station</li><li>School liaison – visits to schools</li><li>Educational projects – such as Crucial Crew, Prison? Me? No Way! and work placements.</li><li>Cadets</li></ul>	<ul><li>Police</li><li>Police</li><li>Police</li><li>Police</li><li>Police</li><li>All</li><li>All</li><li>Police, Armed Forces and fire</li></ul>
Elderly people	<ul><li>Organising concerts and events – using local facilities</li><li>Improving facilities and accessibility</li></ul>	<ul><li>Police</li><li>Police, fire</li></ul>
Disabled people	<ul><li>Supply transport to enable people with disabilities to attend social events</li><li>Adapting and improving accessibility within the community</li><li>Buying/fundraising for specialist equipment (wheelchairs)</li></ul>	<ul><li>Police</li><li>All</li><li>All</li></ul>
Families	<ul><li>Fun days – street parties/festivals</li><li>Regeneration projects</li><li>Raising awareness of the various voluntary support groups</li><li>Careers fair</li></ul>	<ul><li>All</li><li>All</li><li>All</li><li>All</li></ul>

Table 6.6 Community projects in which the public services are involved and which benefit disadvantaged groups

Theory into practice

- Identify which projects your local fire and police service have been involved in over the last year.
- Create a list that highlights the advantages and disadvantages of the public services being involved in community projects.

■ Appropriate language

Promoting appropriate language (also known as politically correct or PC language) is one way of tackling negative attitudes. Appropriate language policies are intended to protect public service workers from making unintentional mistakes in the language they use; to help them interact better with communities; to specifically set out what language is acceptable and what is not; and to provide valuable guidance on how public service workers should respond to inappropriate language both within and outside of their service. The policies cover many issues such as appropriate language to use with regard to race, ethnicity, gender, disability, sexual orientation and religion. These policies take the view that inappropriate language can seriously impact on recruitment and service delivery.

Theory into practice

Write a list with as many PC and non-PC pairs of words as you can. Compare the PC and non-PC words. Do the non-PC words reflect prejudiced or negative views? Do you think that using appropriate terms will lead people to:

- be less personally prejudiced
- cause less offence to the public?

■ Different languages in the UK

There are a number of languages spoken in Britain. However, it's unlikely that you'll be expected to learn

Take it further

Over 250 languages are spoken in London, making the capital the most linguistically diverse city in the world. In a survey of 850,000 children in London schools, a question was asked about their first language spoken at home. The 40 most common languages spoken are:

Language	Approx total	Language	Approx total
English	608,500	Igbo (Nigeria)	1900
Bengali and Silheti	40,400	French-based Creoles	1800
Punjabi	29,800	Tagalog (Filipino)	1600
Gujarati	28,600	Kurdish	1400
Hindi/Urdu	26,000	Polish	1500
Turkish	15,600	Swahili	1000
Arabic	11,000	Lingala (Congo)	1000
English-based Creoles	10,700	Albanian	900
Yoruba (Nigeria)	10,400	Luganda (Uganda)	800
Somali	8300	Ga (Ghana)	800
Cantonese	6900	Tigrinya (Sudan)	800
Greek	6300	German	800
Akan (Ashanti)	6000	Japanese	800
Portuguese	6000	Serbian/ Croatian	700
French	5600	Russian	700
Spanish	5500	Hebrew	650
Tamil (Sri Lanka)	3700	Korean	550
Farsi (Persian)	3300	Pashto (Afganistan)	450
Italian	2500	Amharic (Ethiopia)	450
Vietnamese	2400	Sinhala (Sri Lanka)	450

Table 6.7 The 40 most commonly spoken languages in London

Source: Baker, P., Eversley, J (eds) (2000)
Multilingual Capital: Battlebridge: London

> ▲ One of the ways the public services can communicate with a diverse community is through specialised multilingual publications such as posters, leaflets and multimedia

another language to be a member of the public services. The services employ translators and interpreters to help communicate effectively with non-English speakers.

Take it further

Conduct a survey that looks at the different languages spoken in your area. If it helps, you could focus on a particular age group.

What other questions could you ask to establish the diversity of your local community?

Assessment activity 6.4

The public services for many years have worked towards providing equality of service to all members of the community. This is in addition to creating policies, strategies and procedures which address diversity issues within the services.

You have been asked by the Home Office to review the performance of two public services by taking part in the following activities.

1. Take part in a group discussion which clearly explains the role of two public services in providing equality of services to all members of the community and combating discrimination. **P5**

2. Using your notes from the discussion, create a PowerPoint presentation which analyses how one of the public services has provided equality of service to all members of the community and combated discrimination. **M2**

Grading tips

P5 To achieve P5 you should consider discussing what services are offered to the community and the aims and objectives of the public services. You should show knowledge of relevant statutory legislation such as the Police and Criminal Evidence Act 1984, Armed Forces Act 2006, Fire and Rescue Act 2004. You also need to demonstrate an understanding of some of the key themes such as fairness, personal management, social justice, law and morality and accessibility.

M2 To achieve M2 don't forget to analyse in detail the role of one public service in providing equality of service to all members of the community and combating discrimination.

Policies, strategies and procedures

The uniformed public services have been looking to increase the representation within its workforce of people from the minority groups. This has been tackled at both a national (the Government) and local level (the service) through policies, procedures and strategies. This includes addressing important issues such as ensuring equal opportunities are maintained through the use of grievance procedures and other anti-discrimination policies to deal with harassment and bullying in the workplace. There has been a great emphasis on recruiting and developing a more diverse workforce and many areas have been addressed such as recruitment, support mechanisms, shift patterns and adapting uniform and facilities to meet people's religious and cultural beliefs.

Equal opportunities strategies

A good equal opportunity strategy should ensure that all employees are treated fairly, with respect and without bias and that people are dealt with and supported in a way that doesn't show personal preference for particular characteristics. An equal opportunities strategy shouldn't be about giving certain groups unfair advantage, assuming everyone is the same or having different standards for certain groups.

An equal opportunities strategy should help to create a workplace where the employees are confident they will get fair access to the various opportunities and where advancement is based on their individual skills and competence. It also helps to demonstrate and reinforce the professionalism and image of the organisation to the community.

The public services look to employ a workforce which reflects the vast diversity of background and culture within which they operate. This includes creating a working environment that is free from harassment, victimisation or discrimination. This requires all current employees to demonstrate non-discriminatory behaviour to colleagues and the public, and to challenge behaviour which is unacceptable, especially on grounds of gender, race, ethnic origin, disability or sexual orientation. This includes bullying and inappropriate remarks.

The public services create **policies**, **procedures** and **practices** that reflect these principles and regularly review them. Ensuring that equal opportunity strategies are up-to-date and complied with in the public services means that everyone has access to the services' equal opportunities statement and receives specialist training on equal opportunity issues to raise awareness and help to eliminate discrimination. A senior member of the service is responsible for monitoring the policy, including issues such as recruitment procedures, selection for training, staff appraisal and promotion.

Key terms

Policies These determine what an organisation intends to do.

Procedures These are how it plans to go about it.

Practices These are how it actually does it.

Anti-discriminatory practices Practices that ensure that employees have equality of opportunity and do not experience discrimination or prejudice.

It is critical that public services have effective equal opportunity policies as unfair or unlawful practices within the workplace not only lead to resentment and upset but also affect the public's perception of the services as a possible career for certain minority groups.

Case study: West Midlands Police equal opportunities policy

West Midlands Police has 8125 officers and 3505 support staff. A breakdown of officers from minority groups shows that there are 2017 female officers and 449 ethnic minorities officers. The main points of the force's equal opportunities policy are as follows:

- Equal opportunities shall mean fairness for all; the recognition, development and use of everyone's talents.
- This fairness will run through recruitment, selection, training, promotion, specialisation and career development generally. It should also govern the relationship of all employees to each other.
- Equality of opportunity does not just relate to race, sex or marital status but to anyone who could be disadvantaged.
- No job applicant or employee shall receive unfavourable treatment directly or indirectly on

the grounds of gender, sexual orientation, marital status, race, nationality, ethnic origin, religious beliefs and, where applicable, trade union membership, age or disability.

- Selection criteria and procedures will be frequently reviewed to ensure that individuals are selected, promoted and dealt with on the basis of merit, fitness and competence, subject only to the restrictions imposed by law.
- Training programmes are very important and will be arranged to ensure that staff are fully aware of their roles and responsibilities and have the opportunity to develop and progress within the organisation.

1. **Why is it important to have equal opportunities throughout recruitment, selection, training and promotion?**

2. **Suggest ways in which this could be achieved.**

A successful equal opportunity strategy should work as a mechanism to help resolve any problems that arise in the workplace. This means that any grievances that arise are dealt with quickly and effectively.

Grievance procedures

A **grievance procedure** provides a formal way of dealing with issues and concerns before they develop into major problems. All public services have a written grievance procedure to provide employees with a reasonable and prompt opportunity under the Employment Act 2002 to attempt resolution of grievances through a workplace procedure prior to any application to an **employment tribunal**.

Key terms

Grievance procedure The formal process to deal with an unsatisfactory working condition with reason

for **complaint** or resistance which is dealt with in a certain way.

Complaint An expression of dissatisfaction and something that is the cause or subject of protest.

Employment tribunal A mechanism for resolving disputes which decides on the outcome and action to be taken.

A framework for managing grievances would be:

- Identify the problem and determine how the aggrieved person would like the matter to be resolved.
- Explain the grievance process and give the aggrieved person the opportunity to be accompanied by a colleague or a trade union/staff association representative.
- Undertake an enquiry into the matter.
- Interview the person who is the subject of the grievance and give them the opportunity of being accompanied by a colleague or a trade union/staff association representative.

- Ensure that all the parties are told of the outcome of the enquiry and what action is to be taken.
- Obtain signed confirmation from the person submitting the grievance that the matter has been satisfactorily resolved.

Grievance procedures in action

The police service deals with grievances by applying the Fairness at Work Procedure published by the Home Office in 2004. The procedure's main purpose is to ensure that police officers, police staff, members of the special constabulary and community volunteers who feel aggrieved about the way they have been treated are given every opportunity to have their issue/s resolved in a fair and just manner without fear of recrimination.

The procedure has two formal stages with an additional preliminary informal resolution stage and an optional final appeal stage. The first stage is an initial approach to the person's immediate supervisor by completion of the Grievance Report. The supervisor then has 14 days to resolve it. If no resolution is reached, the Grievance Report, together with any other relevant information, will be forwarded to the divisional/departmental head. After 14 days it enters the appeal stage and the head of human resources will examine the complaint for any procedural breaches. The main purpose will be to examine whether the case was handled correctly and honestly within the framework of the procedure, and ensure that decisions have been made on an informed basis and with due regard to all relevant factors. If there is still no resolution then an application to an employment tribunal will be advised.

Bullying and harassment at work

Harassment is any behaviour that is unacceptable, unwelcome or unreasonable. It can be physical (touching), verbal (offensive language) or non-verbal (gestures) and can even be done through emails and texting.

Bullying is any unwelcome or threatening behaviour. It often takes the form of a person abusing their physical or mental strength, or their position of authority, to intimidate, persecute, humiliate or victimise a person or a group of people.

Victimisation is defined as treating a person less favourably because they have brought proceedings against the discriminator or any other person under the law, given evidence or information or anything else in relation to their or another's proceedings, or made an allegation of discrimination in good faith.

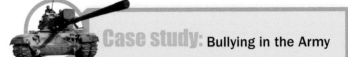

Case study: Bullying in the Army

Alan is on leave after starting his initial training with the Army. After meeting up for a drink with his friend, he breaks down in tears – he is upset at how the corporal has been treating him. He explains that the corporal is always singling him out, finding fault with his performance and criticising him. The corporal does this through belittling, demeaning and patronising him in front of the rest of the soldiers. The corporal has also started to make him do extra duties at night and has made him sleep in isolation from the rest of the soldiers in the barracks.

1. **Highlight where you believe bullying has taken place.**

2. **What would you advise Alan to do?**

Disciplinary action – legal consequences

A breach of the equal opportunities policy by public service workers will result in sanctions depending on the severity of the misconduct and the service in question.

Consider this

- What kind of discipline issues is a commanding officer likely to deal with on a daily basis?
- What punishments can be handed out by a commanding officer?
- What is the role of a standing court martial and what types of cases are they likely to deal with?

(See Figure 6.4 below.) These sanctions apply to all employees while on duty irrespective of rank. A breach of equal opportunities while an officer is off duty may still be punished if the offence is serious enough.

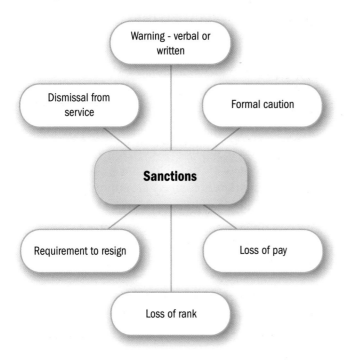

▲ Figure 6.3 Sanctions that may be enforced if the equal opportunities policy is breached by a public service worker

Other anti-discrimination policies

Many changes have taken place within the public services to challenge and eliminate certain types of discrimination, such as the removal of maximum age limits for the fire service and height restrictions from the police service. The Armed Forces now welcome applications from men and women irrespective of their sexual orientation, in line with the Employment Equality (Sexual Orientation) Regulations 2003.

Complaints against the public services

Sometimes members of the public will have grievances against the public services, with regard to their level of service or their behaviour and conduct. All the public services have a complaints procedure which must be made available to the public. The example below is for the police service.

■ Independent Police Complaints Commission

When a member of the public has a complaint against the police service they can contact the Independent Police Complaints Commission (IPCC) (which replaced the Police Complaints Authority on 1 April 2004) if they feel they have not been given sufficient information by the police or if they are unhappy with the outcome of an investigation by the police. This is an independent body and has powers to initiate, run, manage and supervise investigations into complaints or allegations of misconduct and is also responsible for monitoring the way complaints are handled by the police service themselves. It covers all police employees, including support staff and special constables.

The IPCC will automatically investigate the following incidents:

- deaths following police contact
- fatal road accidents involving a police vehicle
- any incident where a member of the public has sustained serious injury
- use of a firearm by an officer on duty
- allegations of aggravated discriminatory behaviour
- allegations that an officer has committed a serious arrestable offence while on duty.

The advantages of this system are:

- It is independent of the police and Government.
- It has greater powers than the Police Complaints Authority.
- People have a mechanism to make a complaint that is free.
- You don't have to be a victim of crime to make a complaint.

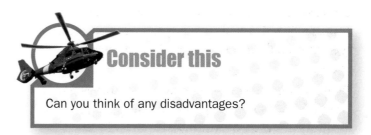

Consider this

Can you think of any disadvantages?

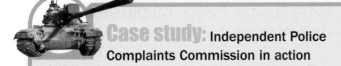

Case study: Independent Police Complaints Commission in action

On 22 July 2005, Jean Charles de Menezes was shot and killed at Stockwell Tube Station on the London Underground after officers mistook him for a suicide bomb suspect.

At the time of the incident, some of the witness and police statements about what had happened were inconsistent or incorrect and lots of different stories appeared in the media. No officers were charged at the time but it has since emerged that the officers involved in the fatal shooting could face charges.

The Independent Police Complaints Commission (IPCC) conducted an investigation into the incident which they may send to the Crown Prosecution Service (CPS) to consider. The investigation by the IPCC aimed to determine whether the findings showed that criminal offences might have been committed. If the report was sent to the CPS, they would then have to decide whether anybody involved in the incident should be charged with those criminal offences.

The IPCC have not provided details of the criminal offences that they believe might have been committed but it is thought that they could include serious offences such as murder or manslaughter.

1. **Should the police have a shoot-to-kill policy in the wake of the Menezes case?**

2. **Should police officers be criminally liable for their actions when in the call of duty?**

The public services also have their own internal complaints procedure for staff who have grievances against others.

Recording and monitoring of equal opportunities data

The public services look to monitor and record the background, culture and characteristics of people applying for jobs within the services. This is usually done in the application process for all applicants and includes candidates who are ultimately unsuccessful.

The reason behind this approach is to ensure that selection is fair and that recruitment is based on merit and ability to do the job. This is in addition to establishing if there are different success rates for men and women and for different ethnic groups and people with and without disabilities.

If there are different success rates it will enable the public services in question to take action to ensure that no group is treated unfairly.

Diversity issues

Developing a diverse workforce

All public services need to have a diverse workforce that represents the community which it supports. The uniformed public services have identified recruitment and retention of employees as key issues that need addressing.

Unfortunately creating a more diverse workforce is much deeper and more complex than just employing more ethnic minority employees or offering benefits such as a pension and medical care.

Creating a more diverse workforce is not just an issue restricted to the police service – the Bain Report reviewed the fire service and set out recommendations for how the service should change in the future to meet the demands of the twenty-first century and one of the changes was 'to encourage a more diverse workforce and develop new national recruitment processes'.

There are many advantages of recruiting a more diverse workforce as it helps a public service gain a greater operational picture of the needs of the whole society and such employees bring with them their own life experience and views which will help to combat discrimination within the workplace.

Take it further

The Government has made the recruitment of more officers from ethnic minorities a priority and in 1999 all police constabularies were set employment targets for the recruitment, retention and progression of minority ethnic officers. These targets are to be met by 2009 and many police services are struggling to meet them.

- Why do you think the police service is struggling to meet these targets?
- Why is it important to attract more recruits from ethnic minority backgrounds?
- Do you think recruiting people from abroad is a good way to meet recruitment targets?

■ Strategies for creating a more diverse workforce

The uniformed public services have looked at various methods of creating a more diverse workforce. Below is a summary of some key approaches that have been adopted by the services in order to try and create a more varied workforce.

1. Increased recruitment from minority groups and positive response to all applicants.
2. Up-to-date training on diversity issues for current and new staff.
3. Sharing of good practice and successful initiatives.
4. Understanding the needs of the current workforce.
5. Reviewing and updating the recruitment and selection process.
6. Improvement of facilities and services delivery.
7. Exit interviews for staff that resign and monitoring of absenteeism/sickness.

8. Creating a positive public image by challenging negative perceptions.
9. Tackling discrimination within the services by having clear grievance and disciplinary procedures.

Case study: Force admits rejecting white men

In 2006, it was reported in the media that the Gloucestershire Police Force had admitted to illegally rejecting 108 applicants for jobs in their force. The reason they gave was that the applicants were white men.

Government targets, set in 1999, state that 7 per cent of police officers in England and Wales should be from minority ethnic groups by 2009 and forces are under pressure to meet these targets.

In September 2005, only 1.6 per cent of officers in the Gloucestershire police force were from ethnic minorities and the Police Federation said that the force was trying to recruit more female officers and more people from minority ethnic groups to meet the targets set by the government.

This particular incident came to light when one of the unsuccessful applicants, Matt Powell, was told that his application had been 'randomly deselected' from the pool of applicants. Mr Powell eventually took legal action against the Gloucestershire police force and the Commission for Racial Equality (CRE) and the Equal Opportunities Commission (EOC) led the investigation. Mr Powell was awarded £2500 in compensation.

The unlawful discrimination evident in the Gloucestershire police force recruitment process is not the only example of its kind. Earlier in 2006, the Avon and Somerset Police Force had also admitted to illegally rejecting nearly 200 applications from white men in order to try and meet government targets.

1. **What positive action could be done to increase the applicants from women and ethnic groups?**
2. **What could be done to increase the number of disabled people working within the services?**

10. Reviewing jobs within the services to see if they can be civilian posts and opened up to part-time workers and disabled people.

11. Screening of all policies and procedures to eliminate any element of discrimination, especially in the recruitment of new officers.

12. Positive media articles in the press or on TV.

13. Placing advertisements for vacancies in specialist publications such as *Gay Times* and *Disability Now*.

14. Community events, open days and familiarisation days to create awareness of the recruitment procedure for under-represented groups and to show them that they are valued.

15. Providing mentors for new recruits.

16. Training opportunities for development and promotion of minority ethnic groups to the more senior ranks.

17. Ensuring that the proportion of people from minority ethnic communities is reflected at all levels of the workforce including the civilian posts.

18. Improving the collection, analysis and use of workforce data on age, gender, ethnicity, race and disability so that services are fully aware of how their service reflects the community they serve.

19. Having an equal opportunities adviser whose role is to advise on developing policies and procedures that help the employment of a diverse workforce.

20. Creating support networks and providing access to support and counselling services.

Familiarisation events and open days

This is a common '**positive action**' that the public services will undertake to raise awareness of a career in, and the role of, the service within society. It has become common for the public services to have familiarisation days and open days which are particularly aimed at under-represented groups.

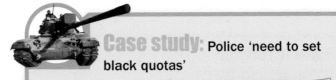

Case study: Police 'need to set black quotas'

As we have seen in the Case Study on page 221, it is currently illegal to discriminate against job applicants on the grounds of race, religion or gender. This makes it extremely difficult for police forces to recruit the number of minority ethnic applicants required by government targets.

Currently only 3.7 per cent of officers in England and Wales come from black and minority ethnic groups. The Association of Chief Police Officers believes that this situation can only be improved if the law is changed to allow positive discrimination, or it will take many more years to achieve a representative workforce than government targets allow.

Some people cite the example of Northern Ireland, where affirmative action has been implemented to ensure that forces recruit equal numbers of Catholics and non-Catholics. This exception was made possible by a provision made under the 1998 Good Friday Agreement.

1. **Is positive discrimination the way forward for the uniformed public services to create a more diverse workforce?**

Key terms

Positive action (Sometimes called affirmative action) This refers to policies aimed at promoting access to education or employment. This is not to be confused with positive discrimination.

Familiarisation days give members of the community an opportunity to visit the service's facilities and to meet people who are currently doing the job that they might apply for, such as police officers or support staff.

The main focus of the familiarisation day is for people to ask any questions and address any issues that might be preventing or discouraging them from applying, such as fear of discrimination or the demands of the job.

These familiarisation days have had some impact in raising awareness and recruitment numbers of under-represented groups such as women and minority ethnics.

Take it further

You have been asked to organise the next familiarisation day which is to be aimed at minority ethnic groups. Create a list of what visitors will do during their visit and what kinds of people they are likely to meet.

Catering for employees' needs

The public services provide a number of support networks for minority groups through a variety of support mechanisms (in addition to on-the-job support through peers and the rank structure). Minority employees can look to a variety of unions, associations and federations. Below are details of some of them.

■ UNISON

UNISON is the biggest trade union in the police service and has over 35,000 members. Trained representatives give police staff protection and advice to ensure they get fair representation and equal opportunities within the public services. They offer advice on issues such as pay, sickness and conditions of service, legal or health and safety advice or representation in grievance and disciplinary processes.

■ Networking Women in the Fire Service (NWFS)

NWFS is an independent voluntary group established in 1993 as a self-help group for women in the fire and rescue service. Its main role is to influence the equality agenda by ensuring the voice of women in the service is heard and to make the service a place where women and men can work together harmoniously and professionally.

■ Black and Asian Police Association (BAPA)

BAPA provides support for black and Asian police officers and works to improve relations between the police and black and Asian people. BAPA exists to provide a support network for minority ethnic staff employed by the police. In addition to working towards improving recruitment, retention and progression of minority ethnic staff, it also provides a social and professional network of other minority ethnic staff from whom advice and assistance can be sought.

■ Police Federation of England and Wales

Police officers are not permitted to belong to trade unions and must not take part in politics. However, every police officer below the rank of superintendent belongs to the Police Federation of England and Wales. It was established by the Police Act 1919 to provide the police with a means of bringing their views on welfare and efficiency to the notice of the Government and the Police Authority. All officials of the Federation are serving police officers.

Individual religious beliefs and needs

In order for the public services to increase recruitment from certain ethnic groups they will ensure, where possible, that an individual's religious and cultural needs are met, for example, by varying uniforms. This includes allowing Sikh men to wear turbans and Muslim women to wear hijabs and ankle length gowns while on duty. Uniform variations including jewellery are considered and accommodated within the public services where there are no significant issues for the employees' health or safety while executing their duties.

Other changes include allowing employees to select other days as religious holidays rather than taking the Christian holidays such as Christmas and Easter or granting leave to allow them to attend key religious events/festivals.

▲ **Employees can be granted leave to attend non-Christian religious holidays**

Employees are allowed to practise their faith while on duty and a quiet and private place will be allocated for the purpose of prayer or meditation within the base or station.

Additional support during religious festivals is offered. For example, employees may have their shift patterns or rest breaks altered to allow them to eat and drink at permitted times during the fast of Ramadan.

General dietary needs can be met simply by providing halal food and ensuring that there is a wide selection of dishes available from the catering suppliers including vegetarian meals.

Consider this

What are the pro and cons of allowing women to wear veils while working within the public services?

Assessment activity 6.5

For many years the public services have worked towards providing equality of service to all members of the community, as well as creating policies, strategies and procedures which address diversity issues within their service.

You have been asked by the Home Office to review the performance of two public services by taking part in the following activities.

1. Create a written report which describes the methodology used by two public services in developing a diverse workforce. **P6**

2. Compare the methodology used by two public services in developing a diverse workforce. **M3**

3. Evaluate the methodology used by the public services to develop a diverse workforce and combat discrimination. **D1**

Grading tips

P6 To achieve P6 you must show awareness of key policies, strategies and procedures such as those linked to equal opportunities, grievance procedures, complaints procedures, bullying and harassment at work, and any other relevant anti-discrimination policies. You must also highlight how employment within the public services has developed to create a more diverse workforce by considering issues such as recruitment and staff selection, catering for employees and their needs

(religious beliefs, diet, dress) through support mechanisms (staff unions, associations and federations).

M3 To achieve M3 don't forget to compare the methodology used by two public services in developing a diverse workforce.

D1 To achieve D1 don't forget to evaluate the methodology used by the public services in developing a diverse workforce and combating discrimination.

Knowledge check

1. State five key dates that have shaped the historical development of Britain and helped to make it more diverse.

2. What is the difference between tolerance and integration?

3. Explain the national composition of the UK in terms of ethnicity, religion, age and gender.

4. List six voluntary support groups that are found within the UK.

5. Explain how women can use the law to help protect their rights and state in what cases the law can be used.

6. What are the main freedoms found under the Human Rights Act 1998?

7. Describe the legal definition of 'disability' in accordance with the relevant law.

8. What range of services does the fire service offer to the community?

9. How do the uniformed public services meet the needs of individuals and groups?

10. How would you go about making a complaint against the police service?

11. What is the difference between bullying and harassment and which is the easiest to prove?

12. What are the common strategies used by the uniformed public services to increase the employment of people from minority groups?

13. In what ways do the uniformed public services cater for minority employees' needs?

Preparation for assessment

The police service is looking to incorporate diversity further into new police officers' training and has asked you to run six one-hour sessions.

You are an experienced police training officer with the responsibility for ensuring that all police officers in the service understand current diversity and cultural issues. You have accepted the offer and have been asked to cover the following issues within your sessions.

Session 1

- Outline the historical developments which have made the UK a diverse society. **P1**

Session 2

- Outline the composition of the local and national community in terms of ethnicity, religion, gender and age. **P2**

Session 3

- Explain how at least one voluntary agency and one statutory agency support members of the community. **P3**

Session 4

- Describe the main legislation that protects human rights in the UK. **P4**

- Explain the relevant sections of two pieces of legislation and how they impact on the public services. **M1**

Session 5

- Explain the duties of two contrasting public services to provide equality of services to all members of the community and combat discrimination. **P5**

- Analyse how a selected public service has provided equality of service to all members of the community and combats discrimination **M2**

Session 6

- Describe the methodology used by two contrasting public services to develop a diverse workforce. **P6**

- Compare the methodology used by two contrasting public services to develop a diverse workforce. **M3**

- Evaluate the methodology used by the public services to develop a diverse workforce and combat discrimination. **D1**

Grading criteria	Activity	Pg no.		
To achieve a pass grade the evidence must show that the learner is able to:			To achieve a merit grade the evidence must show that the learner is able to:	To achieve a distinction grade the evidence must show that the learner is able to:
P1 Outline the historical developments which have made the UK a diverse society	6.1	198		
P2 Outline the composition of your local and national community in terms of ethnicity, religion, gender and age	6.1	198		
P3 Explain how one voluntary agency and one statutory agency support members of their community	6.2	200		
P4 Describe the main legislation that protects human rights in the UK	6.3	206	**M1** Explain the relevant sections of two selected pieces of legislation and how they impact on the public services	
P5 Explain the duties of two contrasting public services to provide equality of services to all members of the community and combat discrimination	6.4	215	**M2** Analyse how a selected public service has provided equality of service to all members of the community and combats discrimination	**D1** Evaluate the methodology used by the public services to develop a diverse workforce and combat discrimination
P6 Describe the methodology used by two contrasting public services to develop a diverse workforce	6.5	224	**M3** Compare the methodology used by two contrasting public services to develop a diverse workforce	

Physical preparation and fitness for the uniformed services

Introduction

A key component in preparing yourself physically for entering a uniformed public service is to understand how your body works. You also need to know what you can do to ensure your body is healthy and operationally capable of performing the complex and difficult tasks that service life may demand.

If you want to be recruited into the public services, you must reach certain levels of health and fitness in order to pass the medical and fitness tests. The public services need individuals who are able to think quickly and respond to a challenge – a good state of health and a reasonable level of fitness are crucial to this.

After completing this unit you should be able to achieve the following outcomes:

- Know the major human body systems
- Understand the effects of lifestyle factors on health and fitness
- Be able to plan a fitness training programme to prepare for uniformed public service
- Be able to undertake a fitness training programme to prepare for uniformed public service.

The nature of public service work is such that your body may be subjected to a variety of stressors including:

- stress
- extremes of temperature
- shift work
- physical exertion
- lack of time leading to poor diet
- disturbed sleep patterns
- physical attack or injury
- fatigue.

If you are not physically fit and healthy, these stressors will be more difficult to deal with and may compromise your job performance.

- How fit are you at the moment?
- Would you be able to meet the physical fitness requirements for your chosen service?
- What can you do to improve your fitness?

Although each individual is unique, the vast majority of people have an almost identical set of body systems, although clearly the reproductive system varies between genders and the skeletal system varies with age (babies are born with many more bones than an adult which fuse as they grow up).

Understanding your major body systems is essential in knowing how to improve your overall health and well-being.

The skeletal system

Structure

The human adult skeleton consists of 206 bones, most of which are paired on the right and left sides of the body. It is an internal skeleton (which means it sits inside the body, unlike some insects who have a skeleton on the outside of their body), which is properly called an endoskeleton.

The skeleton can be divided into two parts:

- the **axial skeleton**, which consists of 80 bones concentrated in the upper central part of the body
- the **appendicular skeleton** which consists of 126 bones concentrated in the extremities.

Figure 7.1 The axial and appendicular skeleton

Key
Axial skeleton
Appendicular skeleton

Key terms

Axial skeleton The bones concentrated at the upper central part of the body.

Appendicular skeleton The bones at the extremities of the body such as the arms and legs.

Function of the skeletal system

The skeletal system is a network of bones, cartilage and joints which performs several major functions.

Function	Detail
Support	The skeleton provides a shape for the body – a framework which takes the body's weight and supports body structures.
Protection	Bones help protect the body from injury, for example, the skull protects the brain and the sternum and ribs protect the heart.
Movement	Bones provide attachment points for muscles. The bones provide a structure for the muscles to work against. As muscles can only contract, the bones are used as levers against which one muscle contracts in order to extend another.
Storage	The bones serve as storage areas for minerals such as calcium and phosphorous which are used by your body.
Production of blood cells	Red blood cells which carry oxygen around the body and some white blood cells which fight infection are produced in long bones.

Table 7.1 The major functions of the skeletal system

■ Bone

A living bone consists of about 35 per cent organic tissue, such as blood vessels, and 65 per cent minerals, such as calcium compounds.

The bone illustrated in Figure 7.2 is called a long bone. It is covered by the periosteum which is like the skin of

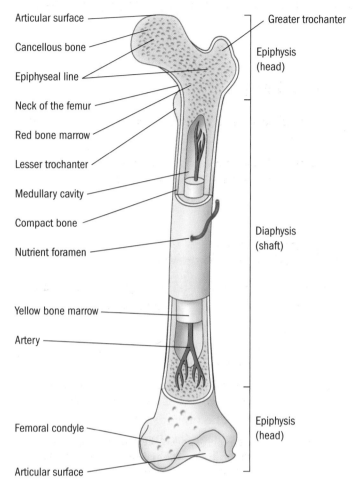

Articular surface
Cancellous bone
Epiphyseal line
Neck of the femur
Red bone marrow
Lesser trochanter
Medullary cavity
Compact bone
Nutrient foramen

Yellow bone marrow
Artery

Femoral condyle
Articular surface

Greater trochanter
Epiphysis (head)

Diaphysis (shaft)

Epiphysis (head)

▲ Figure 7.2 A cross-section of a long bone

with bone marrow; the walls of the diaphysis are made of compact bone which is much tougher than the cancellous bone on the epiphysis.

There are several classifications of bone (see Table 7.2).

Classification	Examples	Purpose
Long bones	Clavicle, humerus, radius, ulna, femur, tibia	To provide support and to act as levers for muscles.
Short bones	Carpals, tarsals	Provide movement, elasticity, flexibility and shock absorption.
Flat bones	Ribs, sternum, scapula	Protection, attachment sites for muscles.
Irregular	Skull, pelvis, vertebrae	Protection, support, movement.
Sesamoid	Patella	Protection of tendons, change the pull of a tendon improving mechanical advantage of a joint.

Table 7.2 Classifications of bone

the bone. The periosteum contains the cells that make new bone. The bone itself is divided into two parts: the **epiphysis**, which is the two rounded end parts, and the **diaphysis**, which is the central, straight part of the bone. The end of the epiphysis is covered with cartilage, which makes it connect and articulate smoothly with any bones that it meets in a joint. The inside of the epiphysis is made up of cancellous bone, which is spongy; the spaces in this spongy bone are filled with bone marrow. The diaphysis has a hollow centre, which is also filled

Key terms

Epiphysis Rounded, end part of the bone.
Diaphysis Straight, middle part of the bone.

Joints

Joints occur at points in the body where bones come together. Joints are areas where flexible connective tissue holds bones together while still allowing freedom of movement. Joints are also called articulations or arthroses. Since the skeleton is not naturally flexible, joints are crucial for movement.

Consider this

What problems would damaged joints pose for a member of the public services?

Figure 7.3 The classification of body joints ▶

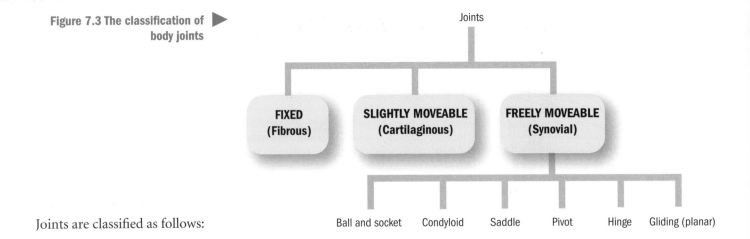

Joints

- **FIXED (Fibrous)**
- **SLIGHTLY MOVEABLE (Cartilaginous)**
- **FREELY MOVEABLE (Synovial)**
  - Ball and socket
  - Condyloid
  - Saddle
  - Pivot
  - Hinge
  - Gliding (planar)

Joints are classified as follows:

Fixed joints (also called fibrous or synarthroses)

These bones are held together by fibrous connective tissue that is rich in collagen fibres. An example of this is the joints' sutures in the skull or the connection between the teeth and the jaw. In adults these joints are not designed to be mobile. They serve their function best when held immovable and firm, for example, in chewing food and in protection of the brain.

Slightly moveable joints (also called cartilaginous or amphiarthroses)

These are joints that are connected by cartilage. Cartilage is a very important substance in the skeletal system. It is a type of gristly connective tissue which performs functions such as:

- preventing bones from knocking together and becoming worn and damaged
- forming a cushion for bones in slightly moveable joints
- acting as a shock absorber
- helping freedom of movement by providing a slippery surface for bones to move against.

Cartilage and ligaments hold the joints together tightly and only permit small movements. Examples of this are in the connection of the ribs to the sternum: the ribs move with breathing but are otherwise unable to move; and the vertebrae, which can move slightly to help you bend but are otherwise immobile.

Freely moveable (also called synovial or diarthroses)

These joints have a cavity called the 'synovial cavity' between articulating bones. The cavity is filled with synovial fluid held in place by a synovial membrane. The fluid acts as a lubricant and reduces friction between the ends of the bone. When at rest the fluid is gel-like but as the joint moves it becomes more liquid. A warm-up before exercise stimulates the fluidity and production of synovial fluid and so benefits the joints.

Most of the major joints in the human body are freely moveable. They fall into six categories (see Table 7.3).

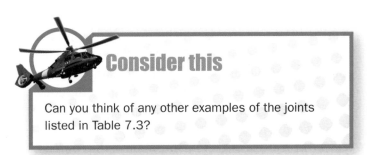

Consider this

Can you think of any other examples of the joints listed in Table 7.3?

Different joints allow for different kinds of movement. There are 17 kinds of movement that the human body can make with the help of the joints:

- **flexion** – bending
- **extension** – straightening
- **dorsiflexion** – the foot bending upwards at the ankle
- **plantorflexion** – pointing the toes away from the ankle

Type	Anatomy (structure)	Example physiology function	Part of body
Ball and socket	A ball-shaped end of one bone fits into a cup-shaped end of another bone	Wide range of movement including rotation Multiaxial	Shoulder Hip
Condyloid	An oval-shaped projection of one bone fits into an oval-shaped depression in another	Biaxial movement (side to side and up and down)	Metacarpals Phalanges Metatarsals
Saddle	Part of the bone is saddle-shaped and the bone it articulates with sits on it	Wide range of movement	Thumb
Pivot	The round or pointed surface on one bone fits into a ring formed by bone and ligament	Monaxial movement (movement around one axis only)	Axis and atlas in the neck (shaking your head to signify no)
Hinge	A convex projection on one bone fits into a concave depression in another bone	Monoaxial movement One direction only	Knee, elbow, ankle
Gliding (planar)	Flat or slightly curved surfaces moving against each other	Nonaxial, side to side and back to front, gliding movements Limited movements	Ribs and vertebrae, carpals and metacarpals

Table 7.3 The six categories of major joints

- **abduction** – the arm or leg moving outwards away from the body's midline
- **adduction** – the movement of a bone towards the midline
- **circumduction** – movement of a distal end of a body part in a circle (for example, moving a finger in a circular motion without moving the hand)
- **rotation** – a bone revolves around its own long axis (for example, turning the trunk from side to side while keeping the hips and legs stationary)
- **pronation** – a movement of the forearm which results in the palm of the hand facing up
- **supination** – a movement of the forearm which results in the palm facing down
- **inversion** – a movement of the soles of the feet so that they face inwards (towards each other)
- **eversion** – a movement of the soles of the feet so that they are facing outwards (away from each other)
- **protraction** – anterior movement of a body part forwards (for example, thrusting out your lower jaw or making your shoulder blades stick out)
- **retraction** – posterior movement of a protracted piece of the body back into its correct anatomical position (for example, relaxing your shoulder blades or jaw back into their natural position)
- **elevation** – upward movement of a body part (for example, shrugging your shoulders)
- **depression** – downward movement of a body part (for example, drooping the shoulders or opening your mouth)
- **hyperextension** – continuation of an extension beyond the anatomically correct position (for example, bending the head backwards or moving the palm backwards at the wrist joint). Hyperextension is usually prevented by a network of tendons and ligaments, or the actual arrangements of bones themselves – it can cause nasty injuries.

Consider this

Consider your movements in the last five minutes. How many of the different types of motion have you used? List and describe them.

The muscular system

Muscles are bundles of protein filaments which work together to produce motion in the body. A muscle fibre is a long thin strand of protein, and within that strand are even smaller strands called myofibrils which are perfectly aligned and give the muscle its characteristic striations (stripes). Muscles have several main functions:

Function	Detail
Movement	The actions of muscles allow you to change position and move around.
Maintain posture	Believe it or not standing upright is a very difficult thing to do because gravity is always pulling at you. The reason you don't fall to the ground is due to the actions of your muscles.
Produce heat	The action of muscles produces heat and this is why you get hot when you are doing physical activity. If you are cold and inactive your muscles will start to rhythmically contract in an effort to keep you warm – this is called shivering.
Regulate blood flow	Your heart is a muscle which pumps blood around your body in accordance with your needs. If you need more oxygen to get to the muscles to enable them to work harder, your heart rate will increase.
Digestion and waste removal	The digestive system moves food through it and eliminates waste due to muscle action in the rectum. Equally, the bladder holds on to your urine until you relax the muscles which allow it to be eliminated.
Support the skeleton	Muscles act as a way to tie the skeleton together. There are muscle attachment points at all joints and this ensures the bones stay in position.

Table 7.4 The main functions of muscles

Muscle tissue typically composes 40-50 per cent of body weight and the human body contains well over 600 muscles, which usually work in pairs. These pairs consist of the agonist, which is the prime mover and the antagonist which works against it. For example, your arm moves by the bicep muscle (agonist) working against the triceps muscle (the antagonist).

Muscle tissue has several characteristics which identify it:

- excitability – the ability to respond to stimuli
- contractility – the ability to shorten
- extensibility – the ability to stretch
- elasticity – the ability to return to original shape and length.

Muscles can only pull, they cannot push. This is why they usually work in pairs. One muscle pulls a limb into the required position and the other muscle pulls it back when required. Muscle action can be **voluntary** or **involuntary**.

Key terms

Involuntary Some muscles in the body are automatically controlled by the brain, such as the heart, diaphragm and intestines. This means that they operate without conscious thought.

Voluntary These muscles are controlled by the individual themselves, such as the biceps and triceps in the arm. You can usually move these muscles at will.

Types of muscle

Our bodies must be equipped to deal with a variety of tasks and we have three types of muscle with which to do these tasks:

- cardiac
- smooth
- skeletal.

■ Cardiac muscle

This is found only in the heart and makes up the walls of the heart or myocardium. It has a branching network of cells which form layers of overlapping spirals. It acts as a single sheet of muscle which operates on an involuntary basis and has its own blood supply. The heart generates its own impulse to beat and so is 'myogenic'. Unlike many muscles in the body the cardiac muscle is attached together rather than to a bone and is designed to resist fatigue.

Consider this

Why is it important to have cardiac muscle which is able to resist fatigue?

Figure 7.4 The microscopic structure of skeletal muscle

Labels: Cylindrical muscle fibre; Connecting tissue covering; Nuclei; Stripes ostriations

■ Smooth muscle

Smooth muscle makes up a large part of our internal organs such as bladder, veins and digestive tract. It is involuntary which means that it works without conscious thought on an automatic basis. Smooth muscle demonstrates two kinds of inervation (movement):

1. multi unit innervation – rapid coordinated contraction, for example, iris of the eye
2. visceral innervation – a wave of contraction, for example, peristalsis (movement of food through the gut).

Smooth muscle contracts very slowly and so it is able to resist fatigue. In addition it can stay contracted for relatively long periods of time.

■ Skeletal muscle

This is the most common type of muscle found in the human body and can make up about 40 per cent of an adult male's body weight. It has stripe-like markings called striations and it is composed of large cells bound together in bundles or sheets. The muscles are served by a system of nerves which connects them to the spinal cord and the brain which control their activation.

Skeletal muscles are attached to bones by tendons at two points: 'origin' and 'insertion'. The majority of skeletal muscles are under conscious control and respond in accordance with an individual's direction. They differ from the two other types of muscle in that cardiac and smooth muscle cells have only one nucleus while skeletal muscle is multinucleated, which means it has many nuclei.

Muscle contraction

Muscle contraction is powered by a chemical molecule called adenosine triphosphate or ATP. ATP is synthesised from the food you eat and it provides energy for cells to use in performing their functions. Muscles need a constant supply of ATP in order to contract. However, there is only a limited supply of ATP in muscles which means it needs to be regenerated quickly. During long periods of muscular contraction body fat becomes the main source of energy to power contractions.

There are three main methods of muscle contraction:

●   **Isometric (or static) contraction** – a muscle produces force without changing its length, i.e. without movement. Examples of static contraction include maintaining your posture standing upright or hanging from a chin-up bar with your arms at a 90° angle. At its maximum level static contraction can only be maintained for about 10 seconds. This is because as force on the muscle increases, blood flow to the muscle is proportionally reduced causing fatigue. However, low-level static contraction can be maintained for a long period of time.

●   **Isotonic contraction** – this kind of muscle contraction is a controlled shortening of the muscle. For example, a bicep curl is a simple example of a contraction that shortens the bicep. Equally, bending at the knee produces an isotonic contraction in the hamstring.

●   **Eccentric contraction** – this is when a muscle actively lengthens, such as the quadriceps (knee extensors) during walking.

Types of muscle fibres

Generally speaking, muscle fibres can be classified into two different types: fast twitch and slow twitch.

- Slow twitch (also known as type I) – these muscle fibres are very efficient at using oxygen to create more fuel (ATP) for continuous physical activity over an extended period of time.

- Fast twitch (also known as type II) – these muscle fibres use anaerobic metabolism to create fuel to power themselves. They are better at generating short bursts of activity such as strength or speed but they tire easily.

Consider this

Having looked at the types of muscle fibres explained above, do you think that each type of muscle fibre is suited to certain physical activities? For example, which type of muscle fibre would benefit a 100 m sprinter and which would benefit a marathon runner?

The cardiovascular system

The cardiovascular system consists of the heart, blood vessels and blood. Oxygen and waste products are carried to and from the tissues and cells by blood. The heart is the mechanism, which allows this by pumping blood around the body through tubes called veins and arteries. The heart pumps continually throughout your life to the tune of around 30 million beats per year. While you are asleep it pumps approximately 10 litres of blood a minute through the 60,000 miles of blood vessels which make up the transport system of your body. The cardiovascular system is one of the most important of all the body systems.

Pulmonary circulation system

Systemic circulation system

Arterioles

Capillaries in lungs

Venules

Arteries

Veins

Left atrium

Right atrium

Left venticle

Right ventricle

Veins

Arteries

Capillaries around body tissues

Venules

Arterioles

Deoxygenated blood

Oxygenated blood

◀ **Figure 7.5 The pulmonary and systemic circulation systems**

The heart

The heart is about the size of a clenched fist and is located in the chest between the lungs with its apex slightly tilted to the left. It is made up of cardiac muscle (myocardium) and is surrounded by the pericardium, which is a fluid-filled bag which reduces friction when the heart beats. It is not really heart shaped at all – it more closely resembles a cone shape. It contains four chambers: the left and right atria which are the upper chambers of the heart and the left and right ventricles which are the lower chambers. These form the basis for the two distinct transport circuits of the body, both of which begin and end at the heart:

- **the pulmonary circuit** which carries blood to and from the oxygen exchange surfaces of the lungs
- **the systemic circuit** which involves blood flow to the rest of the body.

The blood collects initially in the atria which then pump it to the ventricles. The walls of the atria are relatively thin as they are only passing the blood to the lower chambers, but the ventricles have to have enough power to send the blood around the circuits. As a result, the cardiac muscle in the ventricles is much thicker because more muscular power is needed. The right atrium receives deoxygenated blood from the rest of the body which it then pumps into the right ventricle. The right ventricle pumps this deoxygenated blood to the lungs where it drops off any waste gases and picks up a fresh load of oxygen in a system of gaseous exchange. This newly oxygenated blood now returns to the heart where it is pumped into the left atrium. This has completed the pulmonary circuit. The left atrium pumps the blood to the left ventricle which then pumps the oxygen-rich blood to the organs and tissues of the body.

The systemic circuit around the body is much larger than the pulmonary circuit. Consequently the left ventricle is the most powerful chamber in the heart with a thicker muscle wall than the other three chambers.

The heart is divided into left and right by a central wall called the septum and two thirds of its mass lies to the left of the body's midline. The heart weighs about 250 grams in adult females and 300 grams in adult males. It is able to contract independently of a nerve supply because it is stimulated by an area of specialised tissue in the right atrium called the sino-atrial node.

Consider this

How many times will a heart beat in an average lifetime?

Both of the blood-flow circuits described above rely not only on the heart but also on the blood and blood vessels. It is these aspects of the cardiovascular system that we will now explore.

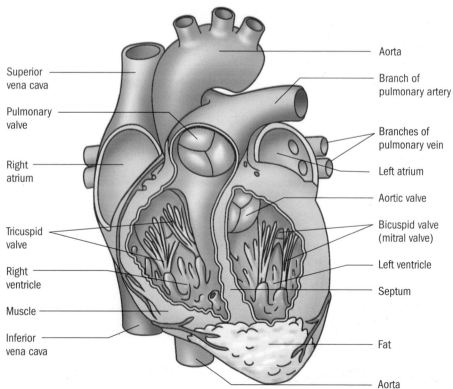

Superior vena cava
Pulmonary valve
Right atrium
Tricuspid valve
Right ventricle
Muscle
Inferior vena cava

Aorta
Branch of pulmonary artery
Branches of pulmonary vein
Left atrium
Aortic valve
Bicuspid valve (mitral valve)
Left ventricle
Septum
Fat
Aorta

Figure 7.6 Structure of the heart

Blood vessels

The blood vessels are the body's transport network. They allow blood to travel to every part of the body and return to the heart. The system of vessels consists of:

- **Arteries** – these are large vessels which usually carry oxygenated blood away from the heart to the rest of the body (the exception being the pulmonary artery). They subdivide to form smaller vessels called arterioles which then branch off again to form capillaries. These vessels are cylindrical and muscular and are able to contract and dilate in order to regulate blood flow.

- **Veins** – these vessels are usually responsible for the movement of deoxygenated blood back towards the heart so that it can be sent on the pulmonary circuit once more. Vessels called venules connect the capillaries where the oxygen has just been deposited to the veins which then return it to the heart. The blood flow in the veins is under less pressure than in the arteries therefore they tend to be slightly less muscular than the arteries.

- **Capillaries** – these are the smallest blood-transportation vessels in the body. They are incredibly thin which allows the exchange of gases through them. Organs and tissues which need a large amount of oxygen and nutrients, such as muscles and the brain, will have lots of capillaries, while other organs which are not so dependent may not have as many.

Consider this

How many miles of blood vessels are in your body?

Blood

Blood is a red fluid which carries oxygen, nutrients, hormones and disease-fighting agents around the body. The typical human has around 5 litres of blood in their body. Blood is made up of several different substances:

- plasma   55%
- cells (red and white) ⎫
- platelets.   ⎬ 45%

Plasma – plasma is what makes the blood a liquid. Without it the cells in the blood would be solid and therefore not able to travel around the body. It is a pale yellow fluid made predominantly from water and a small amount of protein.

Red blood cells (erythrocytes) – these are the most numerous cells in the blood. They are disc shaped with a depression in the centre on each side. They are created by the marrow in the bones and have a lifespan of approximately three months. They carry a substance called haemoglobin which helps transport oxygen around the body. It is haemoglobin that gives the blood its red colour.

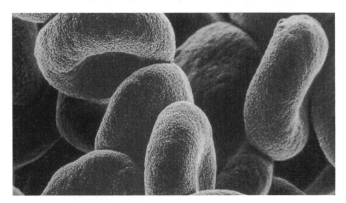

▲ Red blood cells

White blood cells (leucocytes) – white blood cells are the soldiers of the body as they are the cells that fight off bacteria and viruses. They are much bigger than red blood cells and they are irregular in shape. There are several different kinds of white blood cell.

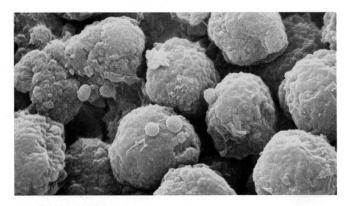

▲ White blood cells

Platelets – platelets play a crucial role in the repair system of the body. They secrete serotonin which restricts blood flow to a damaged part of the body. They also stick together at the site of an injury to plug gaps in broken blood vessels. They activate proteins found in blood plasma which then create a basket-like structure which captures red blood cells forming a natural wound covering called a scab. The scab prevents foreign particles entering the bloodstream and stays in place until the tissue underneath is repaired. It falls off once the tissue is repaired.

Blood performs a variety of functions in the body:

- Repair – platelets within the blood clot at the site of a wound forming a scab to protect the body from bacteria and repair the wound.
- Transport of oxygen – red blood cells are vitally important in transporting oxygen from our lungs to all the other parts of the body.
- Thermoregulation – blood vessels help control our temperature via a process called thermoregulation. When we are warm, blood vessels near the surface of our skin dilate (widen) and allow more blood to flow through to cool us down. When we are cold, the blood vessels near the surface of the skin constrict forcing more warm blood into the core of the body where it is needed most.

- Removal of waste products – the blood contains the waste products of the body. The waste products are transported to the kidneys which filter the blood around 36 times every 24 hours.

The respiratory system

Cells continually use oxygen (O_2) in their reactions and release carbon dioxide (CO_2) as a waste product by a process of diffusion. The body therefore needs a system which provides O_2 for the body and gets rid of CO_2 before it builds up and causes damage. This system is the respiratory system. The exchange of O_2 and CO_2 is completed in three stages.

1. **Pulmonary ventilation** – this is the process of breathing in air (inspiration) and breathing out CO_2 (expiration).
2. **External respiration** – this is the exchange of O_2 and CO_2 between the air spaces in the lungs and the blood in the pulmonary capillaries. O_2 is picked up and CO_2 dropped off.
3. **Internal respiration** – this is the exchange of gases between the blood in the capillaries and the tissues in the body. O_2 is dropped and CO_2 picked up.

The respiratory system is sited within the rib cage. It comprises:

The nose The mouth The pharynx The larynx The trachea	leading to the lungs
The bronchi The bronchioles The alveoli	within the lungs

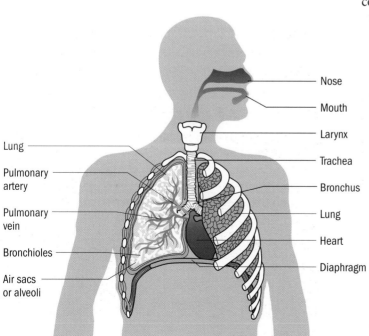

Nose
Mouth
Larynx
Trachea
Bronchus
Lung
Heart
Diaphragm

Lung
Pulmonary artery
Pulmonary vein
Bronchioles
Air sacs or alveoli

◀ **Figure 7.7 The respiratory system**

Inspiration and expiration happen because of changes in air pressure inside the lungs caused by the action of the diaphragm and intercostal muscles.

Inspiration happens when the muscular action of the respiratory system expands the chest causing a decrease in air pressure, which makes air rush into the lungs. Expiration happens when the muscles return to their resting position causing an increase in air pressure which forces air out of the lungs.

Inspired air contains:

Nitrogen (N) = 79%

O_2 = 21%

CO_2 = 0.04%

Other = trace

Water Vapour

Expired air contains:

N = 79%

O_2 = 16%

CO_2 = 4.5%

Water = trace

At rest a typical healthy adult will take 12 breaths per minute with each inspiration and expiration moving about half a litre of air. The function of the respiratory system is therefore to supply O_2 to the tissues and remove harmful waste products before they can build up and cause damage to the body. In order to do this effectively the respiratory system works in partnership with the body's transport mechanism, the circulatory system, in order that O_2 can reach tissues all over the body and CO_2 can be brought back.

Consider this

Why is a healthy respiratory system a requirement of many public services occupations? Why might it be particularly important in the fire and rescue service?

The nose – air usually enters through the nostrils and proceeds to open spaces within the nose called the nasal passages and nasal cavity. The air is filtered by small hairs and mucus in the nostrils and warmed before it reaches the lungs. The mucus also helps moisten the air. This is why it is better to breath through the nose than the mouth.

Pharynx and larynx – moving on from the nose, air moves through the pharynx (throat) and larynx (voice box). Air vibrates the vocal chords which are on either side of the larynx enabling us to make sounds.

Trachea – the larynx connects with the trachea (windpipe) which is a tube approximately 12 cm in length and 2.5 cm wide in adults. It is held open by rings of cartilage and is covered with tiny hairs (cilia) and mucus which help filter the air and move obstructions back up to the throat.

Bronchi – the trachea divides into two bronchi which lead into the lungs and further subdivide and spread like tree branches into bronchial tubes.

Bronchioles – the bronchial tubes divide further and spread becoming smaller and thinner tubes called bronchioles.

Alveoli – each bronchiole ends in a tiny air chamber containing cup-shaped cavities called alveoli. The alveoli are very thin and this allows O_2 and CO_2 to be exchanged through their walls.

Effects of exercise on the systems

Exercise has many short-term and long-term effects across all the systems we have examined in this section. Table 7.5 highlights the most important ones.

Short-term effects	Explanation
Blood flow	Blood flow around the body becomes faster and it is diverted away from areas such as the stomach which are not essential to exercise and diverted towards the heart, lungs and muscles. This is because the blood is required to carry more oxygen and take away more waste products.
Raised heart rate	The heart beats faster, fills up with more blood and moves blood around the body faster. Exercise increases not only heart rate but also blood pressure and **stroke volume**.
Increased respiration	Respiration becomes faster and deeper as it responds to the body's need for more oxygen. It also increases to remove a larger volume of carbon dioxide which is produced during exercise.
Long-term effects	**Explanation**
Muscle tone	Depending on the exercise, the muscles can become bigger and more clearly defined.
Lowered heart rate	At resting state the heart is able to pump blood more efficiently which means it needs to beat less to move the same volume of blood.
Blood pressure	Although the short-term impact of exercise is to raise blood pressure, the long-term effect is the opposite. Long-term exercise has the benefit of generally lowering overall blood pressure as the heart works more efficiently.
Strength	As muscles work hard during a programme of exercise they will become stronger. Again this can depend on the type of exercise.
Stamina	Muscles are able to work for longer without becoming fatigued.
Weight	A long-term exercise plan can have a varying effect on weight. Some exercise will increase muscle mass and lead to a weight gain while other types of exercise will help reduce or maintain the original weight.
Cholesterol	Cholesterol can be reduced by a long-term exercise plan.
Digestion	Exercise stimulates the muscles of the intestinal walls for increased peristalsis.

Table 7.5 The short-term and long-term effects of exercise on the skeletal, cardiovascular and respiratory systems

Assessment activity 7.1

You are required to give a PowerPoint presentation on the body systems which covers the following content:

- skeletal system, joints, muscular system, types of muscle, muscle movement, cardiovascular system, structure of the heart, blood vessels, functions of blood, respiratory system, structure, function, mechanics of breathing, short- and long-term effects of exercise on the body systems.

Use the content you have researched to answer the following questions within your presentation:

1. Describe the muscular-skeletal, cardiovascular and respiratory systems. **P1**

2. Explain the effects of exercise on the muscular-skeletal, cardiovascular and respiratory system. **M1**

Key terms

Stroke volume The volume of blood ejected from the heart ventricles with every beat.

Grading tips

P1 There is a great deal of detail and description you could go into on all these systems which would make your presentation far loo long. Remember that these systems lend themselves to being discussed via diagrams and make sure you include plenty of these in your slides.

M1 For this grade you need to explain in your own words the long-term and short-term effects of exercise on the body systems. You could do this as a table on your slides or as a discussion afterwards.

Each of us makes lifestyle choices which can affect our levels of health and fitness. Lifestyle is the way we choose to conduct our lives from what we eat, to the jobs we do, to the types of relationships we choose to have. The following lifestyle choices impact upon our health and fitness.

Physical activity

It is a well-known fact that individuals who exercise regularly, either as part of their job or in their leisure time, have fewer heart attacks than those who don't. Exercise builds up the strength of the heart, which means it can cope better if you put a sudden physical demand on it. Exercise will also:

- help reduce blood pressure
- keep weight in check
- slow down the bone deterioration in older people (particularly important for women)
- keep muscles strong and joints flexible
- help you deal with stress and depression in more productive ways
- decrease the amount of bad cholesterol in the blood helping keep the heart and blood vessels healthy
- promote psychological well-being and positive self-image.

Smoking

Smoking is a major danger to your health. It can cause heart disease, numerous cancers and bronchial disorders. Over 100,000 people die every year from smoking-related diseases. Smokers have double the heart attack risk of non-smokers and linked with the contraceptive pill in women the risk may even be higher. The body becomes addicted to nicotine which is a stimulant, making the heart beat faster and the blood vessels narrow causing a strain on the cardiovascular system. In addition, the blood becomes more 'sticky' with fats and sugars leading to a 'furring-up' of the arteries. Carbon

monoxide in cigarette smoke can drastically reduce the capacity of the blood to carry O_2 to the tissues which again means that the heart must work harder.

Alcohol

Alcohol has an impact on all of the major body systems and abuse of alcohol can lead to death. Some of the main effects of excessive alcohol are: blackouts, liver cancer, liver disease, diarrhoea, heartburn, cancer of the oesophagus, malnutrition, high blood pressure, loss of libido, reduced fertility, impaired decision making and increased risk of accidents. However, it is important to note that recent studies have concluded that alcohol in moderation is actually good for you, helping protect against heart disease.

In terms of public service work, the abuse of alcohol can directly affect your working performance. Many public service jobs require the operation of complex equipment such as breathing apparatus, weapons and vehicles. The presence of alcohol in your system will impair your judgement, placing yourself and others at risk.

In addition, alcohol is very high in calories and without proper exercise this will lead to weight gain. Carrying excess weight places an additional strain on systems such as the cardiovascular and respiratory systems which have to work harder to perform their functions.

Drug use (abuse)

The abuse of different drugs will lead to a variety of effects on the short- and long-term health and fitness of an individual:

- **opiates (heroin)** – constipation, loss of libido, drowsiness, respiratory distress, an overdose is fatal. It is also linked to the spread of HIV and hepatitis through the sharing of contaminated needles
- **amphetamines (speed, whizz)** – sleeplessness, anorexia
- **LSD** – sensory distortions, hallucinations, a feeling of panic or anxiety

- **ecstasy** – hallucinations, heatstroke, dehydration, panic attacks and depression
- **cocaine** – damage or loss of nasal septum, may cause paranoid psychosis.

Drug abuse may also lead to unwise sexual behaviour or involvement in crime.

In any sports or fitness-related area of study there is also the ever-present danger of performance-enhancing drugs such as anabolic steroids. Steroids are taken by some athletes and bodybuilders to increase their muscle mass and strength but can have significant side effects such as:

- in men – shrunken testicles, baldness, higher voice, prominent breasts and infertility
- in women – a deeper voice, increased body hair and baldness.

Stress

Stress is a constant part of our lives, whether it is worrying about getting assignments in on time or more serious worries such as divorce or bereavement. The kind of stress that is really damaging to your body is a long-term stress, which can be caused by things such as family problems, financial difficulties or being unhappy in your workplace.

Stress can manifest itself physically and emotionally in signs such as indigestion, fatigue, insomnia, feeling irritable or headaches. These symptoms are caused by the increased activity of the nervous system as it responds to your stress and the production of hormones such as adrenaline and cortisol, which trigger your 'fight or flight' response. These hormones stimulate the heart to beat faster and redirect blood to the brain, heart and muscles. This causes an increase in blood pressure, which can lead to the heart and blood vessels being placed under stress. If a blood vessel bursts in the brain it is called a 'stroke' and can have fatal consequences. In addition, the blood becomes 'sticky' with sugars and fats released from the liver in order to give the muscles more energy to power the fight or flight response. However, if you are sitting at a desk fuming at your boss, these fats and sugars are not utilised by the muscles and they can stick to artery walls clogging them up with fatty deposits which put you at greater risk of heart disease.

▲ Figure 7.8 You might need to find different ways of coping with stress

Stress has been linked with many other problems such as eczema, stomach ulcers and depression. The obvious way to deal with this problem is to tackle the cause of the stress so that it no longer exists or to change the way you react to stress. Techniques such as meditation and exercise can help an individual cope with stress more effectively.

It is also worth noting that public service officers may also be at risk of post-traumatic stress disorder (PTSD) if they experience stressful or traumatic events during their working life, such as a major disaster or war conditions.

Consider this

Carry out some research into PTSD. What are the common signs and symptoms of this disorder? Provide examples of documented cases of public service officers suffering it after a major trauma.

Consider this

What are the sources of stress in your life? What strategies do you have for coping with these sources of stress?

Diet

Healthy eating is vital for all our body systems since they rely on the energy from food to run effectively. Diets in the western world tend to contain too much fat, sugar, salt and dairy products, which can cause problems such as obesity, high blood pressure, coronary heart disease and dental decay. Food such as fresh fruit and vegetables, and cereals such as rice and pasta can help fight against diseases such as bowel cancer and gum disease.

■ Diet requirements and recommendations

A well-balanced diet should contain enough of the five food components to keep the body running smoothly.

As you can see a well-balanced diet would consist of enough of each of these components to satisfy the needs of the body. The portions outlined in Table 7.6 are only an indication of the amount of food you should eat to stay healthy as it depends on your current weight, level of physical activity and health. As a general guide, a 10-stone woman should be aiming for around 2300kcals per day and a 11.5-stone man around 3000kcals per day.

A balanced diet can help to improve health and reduce the incidence of heart disease and cancer. A study by the National Audit Office published in February 2001 found that nearly two thirds of adults in England are overweight. This costs the health services over £2.5 billion per year. Obesity is a growing problem across the western world. Obesity is a state in which a person's weight is at a level where it can seriously endanger their health. It is on the increase due to the availability of high-fat and sugary foods and snacks and a decrease in the amount of exercise we take. Obesity increases the risk of heart disease and strokes.

Consider this

Why does having an obese population cost the health service so much money?

Figure 7.9 The five food components ▶

Suggested proportions of different food groups in the UK National Food Guide

Food group	Food types	Serving size	Amount recommended	Main nutrients supplied
Bread, cereals and potatoes	Bread, rolls, muffins, bagels, crumpets, chapattis, naan bread, pitta bread, tortillas, scones, pikelets, potato cakes, breakfast cereals, rice, pasta, noodles, cous cous and potatoes	3 tbsp breakfast cereal, 1 Weetabix or Shredded Wheat, 1 slice of bread, ½ pitta, 1 heaped tbsp boiled potato, pasta, rice, cous cous	These should form the main part of all meals and snacks About a third of total volume of food consumed each day	Carbohydrate, non-starch polysaccharide (NSP) – mainly insoluble, calcium, iron and B vitamins
Fruit and vegetables	All types of fresh, frozen, canned and dried fruits and vegetables except potatoes, and fruit and vegetable juices	1 apple, orange, pear, banana, 1 small glass of fruit or vegetable juice, 1 small salad, 2 tbsp vegetables, 2 tbsp stewed or tinned fruit in juice	At least 5 portions each day About a third of total volume of food consumed each day	NSP – especially soluble, vitamin C, folate and potassium
Milk and dairy products	Milk, yoghurt, cheese and fromage frais	$1/3$ pint milk, 1¼ oz cheese, 1 small carton of yoghurt or cottage cheese	2–3 servings per day About a sixth of total volume of food consumed each day	Protein, calcium, vitamins A and D
Meat, fish and alternative protein sources	Meat, poultry, fish, eggs, pulses and nuts Meat and fish products such as sausages, beefburgers, fish cakes and fish fingers	2–3 oz of lean meat, chicken, or oily fish, 4–5 oz white fish, 2 eggs, 1 small tin baked beans, 2 tbsp nuts, 4 oz Quorn or soya	2 servings per day About a sixth of total volume of food consumed each day	Protein, iron, zinc, magnesium and B vitamins Pulses provide a good source of NSP
Foods containing fat and sugar	Fat-rich: butter, margarine, cooking oils, mayonnaise and salad dressings, cream, pastries, crisps, biscuits and cakes Sugar-rich: sweets, jams, honey, marmalade, soft drinks, biscuits, cakes and pastries	1 tsp butter or margarine 1 tsp vegetable or olive oil 1 tsp mayonnaise	These should be eaten sparingly and, where possible, lower fat options selected Extra energy provided by sugars may be useful in meeting carbohydrate requirements for active individuals	Fat-rich: fat, essential fatty acids and some vitamins Sugar-rich: carbohydrate and some vitamins and minerals

Table 7.6 Food groups and their recommended intake

Nutrition

Nutrition is the study of how the body uses foods and nutrients vital to health in promoting growth, maintenance and reproduction of cells. In essence, it is how what we eat and drink affects our health.

An understanding of nutrition is important as it helps us understand how our body uses the food we eat. There are seven essential foodstuffs the body must be supplied with:

- protein
- carbohydrate
- fats
- water
- mineral salts
- vitamins
- fibre.

Protein

Protein is composed of chains of amino acids which are the building blocks of cells. They provide cells with material with which to grow and maintain their structure. Different amino acids are commonly found in proteins and the human body contains around 20 amino acids.

There are two types of amino acids: essential and non-essential. Non-essential amino acids are made for you by your body and, contrary to their name, they are very essential to your health and well-being. Essential amino acids must be acquired through your food as your body does not make them for itself. So it is important to have a diet that contains adequate amounts of these proteins.

The digestive system breaks down protein in the food we eat and allows it to be absorbed into the bloodstream where it is then utilised for growth. Protein is found naturally in foods such as fish, milk, bread, pulses and meat. Protein is also important as it is responsible for making haemoglobin which as you have already learnt is necessary for the transportation of oxygen in the blood. Protein is also a prime ingredient in the white blood cells that fight off infection and repair wounds.

Carbohydrates

Carbohydrates provide fuel for the body. The digestive system enables the absorption of the sugars and starches that make up carbohydrates and allows them to be carried in the bloodstream to every cell in the body where they are converted into a substance called adenosine triphosphate (ATP) which powers the functions of a cell. Sugars such as glucose, fructose (found in fruit) and lactose (found in milk) are called simple carbohydrates (monosaccharides and disaccharides). They are easily digested and enter the bloodstream quickly.

There are also complex carbohydrates (polysaccharides) which are commonly called starches. This is when simple carbohydrates are bonded to form a chain. Complex carbohydrates are found in foodstuffs such as potatoes, wheat, corn, pasta and rice. The digestive system breaks down the complex carbohydrates into their simple sugars but it takes longer for it to do this. As a result they are released into the bloodstream at a much slower pace therefore keeping you going for longer. If you have an excess of sugars such as glucose they are stored by the body in the liver as a product called glycogen. Any glycogen that won't fit into the liver is stored as fat. When you are exercising for short periods of time your body will use the glycogen in your liver for energy but if you exercise for a long time your body will begin to burn fat instead.

Fats

Fats are also called lipids. A high-fat diet can lead to obesity, heart disease, heart attacks and strokes. However, fat is essential to the body in insulating its systems from the cold and cushioning our hardworking organs against jolts and knocks. It also helps to process some vitamins and minerals and is the major source of the body's energy storage. Generally speaking there are three kinds of fat.

1. **Saturated fat** – the most harmful type of fat to the body as it can cause clogged arteries leading to coronary disease. This fat is normally solid at room temperature such as butter and lard. It is found primarily in animal products such as meat, eggs and milk but also in vegetable products such as coconut milk and palm oil. The excessive use of saturated fat in the diet has links with obesity, high levels of cholesterol, breast cancer, strokes and heart disease.

2. **Polyunsaturated fat** – this has fewer fatty acid molecules than saturated fat and is generally liquid at room temperature, such as sunflower oil and corn oil. It is thought to be less damaging to the body systems than saturated fats. It is also found in oily fish.

3. **Monounsaturated fat** – this is considered to be the best of all three fats as it actively helps to lower cholesterol levels. It is generally found in food such as olive oil, rapeseed oil and nuts and seeds.

Fats that you eat in your food are broken down in the digestive system by an enzyme called lipase which ensures they are ready for transport in the bloodstream; the fats are then either used in muscles as fuel or stored for later in adipose tissue. When we consider ourselves 'fat' it is usually because we have too much adipose tissue. It is important to remember that although some fats have a more damaging effect on our body systems than others, there is no difference in their calorie content. Eating too much monounsaturated fat will make you overweight just as quickly as saturated fat will.

Water

The human body is about 60 per cent water and it constantly needs to be replaced as we lose a great deal through respiration, sweating and urine. At rest, a person loses approximately 40 ounces of water per day. Without water no system in the body could survive. Many people do not drink enough water to replace the losses which occur naturally in the body. This can lead to inattention, headaches and irritability.

Consider this

How much water do you drink each day? Is it enough?

Mineral salts

These are inorganic substances the body must have in order to regulate processes or manufacture specific molecules. They are involved in all body systems and include calcium, iron, iodine, magnesium, manganese, phosphorous, potassium, sodium, selenium and zinc.

Other minerals include chloride, copper, chromium and fluorine. If these minerals are over-abundant in the body then they can have a negative effect. For instance, too much sodium has been linked with high blood pressure. Equally, if mineral levels are low there can be a negative effect, for example, too little iron leads to anaemia.

Vitamins

Vitamins are organic compounds which can provide energy for the body. They assist chemical reactions within the cells of your body and help to regulate metabolic processes. The human body needs 13 different vitamins including A, B, C and D.

Fibre

Fibre is important in maintaining health by assisting in eliminating waste products from the bowel. Foods high in fibre include wholegrain cereals, vegetables, nuts and fruit. Breakfast cereals such as muesli, branflakes and oats are good sources of fibre. Eating a diet rich in fibre is now believed to be crucial in helping to prevent diseases such as bowel cancer, diabetes, irritable bowel syndrome and cancer of the colon.

Theory into practice

Do you know how good your diet is? Keep a food diary for three days, writing down everything you eat and drink. Make a note of how many calories there are in each item and add them up for a daily total. Are you getting a balanced diet? Are you getting enough calories or are you eating too many?

Personal hygiene

Keeping clean is an essential part of any lifestyle. Regular washing removes sweat and dirt, preventing unpleasant smells and, more importantly, reducing the risk of infections. This is especially important for service personnel operating away from their base for an extended period of time, for example, in jungle or desert conditions where bacteria can thrive. Emergency service personnel may also come into contact with contaminated environments where biological or chemical hazards are common in the line of duty, for example, a tanker spillage or a crime scene involving blood or other bodily fluids. These environments can pose a significant threat to health and safety if personal hygiene is not observed.

There are several easy ways of promoting your personal hygiene:

- Daily washing is essential for a healthy lifestyle.
- Wash your hands before eating.
- Shower after physical activity.
- Wash food before eating it if you suspect it may be dirty.
- Wear clean clothes every day if possible.
- Wear any protective equipment you are given, such as gloves or eye shields.

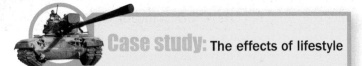

Case study: The effects of lifestyle

Narinda is a 21-year-old university graduate who is applying for a career in the Royal Navy. Her lifestyle at university was not best suited for promoting health and fitness. While at university she:

- predominantly ate takeaway food
- occasionally took illegal drugs
- drank alcohol at least three times per week to excess
- smoked heavily
- did little physical activity.

Fortunately the Royal Navy have given Narinda a start date for training which is six months away and she knows she has to clean up her act if she is going to be successful in training.

1. **What should Narinda's first lifestyle change be?**

2. **Where could Narinda get help to improve her lifestyle?**

3. **What will the consequences be if Narinda does not change her lifestyle, both long-term and short-term?**

4. **What impact will Narinda's current lifestyle have had on her health and fitness?**

5. **Design a lifestyle action plan to help Narinda improve her chances of succeeding in naval training.**

Assessment activity 7.2

For this activity you can take part in an assessed group discussion on the effects of lifestyle on health and fitness and your uniformed service career. You need to examine the following content:

- physical activity, smoking, alcohol, drugs, stress, diet, personal hygiene and the effects of all these on your well-being and future career.

Use this information to answer the following questions:

1. Describe the lifestyle factors that can affect health and fitness and the effects they can have. **P2**

2. Explain the effects that lifestyle factors can have on health and fitness when applying for a uniformed public service and long-term employment. **M2**

3. Evaluate the effects that lifestyle factors can have on health and fitness when applying for a uniformed public service and long-term employment. **D1**

Grading tips

P2 M2 D1 P2 is the main question here – M2 and D1 are extension activities which require you to relate what you learned in P2 to applying for uniformed public service and long-term employment. In order to achieve M2 and D1, you will need to produce a set of detailed discussion notes to support your answer to P2.

Most uniformed public services have a fitness test as part of their selection process. It is used to ensure that:

- all new recruits start training at a minimum standard level of fitness
- applicants have the necessary motivation to perform in the services
- applicants understand that fitness is important to the job
- applicants will be physically able to do the job they are applying for.

The fitness tests are chosen to best represent the needs of each service and are often reviewed. The reviews can lead to changes so it is beneficial to keep up-to-date with the service you wish to join.

Entry fitness requirements for the uniformed services

Please note that the public services tests change regularly. The tests described below were in use at the time this book was published and you should research the tests currently in use when you study this unit.

The police

The test for the police service is now a national standard used by all constabularies. Recruits will have to repeat the test at various times in their training/probationary period, so maintaining fitness is important. At the National Training Centre recruits will undergo more rigorous physical training and tests but this is the entry selection test. It includes:

- **Dynamic strength test**
  This tests your upper body strength in your back and your chest. The equipment used is called a dyno and is similar to a rowing machine but both sides are used. To test the back, sit with your chest against the padding, grasp the handles and pull until your hands are level with your sternum. You then have three warm-up attempts followed by five full strength pulls. The average of the five scores is recorded.

  Pass rate: 35 kg

To do the chest test, go around to the other side of the machine, sit down with your back to the padding, grasp the handles and push. Again, after three warm-ups you get five full strength attempts. Your average score is shown on a monitor.

Pass rate: 34 kg

- **Multi-stage fitness test**
  This is the bleep test used to measure aerobic fitness (stamina/cardiovascular). Cones are set up 15 m apart and you have to run between them. You have to keep time to a series of bleeps played on a cassette. The time between the bleeps is the amount of time you have to run between the cones. As the test goes up in levels, the time between bleeps decreases, meaning you have to run faster.

  Pass rate: Level 5 plus 4 shuttles (you must get to level 5 and continue to run for 4 bleeps at that level)

Consider this

How useful is the police fitness test in assessing the fitness of a potential recruit? Do you think you would be able to pass it?

The prison service

In many ways the prison service is similar to the police service as they both fall under the responsibility of the Home Office; they both deal with offenders and they share a near-identical work-related fitness test. The prison service uses the same dynamic strength test and multi-stage fitness test but also has the following:

- **Speed and agility test**
  This test involves running a slalom course through cones marked out over a 13 m course. The four cones are laid out along the course and there are three lines: start line, finish line and end line. The course is to be run as follows:

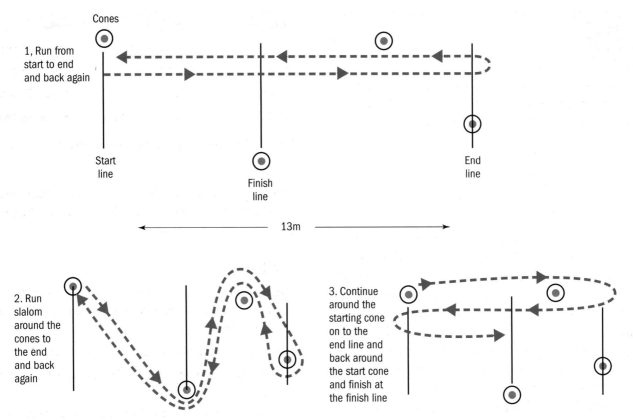

Figure 7.10 The speed and agility test

1. Sprint from the start line to the end line going around the end cone and back to the start.

2. Without stopping you must then negotiate the slalom course sprinting around the cones there and back.

3. After running around the start cone, you again sprint to the end line, around the end cone, back to the start, around the start cone and to the finish line.

Pass rate: 27 seconds

- **Grip strength test**
Grip strength is measured using a grip dynamometer. The dynamometer is held in the hand and the arm raised until it is straight and the hand is above the head. From this position, squeeze the dynamometer as hard as possible while lowering the arm to the side. Stop squeezing when your arm is at your side. The read-out will tell you the score. You have two attempts and your best score is used. This test measures strength in the forearm.

Pass rate: 32 kgs

- **Shield technique test**
You must hold a 6 kg shield during control and restraint techniques.

- **Body mass index**
Applicants are tested on their body mass index to ensure that they are within healthy guidelines for their height and weight.

Key terms

Body mass index (BMI) Body mass index is defined as the individual's body weight divided by the square of their height. BMI = $\dfrac{\text{weight (kg)}}{\text{height}^2 \text{ (m}^2)}$

Consider this

The prison service could be considered to be a more physically static service than some others. Why do prison officers need to pass a fitness test?

Age	Male	Female
16–24	12 mins 20 secs	14 mins 35 secs
25–29	12 mins 48 secs	15 mins 13 secs
30–34	13 mins 18 secs	15 mins 55 secs
35–39	13 mins 49 secs	16 mins 40 secs

Table 7.7 The pre-joining fitness requirements for the Royal Navy

The Armed Forces

Each of the Armed Forces has a distinct and unique role and their fitness tests reflect this. The Royal Marines have to be able to fight in any environment in the world and are usually sent in as shock troops. Consequently, their fitness test is very strenuous and requires high pass levels. The Royal Air Force is the most technical service and the majority of personnel are not expected to engage in contact with the enemy. As a result of this, there is less of an emphasis on fitness. The British Army is the largest of all the services and has a very wide range of jobs, from paratroopers to drivers to engineers. Again this is reflected in the fitness assessments: potential recruits complete the same tests but the pass rates are higher for those wishing to do more physically demanding jobs, with the Parachute Regiment having the most stringent pass requirements.

In the Armed Forces there are two distinct levels of personnel: officers and other ranks. The officers are, in general, in charge of a group of other personnel and make all the decisions about how they are to complete their set tasks. Because of this, officers need to be fitter and more capable than the soldiers or sailors under their command. This is often reflected in the fitness tests.

The Royal Navy

■ Pre-joining

The pre-joining fitness test is an aerobic test performed on a treadmill at a fitness centre and consists of running 2.4 km (1½ miles) in as fast a time as possible. Table 7.7 shows the times required to pass by age and gender.

The purpose of this test is to ensure that recruits pass their Phase 1 training and give them some confidence prior to carrying on training.

■ Phase 1

During Phase 1 training, recruits will have to pass a more involved fitness test before they can move onto trade training.

For ratings (ordinary ranks) the test consists of:

- **aerobic fitness test:** as detailed above with the same pass times
- **swimming test:** swim 40 m, then tread water for 3 minutes, then exit unaided. The Royal Navy is essentially a water-based service so the ability to swim is essential.
- **strength test:**

Men	Time	Women	Time
23–26 press-ups	2 mins	17–19-press ups	2 mins
39–53 sit-ups	2 mins	29–43 sit-ups	2 mins
5 x 60 m shuttle run	53–59 secs	5 x 60 m shuttle run	66–72 secs

Table 7.8 Phase 1 strength test requirements for ratings in the Royal Navy

For officers, the test consists of:

- **aerobic fitness test:** 2.4 km (1½ miles) on a treadmill

Age	Male	Female
16–24	11 mins 13 secs	13 mins 15 secs
25–29	11 mins 38 secs	13 mins 50 secs
30–34	12 mins 05 secs	14 mins 28 secs
35–39	12 mins 34 secs	15 mins 09 secs
Over 40	Special regulations apply	Special regulations apply

Table 7.9 Phase 1 fitness requirements for officers in the Royal Navy

- **swimming** and **strength tests**: as ratings.
Clearly, officers are expected to have a greater level of aerobic fitness than the ratings.

Consider this

Why do you think there might be different physical fitness requirements for officers and ratings? What purpose might this serve?

Consider this

Why does the physical selection test for the Marines have to be so demanding? What does a candidate's determination to complete the difficult three days show a Royal Marines recruiting officer?

The Royal Marines

Applicants for the Marines have to complete the Potential Royal Marines Course (PRMC). This is a non-stop three-day challenge including assault courses, fitness tests, shooting, interviews and drill. Like the Navy, the Marines are experts in water-borne combat and so swimming tests are an essential component of the course. The fitness elements are split between days 1 and 2:

Day 1

- **Gym test:** bleep test (20 m course)
  press-ups: 20–60 in 2 mins
  sit-ups: 30–80 in 2 mins
  pull-ups (overgrasp: palms away from you): 3–6
- **Swimming test:** swim 1 length of breaststroke.
- **Assault course:** complete the high obstacle course and assault course in teams to show teamwork.

Day 2

- **Aerobic test:** 3-mile run in a squad in 22½ mins.
- **Gym test:** individual and team tasks to show teamwork and determination.

The PRMC is one of the most physically demanding selection courses, but is good preparation for the Commando Training Course (CTCRM). At all times during the PRMC recruits are being observed to see if they have the qualities required to be a Royal Marine Commando.

The fire service

Like the police service, the fire service has been making an effort to rationalise recruitment and training. To that end, they too have recently introduced a new fitness test that represents common daily tasks. However, unlike the police test, this test requires more specialised equipment, is more time-consuming and is a much tougher physical challenge.

Potential fire service recruits must undertake the following tasks in order to be successful:

- **Enclosed-space test:** wearing full rescue equipment, including breathing apparatus (12 kg in weight) and a blacked-out visor, applicants must crawl through a 30 m maze.
  Pass rate: less than 4 mins
- **Ladder climb:** applicants must climb a ladder to a height of 9 m. Once there, they are to hook themselves securely onto the ladder and look down to read out a message or other similar task and then climb back down. Safety harnesses are used for this test.
- **Ladder-lift test:** this is a simulated test for strength and skill. An apparatus loaded with 15 kg must be lifted to a required height and lowered again safely.
- **Casualty-evacuation drag:** a 55 kg dummy casualty is dragged around a 30 m course safely and at walking speed.
  Pass rate: less than 41 secs
- **Equipment-carry test:** various items of fire-fighting paraphernalia are to be picked up and carried around a course measuring 25 m. The equipment includes hoses of assorted lengths and weights as well as a 35 kg barbell.
  Pass rate: 5 mins 47 secs

- **Equipment-assembly test:** using the instructions provided, applicants are required to assemble and then disassemble a piece of fire-fighting equipment within a specified time frame.

Some regional fire and rescue services have additional tests for recruits to pass. You may also have to do some of the following:

- **Multi-stage fitness test/bleep test:** using a distance of 20 metres you need to achieve level 9.6.
- **Chester step test:** this test involves stepping up and down on a bench for several minutes, in time with a metronome. The heart rate is monitored and compared to the applicant's maximum heart rate several times during the test.
- **Deadlift:** lifting a 50 kg barbell from the floor using a safe technique.
- **Handgrip test:** using a grip dynamometer the applicant must score 35 kg or above in the dominant hand and 33 kg in the other hand.

Take it further

Not all of the fire service tests are completely fitness-related. Identify those that aren't and explain what the tests show.

Reasons for inclusion of certain tests

As you can see from the physical fitness requirements outlined above, there is wide variation in what is physically required in order to be a potential recruit to the services. It is important to remember that although we talk of the uniformed public services as a whole, each of them performs a highly specialised role with its own set of interpersonal and physical fitness requirements. This is why the services show variation in their testing requirements.

Assessment activity 7.3

For this assessment you are required to produce a poster which looks at the service fitness tests. You must research the following content:

- police, prison service, fire service, Armed Services, different stages of the fitness tests, differences between entry levels, reason for including the tests.

You should use this information to complete the following task:

1. Describe the fitness requirements and tests of three different uniformed public services. **P3**

Grading tips

P3 This is a very straightforward task. You need to describe in your own words the range of tests, why they are used and any differences between entry levels.

Theory into practice

Having researched the physical fitness requirements of the service of your choice, conduct an assessment of how well you perform against those standards. Would you pass the tests? What can you do to improve your performance?

Components of fitness

Being fit is not just about how fast you can run, nor for how long. It isn't just about how much weight you can lift or how many times you can lift it. Fitness is actually all of these things, and more. To be truly fit and able to live healthily, and deal with the rigours of an active life, you need to be fit in several areas. It is these different areas, or components, that make up the sum total of physical fitness.

The components of physical fitness can be divided into two main areas:

- health-related components
- skill-related components.

Aerobic capacity

This is also known as aerobic endurance or stamina, which put simply is the ability to repeat an activity for a length of time without becoming fatigued. This is crucial to performance in many sports whether it be a ninety-minute football match or a three-hour long distance run. Stamina depends on the efficiency of your cardiovascular system (heart, blood, blood vessels, lungs) in terms of how well they provide the muscles with oxygen.

Strength

Strength can be defined as the maximum muscular force we can apply against resistance. It can be demonstrated in three ways:

1. **Static strength** – this involves isometric resistance against a stationary load, for example, pushing as hard as you can against a wall or pulling against an equal force as in a tug of war.
2. **Dynamic strength** – this uses isotonic muscle contractions to move heavy loads, for example, in weight training or power lifting.
3. **Explosive strength** – the use of fast and powerful muscular reactions. An example of this would be the standing long jump (see page 258, Table 7.10).

There are many benefits to improving strength such as:

- Increased strength of tendons and ligaments which may help prevent strains and sprains while taking part in physical activity. This increases strength in an individual's joints and this may also have the potential to help him or her become more flexible.
- Reduced body fat and increased lean muscle mass which helps the body's metabolic system run more

effectively and enables food to be utilised more efficiently.

- It may help to reduce resting systolic and diastolic blood pressure.
- It may help to reduce the amount of LDL cholesterol in the body thus offering some protection from the 'furring-up' of arteries, which can lead to coronary heart disease.

Muscular endurance

Muscular endurance (or stamina) is the ability to repeat an activity for a length of time (for example, press-ups or sit-ups) without becoming fatigued. Muscular endurance can be developed through resistance training or circuit training, both of which are discussed later in this unit.

Flexibility

Suppleness and flexibility is defined as the range of movement possible at joints. Up until the age of 40, ligaments, tendons and muscles are relatively elastic but after this age, movement that is not used frequently can be decreased and eventually lost. This can cause problems and injuries if the body is suddenly asked to do something it has not done for a while.

▲ Developing muscular endurance

In terms of sports performance, suppleness and flexibility will help reduce the risk of injury, improve the execution of sports skills and reduce the likelihood of muscle soreness. Flexibility can be developed and maintained by stretching exercises or activities such as yoga and swimming. It is recommended that an individual should spend 5 or 10 minutes stretching prior to beginning any sport or physical activity, in order to prepare the muscles for what is to follow. Stretching should also be conducted after physical activity since it helps to initiate the recovery process.

■ Body composition

This is a measure of a person's distribution of fat, bone and muscle in the human body. Muscle tissue takes up less space in our body than fat tissue, which means that our body composition, as well as our weight, can determine how lean we appear. Two people at the same height and same body weight may look completely different from each other because they have a different body composition.

Consider this

Can you think of two people you know who weigh about the same, but who look very different in terms of body composition? Why is this?

Measurement of body fat is normally a key area of examining body composition since it has a direct relationship to health and fitness. It is usually measured with skinfold callipers although many gyms now measure it electronically with a device very similar to weighing scales but which measures electrical resistance in the body. Callipers can pose a problem in that they can be difficult to use accurately. Measurements are normally taken in four places:

- bicep
- tricep

- subscapula (below shoulder blade)
- supraillia (just above the waist).

The measurements in mm are then calculated to give a body fat percentage. Generally a reading of 12-20.9 per cent in males would be acceptable and 17-27 per cent for women.

Skill-related components

Skill is the coarse and fine motor control that is required to perform specific abilities. It is a measure of how proficient an individual is at a particular physical ability. Skill is vital to sports performance. For example, it doesn't matter if you have strength, stamina and suppleness if you can't hit a tennis ball with a racket! Skill can be improved by repetition and practice.

■ Speed

Speed is the ability to move a part of the body or the whole body quickly. Speed can be crucial in many sports where the activity is timed or you may be required to outpace an opponent. Speed is not just important for athletes, a quick physical reaction time might help you avoid injury in public service work or perhaps chase and run down criminal suspects.

It is possible to improve speed with speed-training methods such as **Fartlek training** (also known as speed play).

Key terms

Fartlek training Fartlek is Swedish for 'speed play' and it is a combination of both long, slow, distance and interval training.

Consider this

In what services might it be a particular advantage to have speed?

Reaction time

This is how quickly messages are transmitted around the body. The brain receives information from a range of receptors in the body: eyes, ears, skin and nose. The brain then reacts to these stimuli. Putting a hand in a flame results in a pain signal being sent to the brain – this reacts by telling the hand to move away from the flame. How long it takes for the messages to travel from the hand to the brain and back again is the reaction time.

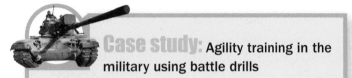

Case study: Agility training in the military using battle drills

Lance Corporal Eric's infantry section has been sent out on patrol when it comes under enemy fire. As soon as the shots are heard, all eight soldiers drop to the ground and crawl away to try to find cover (if the enemy see where the soldiers are they could shoot them, so by crawling away they stand a better chance of not being shot). Eric calls out to see who is injured and if anyone saw where the shots came from. Everyone is fine and someone says they saw muzzle fire from the woods to the west.

The section breaks into two fire teams who take it in turns to practice fire and movement: when Eric's team zigzags towards the enemy position, the other team provides cover by firing at the woods. Eric's team dashes right to left to avoid being shot for a few feet then they dive to the floor and crawl to the side to provide covering fire as the other team get up and zigzag toward the enemy.

The teams continue in this fashion until they reach the enemy and Eric destroys their position with a grenade.

1. **How does this exercise demonstrate the use of agility?**

2. **How would increased agility improve the situation of the section?**

3. **How would the team be disadvantaged if one or more of their members was less agile?**

4. **What activities could the team use to improve their agility on their return to base?**

Agility

This is the ability to move with quick fluid grace and it is critical for improving sports performance. It involves rapid changes in speed and direction while maintaining balance and skill. Like skill it can be developed with practice and is improved by developing strength, stamina and suppleness.

Balance

Having good balance is the ability to avoid falling over, whether standing still (static balance) or when moving (dynamic balance). Much like reaction time, balance relies upon the senses to tell the brain what to do with the muscles. It is a skill often linked with agility.

Coordination

Being coordinated involves using different parts of the body at the same time. Some actions require hand-eye coordination, for example, catching a ball. Again, coordination is strongly linked to agility and can be practised with agility drills.

Power

Speed and strength together provide power. Power is an explosive movement, where the greatest force is moved as fast as possible. Various types of training can be used to develop power including resistance training (weights) or circuit training.

▲ Using weights helps to build strength in the muscles used

Fitness tests

There are many benefits to undertaking a series of fitness tests, for example:

- to establish the strengths and weaknesses of an individual in order to design an appropriate training programme
- to provide a baseline initial fitness level against which future progress can be measured
- to ascertain level of fitness loss after injury, illness or pregnancy

- to allow medical practitioners to recognise and assess some specific health problems such as coronary heart disease.

In the previous section on specific service-related physical fitness requirements we have already discussed a wide variety of fitness tests. Table 7.10 provides a general overview of many of the common fitness tests you might encounter either in the recruitment process or simply as a tool for improving and measuring your own performance.

What is being tested	How
Multi-stage fitness test (MSFT)	• **The multi-stage fitness test** involves continuous running between two markers 20 m apart in time with a set of pre-recorded bleeps. (The MSFT is often called the bleep test for this reason.) The start speed of this test is about 8.5 km/hr which is really just a fast walk, but the time between the bleeps increases every minute or every level. This means that running speed must increase by 0.5 km/hr each time the level changes if the individual is to keep time with the bleeps. The advantage of this test is that large numbers of people can be tested at the same time but the disadvantages are that you need to be highly motivated to run until you can't go any further. Many people drop out earlier than this. Also audio tapes can stretch which may distort an individual's score. Scoring is based on the number of levels and shuttles completed, for example, 7/2 means level 7 has been reached and 2 shuttles completed.
Strength	• **The grip test** measures the strength of an individual's grip by use of a grip-strength dynamometer. The dynamometer is set at 0 and the handle adjusted to fit the size of the palm. Then the dynamometer is simply squeezed as hard as possible. The reading on the gauge tells you how strong your grip is. Most people find the hand that they use more frequently is usually the stronger. • **The Wingate test** is an anaerobic test that uses a specially prepared stationary cycle. After a warm-up session, a resistance is applied to the cycle and the cyclist pedals at full power for 30 seconds, the number of revolutions being counted by a counter on the wheel. The test will show how much energy is produced by the anaerobic pathway before the aerobic system kicks in and is measured in watts. It measures strength, power and muscular endurance.
Muscular endurance	• **The press-up test** is an assessment of the muscular endurance of the chest, shoulders and arms. The total number of press-ups completed in one minute is the score. Traditionally the press-ups for males and females differ as men should be in contact with the ground at their hands and toes while women should be in contact with the ground at their hands and knees or on a slightly raised bar. The resting position is up with elbows locked. • **The sit-up test** is also an assessment of muscular endurance but this time the muscles involved are the abdominals and hip flexors. The test involves the number of sit-ups completed in one minute.
Flexibility	• **The sit-and-reach test** is a flexibility and suppleness assessment. The individual sits down with their legs straight out in front of them and the soles of their feet flat against a box with a measuring device such as a ruler or distance gauge on top of it. They then reach forward with the fingertips to see how far past their toes they can reach. The movement should be smooth and continuous rather than lunging. The test is very easy to administer but it only assesses hamstring flexibility rather than the flexibility of the whole body. The test is usually measured in centimetres and as a rough guide females tend to be slightly more flexible than males.
Speed	• **60 m sprint** A 60 metre course is laid out and runners complete it as fast as possible. The results are recorded. For most people the race should take well under one minute and can be completed without breathing. Of course, this means that the test is purely anaerobic and could be used in place of the Wingate test where specialist equipment is not available.

What is being tested	How
Reaction time	• One of the more common ways of testing reaction time is by rigging up a system where the performer pushes a button when a light comes on. Variations are available on the Internet, where instead of pushing a button the performer clicks the mouse button when the background changes. The time taken to react will be monitored.
Agility	• **The Illinois agility run** is a reasonably simple test to carry out, using only a flat, non-slip 10 x 5 m course, a series of cones and a stopwatch. The performers start at the start line, lying on their front, hands by shoulders. When instructed they leap up and complete the course.
Balance	• **The standing-stork test** is a very simple test that only requires a non-slip, flat area and a stopwatch. The test is performed by lifting one leg and placing the foot on the other knee. The heel of the standing foot is raised and the hands are placed on the hips. The time that the position is held is recorded.
Coordination	• **Alternate hand-wall toss** tests hand-eye coordination. The performer stands at a set distance from a wall (for example, 3 m). A ball is thrown underarm at the wall and the aim is to catch the ball with the opposite hand. The test can be timed and the successful number of catches recorded.
Power	**Vertical and horizontal jumps** in fitness testing are designed to measure explosive power in the legs. • An example of a **vertical jump** is the sergeant jump whereby a subject marks the full extent of their normal reach on a wall or vertical measuring board and then tries to touch a point as far beyond the initial mark as possible using the power of their legs. • An example of a **horizontal jump** is the standing long jump where an individual stands at the edge of a horizontal measuring board and with both feet together jumps forward as far as they can.

Table 7.10 A variety of fitness tests

Remember!

Fitness tests can be influenced and distorted by several factors such as the individual's health, their emotional state, the temperature, lack of sleep, the time of day and the time since the individual last ate or drank.

Consider this

What impact might lack of sleep have on an individual's fitness test results? Explain your reasoning.

◀ The Wingate test measures strength, power and muscular endurance

Training programme

Goals

When you start your programme (or anything, for that matter) you need to decide on what your aims and goals are. To do this you need to give yourself achievable targets, a series of which should lead to your ultimate goal, for example, becoming a police officer or a Royal Marine Commando. Goals can be short-term, medium-term and long-term. For example:

- short-term goal – complete a three-mile circuit, alternating walking and running (walk to a lamp post, run to the next one, walk to the next one, etc.)
- medium-term goal – run the three-mile circuit (this should be achievable after walking and running the course three times a week for four weeks)
- Long-term goal – achieve level 5.4 on the bleep test (this should be achievable after running three miles three times a week for a month).

As you can see in the example, each step towards the ultimate long-term goal builds on what has gone before and uses a plan for success.

In order to be successful with your goal setting, use the SMARTER technique:

- **S** – specific to your ultimate goal
- **M** – measurable, for example, run three miles (so you can see what you've done)
- **A** – agreed with your tutor/trainer, to ensure that it's safe
- **R** – realistic, so that it is achievable and not just wishful thinking
- **T** – time-related, for example, three times a week for a month (so that you know when you should be moving on with your goals)
- **E** – exciting to make sure that you're motivated, such as working with a partner or doing activities that you really enjoy
- **R** – recorded (write down what you've done so that you can track improvements and evaluate your training).

You should try to stick to your goals as much as possible but sometimes life gets in the way or maybe your goals were too hard (or too easy). In this case, sit down and look at your plan; how can you change it to fit the problem?

It is also good practice to use a training diary. This can be used to log each session you have completed so that you can monitor your performance. This will motivate you when you see how you've progressed. You can also note how you felt as you were training as this could have an impact on whether the programme should be changed (you won't do it if you don't like it). Ensure that your goals are clearly marked – that way you can link performance to your progress to achieving those goals.

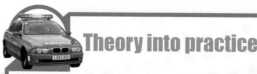

Theory into practice

Keep your own training diary for one month.

Principles of training

In order to build your strength, you need to understand some of the principles of fitness:

- **Overload** – firstly, in order to see gains in strength, your muscles must be stimulated to do more work than they are used to.
- **Progression** – secondly, muscles must continually work against a gradually increasing resistance in order to maintain overload.
- **Specificity** – thirdly, the strength gains you receive from training depend on the particular muscle groups used and the particular movement performed.
- **Variation** – as with anything else, familiarity breeds contempt. In order to stay motivated and interested in your training it is important to vary what you do. Don't keep to the same exercises year in, year out: your body will adapt to them and it will be more difficult to see improvements and it will be very easy to just go through the motions. Try something new instead – it will give you a new challenge and overload your body in a different way.
- **Reversibility** – 'use it or lose it' – improvements in performance start to disappear if you do not keep up the training. If you stop running, your cardiovascular stamina will gradually decrease; if you stop resistance

training, you will gradually lose strength; if you stop stretching, you will gradually lose flexibility. This applies to all of the components of fitness, even the skill-based ones. Once performance is lost, you need to work hard to regain it.

■ FITT principles

Use the FITT system with any training programme:

- **Frequency:** this is how often you train. For example, if you want to develop your cardiovascular stamina you can run up to five times a week. Once you've built it to the required level, you can change to running three times a week to maintain that level and use the rest of the time to concentrate on upper body strength. In another example, you may have been undertaking a simple strength circuit twice a week for the last 12 weeks and now want to devote more time to increasing strength – you decide to go to the gym Monday, Wednesday and Friday, instead of just twice.
- **Intensity:** this is how hard you train. It can be used to adapt training in many ways.
- **Time:** how long your session is. If you have increased the intensity, you may need to train for a shorter time but you have a harder work-out. Or, you may be running further and therefore need a longer session. This will depend upon how much time is available, of course.
- **Type:** you can also change the type of training. For example, to develop cardiovascular fitness, your first programme was to run continuously for 30 minutes. To improve your performance you may try Fartlek training in order to improve your speed at completing your distance. In terms of strength, after completing a programme using a simple circuit of 12 exercises three times a week, you may wish to develop more strength using **pyramid training**.

Key terms

Pyramid training This is just one way to lift weights or engage in any strength-building activity and involves changing your reps and weight for each set of each exercise. In other words, you'll start light and end heavy or start heavy and end light.

Periodisation

Athletes don't keep using the same training techniques all year round and neither should you. As we've seen from the principles of fitness there are benefits to changing the way you train. Another reason for change is to prepare yourself for different goals. This is what periodisation is all about: your training is broken up into a number of different phases or cycles. For an athlete the phases may be pre-competition, competition and post-competition; they need to train in all phases, but the training will be different in each one and they can use the principles of the FITT system to manipulate their sessions.

The longest phase is the macrocycle and this usually covers the whole year, though it doesn't have to (macro simply means big). The macrocycle should take you to the year's long-term goal, for example, complete a uniformed service fitness test.

The training year is broken up into mesocycles, usually four of them (meso means middle). During each mesocycle you will be working to a different short-term goal, such as muscular endurance or strength. Each mesocycle lasts for a number of weeks during which the intensity of training gradually increases. The mesocycle will end in a peak where performance has been improved. All-round performance should peak in the third mesocycle, which is where the long-term goal is, whether it's a competition or a test. The final mesocycle is a recuperation phase to avoid too much stress after the peak and excitement of the ultimate goal.

Between each mesocycle you need to build in one or two rest weeks to allow the body to recover from the increasingly intense training you've been doing. During the rest weeks you can train more lightly or, even better, do some other form of activity to give you a psychological rest as well. You could go hill walking, canoeing or climbing: you're still exercising, just doing it differently.

The mesocycles are divided into microcycles, which translate to your weekly training plans.

■ Resistance training

Resistance training develops strength. The muscles work against a resistance (weight) to develop size and strength. In addition to strengthening the muscles, all the other soft tissues in the area that is worked are strengthened too, i.e. the tendons and ligaments. It is dangerous to jump straight into strength training as it is easy to damage not only the muscles but also the surrounding tendons and ligaments. In order to avoid this, a lightly challenging programme should be put together that gets the body used to lifting weights. The resistance should be reasonably light and repeated about 10-12 times (reps); use a circuit of the gym and aim to work most of the body in between eight and ten exercises. Go around two or three times: this is a simple circuit.

■ Long slow distance (LSD)/ continuous training

This is running, walking, swimming, cycling, etc. at a steady continuous pace. For best gains this should be performed for at least 20–30 minutes and at least three times per week. Due to the nature of the muscles involved (the heart) cardiovascular training can be performed more regularly than anaerobic training and four to six times per week is acceptable. Running is seen as the most effective way of developing this kind of fitness although it does have a higher incidence of injuries than swimming or walking. Good running shoes are essential and they should be replaced every six months if used frequently. Certain activities can be used as alternatives to normal training to alleviate the boredom that can set in to training regimes. Such activities are often very good for LSD training for example:

- canoeing
- hill walking/mountaineering
- vigorous dance
- skiing.

As a rule of thumb, if you can talk while you are walking/running/cycling then you are training at the right level. However, beware of not working hard enough (you'll only be wasting your time). Your heart rate should be between 60-75 per cent of **MHR**.

Key terms

MHR Maximum heart rate – this can be calculated as 220 minus your age.

■ Interval training

This is a technique used by athletes to improve the heart's ability to deliver blood and oxygen. It involves training at a very high level followed by a period of light work. This cycle is then repeated. Interval training is usually associated with running but can be used in cycling and other activities.

During the intense period, work is done anaerobically and the heart works hard to pump oxygen around the body leading to an oxygen debt. In the recovery stage the heart is not working as hard, the oxygen debt is repaid and any poisons created are destroyed. This type of training improves the cardiovascular system, making better use of oxygen and more efficient removal of poisons.

▲ Introduce a different activity to add variety to your usual training programme

This technique is obviously dangerous for those who are unfit or who have heart problems. Start with **LSD** training before moving on to interval training. Heart rates should be between 80-95 per cent MHR for interval training – take care when using this technique!

Key terms

LSD Long slow distance training.

■ Circuit training

This involves going quickly from one exercise apparatus to another and doing a prescribed number of exercises or time on each apparatus. This ensures the pulse rate is kept high and promotes overall fitness by generally working all muscle groups as well as the heart and lungs.

Assessment activity 7.4

This task requires you to plan a personal fitness training programme. You need to include the following content:

- goals, fitness tests, principles of training, variation, reversibility, FITT principles, periodisation, training techniques, training diary.

You should use this information to complete the following task:

1. Plan a personal fitness training programme to prepare for a selected uniformed public service, with support. **P4**

2. The criteria for M3 are identical except you are expected to plan the training programme without support.

There are many considerations you should take into account when undertaking a fitness training programme of your own. This section covers those issues.

Health and safety

The most important part of fitness training and testing is safety. If the activities are not carried out safely there is a high risk of injury, which at best can disrupt and interfere with the training routine or at worst can cause disability or death. Safety also includes checking that the venue and equipment are both in a suitable condition for the activities to be carried out. Last, but certainly not least, are the participants: they must be wearing appropriate clothing and footwear and be safe to perform the activities. This includes assessing recent injuries and illnesses which may affect participation.

Warm-ups

One of the most important, but often under-appreciated, components of the fitness session is the warm-up. It prepares the body and mind for exercise and helps to prevent injuries. Once you have checked the venue and all participants, it is essential to complete a warm-up. This should be done progressively, starting gently and increasing the workload. There are two phases to a warm-up:

1. **Aerobic phase**

   This is used to raise the heart beat. By stimulating the heart and the lungs, blood circulates around the body and literally *warms* the body up. This is important as muscles that are cold can easily be damaged. Any rhythmical activity that can be kept up for the required time is acceptable, for example, running, cycling, rowing, stepping, skipping, etc. This part of the warm-up should last about 5-10 minutes, but obviously depends on the individual and the environment. When you start sweating, you're ready for the next phase.

2. **Stretching**

   This follows the aerobic phase and uses the muscles that are going to be used in the session's activities. For example, if you are climbing you would stretch the arms, fingers, back and legs. Practising the actual skill you will be doing later can be included in the warm-up, so long as it is done gently and not at full speed. This part of the warm-up can prevent strain in the muscles that are going to be used in the session. The stretches should be held for about 10 seconds, with this phase lasting 5-10 minutes.

Once the warm-up is completed, your body will be ready to start working harder. You will also be more ready psychologically to take part in the session as you've had 10 minutes getting used to working your body. This can be important if you haven't been particularly active prior to the session (for example, in bed or sitting in class).

Cool-downs

These are just as important as the warm-up and follow on at the end of the session. The cool-down basically does the opposite of the warm-up by bringing the heart rate down to normal levels and preparing you for leaving the fitness environment. It is also very important in preventing injury and muscle ache. Again, there are two phases:

1. **Light aerobic work**

   This is essential in slowing the heart rate down. If you stop training abruptly, your heart rate will actually continue to increase, which is not healthy. By doing some moderate work the heart starts to calm down and blood flow returns to normal, preventing it from pooling in the muscles used. This has two advantages. Firstly, without a regular supply of oxygenated blood the brain ceases to function and shuts down leading to fainting. Secondly, the blood in the muscles will contain poisons created in the anaerobic energy process; oxygen breaks down these poisons.

   Any rhythmic activity like light jogging, walking, light cycling or rowing will work. Aim for 5-10 minutes to give the heart time to get used to the change in work rate.

2. **Stretching**

This can help the muscles recover from the session and prevent aching. By stretching the muscles used, blood flow is stimulated and fresh oxygen is delivered. Flexibility training is also best done at the end of a session, when the muscles have been worked hard and can be stretched further resulting in an increased range of movement. Stretches in the cool-down should be performed for a minimum of 15 seconds. This part of the training session can be turned into suppleness training, adding another fitness factor into your session.

Cool-downs are also important psychologically as they allow your mind to calm down, removing any stress, aggression, competitiveness, etc. that may have built up during the session or test.

Consider this

Design a warm-up and cool-down for an activity of your choice.

Equipment

Training equipment should be:

- inspected regularly to ensure that it is in good condition and safe to use – if in doubt *do not use it*
- used in the correct manner, for the correct purpose. For heavy weights you may need a spotter (a friend to support the weights if you are struggling and to replace them safely if you cannot complete the repetition)
- properly replaced when no longer needed
- checked before use, for example, collars are properly fitted to bar/dumbbells, suitable resistance (weight) is used, no frayed cables or loose parts, bar/dumbbells are equally weighted
- understood before it is used – ask for an induction or read the instructions.

Monitoring the programme

As you undertake your programme, remember to keep a training diary to log when you trained and what it was like. You need to note the following:

- Date and time.
- Your attitude – did you feel in the mood for the session? Did you feel better afterwards?
- What did you do? Did you complete all of it or only a bit because you were distracted by something?
- Was it difficult or easy?
- Why was it easy or difficult? Does it need to be changed?
- Did you change anything? If so, what? Did it make the session better or worse?
- Did you work with a partner or alone? How did this affect your session?

You can also use your diary to log your performance in fitness tests. Using this data you can compare how you're doing with the public services fitness tests.

Another useful source of information is from your tutor or gym instructors. What feedback have they given you on your programme and on your performance? Don't be afraid to ask – this is part of their role.

Assessment activity 7.5

This activity requires you to undertake a personal fitness training programme to prepare for a selected uniformed public service. **P5**

Grading tips

P5 This is a practical activity which should be monitored by you and your tutor over the duration of this unit. You should take part in a variety of fitness tests and monitor and evaluate your progress.

Reviewing the programme

Once you have completed your programme you can start to review it. This is where it's useful to have kept a training diary. P6, M4 and D2 all require you to know the strengths and areas for improvement in your programme. It is much easier to achieve this if you have a diary of what you did and how you performed.

There are two areas to review:

1. **Fitness training programme**
   - Was it relevant to the service you wish to join?
   - Was it specific to the required components of fitness?
   - Which components of fitness were used?
   - Which principles of training were used in the programme?
   - Was it set at the correct level for you?
   - Was it enjoyable?
   - Did it include fitness tests?

2. **Results achieved**
   - Did you complete the programme or only do part of it?
   - Did you struggle with any parts? Which parts?
   - Why did you struggle?
   - How did you perform on the fitness tests?
   - What was your attitude to the programme? It may be that you didn't like it and therefore didn't carry it out.
   - Did you progress and see improvements in your performance?
   - Did your performance get worse?

Once you have reviewed these areas you can look at the strengths and areas for improvement for both.

Strengths

- Things that worked well – why did they work well?
- Good goals which were relevant to the service fitness test and specific components of fitness.
- Was it well planned?
- Improvements in performance. Which ones and why?

- Improved results on fitness tests. Which results improved and why?
- Used a range of components and principles of fitness.
- Specifically used the FITT system.
- Were you motivated? Why?

Areas for improvement

- What didn't work well? Why?
- Maybe it wasn't relevant.
- Unclear goals.
- Not using SMARTER goal setting.
- Not using a proper plan.
- Maybe your performance got worse. Why?
- You didn't include a fitness test.
- The programme was too short.
- The programme was boring.

The final question to ask is:

- To what extent did the training programme achieve your identified goals? Compare your original goals with the results of your review.

Evaluating the programme

Hopefully, your review will have more strengths than areas for improvement. However, even if it didn't all work out to plan, don't worry – you should now have a good idea why and be able to modify and improve the programme for future use. This is essential to see further improvement and ties in directly to the principles of training.

To evaluate the training programme, you need to look at the following:

Improvements to the programme

- Use the areas for improvement to guide you.
- Do you need clearer goals?
- Was something missing? What was it?
- How can you make the programme more interesting to motivate you more?
- Can you make it more relevant?

- How can you change the programme so that you can carry on using it?
- Do you need to change the components you used?
- How about the principles of training?
- Frequency?
- Intensity?
- Type of training?
- Time spent training?

Goal setting, planning, completing, reviewing and evaluating your training programme should be a continual process. All professional athletes and coaches use this system to continue improving fitness and performance. After a while it should become second nature and you will certainly be reviewing and evaluating your techniques and performance without conscious effort. Make sure that you continue to use a training diary, though. It can be very easy to forget the results of performance and reviews.

Assessment activity 7.6

This assessment requires you to examine the strengths and weaknesses of your personal training fitness programme. You should aim to cover the following content:

- results achieved, strengths and weaknesses, achievement of goals, modifications and improvements to programme.

You need to address the following tasks:

1. Write a 500-word report which describes the strengths and areas for development of your personal training programme. **P6**

2. M4 is a very straightforward extension of P6 where you are asked to explain rather than describe. This means a greater amount of depth and detail needs to be shown. **M4**

3. D2 requires you to evaluate the personal fitness training programme and make recommendations for its improvement. **D2**

Knowledge check

1. Name the four chambers of the heart.
2. Name the three types of muscle.
3. Name the types of joint.
4. How does smoking affect your health and fitness?
5. Describe the fitness tests for the police service.

6. What are the short-term effects of exercise?
7. What are the long-term effects of exercise?
8. What is a training diary?
9. How do you evaluate the success of a training plan?
10. What are the FITT principles?

Preparation for assessment

As a successful recruit into the police service, you have been asked to come back to your old college and give a presentation on how you improved your physical fitness in order to pass the selection tests. You know that there will be students listening to you who have no interest in the police service and you must make sure your presentation covers their needs too. In order to give a full and comprehensive package of information you need to ensure you cover all of the following tasks:

1. Describe the muscular-skeletal, cardiovascular and respiratory systems. **P1**

2. Explain the effects of exercise on the muscular-skeletal, cardiovascular and respiratory systems. **M1**

3. Describe the lifestyle factors that can affect health and fitness and the effects they can have. **P2**

4. Explain the effects that lifestyle factors can have on health and fitness, when applying for a uniformed public service and long-term employment. **M2**

5. Evaluate the effects that lifestyle factors can have on health and fitness, when applying for a uniformed public service and long-term employment. **D1**

6. Describe the fitness requirements and tests of three different uniformed public services. **P3**

7. Plan a personal fitness training programme to prepare for a selected uniformed public service, with support. **P4**

8. Plan a personal fitness training programme to prepare for a selected uniformed public service without support. **M3**

9. Undertake a personal fitness training programme to prepare for a selected uniformed public service. **P5**

10. Describe the strengths and areas for improvement of the personal fitness training programme. **P6**

11. Explain the strengths and areas for improvement of the personal fitness training programme. **M4**

12. Evaluate the personal fitness training programme making recommendations for improvement. **D2**

Grading criteria	Activity	Pg no.		
To achieve a pass grade the evidence must show that the learner is able to:			To achieve a merit grade the evidence must show that the learner is able to:	To achieve a distinction grade the evidence must show that the learner is able to:
P1 Describe the muscular-skeletal, cardiovascular and respiratory systems	7.1	241	**M1** Explain the effects of exercise on the muscular-skeletal, cardiovascular and respiratory systems	
P2 Describe the lifestyle factors that can affect health and fitness and the effects they can have	7.2	248	**M2** Explain the lifestyle factors that can affect health and fitness, when applying for a uniformed public service and long-term employment	**D1** Evaluate the effect that lifestyle factors can have on health and fitness, when applying for a uniformed public service and long-term employment
P3 Describe the fitness requirements and tests of three different uniformed public services	7.3	253		
P4 Plan a personal fitness training programme to prepare for a selected uniformed public service, with support	7.4	262	**M3** Plan a personal fitness training programme to prepare for a selected uniformed public service, without support	
P5 Undertake a personal fitness training programme to prepare for a selected uniformed public service	7.5	264		
P6 Describe the strengths and areas for improvement of the personal training programme	7.6	266	**M4** Explain the strengths and areas for improvement of the personal training programme	**D2** Evaluate the personal training programme making recommendations for improvement

International perspectives for the uniformed public services

Introduction

This unit will provide you with a clear understanding of the importance of international affairs and how international events can impact on the operational work of the public services. The uniformed public services are increasingly being deployed overseas on a variety of missions including peacekeeping, humanitarian aid and disaster relief, as well as their more traditional combat and security role.

During the course of this unit you will examine a variety of international institutions, such as the United Nations and The European Union, and consider the impact they have on the services and the ways in which our services support the work of these organisations. You will also examine in detail the causes of war and conflict and the possible response of the public services to national and international conflict. In addition, you will examine the impact of terrorism and the effectiveness of counter-terrorism measures. This is particularly important in the current international climate as the fight against terrorism is increasingly taking a larger share of the public services' resources.

This unit also looks at the importance of human rights issues and how human rights are protected internationally and how certain countries and regimes infringe them. It is important to remember that we are part of a large and complex network of nations and organisations. Our public services do not operate in a vacuum: they are subject to many kinds of international pressure and a wider range of roles they must fulfil. This unit will help you to understand the complexities of our life in the international arena.

Thinking points

UK public services are increasingly called upon to operate on the international stage. This could be in a variety of situations such as offering humanitarian aid in a natural disaster situation, acting as a peacekeeping force in war torn nations or cooperating with other international agencies in crime detection and prevention. This is a much broader role than they have traditionally held.

- Do you think it is important for UK services to assist others abroad or do you think they should focus their attention at home?

It is extremely likely that if you decide to join the armed services you will end up serving abroad at some point in your career. If you decide to join an emergency service, you will undoubtedly have to deal with international issues which affect the way your service does its job, such as changes to the law which come from Europe.

- What is the likely impact of this on the services?

The role of the public services in the international arena is likely to increase rather than decrease over the coming years. This means that personal skills such as diplomacy and practical skills such as the ability to communicate in another language are likely to become increasingly valuable to the services.

- Do you have these skills?

These are some of the issues you might want to think about before you read on.

After completing this unit you should be able to achieve the following outcomes:

- Understand international organisations that exist and how they impact on the UK public services
- Know the causes of war and conflict and the effects of conflict on UK uniformed public services
- Know how the public services deal with the problem of international and domestic terrorism
- Understand human rights and human rights violations, showing how UK uniformed services are used in a humanitarian role.

The United Nations (UN)

The forerunner of the UN was the League of Nations which came into being after the First World War. It was a mechanism which tried to establish international cooperation, peace and security between nations and so prevent another global war. It was established in 1919 by the Treaty of Versailles. However, the League of Nations failed to prevent World War II and, with its effectiveness in serious doubt, it ceased its activities.

The United Nations was created in very similar circumstances after World War II came to an end. Political and social unity were seen as very important in the post-war climate and, as a consequence, representatives from 50 nations met in the United States to debate the creation of a new global organisation to help maintain friendly international relations and promote peace and security. The new United Nations organisation officially came into existence on 24 October 1945 with 51 members. The UN today has 192 members, all of whom must agree to and be bound by the UN Charter. This is a treaty which sets out the rights and duties of the member states in the international arena and also sets out fundamental practices in international relations.

The UN has many roles and performs many international functions, as shown in Figure 8.1.

Consider this

Consider the roles in Figure 8.1. Which of them could apply to a recent UN situation which involved the UK services, such as the military intervention in Iraq?

The structure of the UN

The UN has six main divisions:

1. The General Assembly
2. The Security Council
3. The Economic and Social Council
4. The Trusteeship Council
5. The International Court of Justice
6. The Secretariat.

All of these divisions are based at the UN headquarters in New York except for the International Court of Justice

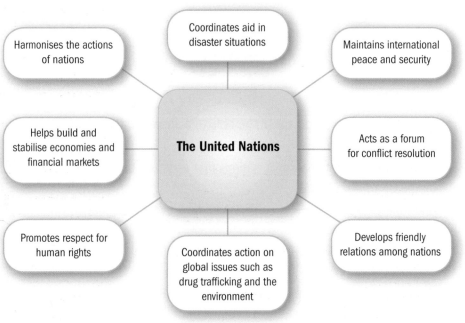

Figure 8.1 The roles and functions of the United Nations ▶

which is based at The Hague in the Netherlands. Each division of the UN has responsibility for a variety of functions and tasks.

The International Court Of Justice

This is the main court of the UN and it is located at the Peace Palace in The Hague. It was established in 1946 to fulfil two primary roles:

- to settle legal disputes between member states
- to provide opinions and advice on international legal issues.

It decides on issues of dispute among the member states. Participation in proceedings is done on a voluntary basis but, if a country does agree to take part, then it must be prepared to abide by the decision of the court. The court consists of 15 judges who are elected from across all member states by the General Assembly and the Security Council. The judges serve a nine-year term of office and no more than one judge from any member state may serve at a time. The judges do not serve on behalf of their respective governments – they are expected to completely independent.

It is not just judges from powerful western nations who are elected to serve the court – all UN nations are eligible to serve. Currently the court has many cases pending, ranging from issues of territorial and maritime dispute, to oil conflict to genocide.

UN Security Council

This division has responsibility for maintaining international peace and security. Members can bring complaints before it, but the council's first action is usually to encourage the parties involved to reach a peaceful agreement themselves. However, it may act as a mediator in the dispute or appoint a special representative to oversee the process. If the conflict has led to violence, the Security Council has a responsibility to bring it to an end and it does this by using measures such as negotiating ceasefires between hostile groups or deploying UN peacekeepers to help reduce tensions in troubled areas. In addition the council may impose other sanctions such as trade restrictions, as with Iraq during and after the first Gulf War, or collective military action such as in Kosovo. It consists of 15 members of which five are permanent members and ten are elected for a two-year term.

The five permanent members are:

- UK
- USA
- China
- Russian Federation
- France.

Each member has one vote. On simple matters, a vote of nine members is needed for action to take place. On more serious issues, such as military action, nine votes are still needed but all of the five permanent members must be in agreement. If they are not then the action cannot go ahead. This is called the power of veto.

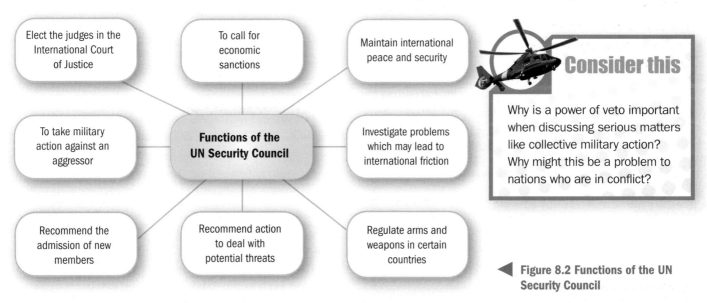

Elect the judges in the International Court of Justice

To call for economic sanctions

Maintain international peace and security

To take military action against an aggressor

Functions of the UN Security Council

Investigate problems which may lead to international friction

Recommend the admission of new members

Recommend action to deal with potential threats

Regulate arms and weapons in certain countries

Consider this

Why is a power of veto important when discussing serious matters like collective military action? Why might this be a problem to nations who are in conflict?

◀ **Figure 8.2 Functions of the UN Security Council**

The UN General Assembly

The General Assembly is like the parliament of the UN in which representatives of the 192 member states sit. The assembly meets to discuss some of the world's most pressing problems such as poverty, human rights and armed conflict. Each member state has a vote and decisions are made on the basis of a majority vote for routine matters and a two-thirds majority on important issues.

The UN General Assembly deals with a tremendous amount of information and queries from all 192 member states, so rather than debate each issue between the 192 members in open forum, which would be very time consuming, the General Assembly has subsidiary committees which deal with many of the issues.

The UN Economic and Social Council

This section comprises of representatives from 54 member states who are elected for a three year term of office. The council has responsibility for discussing economic and social issues and developing recommendations and policies which would help solve some of the more important international economic and social concerns. The council coordinates the work of 14 specialised agencies, such as the:

- World Health Organisation
- International Monetary Fund
- World Bank.

It also coordinates 10 commissions including those which address human rights, the status of women and narcotic drugs. In addition, it coordinates the work of five regional commissions, such as the Economic Commission for Africa and the Economic Commission for Europe.

The work of the Economic and Social Council accounts for over 70 per cent of the human and financial resources of the whole United Nations.

Consider this

Why does the work of the Economic and Social Council take such a large amount of the UN budget?

The Trusteeship Council

This council was established so that member countries with other territories could have assistance in preparing them for independence or self-governance. It consists of the five permanent members of the UN Security Council and until 1994 it met annually. However, on 1 November 1994, the Trusteeship Council suspended its operations after Palau became independent. Palau was the last UN trust territory to gain its independence. Today the council meets only as and when required.

The UN Secretariat

This is the administrative section of the UN. It is presided over by the Secretary General who is appointed for a five year term of office and it conducts the work and operations of the other UN bodies. The Secretariat has about 9000 staff who are drawn from all of the member nations in the UN. They are expected to be independent of their home country and not be biased towards it. The Secretariat may fulfil tasks such as:

- administering peacekeeping operations
- organising international conferences
- public relations
- surveying economic and social trends.

Staff in the Secretariat can be stationed anywhere in the world. Although the UN headquarters are in New York, it has offices in many of its member states. The current UN Secretary General is Ban Ki-Moon from South Korea who was appointed in January 2007.

UK service involvement in the UN

The UK services play a key role in UN peacekeeping operations and military action which has UN support (for instance, in Afghanistan, Kosovo, Cyprus and Iraq). Being part of a collective of nations means that our armed and civilian public services can be utilised by the UN to help maintain peace and resolve conflict globally. The decisions of the UN can have a tremendous impact on UK public services. They may be required to support peacekeeping operations such as those listed above, or to provide and deliver aid in times of large scale overseas disasters such as the Asian Tsunami in 2004.

Remember!

- The UN was established in 1945.
- It aims to promote global peace and cooperation.
- It has six main divisions.
- UK involvement includes peacekeeping and disaster relief.

Consider this

Do we need an organisation like the UN? Explain your reasons.

The European Union (EU)

The EU developed from the Treaty of Rome in 1957, which created the European Economic Community (EEC), although Great Britain did not join until 1973. The EEC was established in a post-war climate to try and ensure that there would be no more European based wars like World War I and World War II. It hoped to achieve this through economic and political cooperation between member nations.

The EU performs a wide variety of functions. For instance, it is the world's largest trade body and is one of the largest providers of funds and humanitarian aid for developing countries. It also sets out rules and guidance for member states on a whole range of important issues such as:

- monetary union
- agriculture
- fishing
- immigration.

Since 1 January 2007, the EU has had 27 members: Austria, Belgium, Bulgaria, Cyprus, Czech Republic, Denmark, Estonia, Finland, France, Germany, Greece, Hungary, Ireland, Italy, Latvia, Lithuania, Luxembourg, Malta, Netherlands, Poland, Portugal, Romania, Slovakia, Slovenia, Spain, Sweden and the UK.

The structure and institutions of the EU

Like the United Nations Organisation, the EU is made up of several different institutions, each of which has specific tasks, see Figure 8.3 below.

■ The European Parliament

The Members of the European Parliament (MEPs) are elected every five years. Each member state elects its own set of representatives to send to the parliament and, just as in a British General Election, MEPs come from a variety of political parties.

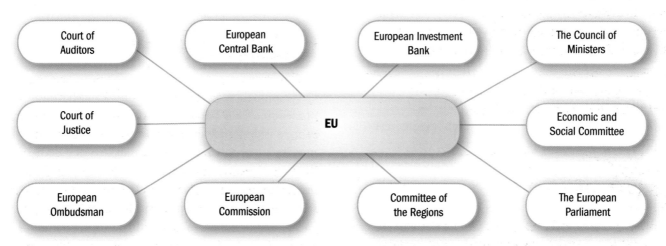

▲ Figure 8.3 Structure of the EU

The European Parliament has three main functions:

1. It shares with the European Council (Council of Ministers) the power to create law which applies to all the member states.

2. It shares authority for the EU's budget with the European Council and can influence how European money is spent.

3. It supervises the European Commission and it exercises political democratic supervision over all of the other institutions shown in Figure 8.3.

■ The Council of the European Union (Council of Ministers)

This is the main decision making body of the EU. It is made up of one minister from each of the member states who is responsible to their own national parliament and its citizens. It discusses issues such as finance, education, health and foreign affairs. Like the European Parliament it has several key roles:

1. It shares law-making power with the European Parliament.

2. It coordinates the economic policies of the member states.

3. It shares authority for the EU budget with the parliament.

4. It takes decisions on common foreign and security policies.

5. It coordinates member states and plays a special role in helping the police and judiciary of member states cooperate in criminal matters. Clearly this is a matter of some importance for the British public services such as the police and customs and excise.

■ The European Commission

This part of the EU is designed to uphold the interests of the European Union as a whole and not any one particular member state. Commissioners are expected to perform their duties without bias to their own member state. It has several responsibilities:

1. It drafts laws and proposals for the parliament and council to consider.

2. It implements European laws.

3. Along with the Court of Justice it makes sure that EU law is followed.

4. It represents the EU in the international arena.

■ The Court of Justice

This court has the task of ensuring that EU law is applied equally throughout the 27 member states. The majority of cases heard by the Court of Justice are referred to it by the national courts of the member states. In order to ensure that European law is followed, the court has wide jurisdiction in the following proceedings:

1. Preliminary rulings – this guarantees cooperation between the European Court and the national courts. If the national courts are in doubt as to the interpretation of a European law they must ask for clarification from the European Court.

2. Proceedings for failure to fulfil an obligation – this allows the court to monitor how the member states are fulfilling their obligations to the European community as a whole. If the member state is found to be failing in their legal obligations to either their citizens or other member states they must rectify this at once.

3. Proceedings for annulment – this allows the European Court under certain circumstances to annul a piece of law set by the other European community institutions.

4. Proceedings for failure to act – this is where member states can lodge a complaint against the European union itself for failing to reach a decision on a given issue. If upheld this is then officially recorded.

Decision making in the EU

Decision making in the EU is a complex and lengthy procedure. Many bodies are involved and because the process is designed to be inherently democratic the movement of policies and proposals between bodies as they are discussed and amended can be very difficult to track. The three main bodies involved in EU decision making are the European Commission, the European Parliament and the Council of the European Union. The European Commission proposes new legislation but it is the Council and Parliament that pass the laws.

There are three main ways that the EU makes decisions, these are:

- co-decision
- consultation
- assent.

Co-decision

In this procedure, Parliament and the Council share the power to make laws. The Commission sends its proposal on law to both institutions and they each read and discuss it twice in succession. If for any reason they can't agree on it, it is put before a committee that tries to resolve the difficulties. This committee is composed of equal numbers of Council and Parliament representatives. Commission representatives also attend the committee meetings and contribute to the discussion since they were the ones to propose the law in the first place. Once the committee has reached an agreement, the agreed text is then sent to Parliament and the Council for a third reading, so that they can finally adopt it as law.

Consultation

Under this form of decision making procedure, the Commission sends its proposal to both the Council and Parliament as we have described in the co-decision procedure, but it is the Council that takes responsibility for consulting with Parliament and other EU bodies such as the Economic and Social Committee and the Committee of the Regions, whose opinions are an important factor in decision making.

In all cases, Parliament can:

- approve the proposal made by the commission
- reject the proposal
- ask for amendments to be made to the proposal.

Assent

This method of decision making means that the Council has to obtain the European Parliament's agreement before certain very important decisions are taken. The procedure is the same as in the case of consultation, except that Parliament cannot amend a proposal: it must either accept or reject it.

EU decisions affecting UK public services

As you would expect, Europe must work together on a variety of issues and the decisions made at EU level can have a great impact on UK public services.

▲ The situation in Kosovo in the mid 1990s highlighted the importance of a rapid reaction force to target trouble spots in Europe

Decision	Impact
European Working Time Directive	The working time regulations have affected all the services as they state that there should be a limit on the average working week for all employees of 48 hours, minimum daily rest periods, a limit on night workers' average working hours and weekly minimum rest periods. The services do have access to some special provisions within the regulations which they can use to protect operational effectiveness – a war or riot doesn't stop in accordance with the regulations and neither should the response to the incident.
European Security and Defence Policy (ESDP)	The European Council meeting in Helsinki in 1999 agreed that a European rapid reaction force was needed to target trouble spots in Europe. The situation in Kosovo in the mid 1990s highlighted the problems of European armed forces strategic cooperation and utilisation of equipment. Most of the equipment used in Kosovo was American, as was most of the telecommunications technology. The rapid reaction force is designed to combat some of these problems. It is a 60,000 strong force able to be deployed within 60 days and operate for up to a year. The rapid reaction force also makes sense for economic reasons – it is better value for money to pool military resources across EU nations and split the cost. This has affected the armed services by potentially enabling a faster, more coordinated response to European incidents of conflict.
Europol	This is the EU cross border police organisation. It coordinates cooperation between all the EU policing agencies including customs and immigration. Europol has several key priorities in assisting the police forces of member states, dealing mainly with drug trafficking, illegal immigration, terrorism, vehicle trafficking and human trafficking. This has affected the police, customs and immigration by providing an information network across 27 nations which can be used to share intelligence and coordinate joint policing operations.
Eurojust	This is an EU organisation which was created to help judicial authorities such as courts in dealing with cross border offences such as organised crime. Eurojust can help with extradition proceedings between member states. As you can appreciate, there are lots of language barriers in bringing someone to justice in a different nation. Eurojust supports investigations and prosecutions across the EU area. Its main aim is to develop Europe-wide cooperation on criminal justice cases.
European Employment Directive 2000	This is an EU initiative which stated that all forms of employment discrimination on the grounds of age, disability, sexual orientation or religion must be removed. It was due to become law in all EU countries by 2003 but the UK government asked for an extension of one year to outlaw disability discrimination and three years to outlaw age discrimination in the workplace. This led to the creation of the Disability Discrimination Act 2005 (which came into force in 2004) and the Employment Equality (Age) Regulations 2006. This directive does not a have a significant impact on the services in terms of operational staff who must be physically fit and operationally ready at all times. The EU directive does exempt armed services from its requirements in any case.

Table 8.1 EU decisions which have affected UK services

Assessment activity 8.1

Working in pairs, research, prepare and deliver a 10 minute presentation which examines the European Union and its impact on the UK uniformed public services. Your presentation should cover the following topics:

- membership, structure and institutions of the EU
- issues that affect the public opinion of the EU
- the decision making procedure of the EU
- UK service involvement.

Once you have researched the content, prepare your presentation ensuring you cover the following questions:

1. Outline the structure and decision making processes of the European Union. **P2**

2. Identify five key EU decisions that have affected UK uniformed public services. **P2**

3. Explain how the European Union has influenced the operation of one of the uniformed public services. **M2**

Grading tips

The North Atlantic Treaty Organisation (NATO)

The North Atlantic Treaty was signed in Washington on 4 April 1949 and it created an alliance of ten European and two North American nations committed to each other's defence. It arose because of the growing strength of the Soviet Union after World War II. The Soviet Union had become powerful under communism and its defensive and offensive capabilities were strong. By contrast, much of Europe in the post-war period was destroyed and vulnerable to external attack. Although the United States implemented 'The Marshall Plan' which aimed to help with the rebuilding of Europe, it was also recognised that any attack which came from the Soviet Union would have to be repelled by the Americans and Canadians until Europe was back on its feet. The treaty itself is not very long and conforms to the United Nations Charter. It states that:

- Member countries of NATO commit themselves to maintaining and developing collective defence capabilities.
- If one of NATO's member states is attacked it will be considered to be an attack against them all.
- Members must contribute to the development of peaceful and friendly international relations.
- Members must eliminate conflict with the economic policies of other member states and encourage cooperation between them.

NATO currently has a membership of 26 countries. These are: Belgium, Bulgaria, Canada, Czech Republic, Denmark, Estonia, France, Germany, Greece, Hungary, Iceland, Italy, Latvia, Lithuania, Luxembourg, Netherlands, Norway, Poland, Portugal, Romania, Slovakia, Slovenia, Spain, Turkey, UK, USA.

Main NATO institutions

Institution	Role
North Atlantic Council	This is NATO's most senior political decision making organisation. It is based in Brussels, Belgium.
Allied Command Operations	This is based at Supreme Headquarters Allied Powers Europe (SHAPE), which is located near Mons in Belgium. This is the part of NATO responsible for all operational duties.
Allied Command Transformation	This is based in Norfolk, Virginia in the United States and has primary responsibility for the training and interoperability of alliance forces. It also has responsibility for the development of new technologies and techniques to improve the performance of NATO operations.

Table 8.2 Main organisations in NATO's military structure

NATO has recently undergone a major restructuring event to make it more efficient and more useful in today's society. It has a distinct military and civilian structure which you can see outlined in some considerable detail on the NATO website.

NATO was originally designed to defend Europe against an attack from USSR (Russia and its allies) after World War II. This developed into its more familiar role of being the first line of defence during the 'Cold War' of the latter part of the twentieth century. However, once the threat from the USSR disappeared at the end of the 1980s, NATO's role became unclear. There were calls for NATO to be disbanded, as the position that it was created to fill no longer existed. However, an adapted role has been created for NATO in collective defence against possible terrorist threats to the US, Canada and Europe and peacekeeping missions.

Key terms

Cold War This was a term applied to the relationship between the US and USSR during the 1950s to the 1980s. The two superpowers were openly hostile and the threat of nuclear conflict was ever present. The situation improved dramatically with the fall from power of the communist regime and the disintegration of the USSR. Russia is now considered to be a friendly nation to NATO and no longer a threat to western nations.

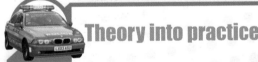

Theory into practice

Go to www.nato.int and examine NATO's new military and civilian structure. It has three levels of command: strategic, tactical and operational. Where might you encounter that kind of operation structure among UK emergency services?

Role of UK services

As Britain is a committed and influential member of NATO, our armed services have to be ready to cooperate with NATO's commands. This means that the British government must be prepared to send our armed forces,

personnel and equipment wherever NATO believes there is a need for them. This primarily means the deployment of peacekeeping forces or rapid reaction forces in missions such as the NATO-led Kosovan Force (KFOR) and the Stabilisation Force (SFOR) both of which used British troops as part of peacekeeping efforts in the former Yugoslavia in the late 1990s.

Security issues at world summits

World summits are occasions where world leaders can come together to discuss international social and economic issues. There are many different kinds of summit with different nations attending each. For instance, the G8 Summit gathers the eight most powerful nations on earth together, while the European Union Summit gathers the heads of the 27 member states together. In recent years these summits have been the scene of rioting and violence by anti-globalisation and anti-capitalism protestors. They would like to see the world economic system being run in a more fair and equal manner so that the poorer people of the world can have the same opportunities which are afforded to the citizens of rich nations. These protestors can cause tremendous disruption to the towns and cities where the summits are held and cause severe problems for the local public services, to say nothing of the damage done to property and businesses in the city.

Consider this

Why do people protest at summits such as the ones described above?

Other institutions

The European Court of Human Rights

The European Court of Human Rights was created to protect the human rights and freedoms of individuals in EU member states. It ensures that if a citizen has a

Case study: Europe and homosexuality in the armed services

The European Court of Human Rights (ECHR) decided in 1999 that the armed services ban on homosexuals serving in the forces was illegal. This was in response to two separate cases which had come before it: the case of Smith and Grady v. UK and Lustig-Prean and Beckett v. UK. These four service personnel had been investigated by the armed services and when they were found or admitted to being homosexual they were discharged from the service. The individuals concerned had to go to the ECHR after the Court of Appeal in London rejected their claim that prohibiting homosexuals from serving in the forces was illegal. The armed service position on the private lives of the four individuals was found to breach article 8 of the European Convention on Human Rights which grants individuals respect for private and family lives. In addition, the court ruled that in the case of Smith and Grady the Ministry of Defence policy had also breached article 13 of the convention which allows individuals the right to have their complaints dealt with in a UK court. The armed services now have no ban on homosexuality.

1. Why did the four service personnel have to go to the ECHR?

2. What were the legal problems with the Ministry of Defence policy?

3. Do you think the ECHR decisions were fair and appropriate? Explain your reasons.

legal complaint concerning a breach of human rights it can be heard by a European-wide court after all national alternatives have been exhausted. The case study above highlights an example of this.

The World Bank

The World Bank is not a single organisation. It consists of five organisations which aim to use their expertise and development specialisms in order to reduce world poverty. The five organisations are:

1. International Bank for Reconstruction and Development (IBRD)
2. International Development Association (IDA)
3. International Finance Corporation (IFC)
4. Multi-lateral Investment Guarantee Agency (MIGA)
5. International Centre for the Settlement of Investment Disputes (ICSID).

As with the EU and NATO, the World Bank developed as a consequence of World War II and one of its main roles was post-war reconstruction in Europe. Today, the focus of the World Bank is on poverty reduction. It provides financial assistance in the form of loans to developing economies. The loans it gives out are intended to finance issues such as:

- education
- agriculture
- industry
- healthcare.

These improvements are designed to establish economic growth in developing countries that is stable and sustainable. However, there are some concerns about the way the World Bank operates: first, loans must be repaid. If a country is already in poverty, how can they be expected to pay back the loan plus the interest it has accrued? This could cause more poverty in the long-term. Secondly, there appears to be some concern over how much actual change the loans bring about. They may provide a short-term solution but this may not create sustained improvement in the society. There is also the risk that the money could be misspent or stolen by an unscrupulous national government.

Amnesty International (AI)

Amnesty International is a non-governmental organisation (NGO) which was established in 1961 by

▲ Amnesty International works to raise awareness of human rights violations worldwide

- *Abolish the death penalty, torture and other cruel, inhuman or degrading treatment of prisoners.*
- *End extra-judicial executions and disappearances.* Extra-judicial executions are where individuals are executed on behalf of the state, but without a trial or hearing. These executions are often conducted by the military or civilian police.
- *To oppose opposition parties who advocate violence to oust a government.*

AI campaigns can take many forms, such as letter writing campaigns on behalf of particular individuals. They also gather information on human rights abuses worldwide. Amnesty pride themselves on their independence and they accept no government funds. Their finances are generated from membership fees and broad public support in the form of fundraising and donations.

Theory into practice

Visit Amnesty International's website at www. amnesty.org which details human rights abuses worldwide. It also gives much greater detail on the origins and purposes of Amnesty and it will be useful later in the unit when we discuss human rights.

Why is an organisation like AI important on a global scale?

a British lawyer called Peter Benenson. Its symbol is a lighted candle surrounded by barbed wire which was inspired by the Chinese proverb 'it is better to light one candle than to curse the darkness'. The main focus of Amnesty International is:

- *To free prisoners of conscience.* These are people who are illegally detained because of their beliefs, ethnic origin, sexuality, religion or political affiliation. Amnesty only works to free those prisoners who don't use or advocate violence.
- *Ensure fair and prompt trials for political prisoners.* Political prisoners are those people who oppose a ruling party or who a ruling party considers to be a threat. Often they may be held in prison for years without trial or access to justice.

Greenpeace

The Greenpeace environmental trust was set up in 1982 but its precursor had been investigating environmental issues for more than a decade prior to this. Like Amnesty International, it is another non-governmental organisation (NGO) which uses non-violent confrontation to highlight global environmental social problems and their causes through specific research and witnessing environmental problems. It was originally established to examine the following issues:

- the effect of human activities on the environment
- making information known to the public

- relieving sickness and suffering of humans and animals caused by environmental issues.

It has also campaigned on many issues such as:

- genetically modified crops
- international whaling
- promotion of renewable energy sources
- elimination of toxic chemicals
- nuclear disarmament
- driftnet fishing.

Greenpeace does not accept funding from governments and it is independent of any political movement. It raises its funds from donations from the public and grants for research.

Grading tips

P1 You need to describe the organisations. This means including information on their role and function, location of headquarters and personnel involved. You must also include information on how the decisions made by these organisations affect the services, such as peacekeeping deployment and counter-terrorism.

M1 This part of the task requires you to analyse. This means you must provide a much greater level of explanation and show the connections between the organisations.

Assessment activity 8.2

Individually research and produce a journal article which describes a range of international institutions and the impact of their decisions on the UK uniformed public services. Your article must include the following content:

- United Nations (structure, institutions, history, role, peacekeeping, peacemaking, UK service involvement)
- NATO (membership, structure, institutions, political and military, post Cold War role, effects on UK services)
- Other institutions (such as ECHR, Greenpeace, Amnesty, World Bank).

Your journal article must use this content to answer the following questions:

1. Describe the key international organisations, showing how their decisions impact on UK public services. **P1**

2. Analyse how decisions made at international level affect the operations of UK public services. **M1**

War and conflict

Very simply put, war is a clash of interests which results in a violent armed struggle. War and conflict are of vital importance in understanding the role of domestic and international public services. This is because conflicts of an ethnic, religious, political and cultural nature are continuing to dominate world attention. Although most of these wars occur within countries rather than between countries, the role of the public services is still crucial in a peacekeeping and humanitarian capacity. One of the major changes in conflict over the last 40 years or so has been the tendency of wars and conflict to occur within nations rather than between nations.

Spectrum of conflict

The spectrum of conflict is a sliding scale of types of war and conflict which can range from small scale terrorist attacks to large scale international conflict. All conflict and instability in the globe can be placed somewhere on this spectrum to highlight its severity in relation to other previous or ongoing conflicts.

Conflict can loosely be categorised into low-intensity conflicts and high-intensity conflicts.

Figure 8.4 The spectrum of conflict

High intensity	Low intensity
These are conflicts in which military action may come in the form of an alliance of nations or a superpower using their military resources to obtain objectives in a highly organised and lethal manner. High-intensity conflict tends to have a limited life span and rarely exceeds 6–10 years. With the end of the Cold War and the decline in the influence of the superpowers, these wars are becoming less common. Examples of high-intensity conflict over the last 100 years include: • The Great War (World War I) • World War II • Vietnam War • Falklands War • Iraq • Chechnya.	Low intensity conflict in contrast can last many decades and often has its roots in cultural and religious issues going back hundreds of years. They tend to involve military skirmishes and low-intensity attacks and retaliation. This is common in areas of ethnic tension, border disputes and as rebellion against a government via terrorist action. This kind of conflict is becoming more common. Examples of low-level conflict have been seen in the following areas: • Northern Ireland • Middle East • Yugoslavia • Kashmir.

Table 8.3 Low-intensity and high-intensity conflict

Consider this

Make a list of as many wars and conflicts as you can and decide, based on the information above, whether they are low intensity or high intensity.

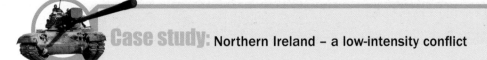

Case study: Northern Ireland – a low-intensity conflict

In 1921, Ireland was partitioned into six Northern counties which remained under British control and 26 Southern counties which were independent. However, this arrangement was seen as a betrayal by some Irish republicans, who were prepared to fight for a united and independent Ireland, completely free from British rule. To this end there were Irish Republican Army (IRA) campaigns in the 1920s, 1940s and 1950s. Constant vigilance was needed by Unionists (supporters of British rule) and the British government to ensure relative stability. The British government created emergency legislation which introduced a predominantly protestant unionist police service and perceived systems of economic discrimination against the Catholic minority in Northern Ireland. It was the dissatisfaction of the Catholics with their treatment that led to civil rights disorders in the 1960s that were the origins of the modern 'troubles', although their presence from 1 August 2007 is a much-reduced force, responsible only for training, not patrolling and policing.

In the 1960s there were many protests by the Catholics such as marches, sit ins and the use of the media to publicise grievances. By 1969 the Northern Ireland administration was increasingly unable to handle the disorder and the British government sent in troops to re-establish order. The Provisional Irish Republican Army (PIRA) was formed in 1969 as a consequence of the violence and riots in Londonderry and Belfast in August of that year. It began a campaign of violence against the British Army and military targets that was designed to liberate Northern Ireland from British rule. The violence hit a peak in 1972 when 468 people died. The British government suspended the Northern Ireland government and began direct control of the province from Westminster, a situation which continued into the 1990s. What began as an Anglo-Irish conflict before 1921 developed into an intra-Irish conflict between Protestants and Catholics.

Causes:
- British colonisation and involvement in the province.
- Political differences between the British and the Irish Republicans and between the Irish Republicans and the Irish loyalists.
- Religious conflict between Protestants and Catholics.

Effects:
- An average of about 100 people died each year in the troubles, both Cathlolic and Protestant and both British and Irish.
- Northern Ireland is a divided society with religious and political differences leading to hatred and mistrust (although this is being overcome with the creation of the Northern Irish assembly at Stormont).
- Irish culture and language have been in decline, replaced by English language and culture.
- There has been an ongoing peace process for the last 20 years in an attempt to re-establish a devolved government for the six Northern counties. This has largely been responsible for the creation of the assembly at Stormont which now operates devolved responsibility for governing Northern Ireland.

British involvement:
Since this is an Anglo-Irish conflict it is expected that British involvement would be high. British public and security services have been operating in Northern Ireland for over 30 years. They began as a support for the police service, the Royal Ulster Constabulary (RUC), in its mission to bring peace and stability to the area. In reality their presence on the streets of Irish cities often caused resentment, hatred and violence, placing the lives of troops and support staff at risk from terrorist attack. Many British soldiers and intelligence personnel lost their lives on the streets of Northern Ireland. However, the British public services were also accused of colluding with loyalist terrorist groups in order to assassinate republican terrorists. In addition, there were many instances where the conduct of the British Army was called into question for their treatment and sometimes killing of Irish individuals.

1. **Describe the origins of the modern troubles in Northern Ireland.**

2. **What have been the effects of the conflict on the citizens of Northern Ireland?**

3. **What impact did the conflict have on British services?**

4. **The devolved government at Stormont has found it difficult to reach agreement on how to rule the provinces. Why do you think this is?**

The Falkland Islands are located in the South Atlantic Ocean about 400 miles from the South American coast and around 8000 miles from the UK. They have been a British territory for over 150 years, although this has been historically disputed by the Argentine government.

On 2 April 1982, an Argentinian military force invaded the islands. This was done for a number of reasons: firstly, the fact that the Argentinians had seen the Falklands as part of their national territory, but secondly, and more importantly, the Argentinian dictatorship led by General Galtieri was in significant political trouble and it needed a cause to unite the people of Argentina behind it or risk losing power.

The British government led by Prime Minister Margaret Thatcher made an immediate decision to fight for the return of the islands to British control and secure the safety of the Falklands citizens, the majority of whom were of British descent. A British task force of 28,000 troops and over 100 ships sailed for the islands and retook the island of South Georgia on 25 April 1982, with a following offensive on the capital of Port Stanley in early May. After several fierce battles, such as the battle for Goose Green in which the British troops were often outnumbered, the Argentine forces surrendered on 14 June and the capital was restored to British control. Diplomatic relations between the UK and Argentina resumed in 1990, and although Argentina still makes a peaceful claim to the islands, the UK has made it clear that there is no room for negotiation on the issue.

Causes:

- The disputed historical sovereignty of the islands.
- An unstable political situation in Argentina including a major economic crisis and large-scale civil unrest.
- Feelings of nationalism and national pride.

Effects:

- 655 Argentine deaths, 255 British deaths and 3 islanders also died as a result of the conflict. The UK lost a total of 10 ships and the conflict is estimated to have cost the UK alone £1.6 billion.
- The failure of the Argentine government to win the conflict made their downfall come much quicker.
- The Conservative government of Margaret Thatcher was strengthened and won the 1983 general election, placing it in power for another five years.
- The UK government re-evaluated its role towards the Falklands and offered more support in developing its political and economic infrastructure. The islands are self sufficient and have several thriving industries such as fishing and tourism.
- Around 1000 British troops are still stationed in the Falklands as a permanent defence force.

1. **Why would the Argentinians believe they have a claim to the Falkland Islands?**

2. **What were the political and economic causes of this conflict?**

3. **What were the political and economic effects of this conflict?**

4. **What was the impact of this conflict on UK public services?**

Areas of global instability

There are several factors that could indicate that war and conflict may appear in a region. Some of these are:

- a government has an oppressive and unaccountable regime
- gross human rights violations
- economic distress
- the military seize power from a civilian government
- demographic pressures such as an increase in population coupled with limited access to food and water.

The Middle East remains a source of instability with frictions over water, oil, religion and military superiority set to increase. There are also long-standing religious conflicts in the area between Palestine and Israel which look set to remain unsolved. There are ongoing

Case study: Kashmir

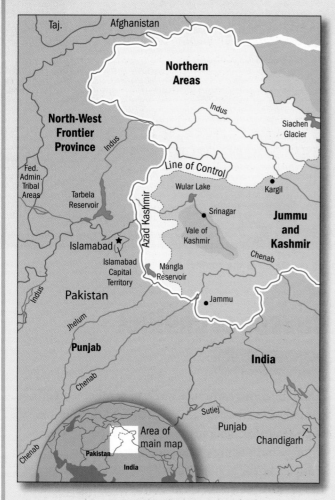

▲ Figure 8.5 The disputed region of Kashmir

The conflict over Kashmir involves two of the world's newest nuclear superpowers, India and Pakistan. The tensions in the region have erupted from a cycle of violence and aggression dating back to 1947 when British Colonial rule ended. The British departure created two new states in the region divided roughly on ethnic and religious lines – Muslims in Pakistan and Hindus in India.

The fate of the region of Kashmir was problematic because the leader at the time was Maharajah Hari Singh, a Hindu, while the majority of the population was Muslim. The choice of the Kashmiri leader to accede to India was not popular with either the Kashmiri Muslim population or the Pakistani government who considered Kashmir part of their natural cultural territory. War in the area broke out in 1947 and continued throughout 1948 resulting in Pakistan controlling one third of the disputed region and India two thirds. The border between the disputed regions is called the line of control and it is hotly contested. The situation is also complicated by the involvement of a third nuclear superpower, China, which claims a controlling interest in the Aksai Chin region of Kashmir.

Causes:

- Disputed border territory across the line of control.
- Territorial control over a politically important region.
- Ethnic, religious and cultural differences.
- Differing political ideologies.

Effects:

- Raised possibility of nuclear conflict in the region.
- Development of armed terrorist and separatist movements in the area.
- Control of the population by measures such as curfews.
- Severe economic costs to both India and Pakistan.
- Military and civilian casualties.
- Human rights abuses by both sides.

1. **What do you think are the main reasons for the Kashmir conflict?**

2. **What are the implications of a conflict involving three nuclear superpowers?**

3. **How could the conflict be resolved?**

4. **What is the impact of the conflict on the people of Kashmir?**

5. **What are the implications on the UK public services?**

▲ War can have a devastating effect on communities and people who are caught up in the conflict

tensions in Iraq and concerns over the development of nuclear capabilities in Iran. Many African nations have political instability caused by the aftermath of European colonialism. These instabilities can lead to civil wars being inflicted on already poverty stricken societies and populations. Currently there are ongoing conflicts throughout Africa, with particular problems in Somalia and Zimbabwe. There are also other areas of instability globally which are worth examining such as Afghanistan, Korea and Kashmir. A case study on Kashmir can be seen on page 287.

It is very important to identify sources of global instability for the public services. This is because areas of the world which are politically and economically unstable are more likely to become breeding grounds for terrorist groups whose ideologies can seem very appealing to citizens who are oppressed by their own or external governments. The consequences of terrorism can be very wide ranging as the 11 September terrorist action has shown. We will examine this in more detail later in this unit.

Causes of conflict

Ethnic relations

Ethnic relations can cause war and conflict if an ethnic group is denied access to resources and the mechanisms of government. There have been instances of some ethnic groups being denied access to facilities that other groups take for granted such as education, healthcare and political suffrage. Clear examples of this are the Jews under the Nazi regime and non-whites in South Africa. In certain circumstances, relations between ethnic groups can deteriorate to such an extent that genocide and ethnic cleansing can occur. This is where the dominant ethnic group undertakes the wholesale extermination of another group, as happened in the former Yugoslavia and also in Rwanda.

International politics

The international political arena is rife with potential sources of war and conflict, such as border disputes and disputes over territory, as can be seen by the ongoing conflict between India and Pakistan over Kashmir. It must also be remembered that many countries exist as part of a greater political and military alliance, such as NATO.

An attack on one of these countries may be seen as an attack upon them all. This was the case with the German invasion of Poland which started World War II. Britain had an alliance with Poland and so was obliged to enter into conflict even though it had not suffered an attack.

Internal politics

Wars can be caused by internal power struggles between sub-groups and divisions in a society, such as classes and tribes. It may also involve certain geographical regions wanting autonomy and self-determination or even full independence from a larger nation. Conflict can also be caused by the tactics and politics used by a government against those who it seeks to represent.

Land and resources

Nations often involve themselves in war over a variety of natural resources, such as oil, gas and water. These assets are immobile: they cannot be moved to another location so preserving them is a matter of enormous

▲ Nations may go to war to secure natural resources such as oil

political and economic concern. In some countries the income generated from natural resources can constitute the majority of money entering a country. Without the resources the economy would collapse. Countries that rely on immobile natural resources are often found in the Middle East and Africa where the land is rich in oil and precious stones and minerals. An example of this kind of war is the Gulf War; Iraq invaded Kuwait in a dispute over oil pipelines. The UN intervened by authorising an attack on Iraq to prevent them from gaining control of the Kuwaiti oil supplies. Wars can be caused because one of the groups desires to acquire the industrial wealth and influence of another. This wealth can take the form of cities or ports, trade routes, manpower, manufacturing industries or financial centres. We live in an information age and conflict over the control of information is not uncommon. Control of this data is usually in the form of computer technology and scientific advancement. Conflict can develop particularly over the development of military technology.

Nationalism

Often people feel so passionately about their way of life that they want to protect it against pollution or dilution by the culture of other groups or societies. Sometimes this feeling may apply to a small tribe and sometimes it may apply to a whole country. When it applies to a country it is called 'nationalism' and it can lead to the persecution of people who do not belong to the dominant culture. It can also cause conflict if the leaders of a society have a different cultural background to the population they lead.

Religion

Religion can often be a great source of stability and cohesion in society by providing moral and ethical guidelines on appropriate ways to conduct your day-to-day existence. However, conflicts between different or competing religions can lead to hatred and mistrust and cause political instability. Equally, the distribution of power between civil and religious leaders can be a source of conflict if either are not happy with the balance of power. An example of religious differences being a contributing factor to conflict is apparent in the Northern Ireland situation.

Ideologies

An ideology is a set of ideas about how things should be organised. For instance, a political ideology is a set of ideas about politics and a religious ideology is a set of notions governing how a belief system may be organised and implemented. Groups of people may have competing thoughts on many different issues and some of the issues are considered so important that the differences cannot be resolved easily or at all in some cases. For instance, the USA and the Soviet Union had competing political and economic ideologies after World War II leading to a state of mistrust and hostility that became known as the 'Cold War'.

Effects of conflict on UK uniformed public services

The role that the British public services play in these conflicts is not always the same. This means that the effects on service personnel will vary from one type of involvement to another. Table 8.4 overleaf lists some of these roles.

It is also important to remember that involvement in some of the conflicts mentioned in Table 8.4 is not only the job of the armed services. During the Hong Kong riots of 1966 and 1967 there were many British police officers serving as part of the Hong Kong police force. Similarly, the situation in Northern Ireland has tremendous implications for all of those involved in any public service, including people such as postal workers who were targets at one point in the troubles. UK police officers are also present in Iraq, training a new Iraqi police force.

▲ UK services may be called upon to send aid to the victims of international disasters such as the Asian Tsunami in 2004

Role	Effects on the individual and the service
Direct military combat	The effects of engaging in direct military combat are well documented. • Individuals may lose their lives, be severely and permanently injured, witness traumatic scenes leading to psychological difficulties including post-traumatic stress disorder (PTSD), alcoholism, depression and suicide. • They may witness the deaths of friends, colleagues and civilians. • There may be after effects from exposure to chemical or biological agents. • The service will be able to reflect on weaknesses in strategy and equipment and improve for next time. It may also retrain personnel in the light of the results of a conflict. This can happen after any conflict such as the situation in Iraq.
Peacekeeping	• Public services who are involved in peacekeeping operations also run the risk of being involved in direct military combat. Peacekeepers are not deployed until there is a ceasefire in place but this does not mean they are safe. Between 1948 and 2007 over 2300 peacekeeping personnel have been killed in action. • Deployment to peacekeeping operations may be a source of pride to the service personnel involved in helping a community to rebuild itself and ensuring the safety of vulnerable civilians. • The effect on the services is the deployment of personnel and equipment to the command of the UN or NATO which may have an operational impact on British responsibilities elsewhere. An example of this would be the UK's involvement in the Kosovo peacekeeping operation.
Evacuation of foreign nationals	• If there is civil war or major civil unrest in a nation then our services may be called upon to ensure the safety and security of British nationals living or working there by evacuating them. This may involve direct combat to protect the lives of civilians. • British nationals overseas are still the responsibility of the British government and they use the military to fulfil this responsibility.
War crimes investigation	• This can be a complex and difficult part of service life. War crimes such as genocide, massacres, systematic rapes and 'disappearances' are often only brought to light by the stories of survivors or by discoveries made by a liberating or peacekeeping force. • This can have a long-term impact on service personnel. First, they may be accused of war crimes themselves and have a responsibility to ensure that their conduct is of the highest possible standard and conforms with all recognised legislation and conventions such as the Geneva Convention. • Secondly, they may be called upon to preserve evidence and secure witness testimony to the war crimes of others. An allegation of war crimes against service personnel can be devastating to a public services organisation and it will lose credibility and respect both nationally and internationally.
Disaster relief and refugees	• Responding to major incidents and disasters and dealing with the flow of refugees can have a large impact on service personnel. They may experience PTSD as a result of what they witness or be subject to long-term health problems due to possible contamination at the site of an incident. • They may also experience an enormous sense of pride from being able to contribute to, and help with, rescue and aid efforts. • The service itself will have to liaise with other agencies and there may well be a significant financial cost. • The UK services were among the first to send aid to the Asian Tsunami in 2004 and Hurricane Katrina in the US in 2006.
Training military and civilian personnel	• Our emergency and military services are often called in to retrain security personnel in other nations, particularly in cases of civil war or ethnic tensions. • This can be a very rewarding job for individuals and many take great satisfaction from the work they are doing. However, the job is not without danger and service personnel might be at risk. • The services will have to release the person concerned and ensure operational effectiveness is not compromised by their absence. • The UK services are currently a key part of the retraining of Iraqi civilian police forces.

Table 8.4 Effect of conflict on the services

Assessment activity 8.3

For this activity you are required to produce a series of fact sheets dealing with aspects of war and conflict, and examining the impact of war and conflict on service personnel. You must include the following content:

- the spectrum of conflict (low and high intensity, areas of instability and risk)
- the causes of conflict (politics, nationalism, religion, ideology, resources, ethnic conflict)
- the effects of conflict on UK uniformed public services (peacekeeping, training, evacuation of British nationals, refugees, war crimes investigation).

Your fact sheets needs to answer the following questions:

1. Summarise the common causes of war and conflict, illustrating the spectrum of conflict and its effects on the uniformed public services. **P3**

2. Compare in detail the causes of a low-intensity and high-intensity conflict and its effects on the public services. **M3**

3. Analyse the causes of two recent conflicts, and their impact on UK uniformed public services. **D1**

Grading tips

P3 For this fact sheet you have to provide a summary of the common causes of war such as religion, ideology, resources etc. You also need to provide a summary of the spectrum of conflict, showing the shift from large-scale international conflict to low-intensity actions such as terrorism. You also need to summarise the effects on the services.

M3 You need to show the differences and similarities in how two different conflicts were caused. One of these should be a low-intensity conflict and the other should be a high-intensity conflict. You should also clearly show how the different intensities of conflict affect the services.

D1 This is the only distinction criteria in the whole unit, so if you are looking for a high grade then it is essential you get this section right. You are required to analyse the causes of two recent conflicts, so really this is an extension activity for the M3 criteria. To analyse means to examine something in detail and make links between different aspects of it. So to achieve this criteria you need to examine the causes of the conflicts in M3 and their impact on the public services in greater detail.

Terrorist organisations and areas of instability

Terrorism can be a difficult concept to define but it includes the idea of violence against a civilian population to inspire fear for political purposes. There are many terrorist groups which operate worldwide: some are national organisations and operate within or near to the borders of their own country; some are global organisations able to strike at foreign targets great distances away. Figure 8.6 highlights some national and some regional terrorist groups.

Irish Republican Army (IRA) in Northern Ireland and the UK.
Aim: To create an Irish republic free of British influence. Responsible for numerous terrorist attacks, including the bombing of a Brighton Hotel during a Conservative Party conference and bombings in Manchester, Birmingham and Omagh.

Islamic resistance movement HAMAS in the occupied territories of the West Bank and Gaza Strip in Israel/Palestine.
Aim: The establishment of a Palestinian state. It is suspected of terrorist attacks against Israel but also uses legitimate means to seek power via elections.

Aum Shinrikyo (aka Aleph) in Japan.
Aim: Global domination. Responsible for the Sarin gas attack on the Tokyo subway in 1995.

Euskadi ta Askatasuna (ETA) in Northern Spain.
Aim: to create an independent Basque nation in NW Spain and Southern France.

Armed Islamic Group (GIA) in Algeria.
Aim: to overthrow the Algerian government and replace it with an Islamic regime.

Khmer Rouge in Cambodia.
Aim: To overthrow the government. They had political power in the 1970s and were responsible for the deaths of over 1 million Cambodians (now Kampuchea).

National Liberation Army (ELN) in Columbia.
Aim: To replace the Columbian Government with a Marxist one. Responsible for politically motivated kidnappings in the 1990s.

Al Qaeda
Aim: To overthrow non-Islamic governments and expel westerners from Islamic countries. Responsible for global activities such as the bombings of embassies, attacks on the UK military and civilian targets such as the World Trade Centre.

Abu Nidal Organisation (ANO).
Aim: The establishment of a Palestine state in the Middle East. Suspected of terrorist attacks in over 20 countries.

Hezbollah.
Aim: To establish an Islamic government in Lebanon. Its main base is in Lebanon but it has cells across Europe, Africa and South America.

☐ Regional Terrorist Groups   ☐ International Terrorist Organisations

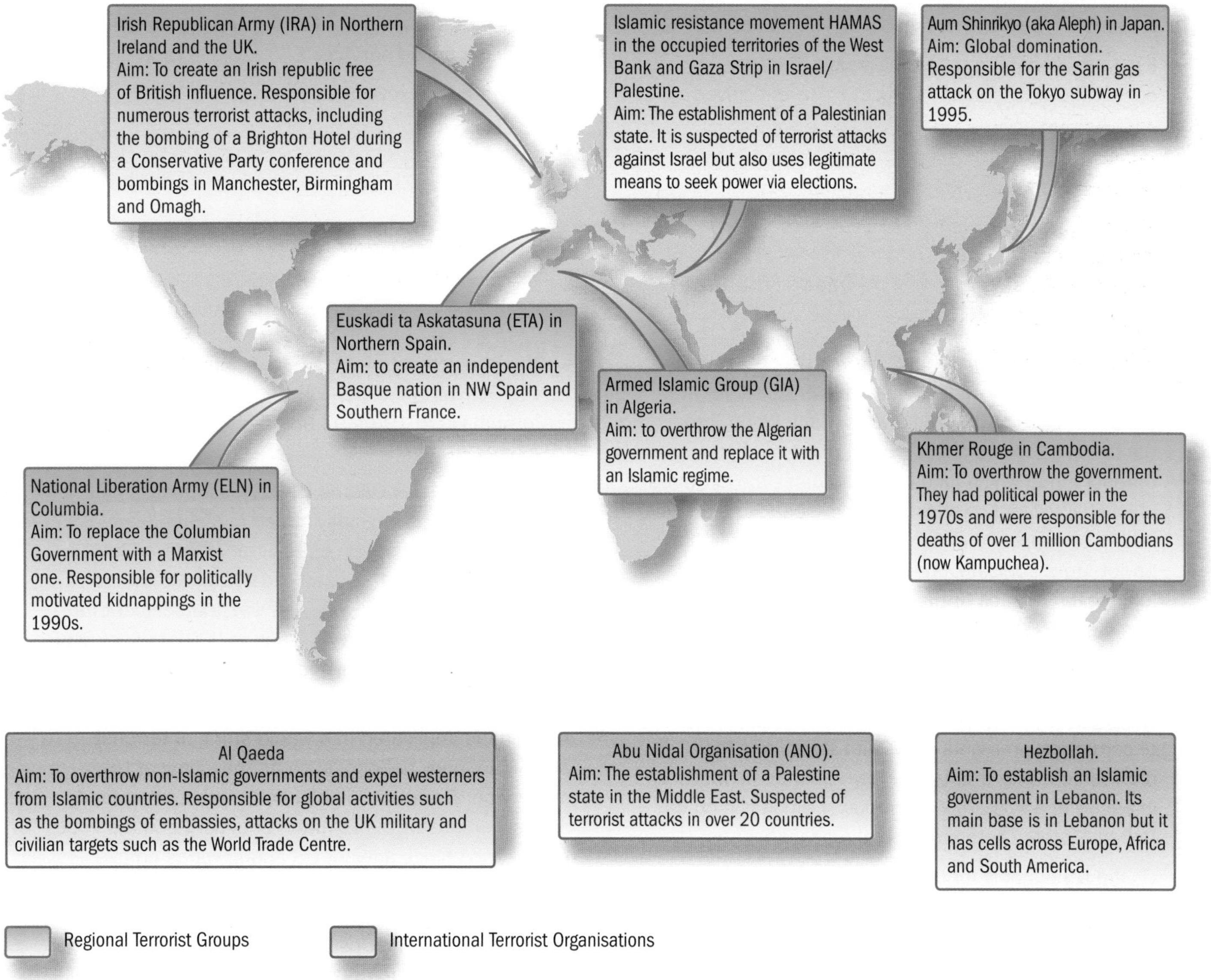

▲ Figure 8.6 Regional and international terrorist organisations

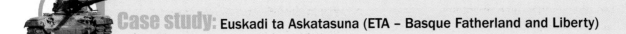

Case study: Euskadi ta Askatasuna (ETA – Basque Fatherland and Liberty)

The Basque region is located in the North West corner of Spain and across the border of the South Western French provinces of Labourd, Basse-Navarra and Soule. ETA was established in 1959 with the aim of creating a Basque homeland, independent of Spanish rule, based around Marxist principles. It arose partly as a reaction to the right wing rule of General Franco in the 1950s and 60s. Their activities include political bombing and assassinations of Spanish government officials, including judges and opposition leaders. It finances its activities from the extortion of Spanish businesses and armed robberies. It also claims ransom on kidnap victims.

ETA has killed more than 800 people since the early 1960s. ETA is also thought to have received training or assistance from Libya and Lebanon, which are countries with a history of sponsoring terrorist activities. It is also possible that it has links with the IRA in Northern Ireland due to the similarity of their political aims and methods. Although many people in the Basque region are in support of self determination for their region, the vast majority of them reject achieving it by terrorist means.

1. **What are ETA's main aims?**
2. **What are ETA's preferred terrorist methods?**
3. **What are the effects of ETA's actions on the Spanish public services?**
4. **Why are they often compared to the IRA?**

Case study: Al-Qaeda (The Base)

Al-Qaeda has become one of the world's best-known terrorist groups since it claimed responsibility for the destruction of the twin towers of the World Trade Centre on 11 September 2001. It is an international terrorist group which funds and organises the activities of Islamic militants worldwide. It developed in the early 1980s to support the war in Afghanistan against the Soviet Army. Ironically, one of the major sources of funding to Al-Qaeda at that time was the United States who gave $500 million to arm and train members of Al-Qaeda and other anti-soviet groups. After the war against the Soviets came to a successful conclusion, the organisation's primary goal became the overthrowing of corrupt governments of Muslim states and their replacement with true Islamic law (Sharia). Al-Qaeda is intensely anti-western with particular emphasis on the United States. There are several reasons for this:

- the US support for Israel at the expense of Islamic Palestine
- the US is seen as providing support for Islamic countries that are enemies of the group such as Saudi Arabia and Egypt

- the involvement of the US in Islamic affairs, such as the Gulf War in 1991–92, Operation Restore Hope in Somalia in 1992–93 and the current US presence in Iraq.

The group is led by Osama bin Laden amongst others and it was originally based in Afghanistan and the Peshawar region of Pakistan. It moved its base of operations to Sudan in 1991 and returned to Afghanistan in 1996 where it was the subject of a campaign by the US and its allies in 2002 to seek and destroy its infrastructure and operations in response to 11 September.

Al-Qaeda is implicated in a whole string of terrorist attacks in many nations, such as the killing of US military personnel in Somalia and Yemen, attempted assassinations of the Egyptian president and the Pope, and car bombings against US and Egyptian embassies worldwide. It is thought to have several thousand members but it also acts as a focal point for other Islamic extremist groups. It is well funded, with Osama bin Laden himself estimated to have a personal fortune of $300 million. The organisation also maintains many profitable businesses and collects donations worldwide.

1. **What are the reasons why Al-Qaeda exists?**

2. **What are its primary aims?**

3. **Why is the US a particular target?**

4. **What are the implications of Al-Qaeda activity on the UK Public Services?**

5. **What are the favoured terrorist methods of Al-Qaeda?**

State-sponsored terrorism

This is when a terrorist group forms to attack the enemies of another nation. Although they would seem to be independent they actually receive funds and resources from countries that are sympathetic to their aims. Countries that sponsor terrorism are often found in the Middle East and their targets are usually powerful western nations.

Methods used by terrorists

Terrorist groups use a variety of methods to inspire fear and achieve their political goals, such as bombings, assassinations and suicide attacks. These have been the traditional tactics of most terrorist groups in the twentieth century but increasingly there is the threat of terrorist groups using non-conventional methods as well. Table 8.5 overleaf highlights a variety of terrorist tactics.

Remember!

Terrorists can use a variety of methods but they are all intended to do the same thing: cause the civilian population to be frightened and cause the government to meet their demands.

▲ Terrorists employ many methods to cause fear and devastation

Method	Explanation
Chemical terrorism	• This is the use of a toxic chemical agent released into the atmosphere or water system in order to create casualties and demoralise the population. In 1995, a terrorist group called Aum Shinrikyo (Supreme Truth) released the chemical nerve agent Sarin on the Tokyo underground killing 12 people and injuring hundreds of others. • Chemical substances are much easier to manufacture or obtain than either nuclear or biological substances. They are also more mobile because they are safer to carry, meaning they can be carried from country to country in relative safety. • However, chemical weapons are very difficult to use effectively. This is because environmental conditions such as wind and rain interfere with their progress. Often just moving out of the area will be enough to counter the immediate effects of a chemical toxin. • To put chemical attacks in context, when Aum Shinrikyo conducted their attack on the Tokyo underground, they had perfect environmental conditions. Even so, only 10% of the people present were injured and only 1% of the injured died. • Chemical attacks are not very effective at mass destruction but, like biological terrorism, they succeed in their primary aim which is to generate fear and panic.
Biological terrorism	• This is the use of biological organisms such as microbes and viruses spread in civilian populations in order to cause casualties and lower morale. The terrorist use of Anthrax spores in the US in 2001 is a perfect example of this particular strategy. • Biological terrorism cannot be used for pinpoint attacks and often the results may be unnoticed for many days, making it very difficult to track down the perpetrators. • However, biological weapons can be rendered almost harmless by a quick and organised medical response and vaccination programme. • Biological weapons are weapons of terror and panic rather than mass destruction. Their primary aim is to demoralise and frighten a civilian population and distract a government from other, more effective, attacks.
Assassinations	• This is the targeted murder of an individual or group of individuals who are perceived to be a source of threat to a group, or whom the group hold responsible for perceived or actual oppression. • The target could also be a high profile or famous person, who is assassinated to generate publicity and increase the fear of the civilian population. • The IRA were responsible for the assassination of Lord Louis Mountbatten, the Queen's cousin, in 1979. Lord Mountbatten and several others, including his 14-year-old grandson, were murdered by a radio controlled bomb attached to his boat. Lord Mountbatten was a target who fitted into both categories of usual assassination targets: he was both a high profile member of the royal family and a part of the British establishment.
Suicide attacks	• This is a terrorist technique where the terrorist him or herself intends to die in the attack. • The most common form is to become a 'human bomb' and detonate explosives carried upon the person when there is a high likelihood of many others being injured or killed, for example, in a crowded place. The hijackings of 11 September 2001 also fall into this category.
Bombings	• Bombs are a tried and tested terrorist technique. They have the advantage that they can be placed in a location which allows the bomber to detonate them from some distance away, ensuring that s/he is not injured. • They have the disadvantage of being detectable if people are observant and they may also fail to detonate on command. An example is the Omagh bomb, which was the worst bombing ever carried out by the IRA. The bomb detonated in the town of Omagh in Northern Ireland in 1998 killing 29 people including several children and a woman who was eight months pregnant with twins. The attack did not inspire fear in the public; instead it created grief, anger and outrage.
Hijackings	• This is usually, but not always, the taking over of a civilian aircraft by a terrorist group. The pilot is forced to fly where the terrorists dictate, or alternatively the flight crew are killed and the terrorists themselves fly the plane. • The most common reason to hijack a plane is to use the passengers as hostages to gain transportation to a particular place or to hold them as ransom until certain political demands are met. • One of the worst examples of a terrorist hijacking was the taking over of 4 planes by 19 terrorists on 11 September 2001. The planes were then used as missiles against several US targets, most notably the twin towers of the World Trade Centre in New York.

Table 8.5 Methods used by terrorists

Counter-terrorism

It can be very difficult to combat terrorist networks. By their very nature, terrorist groups operate in secret and often in small groups that cannot implicate the wider organisation if they are apprehended. The British security service spends well over half its annual funding allocation on combating domestic and international terrorism. Below are some of the possible counter-terrorist measures listed by the United Nations which can be implemented by governments and agencies seeking to end terrorism.

Not all groups will respond to all of these methods and not all countries will be prepared to utilise all of these strategies. It takes more that one counter-terrorism measure to disrupt a terrorist organisation and in reality governments will employ multiple tactics to achieve the result they want. It is difficult to assess the effectiveness of many counter-terrorism methods because details about their use may not be available for security reasons.

Method	Detail
Combating terrorism through mechanisms of politics and government	• Address the specific political grievances of the terrorists. • Engage publicly or privately in discussion to resolve conflict. • Offer political concessions to terrorist groups or to the political parties representing them. • Offer amnesty to active terrorists. • Apply diplomatic pressure on the countries sponsoring terrorist groups.
Combating terrorism through economic and social policy	• Address the specific socio-economic grievances of the group. • Ban terrorist fundraising. • Create a socio-economic climate that disinclines people to violence, by having good standards of living for all. • Apply economic sanctions to countries which sponsor terrorism.
Combating terrorism through psychological and educational strategies	• Establish common values with opponents. • Allow freedom of expression. • Ban interviews and publications by terrorist groups. • Provide training in dealing with terrorist threats. • Media campaigns to condemn the groups' methods. • Educate the public on awareness of terrorist threats.
Combating terrorism through the use of military tactics	• The use of strikes/operations to undermine/destroy groups. • Use public services to protect potential victims and property. • Recruitment and training of counter-intelligence personnel.
Combating terrorism through the use of the judicial and legal system	• Agree and abide by international treaties which denounce terrorism. • Expand extradition treaties. • Introduce and update laws prohibiting terrorist activity. • Give harsh sentences to convicted terrorists. • Provide witness protection. • Increase the speed of justice for terrorists.
Combating terrorism through the effective use of the police and prison service	• 'Target harden' objects or people that might be at risk from attack. • Improve international police relations and coordination. • Run training simulations of terrorist attacks. • Encourage informants and infiltrators. • Ensure terrorist networks cannot recruit in prisons. • Control and regulate immigration/asylum.
Combating terrorism through the effective use of intelligence and security services	• The effective use of technology to monitor terrorist groups. • Improve and maintain links with other intelligence services. • Infiltrate terrorist organisations.

Table 8.6 Counter-terrorist measures

However, where evidence is available, the results are mixed.

Effectiveness of counter-terrorism measures

- **Financial measures and sanctions** – Economic sanctions against Iraq put in place after the Gulf War succeeded only in harming the general population; those who sponsor terrorist attacks have enough money and power to be immune from such sanctions. In addition, international governments are able to seize money they believe belongs to terrorists. Although this may help prevent a particular strategy or attack, it will not resolve the reasons why terrorists are prepared to kill in the first place.

- **Direct retaliation** – The US favoured direct military strikes as a response to 11 September in order to destroy Al-Qaeda. This was the beginning of the US-led 'War on Terror'. This tactic is expensive and time-consuming, and can cost many lives with few visible results. Al-Qaeda is an international terrorist group with independent cells across the world that are well funded and well trained. A military strike against one part of it will not destroy the organisation and may recruit new members to the cause because of resentment against countermeasures.

- **Extra-judicial killing of suspects** – This tactic has short-term success in that the immediate threat from a particular terrorist is removed. However, in some societies the terrorist is martyred, inspiring others to follow in his or her footsteps. Extra-judicial killing by the state is also subject to international condemnation. Many believe that if a government suspects an individual of being a terrorist, they have a duty to try them, but not to kill them.

- **Political negotiation** – In Northern Ireland, diplomacy and political compromise have brought a measure of security to the region in recent years and established a devolved political system.

In essence, the effectiveness of counter-terrorist measures is variable and depends largely on the type of strategies employed by a particular government. Negotiation and compromise is generally a far better tool of resolution than direct military action. This is because the root cause of most terrorism lies in the perceived oppression of one group by another. Negotiation can help lift this feeling of oppression while violence may simply reinforce it. The problem with this is that governments cannot be seen to be forced to the negotiating table by groups who use violence to threaten them and their citizens. It would be a licence for any group with a grievance to commit atrocities simply to get the ear of those in power.

Consider this

What is your view on the fact that most governments refuse to negotiate officially with terrorists? What counter-terrorist measures do you think are most effective and why?

Measures to prevent terrorism in the UK

Since the attacks of 11 September 2001, the UK has been in a state of high alert with regard to a possible terrorist threat on our own soil. The UK was targeted by Islamic extremists on 7 June 2005 who conducted four concurrent bombings on the transport system in London. A total of 52 people plus the 4 bombers were killed in the explosions with hundreds more injured.

Since this time, UK services have undergone extensive training and preparation in order to prevent another attack taking place and to ensure a swift emergency response if we are targeted again. The UK uses many of the counter-terrorism measures described in Table 8.6 including:

- education
- awareness/vigilance campaigns
- promoting freedom of speech
- building relationships with communities who might feel oppressed
- extensive training and exercising of simulations
- control of immigration/asylum
- ensuring the safety of public buildings by 'target hardening' them, i.e. making them less vulnerable to attack.

There is always a political difficulty in balancing the threats to national security with the fundamental human rights of citizens. This is the subject of ongoing debate between the government and various pressure groups and civil liberties organisations. For example, restricting freedom of speech for terrorist groups denies them access to political dialogue and harms their human rights. This needs to be balanced against the benefits of reducing their publicity, which may in term harm the organisation's recruitment and funding mechanisms.

Consider this

Should the human rights of ordinary citizens ever be compromised to combat terrorism? Explain your reasons.

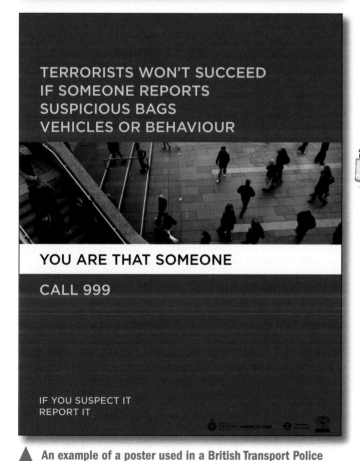

TERRORISTS WON'T SUCCEED
IF SOMEONE REPORTS
SUSPICIOUS BAGS
VEHICLES OR BEHAVIOUR

YOU ARE THAT SOMEONE

CALL 999

IF YOU SUSPECT IT
REPORT IT

▲ An example of a poster used in a British Transport Police campaign to combat terrorism

Source: © 2006 Metropolitan Police Authority

Assessment activity 8.4

In pairs, produce a wall display which examines issues of terrorism and counter-terrorism. Your poster should contain the following content:

- terrorist organisations and areas of instability (national and regional groups, global terrorist organisations, states sponsoring terrorism, areas of terrorist activity)
- methods used by terrorists
- counter-terrorism (methods and their effectiveness)
- measures to prevent terrorism in the UK (training, threat assessments, control of immigration and asylum, security of public buildings, freedom of speech and other human rights issues contrasted with anti-terrorist measures, awareness/vigilance campaigns, relationships with the community, education).

Your wall display should answer the questions below.

1. Describe the methods used by terrorists, identifying the types of counter-terrorist measures used to combat them. **P4**

2. Explain the types of counter-terrorist measures used to combat terrorism. **M4**

Grading tips

P4 You are asked to describe the methods used by terrorists but, as the description can be fairly detailed, make sure you don't simply list the methods as this will not be sufficient to pass. You also have to identify possible counter-terrorist measures; a full list of these is provided for you earlier in the unit.

M4 This is an extension activity for P4 and covers the same type of content in much greater detail. In order to achieve M4, make sure you have offered a full explanation in your own words of the types of counter-terrorist measures used to combat terrorism.

Human rights

Rights are certain things that an individual is entitled to have or do, based on principles of fairness and justice. Many rights are written down in the constitution of a country which lists the basic rights a citizen can expect, but some countries, such as Britain, do not have a constitution and in those countries it is assumed that people have the right to do anything unless the law expressly forbids it. These are called legal rights but they are not the whole story. People also claim rights based on general ideas of fairness and equality which are called moral rights, and they may or may not be supported by the law of the land. It is also important to remember that legal and moral rights can sometimes be in opposition to each other.

Consider this

Can you think of a situation where a person's legal and moral rights might be in opposition?

There are many organisations which examine human rights and monitor how people are treated across the world, such as Amnesty International and the United Nations. There are also many charters or agreements which set out the rights countries should afford their citizens. We will now examine some of these agreements.

The United Nations Declaration of Human Rights

As with many of the organisations and issues discussed in this unit, the UN Declaration is a post-war initiative and it is easy to see why. Two major global conflicts had been fought in less than 30 years and terrible atrocities had been committed against the European Jewish population, prisoners of war in the Far East and the populations of Hiroshima and Nagasaki in Japan, amongst many others. These atrocities had shocked the world and it was felt that a better way must exist for dealing with international problems and treating people in times of both peace and conflict. This was the birth of the United Nations organisation and its charter which emphasises the fundamental importance of human rights. The UN organised a commission to draw up a declaration that would state the importance of civil, political, economic and social rights to all people regardless of colour, religion, nationality, gender or sexuality.

The declaration was agreed in December 1948 and consists of 30 rights or articles (although some of these 30 rights are broken down into sub-sections). You can find a complete list of the rights at www.un.org.

■ Key features

Of the 30 articles in the declaration it has been argued that 3 and 25 are key provisions. Article 3 states that all human beings are entitled to life, liberty and security of the person. These are core political and civil rights ensuring freedom and safety. Article 25 specifies that all people are entitled to an adequate standard of living for themselves and their families. This includes food, clothing, housing and medical care. These would seem to be the fundamental rights on which the others are built. Articles 28 and 29 are also crucial although they are not often discussed. They overarch the others in that they emphasise the responsibility of the international community to put into place a political and social framework in which respect for human rights can flourish. Without this foundation the other articles cannot be effectively implemented. The UNDHR has achieved worldwide prominence and is probably the most important document of its type ever written. It has become an influential standard by which nations are measured.

Theory into practice

Visit www.un.org and read the articles of the UNDHR. Which of the 30 rights do you consider to be the most important?

The Geneva Convention

The Geneva Convention can trace its roots back to 1859 when a Swiss citizen called Henry Dunant witnessed the aftermath of the Battle of Solferino during the Second War of Italian Independence and was horrified at the numbers of soldiers who lay dying and wounded with no one to help them. This experience led him to call for medical relief societies to be set up to care for wounded soldiers and civilians in times of war. Dunant also called for an international agreement to be established which would protect those agencies and the wounded from

▲ The International Committee of the Red Cross seeks to protect the victims of international and internal armed conflicts

further attack. This is how the voluntary relief society of the Red Cross was established.

In 1864, 12 nations signed a treaty in which they agreed to care for all sick and wounded people regardless of nationality and they also agreed to recognise the Red Cross agency as neutral in any conflict. This treaty was called the Geneva Convention. There are now four Geneva Conventions which most countries have signed which cover a variety of issues such as armed forces on land and sea, treatment of prisoners of war and the treatment of civilians in times of war.

■ The First and Second Geneva Conventions

These two conventions are very similar and the main points are:

- the sick, wounded and shipwrecked must be cared for adequately
- each side must treat the wounded as carefully as if they were their own
- the dead should be collected quickly
- the dead should be identified quickly and protected from robbery
- medical personnel and establishments should not be attacked.

■ The Third Geneva Convention

This convention outlines what should happen if a member of the armed forces falls into enemy hands and becomes a prisoner of war (POW). Its main points are that POWs:

- do not have to provide any information other than their name, rank and service number
- must be treated humanely
- must be able to inform their next of kin and the International Red Cross of their capture
- must be allowed to correspond with their family
- must be supplied with adequate food and clothing
- must be provided with medical care.

■ The Fourth Geneva Convention

This deals with the protection of civilian personnel in wartime and its main points are shown in Table 8.7.

Protected civilians MUST be:	Protected civilians MUST NOT be:

• treated humanely
• entitled to respect for honour, family and religious practices
• allowed to practice their religion
• specially protected in safety zones if:
  – under 15
  – sick/wounded
  – old
  – expectant mothers.
	• discriminated against because of race, religion or political opinion
	• forced to give information
	• used to shield military operations
	• raped, assaulted or forced into prostitution
	• punished for offences they have not committed.

Table 8.7 The Fourth Geneva Convention

The European Convention on Human Rights

This treaty was signed in 1950 by members of the Council of Europe. It predates the EEC and the EU, but membership of the EU requires that the treaty is signed. The UK was a founding member of the convention and very influential in its content. It was also one of the first countries to sign and agree it. As with the United Nations Declaration of Human Rights, it arose from the atrocities Europe had experienced during World War II. It is intended to act as the lowest common denominator of rights, which means that it is set at a modest level to encourage compliance with it. It incorporates the right to:

- life
- freedom from torture or inhuman or degrading punishment
- freedom from slavery, servitude, enforced or compulsory labour
- liberty and security of the person
- a fair trial
- respect for private and family life
- freedom of thought, conscience and religion
- freedom of expression
- freedom of assembly and association
- freedom to marry and found a family.

Until the Human Rights Act 1998 came into force, British courts could take note of the Convention but could not directly enforce it.

The Human Rights Act 1998

This piece of law is designed to incorporate the European Convention on Human Rights into domestic (British) law. It provides a package of rights-based law which is in contrast to the traditional English system based on common law prohibitions, i.e. statements about what people cannot do. Under the Act, courts will have to interpret any existing law as being consistent with the convention. This shifts some power away from parliament and towards judges. More information on this act can be found in Unit 1.

Human rights violations

Human rights abuses are committed in every nation around the world. Many people think that human rights violations are the sole province of developing nations in Africa, the Middle East or South America, but they occur in developed western nations such as the UK, Australia and the USA as well.

Theory into practice

Human rights abuses can take many forms such as torture, extra-judicial killing, ethnic cleansing and genocide. Go to the Amnesty International website at www.amnesty.org and look up a case of each of these human rights abuses. Write a short summary of each example.

Assessment activity 8.5

Produce a written report and case study which examines human rights issues. Your report should contain the following information:

- United Nations Declaration of Human Rights
- Geneva Convention
- European Convention on Human Rights
- Human Rights Act 1998.

Your report should focus on the questions below.

1. Produce a written report which describes the key features of the United Nations Declaration of Human Rights. **P5**

2. Produce a case study of how human rights have been violated in one international country. **P5**

▲ Peacekeeping troops in Iraq

Grading tips

P5 This is a very straightforward task which asks you to explain the key features of the UNDHR. It is important to note that all of the features are key – there is no right or wrong answer. Achieving the grade depends on the quality of your explanation, not the particular rights you have identified as being key. The case study should be a clear explanation of a recent abuse of human rights – an important resource for this will be the Amnesty International website. The site has a library function which allows you to search every county in the world for reported human rights violations.

Assessment activity 8.6

Take part in a small group discussion which examines the humanitarian role of the UK services. Your discussion should include the following content:

- humanitarian aid programmes
- peacekeeping
- disaster relief.

Your discussion should address the question below.

1. Describe the humanitarian role played by the UK uniformed services in an international situation. **P6**

The humanitarian role of the UK public services

A great deal of the humanitarian work that the public services do (including peacekeeping and disaster relief) has already been covered several times in this unit. Refer back to those sections for a full account of the public services role.

Grading tips

P6 Your discussion should be clearly focused on the role the UK services play in supporting others in their actions. It is useful to produce a set of notes from your discussion as your evidence.

Knowledge check

1. How did the United Nations Organisation come about?

2. What was the major threat to Europe when NATO was created?

3. What is the impact of EU decisions on the UK public services?

4. What are the principle aims of Amnesty International?

5. Describe the spectrum of conflict.

6. How has war and conflict changed over the past 40 years or so?

7. What are the common causes of war?

8. What is the role of peacekeepers?

9. What roles do UK public services play in war and conflict?

10. What are the common methods used by terrorist groups?

11. Describe in detail at least three counter-terrorist measures and consider how effective they are.

12. Describe the main principles of the various Geneva Conventions.

13. Why do people engage in terrorist activity?

14. What are human rights?

Preparation for assessment

You have been asked to produce a magazine/journal covering a wide range of international issues for distribution to a regiment of soldiers due to be deployed on a peacekeeping mission with the United Nations. The magazine should be informative and provide the potential peacekeepers with the following information:

1. Describe the key international organisations, showing how their decisions impact on the UK uniformed public services. **P1**

2. Analyse how decisions made at international levels affect the operations of UK uniformed public services. **M1**

3. Outline the structure and decision making process of the European Union, identifying five key decisions that have affected UK uniformed public services. **P2**

4. Explain how the European Union has influenced the operation of one UK uniformed public service. **M2**

5. Summarise the common causes of war and conflict, illustrating the spectrum of conflict and its effects on the uniformed public services. **P3**

6. Compare in detail the causes of a low-intensity and a high-intensity conflict and its effects on the uniformed public services. **M3**

7. Analyse the causes of two recent conflicts and their impact on UK uniformed public services. **D1**

8. Describe the methods used by terrorists, identifying the types of counter-terrorist measures used to combat them. **P4**

9. Explain the types of counter-terrorist measures used to combat terrorism. **M4**

10. Describe the key features of the United Nations Declaration of Human Rights, explaining how human rights have been violated in at least one country. **P5**

11. Describe the humanitarian role played by the UK uniformed public services in an international situation. **P6**

Grading criteria	Activity	Pg No.		
To achieve a pass grade the evidence must show that the learner is able to:			**To achieve a merit grade the evidence must show that the learner is able to:**	**To achieve a distinction grade the evidence must show that the learner is able to:**
P1 Describe the key international organisations, showing how their decisions impact on the UK uniformed public services	8.2	283	**M1** Analyse how decisions made at international levels affect the operations of UK uniformed public services	
P2 Outline the structure and decision making processes of the European Union, identifying five key decisions that have affected UK uniformed public services	8.1	278	**M2** Explain how the European Union has influenced the operation of one UK uniformed public service	
P3 Summarise the common causes of war and conflict, illustrating the spectrum of conflict and its effects on the uniformed public services	8.3	292	**M3** Compare in detail the causes of a low-intensity and a high-intensity conflict and its effects on the uniformed public services	**D1** Analyse the causes of two recent conflicts, and their impact on UK uniformed public services
P4 Describe the methods used by terrorists, identifying the types of counter-terrorist measures used to combat it	8.4	299	**M4** Explain the types of counter-terrorist measures used to combat terrorism	
P5 Describe the key features of the United Nations Declaration of Human Rights, explaining how human rights have been violated in one international country	8.5	303		
P6 Describe the humanitarian role played by the UK uniformed public services in an international situation	8.6	303		

Crime and its effects on society

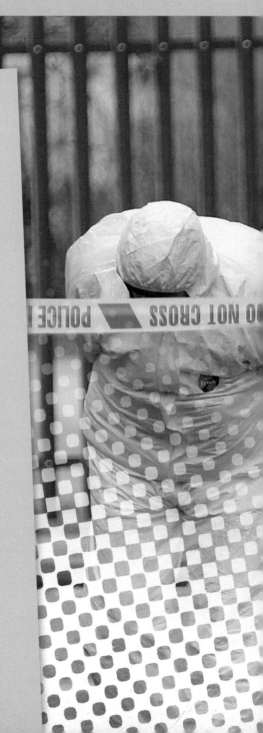

Introduction

This unit aims to provide you with an awareness of the possible theories of criminal and antisocial behaviour, including factors that may contribute to deviance such as socio-economic and environmental influences. You will also explore the consequences of criminal behaviour such as the cost of crime and the fear of it, and how this can impact on individuals and communities.

You will identify the role of the public services and other support and voluntary agencies who offer a variety of services to victims. This will include examining your own local crime reduction strategies, multi-agency crime reduction partnerships and the measures which they take to reduce the fear of crime. It is also necessary for you to explore current legislation that attempts to deal with antisocial behaviour in order to understand the current political influences in this area.

You will also examine how your local police tackle crime using problem solving models such as the National Intelligence Model (NIM), and how they work together with other agencies in joint partnership to reduce crime. This includes the youth offending team, the probation service, the prison service, social services, education services and health services.

After completing this unit you should be able to achieve the following outcomes:

- Know the effects of criminal behaviour on communities
- Understand how the public services support victims of crime
- Know about legislation relating to crime and disorder, including the sentences and orders
- Understand the approaches used to reduce crime, disorder and antisocial behaviour.

Thinking points

Crime has become a national preoccupation over the last few decades. News programmes comment on it every day and our entertainment consists of programmes such as *The Bill*, *CSI* and *Waking the Dead* and numerous true-crime documentaries. The study of criminology seeks to examine crime from every angle – it discusses what crime is and how it can be explained and controlled. Television shows and public attention aside, the concept of crime is more complicated than you might think.

Write down in two sentences or less your own definition of crime.

You might have defined crime as:

- an act punishable by law
- something a person does that is illegal
- behaviour which is contrary to the laws of society.

These answers are not wrong but neither are they entirely right. These definitions do not reflect the fact that what is considered a crime differs from time to time, place to place and culture to culture. Essentially crime is changeable and so is our response to it.

In this section you will explore definitions of crime, theories which may be used to explain why crime happens and the effects of crime on individuals and communities.

The study of crime is called Criminology. It is a multi-disciplinary subject that draws many of its ideas and concepts from other subjects such as:

- sociology
- psychology
- biology
- geography
- law
- anthropology.

There are many ways of explaining why crime happens; these are called 'theories of crime'. Generally speaking, theories of crime fall into three main categories:

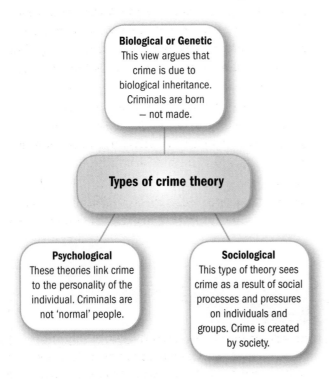

Biological or Genetic
This view argues that crime is due to biological inheritance. Criminals are born — not made.

Types of crime theory

Psychological
These theories link crime to the personality of the individual. Criminals are not 'normal' people.

Sociological
This type of theory sees crime as a result of social processes and pressures on individuals and groups. Crime is created by society.

▲ Figure 12.1 Types of crime theory

We will be examining sociological and psychological theories in more detail.

Sociological theories

Sociological theories focus on society as the primary cause of crime. There are many sociological theories you could examine such as:

- Functionalism
- Marxism
- Labelling theory
- Chicago School/Urban Ecology.

This unit will examine two of these theories: functionalism and labelling theory.

Functionalism

Functionalism developed from the work of Emile Durkheim (1858–1917) who was an active social theorist at the end of the nineteenth century. Durkheim was among the first sociologists to analyse crime and deviance, and the theories he developed have provided a base for later criminologists to build on. Durkheim believed that for societies to exist and work effectively there had to be a strong sense of social order. In other words, there had to be agreement among the members of society about values and rules or norms. He called this agreement a society's 'collective conscience'.

Key terms

Collective conscience This is the collective feeling in a group of people about what is wrong or right. When a group of people share the same morals and values, and they view deviant behaviour in the same way, they could be said to have a collective conscience.

Deviance This can be defined as behaviour which does not match the 'norm'. In essence, it is behaviour which is not considered average. It does not necessarily mean bad behaviour: individuals who behave in a 'saintly' way can be considered to be deviant simply because being saintly is not how the majority of people behave.

Crime and deviance is therefore any behaviour that breaks key social rules or laws. Most people, most of the time, abide by the rules of society but some people break the rules and become criminals. Durkheim argued that:

1. *Crime is universal and normal.* Durkheim and later functionalists have argued that crime exists in every community and society across the globe. In every group of people there will be those who break the rules and transgress the law. Functionalists argue that because crime happens everywhere it can be considered to be a normal part of any given society. Crime in this sense doesn't just mean breaking written law such as we have in the UK, but also the transgression of tribal taboos and the breaching of acceptable standards of behaviour in societies without established legal systems.

2. *Crime is relative.* Crime is not constant and it has changed throughout history, from culture to culture and place to place. The acts that contribute breaches of the law are not fixed and static, they change and shift in response to the needs of the time period, the needs of the culture and the evolving morality of a society. In essence, what was a crime 20 years ago may not be a crime now and what is considered a crime now may not be in 20 years.

3. *Crime is functional and necessary.* Durkheim believed that crime and deviance was both useful and necessary for society, as long as it did not reach excessive amounts. Crime was seen as necessary for society for two reasons:

   - The punishment of rule breakers marks what is considered unacceptable behaviour. It lets us know the boundaries of what we can and can't do.

   - Crime and deviance can contribute towards social change by providing a constant test of the boundaries. If laws are tested often enough, sometimes a change can be made.

Durkheim argued that crime and deviance was more likely to happen in times of rapid social change and pressure, when the collective conscience is weakened and people have less of a clear idea of what is considered right and wrong. He called this state of affairs 'anomie'.

Key terms

Anomie This is a state of social disorganisation which happens when society changes very quickly, perhaps due to a rapidly developing economy. The collective conscience that a society shares is weakened because of the changes and people may have different morals and values – according to Durkheim this can lead to deviance.

Consider this

Can you find an example of a behaviour which was illegal 20 years ago but is perfectly acceptable now? Can you think of any type of illegal behaviour which may be permitted in a few years time?

■ Evaluation of functionalism

- Durkheim argued that crime and deviance was more likely to happen in times of rapid social change and pressure. Some criminologists have argued that crime rates don't increase or decrease during times of great social change.

- Durkheim based many of his ideas on official statistics. There are many problems with using official crime statistics as a basis for investigation, as they can often be extremely inaccurate.

- The concept of 'collective conscience' is vague and relatively undefined. What kinds of values and morals should we share to form one and does this mean there is no room for difference and debate in a healthy society?

Theory into practice

The legalisation of abortion is a social change that was brought about by people campaigning to change the law – and frequently breaking the law. Can you think of more recent examples of changes in society which have resulted from people challenging and breaking the law?

Key terms

Labelling This is the process of giving someone a 'label' based on their behaviour. Labels can either be positive or negative but they can greatly influence how you are treated by others.

Unlike the functionalist theory, this theory sees crime as a result of people labelling an act or a person as criminal. In other words, an act is not wrong or criminal until society says it is. Labelling turns commonsense ideas about crime and deviance upside down. It is not the criminal who is responsible but society:

> 'Social groups create deviance by making the rules where infraction constitutes deviance, and applying those rules to particular people and labelling them outsiders.' (Becker 1966)

Consider this

Consider the quote above from the influential sociologist, Howard Becker. What exactly do you think it means?

Becker points out that most people at some point will commit an act which some would see as deviant. However, it is not committing the act which is significant, it is being caught and labelled a deviant that matters. For labelling theorists, the only difference between criminals and non-criminals is that they have been caught and labelled and we have not. In other words, there are no differences at all between criminals and the rest of the population.

Labelling theorists argue that being stigmatised and labelled because you have broken the rules encourages an individual to begin to see themselves as deviant and behave in an increasingly deviant manner. The process of labelling is influenced by an individual or group's sex, class, race, religion and age and not everyone is subject to labelling equally. We all have ideas of the type of person who is most likely to be a criminal and labelling theorists argue that the people most likely to be labelled criminal are young, male, working class and probably of ethnic origin.

Consider this

Can you think of an example where you were given a label you didn't like or didn't agree with? Have you ever given a label to someone else and realised you were wrong after getting to know them?

Evaluation of labelling

The following criticisms have been made about the theory of labelling:

- Labelling tends to view the offender as a victim of society and loses sight of the fact there may be a 'real' victim that the offender has hurt.
- The theory lacks statistical evidence to back up its ideas.
- Labelling does not explain why some people become criminal and others do not.

Remember!

According to labelling theory:

- acts are only criminal because society says they are
- criminals are ordinary people who have simply received a label
- society's reaction to the act is more important than the act itself
- once individuals are labelled they become stigmatised
- not everyone is equally likely to be subject to labelling.

Psychological theories

Psychological theories examine the reasons why individuals become criminal. They do not look at the problem from the perspective of society but from the perspective of the individual. This might mean examining a person's mental health, how they learned to be criminal or how they were raised by their parents. Although there are many psychological theories, we will examine only two:

- psychoanalytical theory
- social learning theory.

If you are interested in learning more about psychology then *Unit 18: Understanding behaviour in public sector employment*, which can be found in *Book 2*, is a useful resource.

Psychoanalytic theory

Sigmund Freud (1856–1939) argues that all humans have natural urges and drives which could develop into criminal tendencies unless they are repressed. Children are socialised to repress their instinctive impulses by their carers (usually their parents). Freud claims that the human personality consists of three parts: the id, the ego and the super-ego.

- *The id.* The childlike, demanding side of a person. The id responds directly to instincts such as hunger, thirst and need for sexual gratification. It doesn't respond to social norms and values, it only responds to its own needs. According to Freud this is the part that must be repressed if a person is to grow up to be a considerate adult. It is the part of the self that we are born with – a newborn baby has no consideration for its parents, it is hungry so it cries for food. It begins to be repressed in early childhood by effective socialisation from its parents.
- *The ego.* This is the rational, logical part of us and it is governed by reality. It is the part of the id that has been modified by the world around us. It tries to satisfy the id in a socially acceptable way. For example, a baby might want food and cry to get it – this is the id on display. A 3 year old child might ask politely to achieve the same objective – this is the ego being developed. The desire for the food is exactly the same but the method of achieving the desire is more socially acceptable.
- *The super-ego.* This is the moral part of our personality. It judges things as right or wrong or good and bad. It is often referred to as an internalised parent. It develops around the age of 5 years old. It is effectively our conscience.

The relationship between these three elements of our personality is complex but in a simplified manner it may look like this:

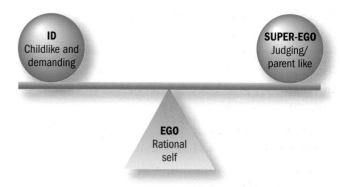

▲ Figure 12.2 The relationship between the id, the ego and the super-ego

The ego is the most important part of the see-saw. It has to balance the demands of the id without causing offence to the super-ego. A well developed ego is essential in a healthy human being according to Freud. Crime can occur when parents or carers do not socialise a child effectively. The result is a poorly developed ego which lacks control over the id, leading to antisocial and destructive behaviour. If the antisocial behaviour is directed inwards, the person may become neurotic and if it is directed outwards, it may lead to criminal behaviour.

■ Evaluation of psychoanalytic theory

The following criticisms have been made about psychoanalytic theory:

- The assumption that crime stems from unresolved childhood conflicts does not take into account the effects of poverty or drugs on individual behaviour.
- Freud's subjects were mainly white middle-class Europeans. It can be difficult to see how his theories can be applied to crime in other racial or socio-economic groups.

- By its focus on the individual, it ignores wider social issues such as power and control which can influence crime.

Consider this

Freud is considered to be one of the most important figures in psychology but there is also much criticism of his approach and treatment for individuals with psychological problems. What is your view on psychoanalytic theory from the snapshot above?

Social learning theory

Social learning theory is based around the principles of behavioural psychology, which states that an individual's behaviour is learned and maintained by rewards or punishments. From this perspective, crime can be seen either as learned behaviour or a failure of the socialisation process which teaches children right from wrong. Sutherland (1939) explains how crime can be normal learned behaviour in his theory of 'Differential Association':

- Criminal behaviour is learned through interaction with others.
- Most of this learning takes place in intimate or close personal groups such as the family or peers.
- Individuals become criminal when they receive more information favourable to lawbreaking that unfavourable to it.

In essence, crime is learned behaviour which does not differ from any other learning experience we might have. Learning theorists argue that deviant or criminal behaviour can be reduced by taking away the reward value for the behaviour and replacing it with a punishment. Hans Eysenck, a learning theorist, states that a child who is consistently punished for inappropriate or deviant behaviour will develop an unpleasant association with the behaviour such as anxiety or guilt which may prevent them from doing it again.

Consider this

Do people only learn behaviour through rewards and punishments or are there other ways of learning?

■ Evaluation of social learning theory

- People are very different and you cannot predict how they will react to negative sanctions (punishments). Some individuals may never commit the behaviour again, while in others it may cause aggression and resentment leading to further deviant behaviour and for some the punishment may not be a punishment at all.
- This theory sees individuals as passive and unquestioning of what is happening around them. They just soak up information like sponges without using their own judgement.
- By stating that most learning is conducted in intimate groups such as peers or family, the theory neglects the influence of the media and wider culture.
- An individual might commit a crime without learning it from anybody.

Consider this

Up to 70 per cent of people who are sent to prison for a crime will end up there again for committing another crime. What does this show about the value of the punishment given to them? Do different people respond to different punishments – or should punishment be a 'one size fits all' response?

More causal factors

There are lots of other factors which may contribute to whether an individual becomes involved in crime. Some of these factors are described below.

Family

Farrington and West (1990) noticed that a small proportion of families tend to account for a large proportion of criminal activity. So it is possible that the family of an individual has a part to play in their criminal behaviour. It may be that the family is so large that the children do not receive the individual attention they need from their parents and instead rely on friends and peers as models of appropriate behaviour. It may be that the stress and disruption involved in family breakdown may lead the young person into a delinquent career.

Political and economic factors

There has been much controversy surrounding the links between economic status and criminal activity. Some studies such as Benyan (1994) and Wells (1995) have claimed that there are clear links between low economic status and criminal activity but Harrower (1998) correctly asserts that the exact nature of the relationship between poverty and crime is still unexplored. The political climate can also influence crime because if the government are in a crisis they might use crime issues to distract the general public's attention away from another matter. Equally, the government might create new legislation on crime which criminalises acts which were previously acceptable.

Peer pressure

The influence of a person's friends and peer group is of vital importance when considering the beginnings of a criminal career. There is evidence to suggest that juveniles commit most of their offences in a group of peers who have regular interaction with each other. It may be that committing criminal or deviant activity is a way of gaining acceptance or status within a group.

- **Education**

- **Drugs/alcohol**

Poor experiences in education may well be linked to juvenile delinquency. If a school does not engage or interest a student they may opt to play truant and become involved in low level criminal activity such as graffiti, criminal damage and causing a nuisance. Persistent truancy increases the likelihood of poor academic performance, which means a young person may not achieve the qualifications they need in order to move away from their criminal activity.

Using drugs and alcohol can lead to an addiction which requires increasing amounts of cash to fund it. Particularly in the case of drugs, the amount needed on a daily basis may be so high that there is no legitimate way to make the money – leaving crime as the only alternative. In addition, the use of drugs and alcohol can lead to extremely poor social behaviour and can promote aggression and violence. It can also leave a person at significant risk of crime themselves.

Assessment activity 12.1

For this activity you are required to produce an information booklet which examines why crime and deviant behaviour happens. You must include the following content:

- theories of crime (sociological and psychological)
- causal factors (family, economics etc.).

Your information booklet must use this content to answer the question below.

1. Describe one sociological and one psychological criminal behaviour theory. **P1**

Grading tips

P1 You are required to describe at least two theories, one of which must be sociological and one of which should be psychological, in your own words. You should also include a description of the other causal factors which may cause people to commit crime such as the family or their economic status.

Effects of crime

Public perceptions of crime can come from a variety of sources such as personal experience, classroom study, hearing about the experiences of others and the media.

All of these sources can have a substantial impact on how we view crime and what effect crime can have on our daily lives.

Antisocial behaviour

According to the Home Office, antisocial behaviour may consist of any of the following:

- nuisance neighbours – this could be neighbours who are noisy, a health hazard or aggressive
- rowdy and nuisance behaviour – this varies from person to person, but could involve groups of young people congregating together at a bus shelter, late night parties, throwing stones, etc
- yobbish behaviour and intimidating groups taking over public spaces – there are few places for young people to socialise which don't cost money so they tend to congregate in public spaces such as shopping arcades and parks; this could be seen as intimidating to the other people using the facilities
- vandalism, graffiti and fly-posting – this can make an area look run down and could attract further criminal activity
- people dealing and buying drugs on the street
- people dumping rubbish and abandoning cars – this can make an area look very run down and may lead to additional anti-social behaviour
- begging and antisocial drinking –begging can be very intimidating for passers-by and alcohol can make people extremely violent, leading to fighting and even assaults
- the misuse of fireworks – this can be a particular problem at certain times of the year and can be upsetting for local residents after hours. If misused, fireworks are extremely dangerous and could cause injury to passers by or buildings.

The public perception of crime

This is the type of behaviour that can lead to fear of crime in the general public, and a perception that crime is out of control, despite year on year reductions in crime figures. The problem is that public perceptions of crime in general come from the media (unless a person has been unlucky enough to have been a victim themselves) and the media may have its own agenda, either political or financial, in reporting crime stories.

Consider this

The media are a business and they have to make money from individuals buying their product. Therefore, their product has to be more interesting to the average TV viewer or newspaper reader than the competition. One way of doing this is to provide entertainment which is disguised as news. This can lead to the public being misinformed about crime and other important social issues.

Can you think of a recent crime news story which has been used as entertainment rather than information? If not check your college/local library for back issues of tabloid newspapers and see if you can find an example there.

■ The media

The mass media includes television, radio, newspapers, the Internet and magazines. Most provide us with information about events outside our social groups and geographical areas and so become a major source of our information. In dealing with crime news, the media can present a distorted view of reality. The media sift all stories for 'newsworthiness' and will tend to choose crime stories which are the most shocking (thus capturing the attention of the public, attracting more viewers/listeners, selling more newspapers and making the media companies more money). It is obvious that a story about a stolen car is not as newsworthy as a brutal murder – the media therefore tend to concentrate on crimes of interpersonal violence. This means that the public may come to believe that these crimes are much more common than they really are.

Consider this

Watch three different crime programmes, such as *The Bill*, *CSI* or *Police, Camera, Action*. Analyse whether each programme oversimplifies and sensationalises crime or actually portrays crime honestly.

Williams (1991) comments that the media simplify and sensationalise events and present the story as a simple division of good versus evil, regardless of the actual facts. The media has a function to inform, entertain and produce profit for its shareholders and as such it presents stories in a biased way. Criminals are presented as very different from the upright citizen reading the newspaper. Broadly speaking there are two forms of newspaper, **tabloids** and **broadsheets**.

Key terms

Broadsheets These often cover issues in great depth and offer a more balanced view. They are often termed 'the quality press' and include newspapers such as the *Guardian*, *Times*, *Independent* and *Daily Telegraph*. They may use fewer images and avoid the use of emotive language in their reporting.

Tabloids Tabloids are newspapers like the *Sun*, *Daily Mirror*, *Daily Star* and *Daily Express*. They provide a broad overview of an issue and often use emotive language and take a clear position of bias on an issue.

The public rely on information from the media to form their picture of crime and criminals and the impact of crime on themselves. Therefore the media can cause moral indignation or outrage in the public.

Statistics often differ in terms of how much crime they show and what kinds of crime appear to be the most frequent. These statistics can be confusing to the public and may cause people to unnecessarily fear crime. In a recent study, 73 per cent of people surveyed believed that crime had risen in the previous two years. This is despite the fact that the crime figures have shown an overall decrease in crime rates every year since 1995 and many people greatly overestimate the risks of being a victim of crime. The table below shows how likely people thought they were to be a victim of crime compared with the actual risk.

Crime	Perceived risk	Actual risk
Theft from a car	25%	6.8%
Burglary	19%	3.4%
Violent attack	13%	4.1%

Table 12.1 People's perceptions of the risk of crime compared to the actual risk

As you can see, the worry that people have over being a victim of crime is not the same as the actual level of risk. This means that the vast majority of people are a lot safer than they think they are. Nevertheless, this fear of crime can have enormous consequences on the everyday lives of individuals and can prevent them from doing all kinds of things.

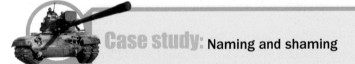 **Case study:** Naming and shaming

In 2000, *The News of the World* disclosed information relating to known paedophiles. Several people, some of them completely unconnected to any cases of child abuse, were injured in the public backlash. In Portsmouth there were violent protests by angry mobs which led to four families who had no connection with paedophile activity asking to be rehoused. Other individuals were beaten and one man committed suicide after an attack on his home left him in fear of his life. The newspaper was accused of deliberately fuelling public protests and encouraging vigilante action rather than obedience to the rule of the law. Sexual abuse of a child by a total stranger is a relatively rare crime in the UK. Far more common is the hidden world of sexual abuse within the family and friendship circle of the child, yet these were not the individuals named and shamed by the newspaper.

1. **Was *The News of the World* correct to release details of known paedophiles to the public?**

2. **What are the consequences of this action for the general public?**

3. **Do you think the information presented by the newspaper provided the public with an accurate view of how and when their children might be at risk?**

The impact of crime on the victim

The impact of crime on victims is explored on pages 321–324.

Effects on lifestyle

Fear of crime can have a tremendous impact on lifestyle. A study by Hough (1995) found that between 1–2 per cent of the population *never* go out at night because they are frightened of crime. Imagine the impact of this on the social life of individuals and communities. It would prevent most of the socialising we take for granted, such as trips to the cinema or pubs. The Crime in England and Wales 2002/3 study by Simmons found that 29 per cent of people never walk alone in their area after dark in the autumn and winter, and 7 per cent of the population say that their lives are greatly restricted by fear of crime. These restrictions on people's lives include the following:

▲ Many people won't consider walking home at night alone – they are more likely to arrange a lift or taxi

- 5 per cent of people carried personal attack alarms
- 5 per cent of people chose to carry weapons
- 30 per cent of people usually travelled with groups of friends for safety reasons
- 35 per cent of people organised special transport arrangements such as a taxi or a lift from family or friends, rather than walking home or using public transport
- 40 per cent of people avoided walking near people who they thought might be a threat.

In addition, people's lifestyles might also be affected because of stress-related health problems, anger and resentment towards the criminals and a withdrawal from social contact with others.

Collective costs to the community

There are also collective costs of crime and antisocial behaviour to the community in the form of funding for the public services such as the police. The costs of the police service in a local area are met from a variety of sources, one of which is the local council tax, which is paid for by the residents of the area. In other words, a high crime area has a clear and direct financial cost to the people who live there.

Consider this

What crime prevention precautions do you take in your day-to-day activities?

Why are people so frightened?

The Home Office has produced a Crime Reduction Toolkit which lists the following reasons why individuals and communities tend to have strong concerns about crime.

1. *They live in a high crime area.* The area in which people live is subject to a great deal of interpersonal and property crime, which causes people to have genuine concerns about their risk of becoming a victim.

2. *They have already been a victim of crime.* Once a person has been a victim of crime they are more likely to be targeted again. Having a crime committed against you makes you much more frightened and concerned, and this fear can affect every aspect of a person's life.

3. *They feel vulnerable.* If a person feels that they are particularly vulnerable to crime they will be much more frightened than usual.

4. *They are poorly informed.* Most people do not know their real risk of being a victim. The majority of the population has a very low risk of being a victim of crime, but they think they are at high risk because of the things they hear in the media and the stories they hear in the community.

5. *They feel powerless and isolated.* If people feel that they are alone and can do nothing to defend themselves or their property, they will feel more afraid of crime.

6. *They have been subjected to antisocial behaviour.* Antisocial behaviour such as verbal abuse, nuisance neighbours or gangs of young people can frighten many people and make them feel more vulnerable to crime. Especially because putting a stop to the antisocial behaviour of others can put a person at more risk of crime. This is because the gangs may then target the person who tried to intervene and direct their antisocial behaviour towards them or their family.

7. *State of the local environment.* If a local environment looks run down, has lots of graffiti, poor street lighting, drug paraphernalia or boarded up windows, it gives an impression of a crime-ridden area and so increases people's fear of crime.

8. *Poor public transport.* If public transport runs infrequently then it can leave people feeling isolated and unable to escape from their local community, unless they have their own transport. In addition, a lack of public transport might mean people face a long walk home, leaving them feeling very vulnerable during the journey, especially if it is at night.

Consider this

Can you think of any other reasons people might be frightened of crime?

This outcome discusses who the victims of crime are likely to be and what the public services, including dedicated agencies such as Victim Support, can do to help and support them.

Victims of crime

The study of victims of crime is a relatively new area of research. Until about 30 years ago, the majority of criminological literature focused almost entirely on the offender, ignoring the victim totally. Recently, however, pressure groups such as victim awareness movements have drawn attention to the role of the victim in a criminal interaction, and the services which exist for their care after they have been victimised.

The notion of being a victim is historically connected with ideas of passivity and helplessness. The archetypal victims who are assumed to be especially in need of protection are children, the elderly and people with disabilities. Their perceived vulnerability is said to make them easier targets for crime. However, these views have increasingly been challenged as stereotypical and inaccurate. In actual fact, the real indicator of whether someone will be vulnerable to crime is a person's lifestyle. People who never go out are unlikely to have to deal with crime, whereas those people who live, work or spend leisure time in public places are at increased risk. Ironically the people who we see as being more at risk may actually be safer than you.

Individuals perceived at most risk of crime

Obviously there are the three groups mentioned earlier, but other groups may also be vulnerable to criminal behaviour, for example:

- women
- prostitutes

- police officers
- casualty nurses
- teenagers
- individuals with mental health difficulties
- members of minority ethnic communities
- members of the gay, lesbian, bisexual and transgendered community
- publicans
- teachers
- businesses.

Consider this

Consider the groups above. Why is each group particularly vulnerable to crime, and which kinds of crime are they most vulnerable to?

Reducing the fear of crime

There are many things that can be done to reduce an individual's and a community's fear of crime. If you consider the eight main reasons why people are frightened of crime (see pages 319–320) then you can come up with strategies designed to tackle them. These strategies are particularly appropriate for the police and local authorities to use in reducing fear of crime and they are adapted from the Home Office Crime Reduction Toolkit, which you can find at www.crimereduction.gov.uk.

Reasons for fear of crime	Ways to reduce fear
They live in a high crime area	• Introduce a programme of effective crime reduction measures. • Communicate to ensure that the community is aware of the action you have taken.
They have already been a victim of crime	• Intervene quickly after the first reported incident to try to prevent a second or third occurrence. • Encourage the person to get in touch with Victim Support.
They feel vulnerable	• Offer reassurance to individuals or groups who are considered to be vulnerable. • Develop positive policies to tackle hate crime which often targets ethnic minorities and lesbian, gay, bisexual and transgender groups. • Try to meet with vulnerable groups on a regular basis to let them know what is being done to help them feel safer. • Talk to vulnerable groups to gather their ideas on what could be done to help them feel safer. • Make sure police officers are visible in communities – it makes people feel safer. • Show vulnerable groups how to keep themselves safer by taking sensible precautions to protect themselves. • Make vulnerable groups feel comfortable reporting crime to the police.
They are poorly informed	• Try to get crime success stories in the local newspapers and on radio stations. • Send out leaflets and flyers to residents letting them know what is being done to reduce crime. • Make every effort to contact traditionally hard-to-reach groups such as minority ethnic elders and older women living on their own.
They feel powerless and isolated	• Consider neighbourhood schemes such as a New Neighbours Scheme, where newcomers are greeted by a resident and told about the area, or Neighbourhood Watch schemes which empower residents to take responsibility for community safety. • Gather the views of the local community to make them feel valued and involved in the efforts to make their community safer. • Develop youth schemes which will have an impact on reducing youth nuisance and make young people feel less isolated.
They have been subject to antisocial behaviour	• Antisocial behaviour can reduce the quality of life – it can be combated by measures such as increased police presence or the use of community wardens. • Police can make visits to primary and secondary schools to warn children about the impact of antisocial behaviour on others.
State of the local environment	• Ensure there is adequate street lighting. • Encourage lots of open, well-kept, highly visible spaces. • Remove graffiti as soon as possible. • Keep roads and pavements in good repair. • Set up regular street cleaning patrols. • Take away abandoned cars as soon as possible. • Repair boarded up windows. • Hold discussions with local community groups. • Use CCTV to monitor the environment where necessary.
Poor transport facilities	• It is important to keep buses and trains safe for travelling, and bus stops and train stations should be well kept, well lit and safe. • Use CCTV and well trained transport staff to encourage users to feel safe. • Provide transport users with up-to-date information and timetables to help them to plan their journey correctly and safely. • Ensure telephones, staff locations and helplines are available to make transport users feel less isolated. • Ensure all groups in a community have access to travel information, perhaps publishing it in some community languages or Braille. • Ensure car parks are safe and secure, staffed and well lit.

Table 12.2 Ways to reduce the fear of becoming a victim of crime

Assessment activity 12.2

You are required to take part in a small group discussion about the effects of crime. Your discussion should cover the following content:

- victims of crime – businesses, communities, minority groups, vulnerable members of the community, individuals.

Your discussion should answer the question below.

1. Describe and analyse the effects crime has on individuals and communities. **P2** **M1**

Grading tips

P2 You should aim to describe the effects that crime has on communities and on the individual in a reasonable amount of detail. Keep a written record of your discussion as part of your assessment.

M1 M1 is basically an extension of P1. The only difference is that you have to analyse the effects crime has on individuals and communities. Analyse means to examine something in detail and see the relationships between separate elements of the discussion. You might also want to address how the public services can minimise the effects of crime on society.

The role of the public services

Survivors of crime can face a range of problems which can affect their lives in the aftermath of the crime. The difficulties individuals face will depend largely on the crime that has been committed against them – a victim of rape will face different issues to a victim of car crime and so on. Figure 12.3 highlights some of the general issues faced by victims of crime.

► **Figure 12.3 The issues faced by victims of crime**

Public service	Support offered
Police	The police provide a great deal of support to a victim of crime. They are usually the service first on the scene of a crime and the first agency to make contact with the victim. This initial contact is crucial in collecting enough evidence to pursue a suspect. The police have specialist family units and officers trained in dealing with sexual crime or crimes involving children. In the cases of serious offences such as murder they can appoint a family liaison officer who will remain in contact with the family of the victim, ensuring they are informed during the process of investigation. The police also have the ability to refer victims to other supporting agencies such as Victim Support and the local authority. The police service also runs extensive crime prevention campaigns in order to reduce victimisation as much as possible.
Social services	The role of social services is not to specifically support victims of crime, it is to help and assist vulnerable members of the community. However, since vulnerable members of the community such as the elderly and children are sometimes victimised, these roles can overlap at times. They can arrange for a range of services from family counselling to assisting with rehousing if necessary.
Probation service	The probation service is not in direct contact with victims of crime. Its role is more indirect – it exists to help rehabilitate offenders so, if it is successful in that role, less victims will be created. The probation service aims to prevent victimisation in the first place.
Local Authority	The local authority can support victims of crime by rehousing if necessary and repairing damaged homes of council tenants. They can also deal with particular problems in an area such as cutting back hedges to ensure there is no hiding place for attackers, or ensuring that repeated nuisance from individuals is dealt with via antisocial behaviour contracts or orders (these will be discussed in more detail later). Since local authorities also have a significant impact on the education system, they can work in partnership with schools to educate young people on avoiding victimisation and what sources of support are available if they do become a victim.

Table 12.3 The support offered to victims of crime

Victims of crime need a great deal of support in the aftermath of a crime to help them deal with some of the problems listed above. There are many agencies which exist to help them in their time of need, including the public services and voluntary agencies.

It is important to remember that all of the public services, whether statutory or voluntary, work in partnership to reduce crime and fear of crime and provide appropriate support to individuals who have become victims of crime.

Consider this

Do you think the government provides enough money to help support victims of crime?

Victim support

In 1990 the first Victims Charter was established in the UK. This was a document which set out the standards of service a victim could expect from the police and courts during the progress of their case. It also set out what a victim could do if they were unhappy with the way they had been treated. This document was replaced in 2006 with the Code of Practice for Victims of Crime. The new code of practice sets out the following rights for victims:

- a right to receive information about their crime in a timely fashion including information about arrests and court cases
- all victims are to be informed about the services of the Victim Support Agency and offered their services
- information provided to victims about the Criminal Injuries Compensation Authority
- a family liaison officer for bereaved relatives.

This offers a system of protection for victims to ensure that they get the best service possible from the criminal justice agencies.

Consider this

Do you think a code of practice that sets out how victims should be treated is important? Explain your reasons. You can find the new code for victims at www.cjsonline.gov.uk in the section on information for victims.

Repeat victimisation

Repeat victimisation is when one particular business, community or individual is repeatedly the subject of crime. The emotional impact of one crime can be terrible; two or more crimes happening in a short space of time can be devastating. The first course of action for the public services is to ensure they are measuring repeat victimisation accurately so that we know how often it happens and who it is most likely to happen to. This will enable an appropriate response to be made by the services in protecting those individuals or their property. Repeat victimisation is common to many crimes such as:

- domestic violence
- sexual offences
- burglary
- car crime
- race hate crime.

In most cases of repeat victimisation, not only is the victim the same, but the offender is the same too. This is apparent in cases of domestic violence and child sexual abuse. How repeat victimisation is tackled depends largely on the individual offence concerned. For example, domestic alcohol abuse leading to violence in the home could not be treated in the same way as repeated alcohol abuse leading to violence in a pub. The best way of ensuring the public services can deal with repeat victimisation of any type is clear analysis of crime data and problem solving skills.

Voluntary agencies

There are lots of voluntary agencies that provide support and information to victims of crime. Some of the main ones are described below:

- Victim Support
- Witness Service
- Women's Aid Federation
- Citizens Advice Bureau
- Rape Crisis
- The Samaritans.

■ Victim Support

Victim Support is a registered charity which focuses on helping victims of crime in terms of emotional support and practical tasks, such as helping with insurance or compensation claims. It receives support from the police who refer victims to it and funding from central government. Victim Support relies on the police to notify them of people who need their aid, but the police do not refer every victim to them, which means that many victims receive no help at all.

■ The Witness Service

The Witness Service exists to ensure that the process of giving evidence in court is as comfortable an experience as possible. It was established in

Victim Support – one of the many voluntary agencies that provide support and information to victims of crime

1989 and is managed and organised by its parent charity Victim Support. There is a Witness Service in every crown court in England and Wales and it performs several functions:

- to provide information on courtroom procedure to witnesses
- to accompany witnesses into the courtroom
- to help and reassure victims and witnesses.

Many witnesses may be very frightened at the thought of giving evidence, but without their evidence many prosecutions would fail and offenders would be able to walk free. It is in everyone's interest to support the Witness Service as good witnesses mean less criminals on the street. The Witness Service is not permitted to discuss the case itself or discuss the evidence the witness will give, this can only be discussed with the police or legal representatives. It can only offer moral support to the witness concerned. Cases of witness intimidation happen regularly, where the defendant tries to frighten the witness or their family to stop them giving evidence, and there are some things which the Witness Service can arrange to make the witness feel safer:

- screens between witness and accused so they cannot see each other
- live TV link to give evidence
- giving evidence privately.

The Witness Service can arrange for a victim or witness to visit the court in advance and be told what to expect so that they feel more comfortable about the process.

■ Women's Aid Federation

This organisation supports the survivors and families of domestic violence by providing them with a place to live in a refuge and offering practical and emotional support from volunteers and trained support workers. As with all charities, they have limited funds and often struggle to cope with the demand for their services. Women's Aid Federation fulfils the following roles:

- providing refuges and support for women and dependent children who have experienced domestic violence or who are in fear of domestic violence
- raising awareness of the issues surrounding domestic violence

- lobbying government for changes in law and policy to protect victims of domestic violence
- training outreach workers to support victims
- sharing knowledge with other public services such as the police.

Each year over 50,000 women and children seek safety in women's aid refuges and many more seek help through telephone support lines such as the National Domestic Violence Helpline, which is also part of the Women's Aid Federation. Women's Aid is a charity and consequently it must rely on the goodwill of volunteers if it is to survive. This also extends to its funding – it must rely on charitable donations, grants and fundraising for all of its income. It is an invaluable service for women and children who are victims of domestic violence.

■ Citizens Advice Bureau (CAB)

The CAB began as an emergency measure during World War II and has now evolved into a much relied upon national agency. The CAB deals with around 6 million queries per year on a wide range of issues such as:

- benefits
- debt
- consumer issues
- legal issues
- homelessness
- immigration.

They can help victims of crime by referring them to legal agencies such as the police or helping them find a civil or criminal solicitor to help represent them. They can also refer people to the Witness Service and Victim Support and give expert advice to victims on their legal rights.

■ Rape Crisis

The first Rape Crisis centre was established in London in 1976 as a response to the fact that female victims of rape and sexual assault were often treated unfairly by the police and often blamed for causing the attack upon them. There are now many Rape Crisis centres around the country operating 'drop in' centres and telephone support, and providing legal and medical information in a safe and emotionally supportive environment.

■ The Samaritans

Often victims can experience significant emotional trauma in the aftermath of a crime being committed against them. They may develop depression, feelings of anxiety, irrational fears or even more serious problems such as Post Traumatic Stress Disorder. The Samaritans are a voluntary organisation which operates a 24-hour service designed to help and support individuals who feel desperate or suicidal. This help is given primarily through a telephone support line.

The Samaritans also offer a service to prisoners who often feel isolated from any other source of support. They have pioneered prisoner listener schemes where inmates are trained to befriend and listen to fellow prisoners who may be experiencing emotional difficulties. In a society where 160,000 attempt suicide each year, the Samaritans provide a vital and necessary service to victims of crime and many others who are troubled and suicidal.

Remember!

Voluntary victim support schemes such as those discussed above are very under-funded. They can't possibly help all the victims of crime who would benefit from their services, and government schemes can only help victims if people are properly informed about them. The public services can often do little to help victims directly due to time and resource issues, but they can and do refer victims to support agencies, such as Victim Support or Rape Crisis, where the support might be available.

Personal safety/household security

Being sensible about your personal safety and security is a key way to avoid becoming a victim of crime. There are many things that individuals can do on a day-to-day basis to enhance their personal safety without compromising their lifestyle too much. The following list describes some of the possible ways of keeping yourself and others safe:

- You should think about how you would act in different situations before you are in them. This will help you plan for and deal with any potential crime situations you might encounter. Imagine how you would defend yourself if you were attacked, how you would get home if your car was stolen or what you would do if you were burgled.
- Stick to bright and well-lit areas – avoid dark alleys or isolated areas where help might not be readily available if you need it.
- Do not look vulnerable to others who might want to commit a crime against you. If you are walking confidently and look capable they might be deterred from selecting you as a victim.
- Do not keep all your personal valuables in one place. This means that if you have your bag stolen or your home is broken into, the thief won't get everything.
- It is always better to run away if you can rather than stand and fight.
- If you are being mugged or burgled, let them have what they want – your property can be replaced but you cannot!
- Scream loudly and make lots of noise if you are being attacked. If you shout for help, people may be afraid to come to your aid – you may get better results if you shout 'fire' instead.
- Don't wear headphones when you are out alone because you will not hear an attacker approaching.
- Be sensible in your choice of clothing – high heels may look good but they won't help you run away from an attacker or defend yourself.
- Carry a personal attack alarm and don't be afraid to use it. Ensure your home has a fully working alarm system.
- Ensure someone always knows where you are and when you will be back.
- Never travel in an unlicensed taxi and always check the ID of any taxi driver you hire. Always sit behind the driver so that you can get out without incident if you feel threatened.
- Make sure you know the times of the last buses and trains.
- Do not display your valuables either at home or when out and about – flashing expensive jewellery and mobile phones can act as an invitation to a thief.

Never travel in an unlicensed taxi – check the ID of any taxi driver you hire. Sit behind the driver so that you can get out if you feel threatened. Don't drink and drive and don't get into a car with someone you suspect may be over the legal drink drive limit or who has used drugs. Do not accept lifts from anyone you do not know

- Do not drink and drive and do not get into a car with someone you suspect may be over the legal drink drive limit or who has used drugs.
- If you drive make sure your vehicle is in a good state of repair and has plenty of petrol – you don't want to be stranded as it can increase your risk of becoming a victim of crime.
- Lock away your valuables in the boot of the car if you drive or use a household safe for your valuables at home.
- Do not accept lifts from anyone you do not know.
- Do not allow strangers into your home.
- Be assertive with anyone who is making you feel uncomfortable or who is invading your personal space.
- Many sexual assaults are committed by someone you know – be wise in your choice of acquaintance. If in any doubt leave the situation or ask them to leave your home and don't worry about appearing impolite.
- If you feel you are being followed, go straight to the nearest public place.
- Do not be afraid to report a crime to the police.
- Never leave your drink unattended in a pub or a club as it can easily be spiked with drugs which will leave you helpless against an attack.
- Do not allow anyone to buy you a drink unless you trust them implicitly or you can see that it hasn't been tampered with.
- On nights out stay with your friends – you are less vulnerable in a group than you are on your own.
- Go to self defence or martial arts classes.

As you can see there are lots of steps that individuals can take to make themselves safe – paying attention to your personal safety and the safety of others is a crucial factor in preventing crime.

Never leave your drink unattended in a pub or a club – don't allow anyone to buy you a drink unless you know them well or you can see that it hasn't been tampered with. On nights out stay with your friends – you are less vulnerable in a group than you are on your own

Consider this

Should you have to take precautions to protect your safety or should the government and the police make society safe for you?

Grading tips

P4 You should choose three public services such as the police, the local authority and the probation service and outline exactly what role each plays in supporting victims of crime.

Assessment activity 12.3

For this activity you are going to produce a large poster that highlights how the public services deal with victims of crime. You must include the following content:

- the role of the public services – police, social services, probation service, local authority, code of practice for victims, multi-agency cooperation, reducing fear of crime
- Victim Support – victim protection, repeat victimisation, voluntary and statutory agencies, preventative measures, personal safety, household security.

You should use this content to produce a poster which answers the question below.

1. Describe the role of three different public service agencies in assisting and supporting victims of crime. **P4**

Crime and disorder has become part of the common vocabulary of the public services since 1998 when they were made responsible for working in partnership with each other to make our society a cleaner, safer place to be. The legislation relating to crime and disorder and the sentences available to help deal with the problem are discussed below.

Crime and disorder legislation

The Crime and Disorder Act 1998

The Crime and Disorder Act 1998 placed a new duty on local authorities, police and other agencies to work together in the development and implementation of strategies to reduce crime and disorder. These statutory partnerships are known as Crime and Disorder Reduction Partnerships (CDRPs), or Community Safety Partnerships (CSPs) in Wales. These partnerships involve statutory, voluntary, community and business groups working together to reduce crime, fear of crime and victimisation. The partnership approach to crime reduction is not a new one. Throughout the 1980s the Conservative government emphasised to all concerned parties that the goal of crime prevention would be better served by utilising a cooperative approach. This approach was supported by the publication of the Morgan Report (1991), which argued for a statutory duty to be placed on crime reduction agencies, such as the police and local authorities, to work together for common targets. This report was acted upon with the creation of the 1998 act.

The Crime and Disorder Act 1998 created 376 local Crime and Disorder Reduction Partnerships in England and Wales. These partnerships have had to develop and implement strategies to tackle crime in three year cycles. The first cycle ran from 1999–2002, the second cycle operated from 2002–2005 and so on. These

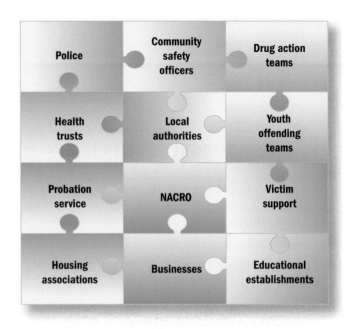

Figure 12.4 Crime and disorder partnerships are made up of many different organisations

strategies must reflect local needs and priorities which means that different crime and disorder partnerships around the country will be aiming to tackle different areas of crime depending on what is a problem locally. The partnerships are made up of many different organisations as shown in Figure 12.4.

The priorities addresses by a multi-agency partnership could be any of a number of issues depending on local needs. Figure 12.5 suggests some of the main ones.

The Crime and Disorder Act is the primary piece of legislation in this area but it is supported by the Police Reform Act 2002 and the Clean Neighbourhoods and Environment Act 2005.

Take it further

Research the Police Reform Act 2002 or the Clean Neighbourhoods and Environment Act 2005 and assess how they improve the safety of communities and encourage a partnership approach to crime and disorder.

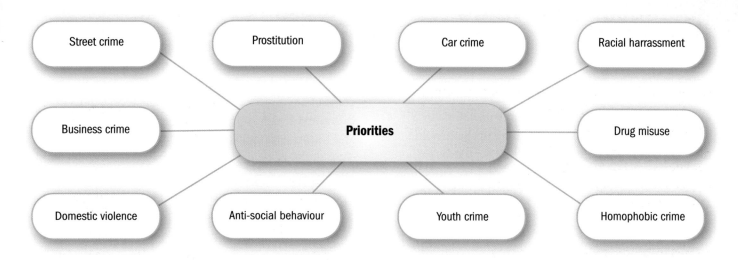

▲ Figure 12.5 A multi-agency partnership might need to address a number of priorities

Assessment activity 12.4

For this activity you will produce a written report on current crime and disorder legislation. You must cover the following content:

- crime and disorder legislation – current legislation, for example, the Crime and Disorder Act 1998.

Use this content to address the questions below.

1. Outline current crime and disorder legislation. **P5**

2. Analyse the implications of two pieces of crime and disorder legislation. **M3**

3. Evaluate the implications of two pieces of crime and disorder legislation. **D2**

Grading tips

P5 An outline is not an especially detailed piece of work but it should include the key features of several pieces of legislation.

M3 M3 is an extension of P5. You should be able to analyse the implications of two pieces of legislation that you outlined in P5.

D2 D2 is an extension of M3 which requires you to evaluate the implications of the two pieces of legislation you have discussed in M3. To evaluate means to weigh up the value of something, so be sure to mention both positives and negatives of the legislation you have chosen.

Sentences and orders

It is important that you understand what happens to offenders once they have been apprehended and found guilty. The first thing that happens is that they are sentenced by the courts. The courts cannot give out any sentence they feel like – they must abide by a set of guidelines provided for them by the Sentencing Advisory Panel which sets out suitable sentences for certain offences. It is important to have these guidelines so that each court in the country is sentencing in the same way. It would be very unfair if, in Yorkshire, an offender was given a fine, but in Surrey they were given a prison sentence for the same crime. There are a variety of possible sentences that the courts can give to offenders once they have been found guilty, as Table 12.4 details.

A caution is an official warning given by the police to an adult who admits they are guilty of an offence. It is designed to act as a deterrent so the offender will not commit any more crimes. Only adults receive police cautions, offenders under seventeen receive reprimands and final warnings instead.

There are two types of caution:

- Simple caution – These are used to deal with offenders who have committed low-level petty crime, such as vandalism or petty criminal damage. They are not processed through the courts system and thus save time and money. They can only be given if the offender admits to a crime and will be recorded on the police database.

Sentence	Explanation
Absolute discharge	This is where an offender is found guilty or has admitted being guilty but no further action is taken against them.
Conditional discharge	The offender has no immediate action taken against them but this is conditional upon them committing no further offences. If they commit further offences within a specific time period they can be brought back to court for sentencing.
Fine	This is where the offender is required to pay a certain amount of money to the court as a result of the crime they have committed.
Compensation order	This is where an offender is required to pay a certain amount of money to their victim in compensation.
Community rehabilitation order	The offender is required to attend regular meetings with a probation officer to ensure their behaviour is monitored.
Community punishment order	The offender is required to give a certain number of hours service to the community, such as getting rid of graffiti or helping council workers to landscape waste ground.
Curfew order	This prevents individuals being out after a certain time, or stops them being in a certain area.
Drug treatment and testing order	The probation service monitor drug rehabilitation and give compulsory drug testing.
Hospital order	A sentence available to be used with 'mentally disordered' offenders (the term adopted by the relevant legislation) where they are placed in a specialist hospital unit so they can be assessed and treated.
Prison sentence	A period of time spent in prison.
Suspended prison sentence	A prison sentence that becomes active if the offender commits another offence.

Table 12.4 Sentences which can be passed by courts when an offender is found guilty

- Conditional cautions – These are also used to deter offenders and keep them out of the courts system, but offenders must comply with a set of conditions in order to avoid prosecution. The conditions are aimed at rehabilitating offenders; for example, dealing with addiction or anger management. The Police and Justice Act 2006 also gave police the power to attach punitive measures to a caution, such as unpaid work or financial penalties.

There are also a range of other orders which can be made as a result of the Crime and Disorder Act 1998, such as:

- Antisocial Behaviour Orders
- child curfew schemes
- child safety orders
- parenting orders.

Antisocial Behaviour Order (ASBO)

The Crime and Disorder Act 1998 says that antisocial behaviour is behaviour which causes or is likely to cause

▲ Antisocial behaviour orders are intended to control the nuisance elements in a community

harassment, alarm or distress to one or more people who are not in the same household as the person causing the disturbance. Antisocial behaviour can include many things such as:

- harassment of residents or passers-by
- begging
- verbal abuse
- criminal damage
- drug dealing
- vehicle crime
- vandalism
- noise nuisance
- graffiti
- dropping litter
- gang behaviour
- racial abuse
- kerb-crawling
- substance misuse
- drunken behaviour in public places
- joyriding
- throwing missiles
- assault
- prostitution.

Antisocial behaviour orders are intended to control the nuisance elements in a community to improve the quality of life for all of the other residents. Sometimes one or two people on an estate can make things miserable for everyone else and this is not fair. ASBOs are applied for by the police or local authority and if there is sufficient evidence a magistrate will grant the order. The order lasts for a minimum of two years and contains certain conditions which must be obeyed, such as staying out of a residential area, not associating with certain people or not committing the same kind of behaviour again. Breaches of ASBOs can be punished with up to five years in prison but it is unusual for this to happen. In fact, one of the major problems with ASBOs is that they have very little power and many people ignore them. It has been argued recently that they have become a 'badge of honour' among certain groups.

Consider this

Do you think ASBOs are a useful tool in preventing offending? Explain your reasons.

Curfews

A curfew is an order that children under a certain age must not be out on the streets after a certain time in the evening. This time is usually somewhere between 6–9 p.m. depending on the age of the child. Like ASBOs, curfews were introduced by the Crime and Disorder Act 1998, although they had existed since 1997 in Scotland. Curfews can be used against all young people under the age of 16 and are applied for by local councils and enforced by the police, who have the power to take young people home who break their curfew and are caught on the street after a specific time. Curfew orders only last for 90 days; after this time the council has to reapply for another order. The idea behind curfews is that, with fewer young people on the streets, there will be less juvenile crime committed and fewer young people will become victims of crime. However, curfews have not proved themselves particularly popular with local councils and they are not used with any great frequency.

Child safety order

This is a part of the Crime and Disorder Act which tries to prevent children under the age of ten becoming involved in antisocial and criminal behaviour. Children under the age of ten cannot be prosecuted for the crimes they commit in this country as they are not considered responsible for their actions. Thus, a child safety order is one of the few things that can be done to help resolve the problems the child is causing. The order can be used if a child under the age of ten has committed an offence, been antisocial or breached a curfew order. The order requires that a social worker or member of the youth offending team monitor the child, make sure that they are being properly cared for and take action to stop the child re-offending. Child safety orders usually last for three months but they can last longer in exceptional circumstances.

Consider this

Children under the age of ten are not considered to be responsible for their criminal actions. What is your view on this?

Parenting orders

Parenting orders were created by the Crime and Disorder Act in order to combat poor parenting being responsible for youth offending. They are applied for by the local council or local education authorities and granted by the courts if a child has committed a criminal offence, played truant or behaved in an antisocial manner. The order requires the parents of the child to go to parenting classes and make sure their child goes to school and does not get into further trouble. The orders can last up to a year and can also be extended to cover children who behave badly at school. In addition to attending parenting classes, the parents can also be fined up to £1000 and in extreme circumstances they could be sent to prison. Like curfews, parenting orders are not popular with councils and are rarely used.

Case study: Imprisoning parents

Patricia Amos was sentenced to 60 days in prison in 2002 for breaching a parenting order by failing to ensure that her two daughters attended school regularly. Magistrates in Banbury decided that a prison sentence was the only option; the first sentence of its kind given in England. The sentence was later reduced to 28 days on appeal. The sentence had a large impact as her daughters pledged not to truant again and Ms Amos pledged that she would ensure her daughters attended school regularly. However, in 2004

Ms Amos was sentenced again for failing to ensure a younger daughter attended school.

1. **Is it fair that parents are punished for their children's behaviour?**

2. **Why is truanting a serious problem?**

3. **How can children be encouraged to go to school?**

4. **How can parents be encouraged to take an interest in their children's education?**

5. **Is imprisonment taking punishment a step too far with regard to truanting?**

Case study: Restorative justice

Restorative justice is a government initiative announced by former Home Secretary David Blunkett in 2003. The main principle is that victims can meet the offenders who committed a crime against them, ask them about their actions and tell them about the long-term effects of their actions. It is designed as an alternative to prosecution and is said to be less expensive than traditional ways of dealing with offenders because it saves on court costs. There are several ways in which mediation can take place:

- restorative conferencing – where the victim and offender meet directly (they are accompanied by others such as parents and loved ones who offer support)
- victim offender mediation – victim and offender meet

with an independent mediator, but are unaccompanied by others
- indirect mediation – the offender and victims do not meet face to face but communicate through a third party.

1. **Is restorative justice a viable alternative to prosecution? Explain your reasons.**

2. **How could restorative justice benefit victims of crime?**

3. **How could restorative justice benefit criminal offenders?**

4. **What do you think are the government's main reasons for piloting mediation?**

5. **Why would mediation and restorative justice not be suitable for all victims and offenders?**

Assessment activity 12.5

Grading tips

For this activity you are required to produce a fact sheet on possible sentences which can be given to someone who breaks the law. Your fact sheet should contain the following content:

- sentences and orders – general, youth, pre-court, antisocial behaviour measures, sentences (financial, custodial and community), restorative justice.

Use this content to answer the question below.

1. Describe the main sentences and orders the courts can impose. **P6**

P6 You should show that you understand what the sentences and orders are but you do not need to go into a great amount of detail. Describe them in your own words from the descriptions you have been given above.

A great deal of time and resources are used by the public services in crime reduction and crime prevention initiatives. It is important to remember that the public services do not just react to emergencies, they are also proactive in developing initiatives and strategies to try to prevent such emergencies from arising in the first place. The section below highlights some of the strategies and techniques currently used.

The National Intelligence Model

The National Intelligence Model (NIM) is a business strategy for law enforcement agencies. It became the policy of the Association of Chief Police Officers (ACPO) in 2000 and was required to be adopted by all forces by 2004. NIM consists of 11 main elements which when applied together make for a coordinated, proactive approach to policing.

Traditionally policing was driven by the need to respond to calls from the public. However, this did not leave a great deal of room for the analysis of crime data and the observation of crime trends and hotspots which could be used by the police to tackle criminal behaviour. NIM helps forces in different geographical areas share information and intelligence to better effect in the fight against crime.

The result of this complex business model is that it becomes easier to identify crime trends in problem areas, enables the targeting of prolific and priority offenders and encourages a culture of problem sharing and solving between forces and other public and charitable services. The gathering and analysis of data is useful because:

- crime data can be incredibly useful to the public services in targeting and coordinating their response to it. For example, the fire service might learn from the statistics that arson is on the increase and develop a strategy for education in schools to highlight the dangers of lighting fires. They can also ensure the availability of staff with fire investigation expertise if

the statistics show the need. The implications for the police are even more profound

- it tells the police which areas in their constabulary have higher crime rates, thus allowing human and physical resources to be deployed to the areas in most need
- it helps the police assess the effectiveness of their current crime fighting strategies to ensure they are getting a return on their crime prevention investment.

The NIM helps the police ensure that information on crime is used in a more effective way, by closing old loopholes in the information-gathering techniques traditionally used. The NIM aids the police in the following ways:

1. Criminals are becoming increasingly mobile. The NIM ensures that crime information is shared and mobile criminals can be tracked and stopped with greater efficiency.

2. The NIM helps police to target the causes of crime rather than reactively dealing with the symptoms. It also helps them liaise better with partner agencies so that non-police matters can be dealt with elsewhere.

Remember that the NIM is only as good as the intelligence and information fed into it. This requires extensive police involvement in the community and excellent community relations so that the police have an accurate picture of what is actually going on in the community.

Safer communities and multi-agency partnerships

Issues of reducing fear of crime and crime prevention are a key aspect of the safer communities initiatives. There are many initiatives that have begun as a result of safer communities legislation in response to these issues. Some of the most important are discussed in Table 12.5.

Initiative	Description
Neighbourhood policing	• This is an initiative where the police work in partnership with individuals, groups and businesses within a community to identify what the policing priorities should be, and to then form strategies to address the problems in partnership with local people. • In effect this has become a form of personalised policing – the needs of communities vary and the type of crimes and antisocial behaviour they experience will also vary. Solving these problems requires a more customised approach, which is exactly what neighbourhood policing tries to achieve. • A neighbourhood team is put into place to help resolve the problems and it can consist of police officers, police community support officers (PCSO's), community wardens, special constables, volunteers from the community and business partners. • Neighbourhood policing blends the high visibility and community involvement of traditional policing with an intelligence-led approach to problem solving. It also gives communities a voice on how to tackle problems in their area. • As a result of this approach it is also breaking down the barriers which exist between the police and some parts of the community which might feel distrustful of the way they have been treated by the police in the past. • It puts the needs of the community and the partnership approach right at the heart of policing.
Neighbourhood Watch	• Neighbourhood Watch is a partnership of people, businesses and groups who come together to make their community a safer place to live in. • It involves a variety of organisations such as the police, local authorities, charities and individuals and families. • The purpose of Neighbourhood Watch is to reduce the fear of crime by improving the security of homes and businesses, and by greater vigilance on the part of residents in watching out for suspicious or criminal behaviour and reporting it to the police if they see anything of concern. • It is usually started and managed by the residents of a particular area. This might be a street or a block of flats or a slightly larger area. • It helps to promote partnerships and cooperation between all of the groups and individuals concerned. It also has links with intelligence-led policing as the police can inform Neighbourhood Watch coordinators of crime trends, and the police receive neighbourhood intelligence in return.

Community Action Teams (CATs)	• Community Action Teams are generally groups of community workers who work with groups and communities in inner city areas.
	• The work involves getting residents to engage in a partnership approach to accessing and improving the services in the area. The principle is that the more people working together, the better the community and its services will be.
	• Some communities are fragmented on religious, cultural or linguistic lines and CATs can help to overcome the barriers which prevent people and organisations from interacting.
	• There are many types of project that CATs can be involved in such as those listed below:
	  – community safety plans – training
	  – community surveys – crime diversion projects
	  – festivals – tenant participation projects.

Police Community Support Officers (PCSOs)	• PCSOs do not have the same powers as regular police officers but they still carry a lot of responsibility and are considered to be a key part of the police services and government crime reduction partnership. • The role of the PCSO can vary from force to force but it generally involves being a visible and reassuring presence on the street in order to reduce the fear of crime among residents in an area. This means they will usually have a beat patrol area to police. • A key aspect of the role is in reducing antisocial behaviour. This could be dealing with minor offences, deterring young people from committing offences and providing crime prevention advice. • They also offer support to regular officers at major events, crime scenes and major incidents.
Community Wardens	• Community Wardens perform a variety of roles largely dependent on the particular problems identified in a community. They are the eyes and ears of the local authority and it is their role to ensure that they work in partnership with local residents to keep an environment safe, clean and tidy. • They are less involved in aspects of crime than PCSOs and CATs but they have some of the same aims which revolve around stopping antisocial behaviour which damages the community. • They have powers to prosecute under the Clean Neighbourhoods and Environment Act 2005 and can issue fixed penalty notices to individuals who allow their dogs to foul the streets, as well as a range of other offences such as fly tipping and littering, all of which harm the community.

Table 12.5 Initiatives that have come into place as a result of safer communities legislation

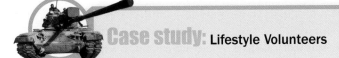

The Crime and Disorder Act 1998 placed a new duty on local authorities, police and other agencies to work together in the development and implementation of strategies to reduce crime and disorder. This partnership involves statutory, voluntary, community and business groups working together to reduce crime, fear of crime and victimisation.

The Crime and Disorder Act created 376 local crime and disorder reduction partnerships in England and Wales. These partnerships have had to develop and implement strategies to tackle crime, reflecting local needs and priorities. This means that different crime and disorder partnerships around the country will be aiming to tackle different areas of crime depending on local problems. The partnerships are made up of many different organisations such as the police, local authorities, the probations service and victim support to name but a few.

Charities

As well as the public services and local authority involvement in crime and disorder partnerships, there are many charities which aim to work together with other agencies to reduce the risk of offending, re-offending and antisocial behaviour. One of these charities is the National Association for the Care and Resettlement of Offenders (NACRO). NACRO is a crime reduction charity that provides services in the following areas:

- resettling ex-offenders and prisoners
- education and employment
- housing
- mental health
- youth crime
- race and the criminal justice system.

Assessment activity 12.6

For this assessment you are required to research, prepare and deliver a 10-minute presentation on crime and disorder strategies. You must ensure you include the following content:

- National Intelligence Model – identification of crime trends, targeting of offenders, coordination of problem sharing and problem solving
- safer communities and multi-agency partnerships – strategies and initiatives to reduce fear of crime, improving community safety, crime prevention and crime reduction, neighbourhood policing, Neighbourhood Watch, safer community initiatives, Community Action Teams, community action groups, PCSO's, Community Wardens, charities, partnerships.

You must use this content to answer the following questions in your presentation.

1. Identify the strategies used by the public services to reduce crime and deal with disorder and antisocial behaviour. **P3**

2. Analyse how the strategies used by the local community public services work to reduce crime, disorder and antisocial behaviour. **M2**

3. Choose one of the strategies or schemes you have discussed and evaluate how successful it has been in terms of reducing crime and its impact on the community. **D1**

Grading tips

P3 You should provide different strategies used by the public services to help reduce crime and disorder. Since you are asked only to 'identify' you don't need to provide a lot of detailed information for this answer.

M2 This is an extension activity to P3 and it is based on the same information. You have to analyse how the strategies you have identified in P3 actually work to reduce crime and disorder. You need to explain in detail how the strategies reduce crime and antisocial behaviour.

D1 D1 is an extension of M2. For a distinction you would be expected to discuss both the positive and negative aspects of your chosen strategy and draw your own conclusions as to whether it has been a success. It would also be useful if you provide a set of supporting notes along with your presentation to show your understanding and depth of knowledge.

Prisoners who are released into the community without a stable home and employment are highly likely to re-offend and cause problems for communities. By providing practical help and support on issues such as this, the hope is that offending can be reduced. Equally offenders with poor literacy are also more likely to re-offend as it can be difficult for them to get a job – so helping with education is a key issue.

Criminal justice agencies

The Crown Prosecution Service (CPS)

The CPS was created by the Prosecution of Offences Act 1985 and became fully operational the following year. It came about as a result of the Phillips Report in 1981, which stated that it was undesirable for the police to both investigate and prosecute crime due to issues of bias and differing practices in police force areas. The police are responsible for deciding on the charge an offender receives and for preparing a case file for the CPS. The CPS then takes over the prosecution from that point and reviews the case files in order to check that the evidence presented justifies the charge given. If it does not, the reviewing lawyer may discontinue proceedings, or charge the offender with a lesser offence. This power to discontinue or downgrade prosecutions was intended to save money by not proceeding with cases that couldn't be proved. In practice what it did was to cause tension and alienation between the CPS and the police when the organisation first started, although this is much reduced today. In addition to this role, the CPS prepares cases for court, prosecutes cases in a magistrates court and instructs counsel in Crown Court.

The decision the CPS makes on whether to prosecute is based on two main 'tests':

1. *The evidential test*. Is there enough evidence that the case is likely to succeed? If there isn't then the CPS are likely to discontinue a case. This happens in about 12 per cent of cases where the police have charged a defendant.

2. *The public interest test*. If the CPS's reviewing lawyer thinks that there is enough evidence for the case to have a reasonable chance of success he or she will then consider whether a prosecution is in the public interest. The factors which influence the CPS decision on the public interest test are laid out in the document 'The Code for Crown Prosecutors'.

The CPS employs about 8,775 people with one third of those being lawyers and the rest legal officers and administrative staff. They deal with 1.3 million cases a year in the magistrates court and approximately 115,000 in the Crown Court. More information about the role of the courts can be found in Book 2 of *Uniformed Public Services*; Unit 22, Section 1.

Prisons and the role of the prison service

There are 138 prisons in England and Wales, which secure and currently take care of over 80,000 prisoners. HM Prison Service has a very specific role and this is reflected in their mission statement:

Statement of Purpose

Her Majesty's Prison Service serves the public by keeping in custody those committed by the courts. Our duty is to look after them with humanity and help them lead law-abiding and useful lives in custody and after release.

Source: www.hmprisonservice.gov.uk

Imprisonment is used to keep the public safe and as punishment for the crime committed. However, as the statement of purpose says, the prison service is required to treat all inmates with dignity and respect and to help to rehabilitate people. This can be achieved through the use of education and training to give them improved job skills. There are several categories of prison that are used to house offenders depending on the level of risk they pose to the public and the likelihood of them trying to escape. The categories are:

- **Category A:** These are for prisoners who are very dangerous and would pose a real risk to the public if they escaped. These are maximum security prisons and house offenders who are guilty of the worst crimes such as murder, rape or terrorism.

- **Category B:** These are for prisoners who are dangerous, but less so than category A prisoners. Security is very tight.

- **Category C:** These are for prisoners who cannot be left in the community but will probably not try a determined attempt to escape.

- **Category D:** These are for prisoners who can be reasonably trusted in open conditions. They may be allowed out during the week to work but have to return to prison in the evenings and at weekends. They are a very low escape risk and they are not considered a danger to the public.

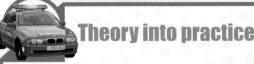

Theory into practice

If category D prisoners are not considered a risk to the public, is prison the most cost effective way of dealing with them?

The government has several aims and objectives which the prison service has to achieve:

- carry out the sentence of the court in order to reduce offending and protect the public
- keep offenders in a safe, healthy and decent environment
- provide education and training to improve the chances of an offender 'going straight'
- deal fairly with prisoners and respect their human rights
- support and promote equal opportunities and combat discrimination
- work in close cooperation with other agencies in the criminal justice system and other organisations that are interested in the welfare of offenders.

■ The prison environment

The prison environment varies according to the type of prison. Prison overcrowding is an issue, with many prisons either near or over capacity. This can lead to staffing issues which, along with poor facilities in older prisons, mean that prisoners spend much of the time in their cells. The majority of prisoners have to share a cell with several other people for the vast part of each day. This means that privacy is very scarce and if there are problems among cell mates it can create a difficult and sometimes threatening environment. Prisons run on a strict timetable and by strict rules, for example, alcohol based toiletries are banned because they might be drunk, wind up radios contain potential bomb making equipment and are banned, as are banana skins which might be smoked. If you are a remand prisoner (this means you have not yet been found guilty and you are awaiting your trial) you can wear your own clothes, apart from football shirts which are confiscated because they might cause fights. If you are a convicted prisoner you must wear a prison uniform which consists of a blue striped shirt, jeans and a maroon jumper.

Regardless of what you might have read, prisons are not like holiday camps. They are highly unpleasant places in which to spend any time. Although prison officers and prison authorities work very hard to promote a positive environment, bullying can be very common in prisons, particularly in Young Offender Institutions (YOI's). The use of drugs in prisons is also an ongoing battle for prison authorities and prisoners are subject to drug testing to try and stamp out the problem, but it can be extremely difficult to stop.

▲ Privacy in prison can be very limited which can lead to a difficult and sometimes threatening environment

Theory into practice

Why would prison authorities be concerned about drug use in prison?

Youth Justice Board

The Youth Justice Board is a government department which oversees the entire youth justice system. This includes work with young people to prevent offending and re-offending and to ensure that if they are placed in custody the environment is safe and secure and the young person has an opportunity to address the causes of their behaviour.

Youth Offending Teams

Youth Offending Teams (YOTs) are another aspect of the Crime and Disorder Act 1998 which have had a big impact on youth crime. YOTs are made up of representatives from a variety of agencies such as the police, probation service, health and education services and local councils. The teams are designed to assess young offenders to find out why they commit crime and design programmes to help the young person stop their offending behaviour. There is a Youth Offending Team in every council area in England and Wales.

Knowledge check

1. List two sociological theories of crime.
2. List two psychological theories of crime.
3. List four other contributory factors to crime.
4. What is antisocial behaviour?
5. Who is vulnerable to crime?
6. What is repeat victimisation?
7. What agencies can support victims?
8. What can be done to reduce fear of crime?
9. What sentences are available for offenders?
10. How does the National Intelligence Model of policing work?
11. What is neighbourhood policing?
12. What do Community Action Teams do?
13. What is the role of a PCSO?
14. What is the role of the Youth Justice Board?
15. Who are the key members of a Youth Offending Team?

End of unit assessment

Preparation for assessment

You have been asked to produce a research project for your local police service on a variety of crime and disorder related issues. They would like to issue it to new probationer police officers to provide them with an overview of the causes of crime and the strategies which can be used to deal with it. The results of your research project should be written up in the form of a formal report which addresses the following questions.

1. Describe one sociological and one psychological criminal behaviour theory. **P1**

2. Describe the effects crime has on communities and the individual. **P2**

3. Analyse the effects of crime on communities and individuals. **M1**

4. Identify strategies used by public services to reduce crime and deal with disorder and antisocial behaviour. **P3**

5. Analyse how the strategies used by the local community public services work to reduce crime, disorder and antisocial behaviour. **M2**

6. Evaluate a local public service strategy or initiative designed to address crime and its impact on the community. **D1**

7. Describe the role of three different public services in assisting and supporting victims of crime. **P4**

8. Outline current crime and disorder legislation. **P5**

9. Analyse the implications of two pieces of crime and disorder legislation. **M3**

10. Evaluate the implications of two pieces of crime and disorder legislation. **D2**

11. Describe the main sentences and orders the courts can impose. **P6**

Grading criteria	Activity	Pg no.		
To achieve a pass grade the evidence must show that the learner is able to:			To achieve a merit grade the evidence must show that the learner is able to:	To achieve a distinction grade the evidence must show that the learner is able to:
P1 Describe one sociological and one psychological criminal behaviour theory	12.1	316		
P2 Describe the effects crime has on communities and the individual	12.2	323	**M1** Analyse the effects of crime on communities and individuals	
P3 Identify strategies used by public services to reduce crime and deal with disorder and antisocial behaviour	12.6	339	**M2** Analyse how the strategies used by the local community public services, work to reduce crime, disorder and antisocial behaviour	**D1** Evaluate a local public service strategy or initiative designed to address crime and its impact on the community
P4 Describe the role of three different public services in assisting and supporting victims of crime	12.3	329		
P5 Outline current crime and disorder legislation	12.4	331	**M3** Analyse the implications of two pieces of crime and disorder legislation	**D2** Evaluate the implications of two pieces of crime and disorder legislation
P6 Describe the main sentences and orders the courts can impose	12.5	335		

Command and control in the uniformed public services

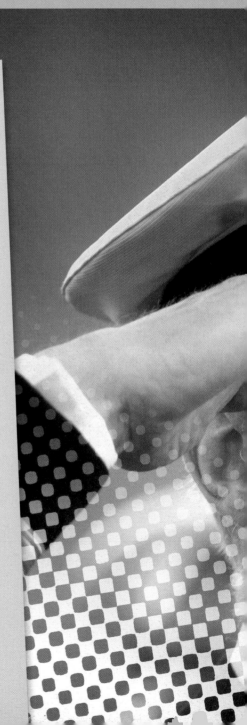

Introduction

This unit will enable you to explore the command and control structures of the various uniformed public services, together with the different skills and qualities required for effective control.

You will begin by looking at the different rank structures before looking at chains of command and responsibilities of the services. You will then look at the skills and qualities, as well as different attributes that are needed by good commanders. The unit then examines a range of ways in which individuals can exercise command and control.

Finally, you will be able to look at the skills that commanders need to demonstrate in order to be effective. These include command and control skills, as well as types of command tasks and problem-solving skills.

After completing this unit you should be able to achieve the following outcomes:

- Know how the principles of rank, responsibility and the chain of command relate to the command structures of the uniformed public services
- Understand the skills and personal qualities required for command and control
- Understand how an individual can exercise command and control
- Be able to demonstrate command and control skills through command task activities.

Thinking points

On 7 July 2005, London came to a standstill when three bombs exploded on three trains on the London Underground during the morning rush hour. The first bomb exploded at 8.50 a.m. and two more exploded within a minute of the first. A fourth bomb exploded on a bus almost an hour later. The explosions were believed to be the work of suicide bombers.

A total of 56 people, including four suspected terrorists, were killed and 700 people were injured. London's transport system was closed down for the day while the emergency services undertook the huge task of dealing with the incident.

This is an example of the implementation of command and control, without which, the operation would not have been concluded as swiftly and successfully as it was.

- Have you ever wondered how the uniformed public services organise themselves to control situations like this?
- How do they know who is responsible for taking overall charge of the incident and how do they know who is responsible for which task?
- How do they prepare for such eventualities?
- Have you thought about the personal skills and qualities that make commanders effective in such situations?
- Do you have the necessary skills and qualities to make quick and vital decisions?

This unit will help you to answer questions like this, as well as giving you a good insight into the command structures of different uniformed public services. Even if you do not apply for the uniformed public services you will acquire knowledge of management and leadership techniques that could benefit you in any walk of life.

Rank structures

Identifying which uniformed public services have a rank structure

Rank structure is the way in which the hierarchy of authority is arranged within an organisation. A rank is a position within the hierarchy and the higher the rank or position, the greater the authority and responsibility. The uniformed public services include the emergency services (police, fire and ambulance) and the Armed Forces, which are comprised of the Royal Navy (including the Royal Marines), Royal Air Force and British Army . They all have rank structure so that orders and instructions are followed, thus making the services efficient.

You should note that the rank structure of the police service in the provinces is slightly different to that of the Metropolitan Police (see *Unit 5: Discipline within the uniformed public services*).

Army	Royal Air Force	Police	Fire
Field Marshall (honorary rank or wartime only)	Marshall of the RAF	Chief Constable	Brigade Manager
General	Air Chief Marshall	Deputy Chief Constable	Area Manager
Lieutenant General	Air Marshall	Assistant Chief Constable	Group Manager
Major General	Air Vice-Marshall	Chief Superintendent	Station Manager
Brigadier	Air Commodore	Superintendent	Watch Manager
Colonel	Group Captain	Chief Inspector	Crew Manager
Lieutenant Colonel	Wing Commander	Inspector	Fire Fighter
Major	Squadron Leader	Sergeant	
Captain	Flight Lieutenant	Police Constable	
Lieutenant/2nd Lieutenant	Flying Officer/Pilot Officer		
Warrant Officer Class 1	Warrant Officer		
Warrant Officer Class 2			
Staff Sergeant	Flight Sergeant/Chief Technician		
Sergeant	Sergeant		
Corporal	Corporal		
Lance Corporal	Leading Aircraftman/woman		
Private	Aircraftman/woman		

Table 13.1 The rank structures of the British Army, Royal Air Force, the police and fire services with the highest ranks at the top of the table *(Please note that ranks across each row are not at a comparable level.)*

Figure 13.1 Rank badges for senior officers in the police service ▶

Chief Constable Deputy Chief Constable Assistant Chief Constable Chief Superintendent Superintendent

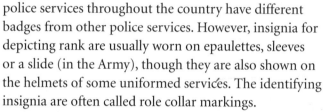

Badges of rank

It is important for you to realise that not all badges (or insignia) are badges of rank. For example, each regiment and corps within the British Army has its own badge (which is usually worn on a cap, beret or belt) but they are not badges of rank. Similarly, different police services throughout the country have different badges from other police services. However, insignia for depicting rank are usually worn on epaulettes, sleeves or a slide (in the Army), though they are also shown on the helmets of some uniformed services. The identifying insignia are often called role collar markings.

Look at the rank badges for senior officers of the police service in Figure 13.1.

Similarities and differences between public services

All of the public services have rank badges on their uniform so that they can be identified and individuals can recognise where they fit into the hierarchy; they know whether they are senior or subordinate to a particular rank even if they do not know the person of rank.

Some of the rank badges of several of the uniformed public services are very similar. In many cases it is only the colour of the epaulettes that distinguishes the badges of one service from another, although different services sometimes have the same colour epaulettes (for example, the police and the Royal Marines' dress uniform).

However, even though the rank badges of different services are similar, you should remember that they do not identify the same rank in different services. The Armed Forces are different from the emergency services, which are different from the prison service and HM Revenue and Customs. Any similarity in rank badges is merely coincidental and you cannot identify someone

as the same rank as another in a different service simply because they have similar rank badges. The only exception to this is the Royal Marines, which is the Royal Navy's infantry, yet it has the same rank insignia as that of the Army.

Take it further

Go to the website www.uniforminsignia.net where you will find rank badges for the Royal Marines, Royal Navy, RAF and British Army.

Look at the rank insignia of the Royal Marines and the Army – the only difference is the colour of the epaulettes and the 'RM' up to and including the rank of lieutenant colonel. However, in combat dress, the insignia would be worn on a slide and the colour would be the same as the Army and more difficult to identify.

Now look at the army ranks of major, lieutenant colonel and field marshall and see which of the police ranks are very similar. Remember, though, that the responsibilities and job roles for each service are very different and so are the ranks. You do not have the rank of superintendent in the Army, just as you do not have the rank of warrant officer in the police service.

Responsibilities

While the responsibilities of different uniformed public services vary, there are several similarities. For example,

Figure 13.2 Each of the emergency services has its own responsibilities when they are working together at a major incident.

Police
- Investigate the causes of incidents
- Coordinate major incidents
- Take witness statements
- Preserve the scene for evidence
- Identification of deceased
- Prosecute offenders
- Traffic control
- Establish temporary mortuary
- Press liaison

All three emergency services attend major incidents and:
- Save lives in conjunction with each other
- Administer first aid

Fire
- Fight fire
- Investigate causes of fire
- Perform search and rescue
- Deal with hazardous substances
- Rescue trapped people using specialist equipment
- Advise other services on health and safety issues
- Perform decontamination

Ambulance
- Perform triage
- Take injured to a designated hospital
- Order medical resources
- Establish a casualty loading area

in the emergency services, it is the primary responsibility of the police, fire and ambulance services to save lives, but each service has other responsibilities, especially when working together at major incidents.

Senior officers from the emergency services form incident command and control.

Case study: The Kegworth air disaster

At 7.52 p.m. on 8 January 1989, a Boeing 737 was en route from London's Heathrow Airport to Belfast International Airport, carrying 126 people (including flight staff). It developed engine trouble as it climbed to over 28,000 feet. The captain closed down what he believed to be the faulty engine and on the suggestion of British Midland Airways Operation, attempted an emergency landing at nearby East Midlands Airport.

Unfortunately, the captain shut down the remaining working engine and as it descended on approach to the runway, the aircraft was, in effect, gliding. With only a few hundred yards to the airport's runway, the aircraft crashed onto the M1, narrowly missing the village of Kegworth. On impact with the ground, the aircraft broke into three pieces and a total of 39 passengers died and 74 received serious injuries.

All the emergency services attended the scene and before rescue operations could begin, the fire service sprayed the fuselage with foam to minimise the risk of fire from leaking fuel. The motorway was closed and remained so for a week while the wreckage of the aircraft was removed. The Army and Royal Air Force assisted in recovering and transporting the wreckage.

1. Which of the emergency services would be responsible for redirecting traffic and how might this have been done?

2. Which service would use specialist equipment to rescue people in the case just described and what type of equipment might it be?

3. Apart from transporting the injured to hospital, what else would the ambulance service be responsible for?

Table 13.2 shows a breakdown of the ranks and responsibilities within the British Army.

In the police service, the chief constable is the ultimate commander and is assisted by a deputy chief constable and two or three assistant chief constables. Officers above the rank of chief superintendent are considered to be non-operational officers. This means that they are not involved in a hands-on approach to policing; they are strategic commanders whose main role is to implement service policy and plan strategies, such as how to meet Home Office targets. They also form the senior command when dealing with major incidents.

A chief superintendent is the commanding officer of a divisional headquarters (sometimes referred to as districts), which would contain somewhere in the region of 400 officers, depending on the size of the division. The chief superintendent would be expected to implement the force's policy regarding the safety of the community, maintain discipline over those under their command and ensure the welfare and professional development of their staff.

General Officers (these are administrative commands and these officers would not normally lead soldiers into action)	
Rank	Typical command
Field Marshall	British Expeditionary Force
General	British Army
Lieutenant General	Corps (two divisions)
Major General	Division
Brigadier General	Brigade
Colonel	usually an administrative command
Field Officers (these lead troops in the field of battle)	
Rank	Typical command
Lieutenant Colonel	An infantry (cavalry regiment or artillery brigade)
Major	Company (four platoons)
Captain	Battalion's adjutant
Lieutenant	Infantry platoon (four sections)
2nd Lieutenant	Same as for Lieutenant
Other ranks in the British Army	
Rank	Appointment or role
Warrant Officer (1st Class)	Regimental Sergeant Major (in charge of Army discipline)
Warrant Officer (2nd Class)	Company Sergeant Major (company discipline)
Colour/Staff Sergeant	Company Quartermaster (supplies and pay)
Sergeant	Platoon or troop administration
Corporal	Infantry/Cavalry section commander
Lance Corporal	Infantry/Cavalry 2nd in command
Private	A rifle-armed soldier

Table 13.2 Ranks and responsibilities within the British Army

In the context of the uniformed public services, a post can mean an area where personnel perform their duty (for example, a posting to Iraq if you are in the Army) or it can mean being assigned to a specific task (such as a weapons instructor). Some posts carry a lot of responsibility and there is a relationship between the post and rank whereby seniority of rank does not always take command. For example, at a crime scene, a detective sergeant would take seniority over a higher ranking uniformed inspector, because the detective sergeant has had the necessary training to protect and examine crime scenes. Hence, the officer in charge of a crime scene is not necessarily the highest ranking officer at the scene. Similarly, the commander of a Royal Air Force aircraft is not necessarily the most senior rank onboard.

Chain of command

Organisations that operate within the command structure

The uniformed public services consist of a collection of units that can join with others to form larger units or that can operate independently within the command structure. Each unit has a leader or commander and

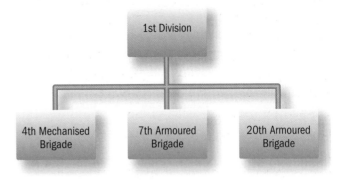

Figure 13.3 An Army fighting division is traditionally comprised of three or four brigades, with each brigade containing approximately 5000 men

when units combine to form larger units, the larger unit has a higher commander. For example, an infantry regiment is a unit that can work alone or join with other regiments to form a brigade. The 7th Armoured Brigade, also known as the Desert Rats, is comprised of 12 regiments and supporting units.

Each brigade is made up of regiments, which are a collection of battalions, each containing about 700 soldiers.

The Army is organised into five divisions: two fighting divisions and three administrative support divisions. A fighting division is a complete, self-sufficient force consisting of soldiers, support staff, cooks, medics, clerks and a headquarters. It is traditionally comprised of three or four brigades, with each one containing approximately 5000 men.

Battalions, regiments, brigades and divisions are links in the chain of command that operate within the command structure of the British Army.

The command structure of the 43 police services throughout England and Wales is very different from that of the Army, although they do have a chain of command. Like the Army, our police services have divisions (or

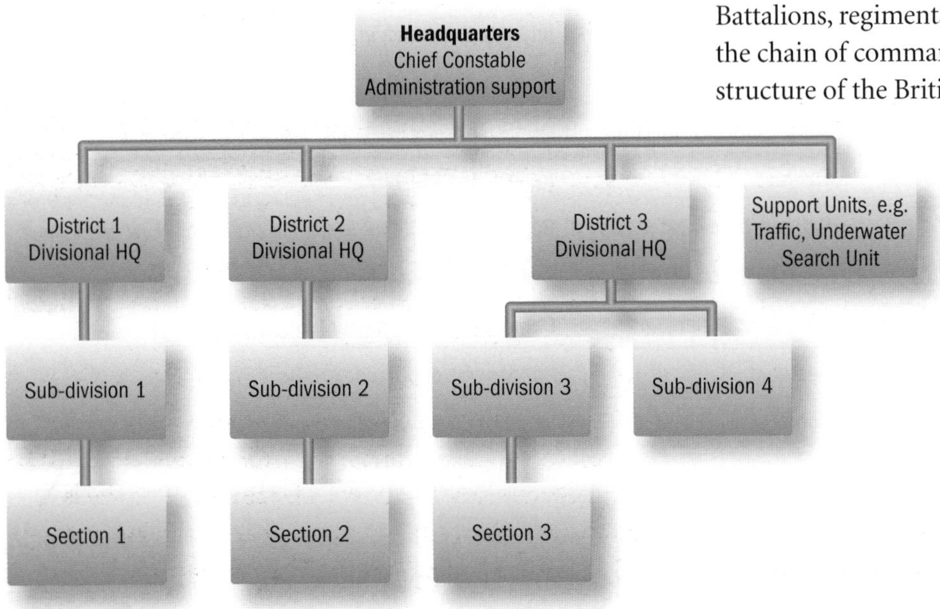

Figure 13.4 The organisation of a police headquarters showing divisions/districts, support units, sub-divisions and sections

districts) but these usually refer to a city or town within the county for which the police service is responsible; and each division will have a police station. If, for example, a county has four towns within its boundary, then the police service will usually have four divisions or districts, that is, one division for each town, though a large city may well have two divisions.

Unlike the Army, police services do not have a headquarters within each division but they do have a separate divisional headquarters which provides administrative support for each division. Police headquarters is usually a separate building which contains administrative support and special services, such as Criminal Records Offices, Scenes of Crime Department, Fingerprint Department, Underwater Search Unit and so on, though some support units might be based in a central location other than at headquarters.

The outlying areas of the towns, especially the heavily populated areas, will also have police stations, although these will be smaller establishments than divisions and will be known as sub-divisions. Depending on the size of the police service area (in terms of geography and population) a division could have more than one sub-division. Sub-divisions can be further divided into sections, which are smaller police establishments (more like small offices than police stations) which serve the more rural areas. Section stations are not always staffed 24 hours a day and they serve the smaller communities which, because of distance, could not practically be served by sub-divisions or divisions.

Take it further

Carry out some research and find the command structure of:

- Royal Air Force
- Royal Navy
- Royal Marines
- HM Coastguard
- HM Revenue and Customs

Relative levels of control

Each unit of the uniformed public services, whether it is one of the armed services, emergency services or other uniformed services, has a commander. The rank of the commander will depend upon the size of the unit.

In the army, a general will be in command of a division, while a brigadier is in command of a brigade. A regiment is commanded by a colonel and the officer in charge of a battalion is a lieutenant colonel.

In a battle group, some smaller units are used and these are:

- company – a unit of about 100 soldiers and commanded by a major
- platoon – a unit of about 30 soldiers and commanded by a second lieutenant or lieutenant
- section – a unit of between 8 and 10 soldiers and commanded by a corporal.

In the police service, a division is commanded by a chief superintendent with a sub-division commanded by a superintendent. A section station would normally be commanded by a police sergeant.

Take it further

Carry out some research and answer the following:

1. In the RAF, what is a squadron and who is in command of one?
2. In the RAF, what is a wing and who is in command of one?
3. How many divisions are there in the London Fire Brigade?
4. What is the rank of the officer in charge of a division in the London Fire Brigade?

Control of the public services by non-uniformed organisations

You have seen how the uniformed public services operate within a chain of command but there is a higher authority to which they are accountable.

All of our Armed Forces are controlled by the Ministry of Defence (MOD), which is a department of central government. The cabinet minister in charge of the MOD is the Secretary of State for Defence and he or she is ultimately responsible for making and carrying out the UK's defence policy. The Secretary of State for Defence is also the Chairman of the Defence Council which has three boards: the Admiralty Board, the Army Board and the Air Force Board.

To assist in the huge task of organising defence, the Secretary of State is supported by three junior ministers, one of whom is the Minister of State for the Armed Forces.

Just as it is the Government's responsibility to defend the UK's interests at home and abroad, it is also their responsibility to provide us with a safe and secure environment in which to live and work. The government department in charge of ensuring our safety in the community is the Home Office, headed by the Home Secretary. The Home Office is responsible for providing us with an efficient police service, and prior to Government restructuring in May 2007 was responsible for the prison and probation service.

While it is chief police officers who are responsible for their individual services in terms of control, discipline and direction, it is the Home Office that funds and coordinates the 43 police services within England and Wales. Our police services are monitored by HM Inspectorate of Constabulary, which reports to the Home Secretary and makes recommendations for their increased efficiency.

▲ Figure 13.5 The Secretary of State for Defence is supported by the Minister of State for the Armed Forces and the Defence Management Board

Assessment activity 13.1

For this assignment you are to design a leaflet that will show how the ranks are structured in two contrasting uniformed public services and which describes the chain of command for one service. The leaflet should include, for one service, the uniform structure and the role of non-uniformed personnel, for example, members of the Ministry of Defence. **P1**

Make sure you cover the following content:

Section A

- *Rank structures*: identifying which uniformed public services have a rank structure (for example, police, Royal Air Force); similarities and differences between public services (for example, both the police and the Army have similar rank badges but they have different titles and mean different things); badges of rank (for example, identifying a badge and relating it to a title); responsibilities (for example, what would normally be expected of a particular rank); relationship between posts and ranks (for example, the commander of a Royal Air Force aircraft is not necessarily the senior rank onboard).

Section B

- *Chain of command*: organisations that operate within the command structure (for example, within the Army, there are regiments, brigades, divisions); their relative level of control (for example, what individuals would be responsible for); control of the public services by non-uniformed organisations (for example, Ministry of Defence, Home Office).

Grading tips

P1 To achieve P1 you should select two contrasting ranks from Section A of the content and one uniformed service as well as one non-uniformed service from Section B of the content.

Command and control are used by the uniformed public services to deal effectively with many situations. For example, a major incident, such as a plane crash, would require proper command and control in order for the emergency services to respond quickly and efficiently to the recovery operation. The Armed Forces also rely on command and control for successful military exercises, especially in a war situation.

Key terms

Command and control The term used whereby instructions are given to control or manage certain situations, or to achieve objectives.

Skills and qualities

Technical skills

We live in a very technical age and the uniformed public services have access to some of the world's most advanced equipment, which helps enormously in a command and control operation.

Technology allows high ranking officers to make informed decisions and prepare battle strategies which, before the development of science and technology, were unavailable. For example, a naval captain and warfare officer can draw up a tactical strategy based on the information from an operations mechanic, who has tracked the position of enemy ships, aircraft and submarines on the ship's computers.

It is the responsibility of commanders to keep up-to-date with new technology and know how to use it effectively.

Specialist skills

As well as having good technical skills, specialist skills are often required in command and control for a variety of reasons. For example, in the Royal Marines, a landing craft officer must be skilled in seamanship, sea survival, navigation, boat handling, communication and management. In times of conflict, these specialist skills could prove vital in safeguarding personnel.

Case study: Submarine technology

The Royal Navy is due to acquire shortly three Astute class nuclear-powered attack submarines (to be named Astute, Artful and Ambush). The submarines will have onboard newly developed combat managing systems which will receive and interpret data from sonar and sensors through advanced algorithms and data handling.

Propelled by nuclear power, each submarine will never need refuelling throughout its service history and it will be capable of circumnavigating the world 40 times. It is to be equipped with Tomahawk cruise missiles and Spearfish torpedoes, as well as having the latest in electronic counter-measure technology.

1. Would you expect the commander of such a submarine to be familiar with it just because he has technical skills?

2. The crew would also need technical skills but do you think you have to have an interest in such advanced technology before you could become a vital crew member or would it just be a case of receiving some training?

3. What are the advantages of a nuclear-powered submarine?

In the Royal Air Force, a regiment officer who is responsible for defending RAF bases must be skilled in military tactics, communications, signalling, weapons handling and deployment. Without these specialist skills, RAF bases would be vulnerable.

The Armed Forces have certain members who are trained in mountain leadership; they are able to navigate and lead groups safely through dangerous mountain regions, using specialist climbing and belaying equipment. Furthermore, the Special Air Services (SAS) are renowned for their success and professionalism because of the specialist skills they possess, such as communications, survival in extreme temperatures, explosives, negotiation skills and even foreign languages.

As well as having good technical skills, specialist skills are often required in command and control for a variety of reasons. It would be unreasonable to expect commanders to possess lots of specialist skills but it is important that they can deal with a situation by calling on the people who do have the necessary skills.

Theory into practice

Consider which of the uniformed public services you would like to join. Research some jobs within that service and find out about:

- entry requirements
- pay
- training required
- qualities needed.

Consider this

Look at the following examples and say what specialist skills would be required to successfully resolve the situations.

- A hostage situation where the hostage-takers do not speak English.
- A shopping complex has been evacuated because a suspect package has been found by a shop assistant.

Leaders are usually people who have been selected for the qualities they possess and for their ability to bring out the best in others.

Personal quality	Description
Role model	Someone who is regarded by others as a good example for a particular role; it is someone who is admired and respected by others and very often others measure their performance by comparing themselves to a role model.
Courage	Someone who is brave and disregards fear in order to do their duty, even in the face of great adversity.
Confidence	Someone who is self-assured and bold in their manner and execution of duty.
Integrity	Someone who is honest, of sound judgement and morally upstanding.
Determination	Someone who is firm and resolute in what they do and who will overcome obstacles to succeed in a task.
Decisiveness	Someone who can make a decision quickly and effectively without having to rely on or consult with others in making that decision.
Mental agility	Someone who has an active and quick mind with the ability to read situations and know exactly what is required to achieve a positive result.

Table 13.3 The personal qualities of leaders

Good commanders are well-informed about people, especially those under their command – they know how people react to certain conditions and they know how to instil qualities in others.

■ Trust

If you trust someone, then you have a strong belief in their reliability; you can depend upon them without fear or hesitation. However, that trust has to be justified in the first place. You should remember that if a person holds the rank of a commander, that in itself is justification that they can be trusted; they will not ask lower ranks to do something that they have not done or are not capable of doing themselves. However, good commanders will not always take this for granted. They will give those under their command good reason to trust them, through words and deeds, and by displaying the qualities listed in Table 13.3.

Trust is a mutual thing, especially in the uniformed public services and it is only because trust is reciprocated that command and control is successful.

Loyalty

In the context of the uniformed public services, to be loyal means to be faithful to your duty and to remain committed to your task. The very nature of the work of the uniformed public services means that there are many occasions where members of the services are under extreme pressure. For example, soldiers in Iraq have witnessed hostile resistance by insurgents when, no doubt, they would rather be at home with their families and friends. However, they remain committed to their duty and responsibilities because they have commanding officers who understand their feelings and, besides leading by example, make them realise the value of their work.

Discipline

Discipline in the uniformed public services is needed for many reasons but, in a command and control situation, it is especially necessary for maintaining order and for ensuring that rules and regulations are followed and orders are carried out. Without this assurance, there would be no command and control because the hierarchical structure would collapse, leading to chaos. A good commander has the skill of ensuring that discipline is maintained so that operations run smoothly and effectively. (For more information on the need for and role of discipline see *Unit 5: Discipline within the uniformed public services*.)

Morale

Morale is a state of mind that can affect the way you and the team, or even the service, work. Low morale can be unproductive and is one of the worst things for the uniformed public services because it leads to poor team spirit and lack of motivation. It is part of the commander's role to maintain high morale to ensure that the lower ranks are effective in their tasks.

A good commander, because they have a good understanding of people, knows what causes low morale amongst lower ranks and will take steps to ensure high morale is maintained.

It is particularly important to maintain order in a control and command situation ▶

Case study: Raising morale

Prior to the war with Iraq in 2003, the Ministry of Defence conducted an attitude survey into the morale of British troops about to be deployed in Iraq. The survey revealed that more than a third (36 per cent) of the Army's soldiers was experiencing low morale. The survey of Royal Navy personnel showed that 27 per cent were dissatisfied with the conditions of their service and 22 per cent stated that their own morale was poor.

A politician said the cause for low morale was the concern over jamming SA-80 rifles and ineffective personal equipment. The politician added that, 'The MoD has a great deal to do if we are to have the motivated and satisfied armed forces that we require, particularly in view of their current obligations.'

However, some believe that serving personnel did not have the confidence that they were being fully supported by the public. Many people feel that we do not have the right to invade a country just because we do not agree with their system of government.

1. **How would officers commanding and controlling the troops maintain morale?**

2. **What problems would low morale cause in the situation mentioned above?**

3. **Imagine you are a platoon commander deployed in Iraq and your platoon is constantly under threat of insurgent uprisings, which can be very violent. Many soldiers in the platoon have not seen active service before and they have seen some of their friends seriously injured. How would you keep morale high?**

■ Motivation

Lack of motivation, just like low morale, can be very damaging to the uniformed public services because it means that there is no interest in the job to be done. Even if the lack of motivation is experienced by an individual (and not the whole team), this can have an adverse effect on team spirit because not everyone is trying their best and a burden is placed on the remainder of the team.

A good commander will motivate individuals and teams to ensure they maintain an interest in their work, thus ensuring the smooth operation of that particular service.

■ Respect

Lack of respect for those of a higher rank in the uniformed public services can lead to low morale and lack of motivation, which, for the reasons just given, can affect the smooth operation of a service. You may have heard the phrase 'respect has to be earned', which means that someone has to show that they are of a certain quality in order to gain the esteem of others. In the uniformed public services, promotion to a particular rank is given for that very reason – because the member of that service has shown qualities that are to be admired and which make them a leader.

You should remember that it is the rank that is respected, not necessarily the person who carries that rank. While it is natural not to want to respect someone you do not like, you must respect the authority of the rank.

Motivational strategies

Instigate and maintain command

Key terms

Instigate To bring about or to make something happen by persuasion or urging someone to do something.

By virtue of their higher rank, commanders in the uniformed public services have the authority to demand that lower ranks carry out their orders and it could be said that as long as orders are carried out, then the end justifies the means. That is to say that it does not matter how people feel as long as they do what they are told. However, this authoritarian style does nothing for individual or team morale; it can make members of the lower ranks feel as though they are not valued at all.

A good leader would not 'pull rank' in order to have their orders carried out unless it was absolutely necessary. Instead, they would stimulate their colleagues into complying with the line of command by recognising and appreciating their individual talents and skills. By instigating command in this way, leaders enable others to feel valued while achieving their organisation's objectives. And if morale and motivation are high, then it is easier to maintain command.

Inspire loyalty and obedience

Just as command can be maintained by an authoritarian style of discipline, both loyalty and obedience can be enforced in the same manner. However, a good leader does not force someone into being loyal and obedient by threatening punishment. A good leader is inspirational

Case study: Fire fighter attacks go unreported

In April 2005, the media revealed that attacks on fire fighters in the Greater Manchester area were being hugely under-reported, according to the Fire Brigade's Union (FBU).

A national report issued by the FBU aimed to bring to the government's attention the fact that incidents of violence and abuse against fire fighters could be up to three times higher than the official figures from the Office of the Deputy Prime Minister (ODPM), and that figures in Greater Manchester could be up to 15 times that figure. This indicated that there were a huge number of unreported incidents of violence against fire fighters in that area.

Examples of the incidents being reported by the FBU included youngsters throwing stones at fire crews as they fought a rubbish fire at the Daniel Fold estate in Rochdale and a physical assault against fire fighters from Agecroft as they tried to put out a fire in Eccles on Good Friday.

These types of incidents are extremely frustrating and upsetting for the fire fighters involved, who cannot fight back against their assailants.

The FBU called for adequate funding to allow a national strategy to be implemented; they asked that incidents involving violence or abuse were recorded more accurately and that training was provided to help deal with the associated problems. They also called for the government to assist fire brigades in educating the public.

1. **How would you feel if you were a fire fighter in Greater Manchester?**

2. **How would you motivate your team and inspire loyalty?**

3. **Why do you think the fire fighters would not fight back?**

4. **Would educating people make it easier for fire fighters to do their job?**

and makes others feel proud to belong to a particular service. Again, this raises morale and team spirit and makes members of the lower ranks want to be loyal and obey orders. However, to maintain morale and team spirit in adverse conditions requires skill on the part of the commander.

Consider this

A team of police constables work in an area where there is a lot of youth crime and antisocial behaviour. When they have apprehended the youths responsible they have given them a caution but this has not stopped the trouble. Team morale is very low and the general feeling is that the police are fighting a losing battle.

- If you were a commanding officer, how would you motivate them and ensure loyalty?
- If you were a member of the police service in the above example, would you expect your commander to be strict or sympathetic?

▲ Figure 13.6 Ranks in the Army must carry authority

Practical consequences of orders not obeyed

There are many practical consequences of failing to obey orders. Orders are not given for fun or to flaunt

Maintenance of authority

Need for authority

Authority is needed to ensure the smooth and efficient running of the uniformed public services. It gives certain ranks the right to make decisions and give orders, which should be carried out as directed by lower ranking personnel. If orders are not obeyed, then authority becomes undermined and the entire hierarchical structure would collapse. For example, if a corporal in the infantry ordered a private to clean his dirty weapon, then the private is obliged to comply with that order. If the private refused to obey the order and the corporal had no means of enforcing it, then there would be no point in having the rank of corporal since the rank would carry no authority.

Consider this

Imagine what would happen if you were in the fire service and you were ordered to check that the recently installed smoke alarms in a residential home were fully operational. However, you merely assumed that because they were fine when they were last inspected, they would still be in good working order. During the night a fire broke out in the residential home and, because there was no warning of smoke, the residents' lives were put at risk.

- How would you feel if anyone died as a result of the fire?
- What would it do for the name of the fire service when it transpired that the smoke alarms had not been properly inspected?
- What would it do for team morale?

authority – they are given for a reason. They could be given for health and safety reasons, where failing to obey could endanger a member of the uniformed services or members of the public. Orders are also given to ensure the good name of the uniformed public services is not brought into disrepute.

You should remember that all the uniformed public services have a purpose and that purpose can only be fulfilled by having a hierarchy of authority whereby orders are given and carried out correctly. The practical consequences of not obeying orders are that the services' purposes cannot be fulfilled effectively and the hierarchy of authority will have little effect.

Course of action if orders not obeyed

Failing to carry out a lawful order amounts to misconduct and any member of the uniformed public services who is reported for misconduct will have their case considered by a senior officer and may be called to a disciplinary hearing, which is usually presided over by a commanding officer. However, in a military hearing, known as a court martial, serious cases are presided over by a judge advocate.

Disciplinary hearings follow similar lines to that of a court hearing and the person accused can have legal representation if they so require. If the case is proven, then a range of punishments can be administered including: a caution, fine, reduction in rank, reduction in pay, dismissal from the service or, in Armed Forces cases, imprisonment.

Credibility as a commander

Be fair

All good commanders should have, and be able to demonstrate, a sense of fairness, either when commanding situations or when dealing with the welfare or discipline of colleagues. It is essential for the integrity of a commanding officer, as well as the morale and trust of the lower ranks, that they are seen to be fair. However, you should recognise that to be fair does not necessarily mean that everyone should be

treated in the same way – to do so would could mean that no consideration had been given for individual circumstances.

Case study: Being fair

Fire fighters Jordan and Greenslade were both ten minutes late for the start of their shift. Fire fighter Jordan had overslept, whereas fire fighter Greenslade was delayed because she assisted with a road traffic accident and did not have access to her mobile phone.

1. **Should the watch manager treat them both in the same way in terms of disciplinary proceedings? Explain.**

Private Muscroft's application for 48-hour leave was turned down by the company sergeant major (CSM), even though he knew how much Muscroft wanted to watch his favourite football team playing in a cup competition. Private Mumby's application was also turned down so he could not go and visit his newborn son. The CSM told him, 'I refused Muscroft so, to be fair, I have to refuse you'.

2. **Was the CSM being fair? Explain.**

Police Constable Waring was a very bright woman with a flair for detecting crime and after just two years in the service her application to join the CID was accepted on the recommendation of her inspector. However, Police Constable Burton, who had five years' service and showed an aptitude for criminal investigation, had applied for CID six months ago and on this occasion had his application rejected. The reason why Police Constable Burton was not successful was because his inspector had stated in the reference, quite truthfully, that Burton had taken more than average sick leave in the last 12 months. The constable pointed out that the sick leave was because of various sports injuries he had received whilst playing rugby for the police service.

3. **Was the inspector who gave the reference being fair? Explain.**

Do not favour individuals

Good commanders do not have favourite individuals; everyone should be given the same consideration, regardless of gender, religion, colour or creed. If a commander were to show favouritism, then this would undermine their integrity as well as the morale and trust of the team.

In the uniformed public services, promotion comes from merit, loyalty and devotion to duty, amongst other things; it is not simply given to someone who is a favourite of the commanding officer.

Consider this

Explain how favouring individuals could lead to:

- resentment (of the individual who is being favoured and of the commanding officer)
- lack of motivation
- low morale
- low productivity.

Know the strengths and weaknesses of direct reports and managers

A good commander makes the time to get to know the people they command, including those who report directly and those who manage others on the orders of the commander. Only by doing this can a leader command effectively because by knowing the strengths and weaknesses of lower ranks, the leader can form a

Remember!

What you may regard as weaknesses could, in some situations, be seen as strengths, and vice versa – it depends on the task.

Theory into practice

Look at the following scenarios and select from the grids one person who you would like to be in your team under your command. Give reasons for your answers.

1. You are a lieutenant in charge of a platoon from which you need to select a team to rescue a colleague who is being held in a makeshift prison ten miles away. The prison is guarded by six members of a local militia, who are armed with rifles.

Rank	Strength or weakness
Private	Extremely courageous and expert rifleman but does not work well as part of a team
Corporal	Likes to be one of the boys and gets on well with privates but not very assertive
Private	Good team player but soon loses interest if things aren't going as planned
Corporal	Renowned for disciplining privates who do not obey promptly but has the respect of the section

2. You are a chief inspector in the police service and you need a team of police officers to carry out a fingertip search of a playing field and hedgerows for a button that is vital evidence.

Rank	Strength or weakness
Police Constable	Desperately wants promotion and is very capable but likes to take all the glory. Once received a commendation for an act of bravery when he rescued a child from a burning car with no thought for himself.
Police Sergeant	Ready for retiring and still dedicated but would sooner work inside. However, if called to do something he is very dependable.
Police Constable	Still on probation but can follow orders to the letter without distraction; she does not get on well with some female team members.
Police Sergeant	A newly promoted female sergeant who is destined for a high rank. Knows all the rules and regulations but lacks people skills, especially with colleagues.

strategy that takes into account those strengths and weaknesses. Furthermore, the commander will know who is best suited to execute the plan.

Understand the group's role or function

It seems quite obvious to say that a commander should understand the group's role or function but it is not simply a case of understanding what the group has to achieve.

It is important for the commander to understand the task or function of the group because, with their knowledge of the individual group members, they will know if it can be achieved without further resources and in the time that has been allocated. In deciding this, the commander must consider if the group has the mental, physical and technical ability to perform the task, as well as considering the impact of the task on the welfare and morale of the group.

Furthermore, the group's function may be a small part of a larger plan and while it is important for the commander to know the group's role, it is equally important for them to know how that role contributes to the overall plan.

It is only by understanding the role or function of the group, as well as the individual characteristics of the members, that the commander can match the roles to the individual members best suited to them. Without these considerations, the group, and the commander, could fail.

Demonstrate confidence

Commanders are only human and have feelings like anyone else but they must demonstrate confidence for the good of morale, team spirit and to maintain the team's trust and belief. One of the qualities that good commanders possess is to think and make decisions quickly, even though they may have had no time to plan; it could be that something has happened unexpectedly. However, it is the confident manner in which commanders conduct themselves, both verbally and non-verbally, that instils confidence in the team and enables them to take the right course of action at the right time.

Case study: The sinking of the Sir Galahad

On 8 June 1982, during the Falklands conflict, two naval vessels, Sir Galahad and Sir Tristram, were anchored off Fitzroy in the Falkland Islands. They were unloading equipment, ammunition and military personnel so that an advance could be made on the occupied eastern side of the island. However, before the personnel and supplies could be unloaded, both ships were attacked and bombed by Argentine Air Force A-4 Skyhawks.

Both ships caught fire and were engulfed in flames and thick, choking smoke, with Sir Galahad sustaining the most damage and resulting in the ship being abandoned.

A total of 50 personnel, mainly Welsh Guards, were killed or missing and this might have been worse had it not been for the helicopters and boats that had been unloading the ships but which quickly turned their efforts to rescuing and treating survivors.

It is very difficult for anyone to imagine the horrendous experience of that event but even in all the confusion a rescue operation still had to be attempted and it needed coordinating.

1. From a survivor's point of view, what might they have found most reassuring during those terrible moments?

2. From a rescuer's point of view, what would have been most important about the coordination of the rescue operation?

3. From the point of view of the officer who was commanding and controlling the operation, what would have been one of the most important aspects?

point they should be told – information overload could have a negative effect on the team's performance.

While the commander may be selective in the information they share with the team, they must ensure that all orders are passed on promptly and accurately. This is especially important where a leader is commanding a team or unit as part of a higher or strategic command involving lots of units. The success of the operation is wholly dependent upon every unit following orders promptly from senior command.

▲ Commanders must conduct themselves in a confident manner to instil confidence in their team

Ensure information is shared and orders disseminated

In a command and control situation, it is important for commanders to share information with the team so that everyone knows exactly what is happening and is aware of any progress. This gives the team a sense of purpose, especially when they are becoming tired; news that their efforts are having a positive effective on the organisation's overall objectives can be motivating. It would be bad for morale if a commander continued to make demands of a team without keeping them informed of developments – they would have no idea whether or not they were working in vain.

However, the commander must decide which information is relevant, what the team needs to know and at what

Assessment activity 13.2

Prepare and deliver a presentation to the group in the form of a debriefing identifying the qualities and skills necessary for command and control and describing how each skill or quality is important. You should ensure that you include the following content:

- *Skills and qualities:* technical skills; personal qualities, for example courage, confidence, integrity, determination, decisiveness, mental agility; qualities instilled by a good commander, for example trust, loyalty, discipline, morale, motivation, respect
- *Motivational strategies:* instigate and maintain command; inspire loyalty and obedience
- *Maintenance of authority:* need for authority, for example failure to obey orders promptly undermines authority; practical consequences of orders not obeyed; course of action if orders not obeyed
- *Credibility as a commander:* be fair; do not favour individuals; know the strengths and weaknesses of direct reports and manager; understand the group's role and function; demonstrate confidence; ensure information is shared and orders disseminated. **P4**

Grading tips

P4 In your presentation, you must first identify the skills and personal qualities required for command and control in the Uniformed Public Services. Then you should describe how each skill or personal quality is important.

Sequence of events

In the uniformed public services, there are several occasions when command and control need to be established. While it is generally assumed that the senior officer takes command of a situation, this does not necessarily mean they take control of everything. For example, the first police officer to respond to a crime scene, regardless of rank, would be in control of the scene and responsible for preserving it until it could be forensically examined and until supervisory officers arrived.

In the uniformed public services, individuals are able to exercise command and control by virtue of rank and status within the hierarchy of a particular service. Command and control scenarios are widely practised so that the services know how to respond efficiently during a real situation.

A good example of a command and control situation is where there is a major incident on land. It is usually the police who have overall control in these situations and who are responsible for coordinating all the emergency services and other organisations. However, there is a lot of individual control and command which combines to form a chain of command.

The case study below is a fictitious scenario but it will illustrate the command and control involving several organisations and individuals.

Who is responsible for assuming control and how they would do it

As we have already established, it is universally accepted that the police have overall command in such incidents and this is outlined in the Emergency Procedures Manual,

Case study: Dealing with disaster

During the early hours, a commercial airliner has crash landed in fields, four miles from an industrial town in northern England. Just before it landed and broke up, the airliner demolished a chemical processing plant causing toxic fumes to be released into the atmosphere. Debris from the airliner seems to be confined to 200 metres of open land and there are several small fires where aviation fuel has ignited on impact with the chemical plant. Power lines serving the local town have been brought down and it is feared that local drinking water supplies may be contaminated.

The airliner's fuselage is broken in half and while it is believed that several of the 200 passengers could not possibly have survived the landing, there is a strong chance that many are still alive and require urgent medical attention.

It is not known at this stage what long-term effects the chemicals could have on humans, animals and the environment but it is known that they cause respiratory problems and skin irritation, as well as mineral damage to soil.

The nearby town has a population of 200,000, with a full divisional police service, a fire service, general hospital and local authority department. There are four comprehensive schools, twelve junior schools and three further education colleges, as well as two leisure centres.

1. **If you were the first member of the uniformed public services to arrive at the scene, apart from radioing for help, what would be your initial actions?**

2. **What sort of information would you communicate to your control room to ensure the right response was activated?**

3. **Once you had called for assistance, would it be wise to attempt a rescue by yourself? Explain.**

published by the Association of Chief Police Officers. However, in a fire situation or situation involving hazardous materials or unstable structures, the fire service are specialists and would, therefore, have control.

The first member of the uniformed public services to attend an incident is usually a police officer who then, regardless of rank, assumes the role of initial police incident officer. He or she assesses the situation, contacts their control room and a major incident is declared, drawing a coordinated response from all of the emergency services. The initial police incident officer will then protect the scene, unless conditions dictate otherwise, and will remain with their supervisor to maintain continuity of procedures and to act as staff officer.

In the scenario described above, the immediate area would be cordoned off by the police in order to establish control of it, ensuring there is access to and from the area for rescue work to be carried out. Command vehicles would be brought to the scene and sited in a safe location on the advice of the fire service.

The chief of police for the area, in liaison with chiefs of other services and organisations, would act as incident coordinator from strategic headquarters, away from the immediate area. They would formulate a plan of how best to deal with the incident.

At the scene, an officer of the fire service could decide that the incident is likely to escalate and, therefore, an outer cordon is required to secure the site. The incident coordinator, in conjunction with the fire service, would decide who should enter the inner cordon together with authorisation identification, as well as the safe routes for entering and exiting the cordon. All personnel entering the inner cordon must be briefed about hazards, an evacuation signal, control measures and other issues relevant to the incident. It is important, therefore, to designate a member of the uniformed public services to record all personnel entering and leaving the inner cordon. The officer in charge of this task, regardless of rank, has the authority to admit or refuse personnel into the inner cordon.

Where it is known that people have died, it is essential to inform Her Majesty's Coroner before the bodies are removed from the scene. The bodies require formal identification and documentation and this is carried

out by the police – usually a police constable – who act as agents on behalf of the coroner and are known as coroner's officers. Depending on the size of the incident, there could be more than one coroner's officer – they have the authority to ensure that bodies are not disturbed or moved unnecessarily. Hence, coroner's officers can control members of the uniformed services of a higher rank when it comes to dealing with fatalities.

Take it further

1. In the case study on page 365, why would it be dangerous to allow rescue workers to go into the inner cordon without personal protective equipment?
2. If you were coordinating the incident, would you take any precautionary measures regarding the toxic chemicals before you allowed any rescue work to commence? If so, what would they be?
3. Why is it necessary to keep a register of all those who enter and leave the inner cordon?

Remember!

Where there is an incident at sea, it is coordinated by HM Coastguard.

Comparison of the methods used by the services

The emergency services use similar methods of command and control, especially where a large incident calls for a combined response. The initial command and control of each service is initiated by the first vehicle to attend at the scene. The police would use the first police vehicle until a specially designed command and control vehicle was brought in as the incident developed; this would form the incident control post and be located with other command and control vehicles.

The fire service forward control vehicle would be the first fire tender to arrive at the scene and this would be identified with a red flashing beacon. As more resources arrived, this would be replaced with a command support unit, which would serve as the formal command support point.

The ambulance service uses specially equipped communications vehicles, identified by a green flashing beacon. This provides the focal point for all ambulance, medical and voluntary personnel. St. John's Ambulance personnel volunteer their services at major incidents and are coordinated by the ambulance service.

All the control vehicles for each of the services are parked together and are recognisable by the fact that they are the only vehicles displaying flashing lights.

A chain of command is established by dividing the incident into sectors or levels of command. Each of the emergency services appoints a sector commander who operates in that sector with a team of personnel from their service. Hence, there will be three sector commanders and at least three teams of emergency service personnel. The sectors are known as:

- strategic
- tactical
- operational.

The Armed Forces use a different type of command and control, especially during a huge military operation such as war. It very much depends upon the type of war as to who will command the Armed Forces. This means that if the conflict is mainly a land-based operation, then the Army will take control but if the conflict is mainly a sea battle then the Royal Navy would be in command.

The Falklands War of 1982 was commanded and controlled by the Admiral of the Fleet, who was situated in Whitehall. He was assisted by other commanders located outside London. Overall control was taken by the Royal Navy, not because the operation was a naval one, but because the war mainly involved a conflict at sea. Over 30,000 Armed Forces personnel were engaged in the conflict, including a large proportion of the Royal Navy, five Army battalions and RAF squadrons. Operational command was carried out by the commanders at the scene, under the control of the commanders in the UK.

However, as stated, where the conflict is predominantly a land battle, the commander of the operation would be an Army officer, as in the Gulf conflict. In the case of the conflict in Iraq, strategic command is controlled away from the conflict zone by several commanders who form the Multinational Force – Iraq, while tactical command is headed by a US Army general.

Levels of command and control

It is important to understand that while 'levels of command and control' seems to imply a hierarchy of command, the following levels of strategic, tactical and operational command do not represent seniority, they signify functions. The senior officers in charge of each level could all have the same rank.

Strategic command

Key terms

Strategic To do with planning to gain an advantage, whereas 'strategy' means a plan.

A strategic commander is involved in formulating plans or strategies in order to decide on the best way to achieve an organisation's objectives. The strategies could include such things as planning for war, combating terrorism, reducing crime or dealing with a major incident.

Strategic command usually involves several chiefs of different uniformed public services because some plans affect more than one service. For example, the conflict in Iraq would have taken meticulous planning and would have meant months of collaboration with senior officers from the Army, Royal Navy and Royal Air Force, since the conflict entailed a combined response from our Armed Forces.

Strategic command in a major incident would involve the heads of the emergency services formulating a plan of how best to deal with it. This level of command is also known as 'gold command' by the police and ambulance services.

Strategic command headquarters are normally established away from the incident, or spread over one or two locations. For example, during a major incident, strategic command might be located at a local police headquarters or local authority council offices, or both. Strategic command for the Armed Forces would normally be established in London.

Tactical command

Key terms

Tactical The way in which a plan is carried out with the desire of bringing about a successful conclusion.

A tactical commander is involved in implementing the plan formulated by strategic command. There may be several tactical commanders, especially where there is more than one service. Tactical commanders are responsible for ensuring that members of their service are aware of the strategy and how to put it into operation. Tactical command is not involved in direct hands-on operations; that is to say they are not involved directly at the scene of an incident. Their involvement is more of a planning and coordinating role and in a conflict situation it is important that tactical commanders should remain detached and not allow themselves to become personally involved. They would be located away from the front line because it is their job to support and liaise with strategic command on any issues or changes that may develop and to ensure these are carried out.

In a major incident situation, tactical command is also known by the police and ambulance services as 'silver command' and serves the same function outlined above.

Operational command

In a conflict situation, this would be the front line where operational commanders would deploy and control the resources of their respective services, implementing the tactics relayed to them by their tactical commander, thus following the plan set by strategic command.

In a major incident situation, this is known as 'bronze command' by the police and ambulance services and it is the area within the inner cordon where rescue work is being carried out or measures are being taken to prevent the incident from escalating.

Planning

Clear objectives

Successful strategies are formulated by individuals who have clear objectives that can be realistically achieved in a given time. This does not necessarily mean that they have to be leaders of organisations; individuals can formulate strategies for a variety of reasons, including personal development. One of the most popular models for formulating successful plans has the mnemonic (an aid to memory) SMART.

SMART objectives are:

- **Specific** – objectives must be specific and clearly set out. Vague objectives are difficult to follow and could be ambiguous. For example, a specific objective in your plan could be to pass the promotion exam.
- **Measurable** – objectives must be measurable so that you can gauge the progress of your plan and see how far you have travelled towards achieving it. If you cannot measure progress, then you have no way of knowing if you are heading in the right or wrong direction. For example, you could measure your progress by passing the promotion exam.
- **Achievable** – objectives must be achievable otherwise there would be little point in setting them as goals.

When something is achievable it means it is capable of being accomplished or reached, even though it might involve lots of hard work and dedication. Something that is achievable can motivate a person to strive towards it, whereas if something is impossible or impracticable to achieve then there could be no motivation.

- **Realistic** – objectives must be realistic, which means you must be reasonable in what you want to achieve. If you set your targets too high they might not be realistic and you will lose heart when you cannot achieve them. Would it be realistic for you to pass the promotion exam as one of your targets?

- **Time-related** – objectives must be achievable over a certain period of time. You cannot measure success if there is no time limit on your objectives. You could set a realistic target to pass your promotion exam within two years.

This model is used in the uniformed public services, as well as other organisations, to empower individuals to achieve their potential. It allows individuals to set their own targets and plan their development within an organisation, thus enabling them to be in charge of their own future.

▲ Civilian lives could be at risk if a briefing is not properly understood

of a bombing plan for the Royal Air Force and if the instruction is not understood, then civilian lives could be at risk. This would be devastating, not to mention the discredit and disrepute brought upon the service.

Theory into practice

You could devise a SMART plan for the course you are doing at the moment.

- What would be your specific objective?
- How would you measure it?
- Is it achievable?
- Is it realistic?
- What is the time scale?

Key terms

Briefing A meeting where instructions or information is given. For example, it could be a briefing about a mission to gather information on enemy positions.

SMEAC

There are several points that constitute an effective briefing and another mnemonic that will help you to remember those points is SMEAC.

- **Situation** – this is an explanation of the state of affairs and the reason why the forthcoming operation is necessary. The situation could be that a unit of soldiers have been cut off from their section by the enemy and they need to be rescued from their current position.

- **Mission** – this is where the assignment or task is explained. For example, a rescue party may be

Briefing

A **briefing** is an instruction given for a task or operation. In the uniformed public services, a briefing is very important as it can mean the success or failure of an operation. For example, a briefing could be in the form

required to penetrate enemy lines in order to rescue their colleagues.

- **Execution** – this is where the means of carrying out the mission is explained in great detail. It would include coordinates, timings, rendezvous points, etc.
- **Any questions** – this gives personnel the opportunity to clarify any queries about the situation, mission or execution. For example, 'What if we miss the rendezvous point?'
- **Check understanding** – this allows the officer giving the briefing the chance to test the understanding of the personnel who have been briefed. The officer will ask questions and judge understanding from replies to questions, as well as making a note of body language. If there is any doubt that everyone has understood, the briefing will be repeated.

Remember!

A mnemonic is an aid to memory. Remember SMART and SMEAC.

Consider this

Why is it important that briefings have clarity? Why is it important that briefings are accurate and concise?

Effective control

Receiving and giving orders directly

The most effective way for a commander to control is by receiving and giving orders directly. In other words, there is no go-between or relaying of orders through another person. However, this is not always possible. For example, where there is a breakdown in radio or electronic communication, a system of runners might be used to relay orders and instructions. If they are not written down at the time they could be misinterpreted or distorted, resulting in something like Chinese whispers! There is a well-known story that, while probably false, perfectly illustrates the point of receiving and giving orders directly. During World War II, an instruction was passed verbally along the trenches for the radio operator to: 'Send reinforcements, we're going to advance.' However, by the time the message reached the operator, he sent: 'Send three and four pence, we're going to a dance.' Not the original instruction at all!

Noise, stress, hunger and lack of sleep can affect people's perceptions and they may hear incorrectly, or they may not relay the message clearly enough for people to understand. This can lead to ineffective command and control so the best way to ensure that orders are carried out correctly is for the commander to receive and give orders directly.

Monitor teams effectively

Monitoring a team means checking that it is fulfilling its function in accordance with objectives. However, to monitor effectively includes checking that the welfare of the individual team members is as it should be. This would include checking that team spirit and enthusiasm are maintained because, while the team might be fulfilling its function, low morale could quickly lead to an unsettled team.

The manner in which a commander monitors a team is also important. It would have a bad effect on the team if they thought they were being watched to see if they were doing their job correctly.

Maintain a physical position of control

Maintaining a physical position of control serves two purposes:

1. It allows the commander a direct view of the operation where they can assess and reassess progress and make changes where necessary.
2. It is good for team morale to know that the leader is there to offer support and guidance when required.

Commanders in certain organisations have a natural position of command where they can view progress.

For instance, the captain of a ship has a good position of control from the bridge and a squadron leader has an excellent position of control over a squadron, as a squadron leader or wing commander is usually located at the front and centre of a formation.

Not all commanders have such advantageous positions but this does not mean they are not maintaining a physical position of control. A good commander would want to be with their team, whether this means hiding in a swamp with them or swimming across an icy cold river with them in the middle of the night.

Essentially, a commander is there for the team and the team can rely on him/her to help achieve its objectives.

Issue clear orders and commands

Consider this

Why do you think it is important to issue clear orders and commands? What are the consequences of not doing so?

Maintain a strong command presence

You should not confuse this with maintaining a physical position of control. To maintain a strong command presence means to maintain a strong personality – the type of personality that befits a good commander. A good commander speaks with confidence and conviction while looking people in the eye, which gives team members belief and trust in their commander. A commander with a weak presence or character will lose trust and respect.

Influence the tempo

The tempo of something is the speed at which it is being done – it could be slow, moderate or fast. To do something too quickly (for example, typing out a report) could lead to errors. On the other hand, to do something too slowly can also have a negative effect, as well as putting people at risk. A good commander recognises when the tempo of a task is wrong and skilfully alters it for the good of the group, the organisation or the general public.

Case study: Floods in South Yorkshire

In June 2007, torrential rain caused severe flooding in parts of Rotherham, as well as other regions of South Yorkshire. In an elevated position to the east of the town was the Ulley Reservoir which, according to engineers, had a weak section in the dam wall. It was feared that the water in the dam could breach the wall, releasing millions of gallons of water into the valley below and putting the homes and lives of nearby villagers at risk. In addition, any breach in the dam wall would mean that a section of the M1 would flood and cause a serious risk to those travelling along it. Furthermore, an electricity sub-station below the reservoir was in imminent danger of flooding, which would result in a large section of the town losing electricity.

A large evacuation was put into operation whereby people were evacuated from their homes in the early hours of the morning and taken to alternative accommodation.

1. **If you were the commander of the evacuation operation described above, what tempo would you implement?**

2. **How would you know if the operation to evacuate was succeeding?**

3. **Would you, as commander, become physically involved in the evacuation process? Explain.**

4. **How would you tell your team to approach the people they were evacuating in the early hours of the morning?**

Delegate

To delegate means to pass on a task to another person. This is a good management tool and a commander can motivate a team by delegating tasks to the team or individual members. It gives them a sense of responsibility and value, as well as a recognition of the fact that the commander trusts them.

However, the commander has to ensure that the team is capable of carrying out the delegated task otherwise this can make the group feel inadequate or incompetent.

Functional command methods

Functional command methods are practical ways of ensuring commands are carried out effectively. For commands that involve a task, it is sometimes easier to break it down into manageable stages and one such method has another mnemonic to help you remember those stages – PICSIE.

- **Plan** – a strategy or plan is drawn up, either by a team or by the leader, with the purpose of achieving a mission. The plan will contain aims and objectives and means of measuring progress. For example, the mission might be: 'Rendezvous with 4 Section at 749046 at 0230 in one week and construct a rope bridge over the River Fury between 0300 and 0330 at 751049. You must not be discovered.'

  The plan will involve measuring the distance of the coordinates from the present location and estimating the travelling time, including arrangements for travelling, bearing in mind the instruction stated that the team should not be discovered.

It is the responsibility of the leader to ensure that proper steps are taken so that the mission is accomplished.

- **Initiate** – this is the first stage in carrying out the plan and it would begin with a full briefing to the rest of the team (remember SMEAC).
- **Control** – the plan is put into operation and the leader, who is aware of every stage of the plan, controls the task by ensuring each member of the team knows their role. A good leader should not become personally involved in the task but should maintain a supervisory role.
- **Support** – the leader, besides ensuring that team members support each other, will maintain morale and team spirit by praising and encouraging, as well as maintaining discipline.
- **Inform** – this involves effective sharing of information within the team and with the leader. The team needs to be informed of any change in the plan or mission and the leader needs to be informed of any changes that the team thinks are necessary.
- **Evaluate** – this involves an assessment by the leader of the team's progress, both in terms of objectives achieved and overall team performance. If targets are not being met and the team is performing badly then the leader may alter the plan and reassess at intervals.

Assessment activity 13.3

For this assignment you are required to prepare and deliver a presentation to show how an individual can exercise command and control and why it is important.

You should ensure that you include the following content:

- *Command and control*: sequence of events (for example, who is responsible for assuming control and how they would do it), comparison of the methods used by the services (for example, emergency services, Armed Forces, other uniformed public services)
- *Levels of command and control*: strategic, tactical and operational
- *Planning*: clear objectives (SMART objectives)

- *Briefing*: methods (for example, SMEAC); importance of clarity, being accurate and concise
- *Effective control*: receiving and giving orders, directly monitoring teams effectively, maintaining a physical position of control, issuing clear orders and commands, maintaining a strong command presence, influencing the tempo, delegating, functional command methods (for example, PICSIE).

You should use this content to:

1. Explain how an individual can exercise command and control.

2. Analyse the importance and use of command and control within a uniformed public service.

3. Evaluate the importance and use of command and control within the uniformed public services. **D1**

Grading tips

P2 Using the content to guide you, explain how individuals establish command and control.

M1 Using your answer from P2, explore the reasons why command and control is important in the uniformed public services. Break down your answer into detailed sections and try to give examples of what would happen without command and control.

D1 This is a direct progression from M1 but now you need to weigh up the importance of command and control and give conclusions.

Command and control skills and qualities

There is a difference between understanding the required command and control skills and qualities and demonstrating them. Good leaders not only understand the skills and qualities, they are also able to demonstrate them through command task activities.

Personal qualities

We have already looked at some of the personal qualities required for command and control in section 2. Have a look again at those qualities to refresh your memory and then add the following:

- **Knowledge of people** – a good leader can command and control effectively because they are knowledgeable about people and know how to bring out the best in them. They have the wisdom to understand what makes people happy, what motivates them, and what upsets them. Knowledge of people enables a good leader to demonstrate patience and understanding because they are aware that people make mistakes, especially when under pressure, and they help and encourage them to improve.
- **Belief** – a good leader will truly believe in their organisation and all that it stands for. This belief gives them commitment and loyalty to their service and the conviction to command and control with confidence. Without this fundamental belief, a leader would be unable to demonstrate dedication and enthusiasm which are vital in command and control.
- **Strength of character** – leaders, like anyone else, are accountable for their actions and a good leader has the strength of character to accept responsibility for their actions without having to apportion blame.
- **Creativity** – good leaders are creative and resourceful. Their mental agility enables them to think of original ideas to solve problems where others

might fail. This is one of the reasons why leaders should not get personally involved in team tasks; they are required to see the whole picture without becoming distracted.

- **Personality** – a good leader has a personality that can adapt to any situation. For example, there may be times when a leader has to be assertive because being forceful might be the only way forward. However, at other times, the leader might have to show compassion or appear charismatic. This is because situations and moods can be very different, including the mood of the team. A good leader can read a situation in terms of atmosphere and mood and can demonstrate personality by adapting to it.

Effective control

By utilising their personal skills and qualities to their best advantage, leaders should be effective in commanding and controlling. To be effective means to bring about a successful outcome to the task in hand. No matter how many skills the leader possesses, they will not be of use unless they can bring about a successful mission.

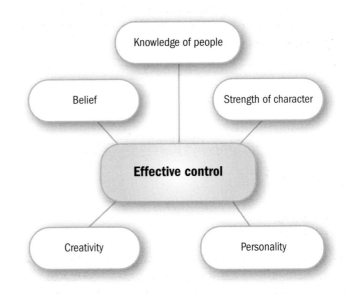

▲ Figure 13.7 The elements of effective control

Effective communication

Effective communication involves many things. It is not only the ability to speak clearly and at the right pace and tone, it also includes non-verbal communication such as body language, eye contact and correct body posture. Negative body posture and lack of eye contact can contradict words of praise and encouragement; body language is often more powerful than the spoken word. A good leader will appreciate the importance of demonstrating positive body language, especially when they encounter someone who does not speak the same language.

Good communication also entails sending the right message at the right time to the right person. Messages sent too late are ineffective and messages sent too early can be forgotten or cause a backlog.

Consider this

Some leadership skills and qualities are more practical than others. For example, to have a pleasing personality is a type of skill but it has no practical application. A commander might be a nice person to work with but, unless they can demonstrate practical skills and qualities, they will be no good at command and control. Look at the various skills and, as well as thinking of some of your own, try to classify them as practical or non-practical.

Types of command task activities

Combat

To engage in combat means to engage in a fight or battle and, in a conflict situation, combat usually means an armed encounter. Therefore, out of all the different command tasks, this is perhaps the most important for

both the commander and those being commanded and controlled. In this type of command task, a commander must use all their skills and qualities – courage, mental agility, decisiveness, creativity and commitment – to ensure the safety, as far as possible, of all those under their command.

While strategies and objectives will have been drawn up, in a combat situation there will certainly be events that have not been planned for. This is where mutual trust between the leader and the team will be at its greatest. The team will trust the leader to command and control and the leader will trust the team to respond promptly to commands.

Rescue

All of the uniformed public services take part in rescues of some form or another. For example, HM Coastguard personnel regularly perform rescue operations at sea, as well as the RAF and RNLI. The fire service frequently rescues people from burning buildings, road traffic accidents and train crashes, in conjunction with the police. And all the emergency services join to rescue people during major incidents.

In all these situations, the uniformed public services are professional and dependable because, apart from the personal skills and qualities they possess, they know their role within the command and control system.

Containment

Containment refers to the policy of preventing hostilities or a bad influence from spreading through a country. While this could involve the police service in a riot situation, it is a procedure that is usually carried out by the Armed Forces, who act in a peacekeeping capacity. Such operations have been taking place in Northern Ireland, Kosovo, Afghanistan and Iraq, to name but a few. These manoeuvres are very dangerous, especially in highly volatile areas (for example, Iraq at the time of writing) and strategies have to be carefully drawn up to minimise casualties.

Here again, the skills of a commander are tested to the full because the operations can involve innocent civilians and children who become embroiled through no fault of their own. This can serve to worsen an already grave situation and can cause even greater hostility to our uniformed public services. A commander has to exercise diplomacy, compassion and understanding, as well as remaining focused on the task in hand, knowing that an insurgent could take on the guise of an innocent civilian, thereby threatening the safety of one or more of their team.

Situation control

There are many situations that call for control by the uniformed public services. These can either be civilian or military situations. For example, a prison riot would be a civilian situation that requires control, while a natural disaster, like flooding, could involve the military and the civilian police, as well as other agencies. Situations like these call for command and control so that the situation can be monitored, controlled and returned to normal.

Accident

Unfortunately, road traffic accidents are all too frequent and multiple-vehicle accidents invariably call for command and control because of the amount of work involved in dealing with them. For example:

- roads need to be blocked while the emergency services rescue the injured from the scene
- relatives need to be informed and told which hospitals their relatives have been taken to
- property at the scene needs safeguarding
- photographs of the scene will be required, etc.

However, accidents do not only involve traffic. There are accidents such as chemical explosions, accidents on oil rigs, mining disasters, all of which need command and control for dealing with them effectively.

Recovery

Recovery entails restoring the community to normality after, for example, a major incident. The community is often the centre for social, leisure and spiritual life and any upheaval can devastate its fabric. It usually falls to the uniformed public services to help the community to recover. This is particularly difficult in the event of, for example, a flood, where properties including houses, shops and community buildings have been destroyed. To restore a community is a huge operation and requires proper command and control.

Lead and support people to resolve operational incidents

It is an unfortunate but true fact that operational tasks can themselves result in incidents. For example, military aircraft have been known to develop technical problems and crash. In the Falklands conflict, some Royal Navy vessels came under enemy fire, resulting in fires and horrendous burns to crew members.

In such incidents, the commander has the task of organising and leading teams to deal with them. Again, the skills of the commander are crucial because, as you may imagine, the morale of the team can suffer greatly.

Other operational incidents call for lead and support even where serving personnel have not been injured. For example, the alleged manner in which prisoners of war are treated during a conflict situation could bring about low morale. The ill-treatment of Iraqi prisoners a few years ago brought the good name of the US Army into disrepute, which called for lead and support to resolve the incident.

Problem solving techniques

As we have already seen, commanders routinely solve problems for a whole range of situations. It is not by accident that commanders do this; they expect problems as part of their responsibilities and solving them becomes second nature to them, although some situations are more complex and involved than others. Whatever the problem, it is easier to solve if you use some sort of plan and, while not everyone uses the same techniques, the manner in which a problem can be solved successfully usually involves a number of stages, as we shall explore in the Theory into Practice on page 377.

Theory into practice

You and three of your friends live in the south of England. You are going on a three-day hill-walking and camping expedition to the Lake District in July and you haven't worked out how to get there. Furthermore, you're not sure what food to take and how it will be affected by the anticipated warm weather. You will also need to consider getting home.

Working in small groups, consider the problems presented by this scenario and test your skills at solving them by using the following points to guide you:

- define the problem
- gather all the relevant information
- list the possible solutions
- test the possible solutions
- select the best solution.

▲ Figure 13.8 Solve any potential problems before you set off!

Take it further

Carry out an inventory of your own skills and check it with your peers to see if they agree with you. You could list the skills in a table like the one shown below (but make it larger so you can include more skills and qualities). Ask your peers to use a scale of 1 to 5 to show how much they agree with your own assessment of your skills where 1 is 'strongly agree' and 5 is 'strongly disagree'.

I believe I have the following skills and qualities	Rate your agreement from 1 to 5 where 1 is 'strongly agree' and 5 is 'strongly disagree'			
Communications				
Assertiveness				
Strength of character				
Creativity				

Table 13.4 Personal skills inventory

Assessment activity 13.4

For this assignment you are required to take part in a group role play where you will identify and demonstrate the skills and qualities required for command and control.

You should ensure that you include the following content:

- *Command and control skills and qualities*: personal qualities, effective control, effective communication
- *Types of command task activities*: combat, rescue, containment, situation control, accident, recovery, lead and support people to resolve operational incidents
- *Problem solving techniques*: define the problem, gather all the relevant information, list the possible solutions, test the possible solutions, select the best solution.

You should use the content to:

1. Demonstrate, with support, the use of command and control skills in four different situations. **P3**

2. Identify the skills and personal qualities required for command and control within a uniformed public service, describing how each skill and personal quality is important for command and control. **P4**

3. Demonstrate practical command and control in four different situations for a specific public service. **M2**

4. Identify the skills required for practical command and control scenarios and compare these to your own performance. **M3**

5. Evaluate your own performance in command and control situations, identifying areas of personal development. **D2**

Grading tips

P3 You should choose four command task activities from the content and assume the role of leader to demonstrate the use of command and control skills to bring about a successful conclusion. For this grade you may receive support.

P4 After the role play you could give a presentation to the group in the form of a debriefing, where you identify the qualities and skills necessary for command and control, and describe how each skill and quality is important.

M2 You could achieve this from P3 by deciding which service you want to represent for the role play and by understanding the role of that service.

However, unlike P3, you may not have support in the demonstration of command and control skills. Make sure that you understand the role of the service.

M3 This is an extension of P4 but make sure you draw the distinction between theoretical and practical skills.

D2 To achieve this you could write an evaluation of your performance in the role play and ask your peers for feedback. Analyse the feedback and highlight any qualities that you need to develop.

Knowledge check

1. The Royal Marines have the same rank insignia as the Army but which of the Armed Forces do the Royal Marines belong to?

2. Who is responsible for army discipline?

3. Which rank in the police service would command a division or district?

4. Why is integrity a good quality to have for command and control?

5. Name three qualities that a good commander can instil in others.

6. What does 'disseminate orders' mean?

7. What are the three levels of command and control?

8. What does the acronym SMART stand for?

9. When would you use the acronym SMEAC?

10. PICSIE is an acronym for a functional command method. What does the acronym stand for?

11. Name five command tasks.

12. What are the five stages of good problem solving techniques?

Preparation for assessment

Produce a report to your immediate superior that will answer the following questions:

1. Identify the rank structure in two contrasting uniformed public services and describe the chain of command for one, including its uniform structure and the role played by non-uniformed personnel in its structure. **P1**

2. Explain how an individual can exercise command and control. **P2**

3. Analyse the importance and use of command and control within a uniformed public service. **M1**

4. Evaluate the importance and use of command and control within the uniformed public services. **D1**

5. Demonstrate, with support, the use of command and control skills in four different situations. **P3**

6. Demonstrate practical command and control in four different situations for a specific public service. **M2**

7. Identify the skills and personal qualities required for command and control within a uniformed public service, describing how each skill and personal quality is important for command and control. **P4**

8. Identify the skills required for practical command and control scenarios and compare these to your own performance. **M3**

9. Evaluate your own performance in command and control situations, identifying areas of personal development. **D2**

Grading criteria	Activity	Pg no.		
To achieve a pass grade the evidence must show that the learner is able to:			To achieve a merit grade the evidence must show that the learner is able to:	To achieve a distinction grade the evidence must show that the learner is able to:
P1 Identify the rank structures in two contrasting uniformed public services and describe the chain of command for one, including its uniform structure and the role played by non-uniformed personnel in its structure	13.1	354		
P2 Explain how an individual can exercise command and control	13.3	373	**M1** Analyse the importance and use of command and control within a uniformed public service	**D1** Evaluate the importance and use of command and control within the uniformed public services
P3 Demonstrate, with support, the use of command and control skills in four different situations	13.4	378	**M2** Demonstrate practical command and control in four different situations for a specific public service	**D2** Evaluate your own performance in command and control situations, identifying areas of personal development
P4 Identify the skills and personal qualities required for command and control within a uniformed public service, describing how each skill and personal quality is important for command and control	13.2 13.4	364 378	**M3** Identify the skills required for practical command and control scenarios and compare these to your own performance	

Index

Note: Page numbers in **bold** indicate where key terms are defined.

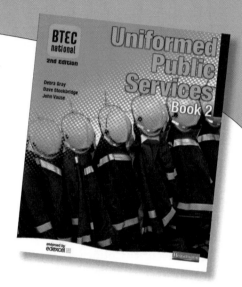